EMPIRE AND FRONTIER

Colonel Peter Schuyler and the Valiant Iroquois in King William's War: 1689–1701

SAMUEL MARQUIS

PEGASUS BOOKS
NEW YORK LONDON

EMPIRE AND FRONTIER

Pegasus Books, Ltd.
148 West 37th Street, 12th Floor
New York, NY 10018

First Pegasus Books cloth edition August 2026

Interior design by Maria Fernandez

Maps by Gene Thorp

Library of Congress Cataloging-in-Publication Data is available.

ISBN: 979-8-89710-154-2

10 9 8 7 6 5 4 3 2 1

Printed in the United States of America
Distributed by Simon & Schuster
www.pegasusbooks.com

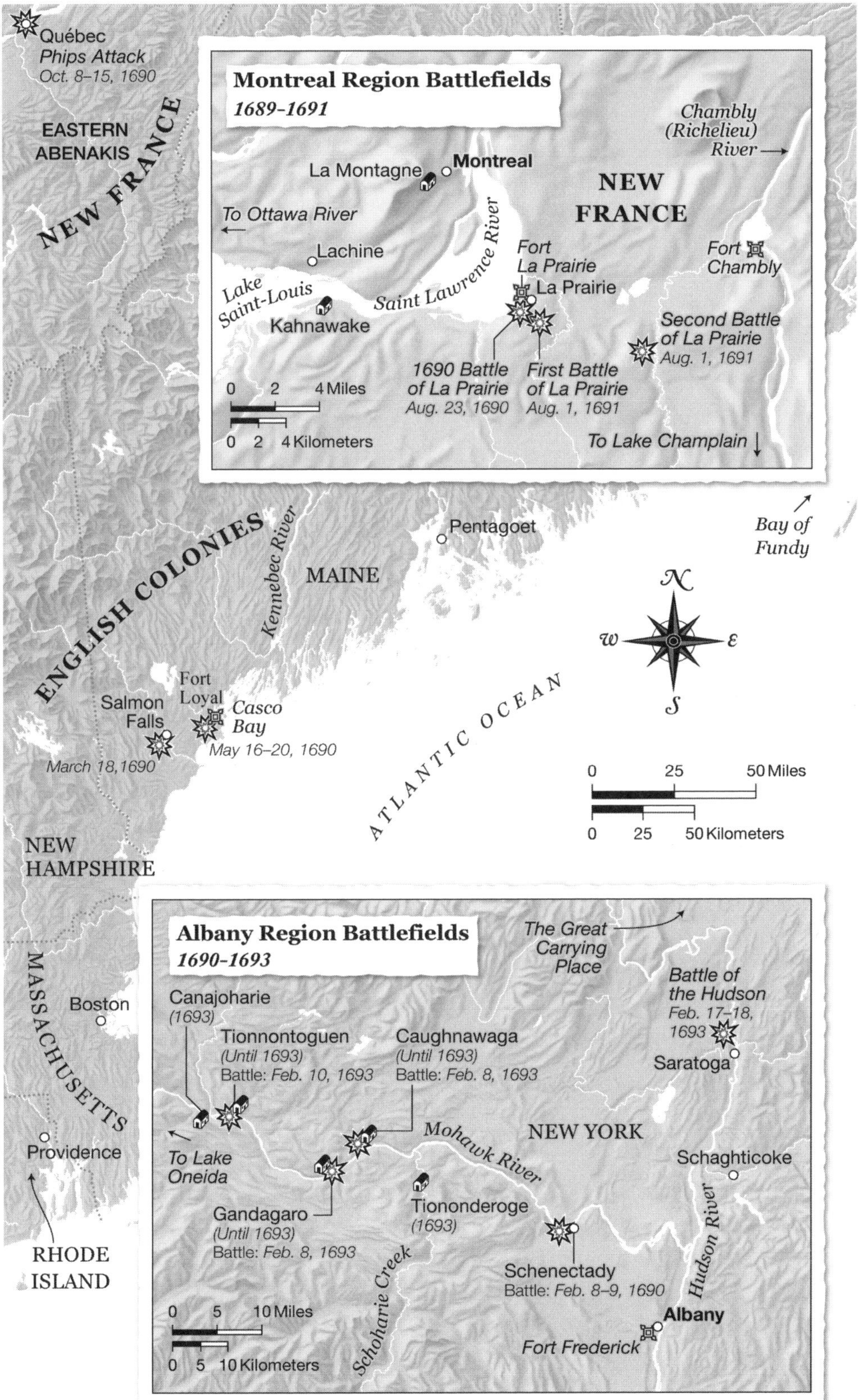

Québec
Phips Attack
Oct. 8–15, 1690
EASTERN ABENAKIS
NEW FRANCE
Montreal Region Battlefields
1689–1691
Chambly (Richelieu) River
La Montagne
Montreal
NEW FRANCE
To Ottawa River
Lachine
Saint Lawrence River
Fort La Prairie
La Prairie
Fort Chambly
Lake Saint-Louis
Kahnawake
Second Battle of La Prairie
Aug. 1, 1691
1690 Battle of La Prairie
Aug. 23, 1690
First Battle of La Prairie
Aug. 1, 1691
0 2 4 Miles
0 2 4 Kilometers
To Lake Champlain
Bay of Fundy
Pentagoet
ENGLISH COLONIES
Kennebec River
MAINE
N
W
E
S
Fort Loyal
Salmon Falls
March 18, 1690
Casco Bay
May 16–20, 1690
ATLANTIC OCEAN
0 25 50 Miles
0 25 50 Kilometers
NEW HAMPSHIRE
MASSACHUSETTS
Boston
Providence
RHODE ISLAND
Albany Region Battlefields
1690–1693
The Great Carrying Place
Battle of the Hudson
Feb. 17–18, 1693
Saratoga
Canajoharie
(1693)
Tionnontoguen
(Until 1693)
Battle: Feb. 10, 1693
Caughnawaga
(Until 1693)
Battle: Feb. 8, 1693
To Lake Oneida
Mohawk River
NEW YORK
Schaghticoke
Gandagaro
(Until 1693)
Battle: Feb. 8, 1693
Tiononderoge
(1693)
Schoharie Creek
Schenectady
Battle: Feb. 8–9, 1690
Hudson River
Albany
Fort Frederick
0 5 10 Miles
0 5 10 Kilometers

Praise for
EMPIRE AND FRONTIER

"Samuel Marquis recovers a pivotal but long-neglected chapter of early United States history. Marquis writes with the narrative drive of the best popular historians, and his eye for character, human complexity, and cross-cultural nuance makes this essential reading for anyone interested in how empires were made and unmade on the American frontier."

—Greg Grandin, PhD, Pulitzer Prize–winning historian and author of *America, América: A New History of the New World*

"A gripping, well-researched narrative that illuminates one of the more overlooked chapters in early American history: the unlikely alliance between Dutch-American frontiersman Colonel Peter Schuyler and the Five Nations of the Iroquois (Haudenosaunee). Marquis humanizes this cultural collision without romanticizing the era, bringing to life high-stakes diplomacy, friendships, and raw battlefield realities. Vivid and insightful, this book puts you on the gritty edge of the frontier."

—Patrick K. O'Donnell, historian and author of *The Unvanquished* and *Revolutionary Snipers*

"Marquis creates a rich narrative interwoven with individual heroism, wartime brutality, political subterfuge, and cultural interconnection. A valuable addition to the canon."

—J. D. Dickey, author of *Boston, 1776* and *Empire of Mud: The Secret History of Washington, DC*

"A highly momentous tale, filled with deadly skirmishes and shifting alliances with local Indian tribes along the Albany frontier. Marquis reveals, in meticulous detail, how invaluable this Iroquois partnership was in protecting English settlements in the Province of New York and the northeastern colonies. Essential reading for anyone interested in great power rivalry during the seventeenth century."

—John Reeves, author of *Grant's Betrayal: Power, Corruption, and the Theft of the Black Hills*

"Training a storyteller's imaginative eye on period documents and other historians' research, Samuel Marquis brings to life three seventeenth-century characters. The result is a compelling tale about the colonial world that Indigenous, Dutch, English, and French powers bloodily created together. Fast-paced, quirky, and opinionated, this is a book to be noticed."

—Daniel K. Richter, PhD, professor at the University of Pennsylvania

"Fascinating and richly detailed. Out of this polyglot and often brutal frontier came the beginnings of a new kind of politics, for a brand-new kind of nation."

—Scott Ellsworth, author of *Midnight on the Potomac*

"Samuel Marquis has peopled his vivid history of King William's War with memorable characters, including a fascinating Mohawk-Dutch interpreter named Hilletie van Olinda, as well as better-known politicians, military leaders, and even pirates. This fast-paced narrative shows how the Haudenosaunee controlled the fate of European colonists who had been desperate to create profitable communities in the Northeast since Henry Hudson sailed upriver in 1609."

—Peter C. Mancall, PhD, author of *Contested Continent: The Struggle for North America, c. 1000–1680*

"*Empire and Frontier* combines the charm and accessibility of biographical writing and the analytical probing of academic scholarship. By narrating the forging of the Anglo-Iroquois military alliance with a focus on the dramatic interactions between captivating individuals, Samuel Marquis does a great service to the field of diplomatic history. This biographical approach highlights the role that individuals play in shaping the fates of nations."

—Guy Chet, PhD, professor of history at the University of North Carolina and author of *The Ocean is a Wilderness* and *The Colonists' American Revolution*

To the memory of the legendary Dr. Kennard B. Bork—
Professor of Geology and Paleontology at Denison University,
a true Renaissance Man, and my most inspirational teacher and mentor.

We remember how it was in former times when we were a strong and powerful People. Colonel Schuyler used frequently to come amongst us, and by this means we were kept together.

—Mohawk headman Hendrick Tejonihokarawa
of the Wolf Clan, 1754

My heart is broken to see so much of my Brethren's blood shed and I will take some of the prisoners back again either by force or by stratagem [adroit diplomacy].

—Mohawk War Captain Lawrence of the Wolf Clan,
following the devastating February 1690 attack on Schenectady,
vowing to hunt down the retreating French and Indian war party
and to recover the twenty-seven captured American prisoners

CONTENTS

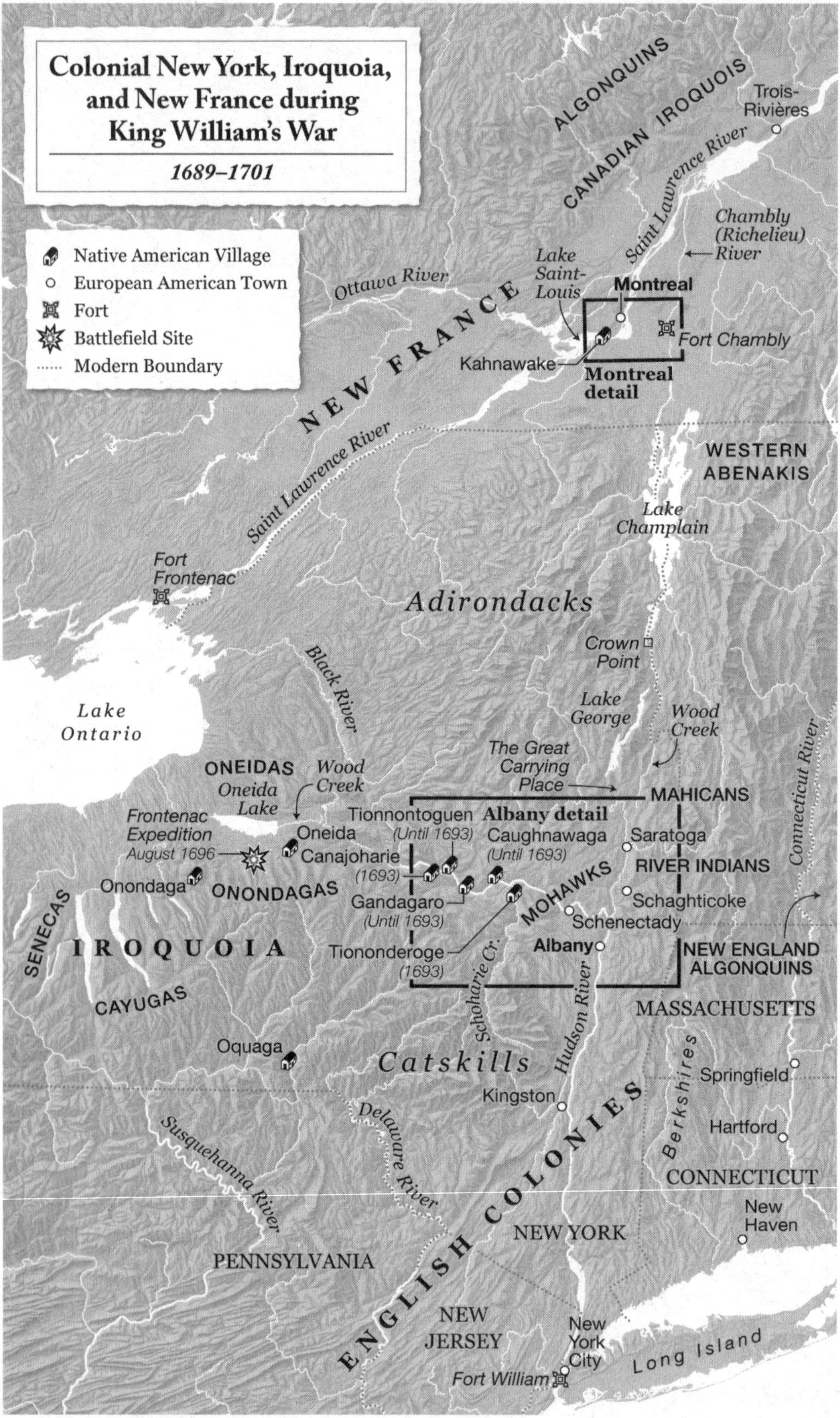

Colonial New York, Iroquoia, and New France during King William's War
1689–1701
Native American Village
European American Town
Fort
Battlefield Site
Modern Boundary
ALGONQUINS
CANADIAN IROQUOIS
Trois-Rivières
Saint Lawrence River
Chambly (Richelieu) River
Lake Saint-Louis
Ottawa River
NEW FRANCE
Montreal
Fort Chambly
Kahnawake
Montreal detail
WESTERN ABENAKIS
Lake Champlain
Fort Frontenac
Adirondacks
Crown Point
Black River
Lake Ontario
Lake George
Wood Creek
The Great Carrying Place
ONEIDAS
Oneida Lake
Wood Creek
Frontenac Expedition
August 1696
Oneida
Canajoharie
Onondaga
ONONDAGAS
Tionnontoguen
(Until 1693)
Albany detail
Caughnawaga
(Until 1693)
MAHICANS
Saratoga
RIVER INDIANS
(1693)
Gandagaro
(Until 1693)
MOHAWKS
Schaghticoke
Schenectady
Connecticut River
SENECAS
IROQUOIA
Tiononderoge
(1693)
Albany
NEW ENGLAND ALGONQUINS
Schoharie Cr.
CAYUGAS
MASSACHUSETTS
Hudson River
Oquaga
Catskills
Springfield
Berkshires
Kingston
Delaware River
Susquehanna River
ENGLISH COLONIES
Hartford
CONNECTICUT
New Haven
NEW YORK
PENNSYLVANIA
NEW JERSEY
New York City
Fort William
Long Island

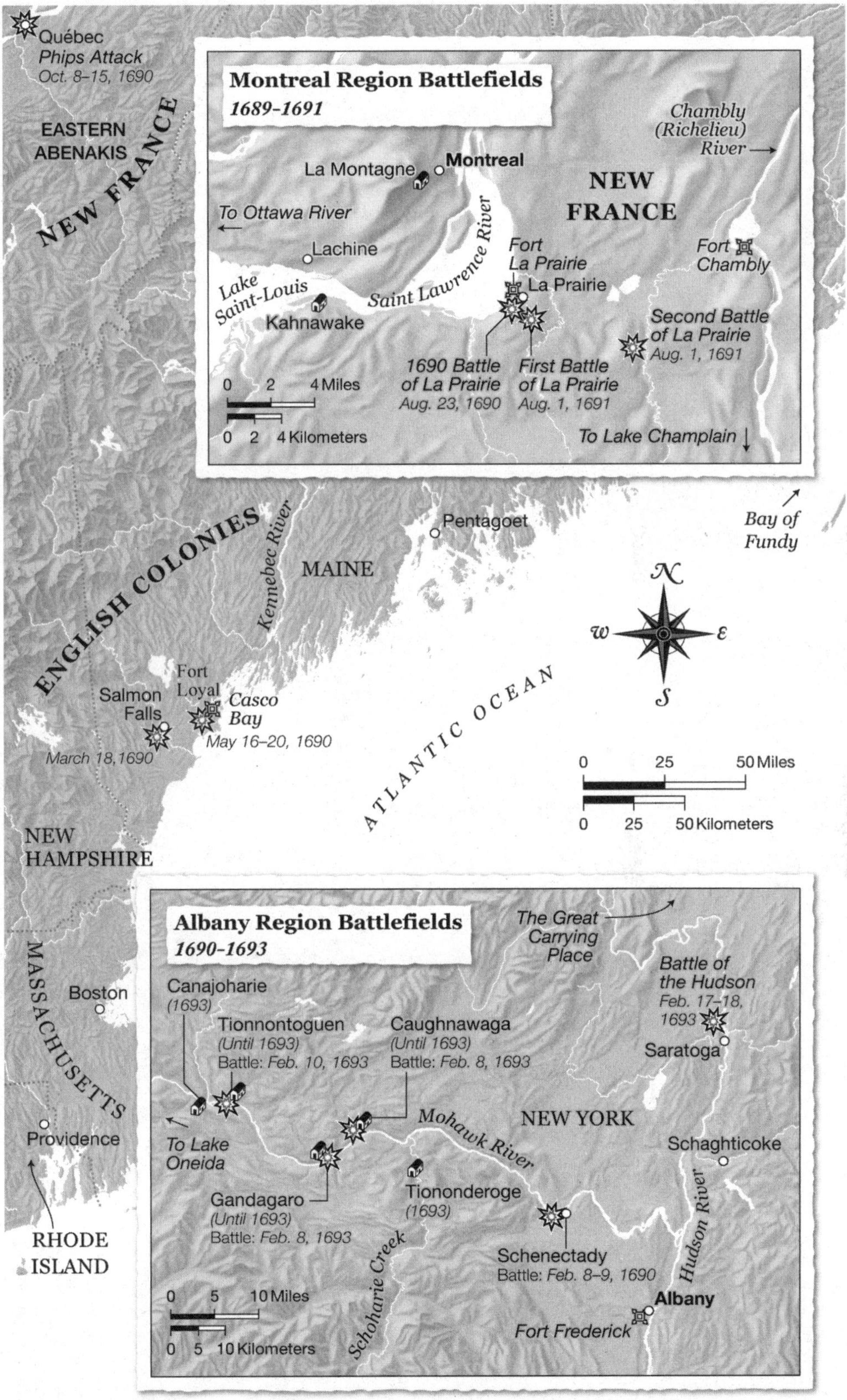

Québec
Phips Attack
Oct. 8–15, 1690
EASTERN ABENAKIS
NEW FRANCE
Montreal Region Battlefields
1689-1691
Chambly (Richelieu) River
La Montagne
Montreal
NEW FRANCE
To Ottawa River
Lachine
Saint Lawrence River
Fort La Prairie
La Prairie
Fort Chambly
Lake Saint-Louis
Kahnawake
Second Battle of La Prairie
Aug. 1, 1691
1690 Battle of La Prairie
Aug. 23, 1690
First Battle of La Prairie
Aug. 1, 1691
0 2 4 Miles
0 2 4 Kilometers
To Lake Champlain
Bay of Fundy
Pentagoet
ENGLISH COLONIES
Kennebec River
MAINE
N
W
E
S
Fort Loyal
Salmon Falls
Casco Bay
May 16–20, 1690
March 18,1690
ATLANTIC OCEAN
0 25 50 Miles
0 25 50 Kilometers
NEW HAMPSHIRE
MASSACHUSETTS
Boston
Providence
RHODE ISLAND
Albany Region Battlefields
1690-1693
The Great Carrying Place
Canajoharie
(1693)
Tionnontoguen
(Until 1693)
Battle: Feb. 10, 1693
Caughnawaga
(Until 1693)
Battle: Feb. 8, 1693
Battle of the Hudson
Feb. 17–18, 1693
Saratoga
To Lake Oneida
Mohawk River
NEW YORK
Schaghticoke
Gandagaro
(Until 1693)
Battle: Feb. 8, 1693
Tiononderoge
(1693)
Schoharie Creek
Hudson River
Schenectady
Battle: Feb. 8–9, 1690
Albany
Fort Frederick
0 5 10 Miles
0 5 10 Kilometers

CAST OF HISTORICAL FIGURES (1689–1701)

Principal Point-of-View Historical Characters

Major-Colonel Peter Schuyler: Dutch-American mayor of Albany, Indian Affairs commissioner, and commander of New York militia; born in 1657 in Beverwyck (Albany), New Netherlands, into a powerful Dutch immigrant family of humble beginnings; fluent in Dutch, English, and Mohawk; led joint English-Iroquois military expeditions against New France (French Canada); respected and beloved by the Five Iroquois Nations, who referred to him as "Brother Quider."

War Captain Lawrence: Mohawk war leader, peace negotiator, and Protestant Christian member of the Albany Dutch Reformed Church; born around 1663 into the Mohawk Wolf Clan near Tionnontoguen in the Mohawk River Valley; led Five Nations in several important war expeditions against the French with Peter and Johannes Schuyler; conducted peace conferences and negotiated with French-Canadian leaders for the return of colonial American and Iroquois prisoners.

Hilletie van Olinda: Biracial and multilingual Mohawk-Dutch woman in Schenectady and Albany; important council interpreter, Protestant Christian religious text translator, and messenger between the Iroquois and New York Indian officials; born around 1646 as fourth child of matriarch

Ots-Toch of Mohawk Wolf Clan and Dutch trader Cornelius van Slyck; moved to Schenectady in 1663, where she became a household servant, was taught to read and write Dutch, was baptized, and became paid government interpreter and key cross-cultural facilitator in Anglo-Iroquois diplomacy.

New York Royal Governors

Richard Coote, 1st Earl of Bellomont (1698–1701): Irish-born Whig nobleman and colonial governor of New York, Massachusetts Bay, and New Hampshire; bombastic pro-Leislerian governor disliked by the Iroquois; ousted his predecessor Benjamin Fletcher and led anti-piracy crusade in American colonies; enemy of Peter Schuyler and Hilletie van Olinda; lead sponsor of Captain Kidd's ill-fated 1696–1699 Indian Ocean pirate-hunting expedition.

Colonel Benjamin Fletcher (1692–1698): Tory royal governor and commander in chief of New York Province and northeastern English colonies during King William's War (1689–1697); longtime English soldier and friend of Peter Schuyler; called Cayenquiragoe (Great Swift Arrow) by the Iroquois, who respected him; as governor, he enriched New York but lined his own pockets by condoning the lucrative Madagascar pirate trade.

Richard Ingoldsby (1691–1692): Major-Colonel of English troops in New York Province; acting governor from July 1691–August 1692.

Henry Sloughter (1691): Royal governor briefly from April–July 1691 who put down Leisler's Rebellion; godfather of Mohawk war leader Lawrence's baptized son Henry.

Jacob Leisler (1689–1691): German-born merchant, New York City militia officer, and leader of Leisler's Rebellion; acting lieutenant governor from June 1689–March 1691; fiercely anti-Catholic, militant Calvinist

Protestant; corrupt, incompetent, and despotic colonial administrator; enemy of Peter Schuyler, Lawrence, and Hilletie van Olinda.

Francis Nicholson (1688–1689): Tory lieutenant governor of the Dominion of New England, serving under Edmund Andros; de facto ruler of New York Province until Leisler's Rebellion in June 1689, when Nicholson fled to London.

Five Tribes of the Iroquois Confederacy (Haudenosaunee)

Sanonguirese: Anglophile Mohawk headman, member of Bear Clan, and frequent Albany council spokesman; one of the elderly "principal sachems" of the Five Nations and unbaptized traditionalist throughout his life; friend of Lawrence.

Onnonouagaren: Anglophile Mohawk war captain, council spokesman, and peace negotiator; friend and fighting comrade of Lawrence.

Sadekanaktie: Anglophile Onondaga Iroquois headman and council spokesman.

Teganissorens: Onondaga headman and orator of the Five Nations who became the leading advocate for the neutralist faction, the leading Iroquois council spokesperson of his generation, and a key figure in the Grand Iroquois, English, and French Settlement of 1701.

Rode: Elderly Anglophile Mohawk chieftain and Five Nations council spokesman born in 1615; member of the Mohawk Turtle Clan; baptized in the Protestant Christian faith late in life in 1695.

Togouiroui: Francophile Kahnawake Mohawk war chief known as the Great Mohawk; led French and Indian war party in 1690 attack on

Schenectady; baptized by Canadian French Jesuits as Joseph and known by the Dutch of Albany as Kryn; knew Lawrence from their time together at Kahnawake mission outside Montreal.

Ourehouare: Cayuga Iroquois headman and war leader born in 1650; favorite of French royal governor Count Frontenac; served two years as a galley slave aboard a French warship fighting the Barbary pirates in the Mediterranean, along with fifty other captured Iroquois warriors.

Maria Iose: Wife of Mohawk war leader Lawrence; daughter of the powerful Mohawk Turtle Clan matriarch Karanondo (Lifter); mother of Sagonorasse (baptized Adam), Henry, and Hendrick.

Crown-Colonial Officials and Citizens

King William III: Dutch Prince of Orange who became King of England, Ireland, and Scotland from 1689 until his death in 1702; commander in chief of English forces during King William's War; ruled alongside his wife Queen Mary II, until her death from smallpox in December 1694, in the joint reign of William and Mary.

Louis de Buade, Comte de Frontenac: Governor general of New France (French Canada) from 1672 to 1682 and again from 1689 to his death in 1698; former soldier and architect of French expansion in North America; commander in chief of Franco-Indian attacks on New York and New England colonies during King William's War and defender of New France against joint Anglo-Iroquois attacks by New York and New England colonies; called Yonondio by the Iroquois.

Robert Livingston: Scottish-born merchant and New York government official in Indian affairs and supplying English troops; first lord of Livingston Manor in Hudson River Valley; accumulated much of his fortune by selling "illegal cargoes" to the French in wartime and siphoning money that was supposed to be used to feed the English soldiers of Albany; chief promoter and manager of Captain Kidd's ill-fated 1696–1699 Indian Ocean pirate-hunting expedition.

Reverend Godfredius Dellius: Clergyman of the Albany Dutch Reformed Church and missionary to the Mohawks; staunch opponent of Jacob Leisler during Leisler's Rebellion; worked closely with Mohawk interpreter Hilletie van Olinda; architect of shady land deal with Mohawks in 1690s that ended his career in New York in disgrace and forced him to return to the Netherlands.

Jacob Milborne: English-born New York militia captain and second-in-command to Jacob Leisler during Leisler's tumultuous 1689–1691 administration; married Leisler's daughter Mary to become his son-in-law; served as an indentured servant in Barbados and Connecticut before immigrating to New York in 1668; known for his extreme Protestant Calvinist beliefs and being a hothead in public affairs.

Captain Johannes Schuyler: Dutch-American captain in New York militia; youngest brother of Colonel Peter Schuyler; led joint English-Iroquois military expedition against New France in 1690, fighting alongside Mohawk war leader Lawrence.

Captain William Kidd: New York privateer, merchant sea captain, and former Caribbean buccaneer; wealthy gentleman, civic leader, and founding father of Trinity Church; commander of Crown-sponsored 1696–1699 Indian Ocean expedition to hunt pirates and French merchant ships during King William's War.

Frederick Philipse: Wealthiest merchant in New York Province from both licit and illicit transoceanic trade from 1675 until his death in 1702; anglicized Dutchman who arrived on American shores in the mid-1650s as a carpenter and rose to become first Lord of the Manor of Philipsburg and patriarch of the Philipse family; anti-Leislerian member of New York governor's council; known as "the Pirate King" for pioneering the lucrative Indo-Atlantic Red Sea pirate trade between New York and Madagascar.

Nicholas Bayard: Wealthy anglicized Dutch merchant and governor's council member in New York City; former head of New York City militia imprisoned by Leisler for being an outspoken critic; friend of Peter Schuyler, Frederick Philipse, and Captain Kidd, and enemy of Leisler and Lord Bellomont.

William Blathwayt: Tory Secretary of War and powerful member of the English Privy Council, the king's cabinet in London charged with colonial administration; one of the primary wheeler-dealers in imperial patronage in London in the 1690s.

Charles Talbot, the 1st Duke of Shrewsbury: English Whig secretary of state for the Southern Department, responsible for Southern England, Wales, Ireland, and the American colonies during King William's War; acting regent whenever the king was absent from England; affectionately referred to as the "King of Hearts" by William III; key backer of Captain Kidd's 1696-1699 Indian Ocean voyage.

1
LEISLER'S REBELLION

On June 10 of the Year of Our Lord 1689, the City and Province of New York were not only in a state of open political rebellion that verged on bloody anarchy but stood on the cusp of a grueling nine-year war with imperial France. Peter Schuyler—the Dutch-American mayor of Albany, lead commissioner of Indian Affairs, and major of the New York militia—would soon be on the front lines of both the rebellion and war, but at this moment he was 150 miles upriver from the burning cauldron of New York City and had no idea how dramatically his life was about to change. Though the born-and-bred American backwoodsman had risen to become one of the wealthiest individuals in the colony, was currently one of its most respected citizens, and had witnessed just about everything in his thirty-one years of war and peace on the Indian frontier, nothing could have prepared him for the current turmoil taking place on the oyster-shell-strewn streets of the City. Though he spent most of his time in Albany as the town's mayor and militia leader, he often conducted political and business affairs in New York City, where his younger brothers Brandt and Philip Schuyler lived as full-time residents.[1]

When he sailed downriver from Albany, he often stayed at his brother Brandt's glazed-brick, Dutch-style home on Broad Street in the City's South Ward. If he had been there on this historic day of June 10, 1689, Major Peter Schuyler would have looked out upon Fort James to the south, which had long been a source of reassurance for New Yorkers but today rose from the southern tip of Manhattan Island like a menacing enemy castle. The fort was stoutly built with four sides, a bastion at each corner, and walls of hard-packed earth, oyster shells, and rubble instead of stone masonry to absorb cannon fire without collapsing. However, that would have meant nothing to Schuyler because the fortress was occupied by Jacob Leisler, the leader of the rebellion, and his provincial troops, who had taken over the City.

The fifty-year-old merchant, militia captain, and ultraorthodox Calvinist Protestant of German extraction had in the past month capitalized on the unsettled state of New York Province in response to the Glorious Revolution, the ongoing political struggle in Europe between Protestants and Catholics over the English throne that had sent several American colonies into disarray. An English Jack fluttered in the crisp breeze above the garrison and her 12-pound cannons mounted on the palisades, but with Leisler and his troops occupying Fort James, Schuyler would not have found his country's flag comforting.[2]

Leisler's rebellious force had captured the fort on May 3 and by June 8 had created a Committee of Safety and elected Leisler commander in chief of the militia and captain of the fort. Within a day of being seized, the stockade was transformed into the primary military command post of the rebellion. Dozens of Leisler's militiamen now guarded the northern entry gate to the fort, marched along the perimeter, and stood at the ready at the ramparts and battlement cannons. Dispatch couriers and riders on horseback came and went before the heavily armed sentinels clutching pikes, swords, and bayoneted muskets. New York City appeared on the verge of a foreign invasion.[3]

The fledgling but burgeoning metropole was at this time an English possession with a multiethnic but predominantly Dutch population of some five thousand souls. Conceived by the Westindische Compagnie, or Dutch West India Company (WIC, 1621–1815), to take advantage of the North American fur trade and protect the mouth of the Hudson River, New York City had been founded in 1625 as the Dutch trading post of Nieuw Amsterdam within the colony of New Netherland and was the twelfth oldest continuously occupied European settlement on what would become US soil. Though the English had seized control of New Amsterdam, the Dutch capital of New Netherland, in 1664, renaming it New York, the quintessential Dutch architectural character of the City had been preserved.[4] Many of the houses on nearby Stone, Duke, and Pearl Streets were of a three-story Dutch design similar to those of crowded Amsterdam to make use of space and were constructed of both wood and imported red, white, and yellow brick. Along with deeply canted, shingled gable rooftops and facades of dormered brick, the colonial homes had flaring eaves, double-hung sash windows with outward swinging wood shutters, and six-foot stoops up to the front doors, in case of flooding from the nearby East River and North (Hudson) River to the west.[5]

Though Peter Schuyler continued to spend most of his time in Albany, he and his fellow family members of the powerful Schuyler clan who continued to make the upriver fur-trading outpost their primary residence did considerable business and maintained houses in the global trading center of New York City. Many of them had to come to love the growing, multiethnic port town almost as much as Dutch Albany. But today, with the companies of enemy soldiers carrying muskets with fixed bayonets stomping aggressively about the streets, turning what would one day be known as Lower Manhattan into a police state, Schuyler and his fellow family members who had made New York Province their home for decades would have been in a state of shock. The militarized conditions had put the whole City under strain, not just Schuyler's younger brothers Brandt and Philip, who lived full-time in the City. Many New Yorkers feared that they would soon be rounded up and stuffed into the Fort James prison.[6]

Soon, very soon, Peter Schuyler, upriver in Albany, would learn that his cherished colony, the place where he had carved out a life for himself and his wife and children in the New World, was being taken over by a tyrant. And once he received this critical information, he would find himself embroiled in an epic political struggle that would pit him directly against Jacob Leisler. The "great usurper,"[7] as many Manhattanites were now calling Leisler, was well on his way to seizing control of the entire royal province in the name of the Glorious Revolution.

The political unrest that would divide Peter Schuyler and his fellow New Yorkers into two bitter, warring factions for the next decade had begun across the Atlantic much earlier, in the fall of 1688, when the Catholic King James II was usurped in a coup by English Protestant leaders, his own daughter Mary Stuart, and her Dutch husband, Prince William of Orange. James had angered much of England's Protestant aristocracy by his pro-Catholic stance, his arbitrary rule, and his absolutist concentration of power at the expense of Parliament. But the last straw occurred in April 1688 when his wife, the queen, gave birth to a son, threatening to force a Catholic dynasty upon England for decades through a legitimate male heir to the throne.[8]

Recruited by Anglican bishops and England's political and military elite, the two ardent Protestants William and Mary vowed to rule as equals and accept limits imposed by Parliament to their imperial powers. As the nephew and son-in-law of James, William stood as a viable Protestant alternative for the English throne, and as the military commander of the Netherlands, his goal was to make England an ally in the Dutch war against powerful France. The French were under the rule of Louis XIV—the Roi Soleil, or Sun King, as he was popularly known, the feisty defender of the Catholic faith and a longtime thorn to the English Crown.[9]

In a bold military gambit and political takeover, William invaded England at the head of fifteen thousand Dutch, Danish, and German troops, and marched for London to seize control of the Protestant nation's extensive financial and military assets and integrate them into his Dutch alliance. Supported by disgruntled senior English army and navy officers, the Dutch prince and his invasion force crossed the English Channel and made a landing at Brixham in Devon without opposition on November 5, 1688. Switching allegiances from their Catholic monarch to the stronger alliance, most high-ranking English officials abandoned their king and joined William and his wife, Mary. At the same time, James II escaped to France and sought refuge at the court of Louis XIV, who provided him protection and became his guardian.[10]

Once Prince William's Dutch forces took control of London, Parliament transferred the throne to William and Mary as joint monarchs after the royal couple signed off on a Bill of Rights ensuring constitutional and civil rights protections. A short time later, the new queen chose to step back from co-rule and allow her Dutch husband to take the lead in Crown affairs. The Whig Protestant political leaders who coordinated the takeover, known as the Whig Junto, were fervent adversaries of the pro-monarchist Tory Party and declared the seizure of power a "Glorious Revolution."[11] Thus, the takeover was skillfully depicted as a spontaneous uprising by united Britons when it was, in truth, a bloodless usurpation spearheaded by Dutch military forces and a rebellious, fiercely anti-Catholic Whig wing of England's Parliament.[12]

The outcome of the coup d'état was the security of the Protestant succession, the death knell of royal absolutism, and the establishment of the supremacy of Parliament over the monarchy in England. With the steadfast backing of the Whig aristocracy, King William III formally declared war upon France in May 1689, plunging England into what would turn out to be a prolonged global conflagration of unprecedented cost requiring heavy new taxes. To compete with France, England was forced to build up her army and navy on a massive scale, managed by a cumbersome state bureaucracy and funded by higher taxation.[13]

While the Glorious Revolution radically transformed the monarchy and ushered in historic constitutional reforms in England, the flight of King James II from the throne and ordination of William and Mary as joint sovereigns had just as dramatic repercussions in colonial America—and Peter Schuyler's New York Province, in particular. When word of the Revolution had reached American shores back in March and April, political power struggles erupted in New York, Massachusetts, Maryland, and Virginia between those who had served in the regime of the deposed Catholic Stuart king and the Protestant promoters of the new monarchy. The Dominion of New England—James II's mega-colony that bundled together the eight northern colonies of New Hampshire, Massachusetts Bay, Plymouth, Rhode Island, Connecticut, New York, and East and West Jersey by royal fiat—was dissolved and Sir Edmund Andros, the Dominion's autocratic royal governor, was thrown in jail. The result was several northeastern colonies reverted to their pre-Dominion forms of governance and remained in a state of political crisis and anti-Catholic hysteria.[14]

The rebels of New York and New England took matters into their own hands by rejecting Sir Edmund Andros and other English officials appointed by James. In New York, the news of the London coup sparked discontented Dutch and other fervently Protestant ethnic groups to rebel against the local officials they associated with Catholic Stuart tyranny. While in Massachusetts and Maryland the citizens quickly united to seize the provincial governments and cast out tainted officeholders, New York was a far more socially and religiously diverse colony, with pent-up tensions and competing factions that had existed for decades. Consequently, its divided citizenry fought violently over who should control political power.[15]

Political factionalism was also more pronounced in New York because, unlike the New England colonies, New York did not possess a preexisting charter upon which to base the legitimacy of its rebel government. Administrative authority in New York had always been vested in the Catholic James: first as the Duke of York following the English conquest of New Netherland in 1664 and ceding of the Dutch colony to England; and later, in February 1685, when he ascended to the English throne as King James II and his colony became a royal province. Because he had added the royal colony of New York to the Dominion of New England in May 1688, the provincial government lacked constitutional legitimacy with his removal from power and the dissolution of the Dominion of New England.[16]

After capturing Fort James, forming a Committee of Safety, and electing Leisler commander in chief of the militia and captain of the fort, New York's hardline Protestant insurgents had removed Lieutenant Governor Nicholson, Andros's second-in-command and an Anglican, and his former Dominion political appointees, including sheriffs and clerks. Leisler and his supporters claimed that pro-Catholic enemies of the people had joined in a conspiracy with the deposed James II to join with New France, conquer New York, and put it under Roman Catholic rule. The viceroyalty of New France was the North American territory controlled by France in the 17th century, in what is today Canada and a vast swath of the US continental interior extending to Louisiana. With the Dominion of New England dissolved and Fort James seized by Leisler and his troops, Nicholson feared for his life and fled to England. Before his departure, he entrusted the government to his three councilors—Frederick Philipse, Stephanus van Cortlandt, and Nicholas Bayard, all friends of Peter Schuyler—but they, too, were repudiated. Having arrived on American shores in 1653 as a mere carpenter, Philipse had risen to become the wealthiest merchant and property-owner in the colony and the leading voice of the governor's council.[17]

Now, on June 10, 1689, with Leisler having assumed full command of the New York militia, a mob mentality had taken hold of the City. For the past two days, Committee of Safety militiamen had lorded over Manhattan like prison guards, standing at the ramparts of the fort and marching about the streets armed with muskets, swords, and pikes—as if the French in Canada and their Catholic sympathizers in New York and New England would invade at any moment. The militiamen continued to root out, publicly harass, and rough up those who questioned their actions, stood against them, or had previously held commissions under Andros and Nicholson. Philipse and his fellow governor's council members had protested the abuse of the town's public officials, sailors, and citizens, but to no avail.[18]

As tensions had escalated in the past two days, Leisler and his militant followers had become increasingly impatient for Frederick Philipse and his fellow members of the ruling Anglo-Dutch elite to declare their unequivocal loyalty to William and Mary. Because Philipse and the other leaders were uncertain if the Dutch prince and his Stuart wife were truly in power and the legitimate heirs to the English throne, they were reluctant to commit to the new king without more definitive information and clear-cut orders from London. Because many of the City's merchants belonged to New York's Dutch Reformed Church or the Church of England, they also opposed the rebellion on the grounds that it brought unnecessary violence, panic, and instability to the province. They wanted to slow the process down and not be forced to make a rash decision, especially given that it took six to eight weeks for news to cross the Atlantic. The situation in London might have changed since the initial pronouncement.[19]

But now, with blood on the streets all but inevitable, Peter Schuyler's friend Frederick Philipse—who also kept a home in the fur-trading outpost of Dutch Albany—was running out of time. Alarmed at how swiftly the City was sinking into chaos and unsure of what the future portended under the unpredictable Jacob Leisler, Philipse called an emergency meeting with his fellow governor's council members, Stephanus van Cortlandt and Nicholas Bayard. They quickly decided to prepare a detailed letter for Charles Talbot, the Duke of Shrewsbury, the English secretary of state for the Southern Department who administered the American colonies, warning the Mother Country of the precarious situation. Because of Leisler and "other disaffected and dangerous persons," wrote Philipse and the council members, "all manner of Government" was overthrown, "no person" or "estate" was safe, and the City would be in "utter ruin" unless the Crown sent "sudden relief."[20]

But as the councilors stamped the letter with the official royal seal, it seemed highly unlikely that the City and Province of New York would even be in existence by the time their letter reached London.

On June 22, Leisler and his militiamen proclaimed that they were holding Fort James in the name of the new Protestant King of England and swiftly consolidated their power. Six days later, the Committee of Safety appointed Leisler as permanent captain of the fort, and on August 15, they granted him the authority of commander in chief.[21] Once firmly in power, Leisler stripped Philipse, van Cortlandt, and Bayard from the governor's council and removed other Dominion appointees from their offices, inserted new pro-Leislerians in their place, and began arresting and imprisoning his most ardent opponents. Leisler also took steps to refurbish the fort and requisition supplies for the colony's defense against Louis de Buade, Comte de Frontenac, the governor-general of New France, and his Gallic legions in Canada, since he knew war with France was inevitable. Leisler also renamed Fort James Fort William in honor of England's new Dutch king.[22]

Religion, more than politics, was at the heart of both the Glorious Revolution and Leisler's Rebellion. On both sides of the Atlantic, no issue stirred the suspicions or sparked the passions of devout English and Dutch

Calvinist Protestants more than the fear of Roman Catholicism. In England and colonial America, the Glorious Revolution pitted Protestants and so-called "Williamites," or supporters of King William, against Catholics and so-called "Jacobites" or "papists," or those who supported King James and the restoration of the House of Stuart to the English throne.[23] For Leisler and his pious followers, "the threat of Catholicism meant not only the specter of heresy but also the yoke of tyranny."[24] He and his fellow Calvinists placed emphasis on the supreme power of God, the sinful tendency of mankind, and the doctrine of predestination, believing that all human events were controlled by God, thus denying free will. Fiercely anti-Catholic, they viewed the world through the narrow prism of a never-ending, apocalyptic struggle between so-called "papists" and Protestants.[25]

At the same time, political affiliation, class, ethnicity, and family connections also played a role in the rebellion. The Leislerians tended to be more Dutch or German than English or Scottish; were more likely farmers, artisans, and second-tier merchants than upper-rung merchants or landholders; and were more likely to be conservative Calvinist Protestants than belong to the Anglican Church or practice any of the other more progressive versions of Protestantism. Factional tensions between the elite and second-tier Euro-American families jostling for power and preeminence also played a role in the unrest in New York City, Albany, Long Island, and elsewhere.[26]

But for Jacob Leisler, religion was the driving force for the revolution waged in his name. His main conflict was between New York's Calvinist Protestants and the City's English and Dutch colonists who belonged to the Church of England or Dutch Reformed Church. He wanted hard-line Protestantism to triumph over Anglicanism because he believed the Anglican Church would eventually submit to Roman Catholicism, whose political and religious leaders under James II had governed arbitrarily and had persecuted Protestants for their religious affiliation.[27] He had acquired his longtime fear of Roman Catholics from the abuse inflicted upon his father, Reverend Jacob Victorian Leisler, who had been harassed by the Spanish Catholics during the Inquisition and Europe's Thirty Years' War in the late 1630s. After two years of ministering to and aiding the French Protestant community in the Spanish-occupied Palatinate city of Frankenthal, his parents were forced to flee to Frankfurt am Main, Germany, where Leisler was born in 1640. The persecution of his Calvinist family and the local French Huguenots by Spanish Catholics made a lasting impression on young Jacob, setting him on a path of lifelong suspicion and hatred of Catholics.[28]

Despite Leisler's populist and anti-elitist appeal, he came from a long line of upper-middle-class Germanic nobles, magistrates, and clergy and was the proud owner of an ancestral family coat of arms. Well educated, he was versed in Latin, fluent in German, French, English, and Dutch, and had close business ties to the wealthy Dutch and English merchants of New York City. In many ways, Leisler was the perfect example of the American Dream. Sailing to North America from Amsterdam aboard *Gilded Otter* in the spring of 1660, he arrived in New Netherland at age twenty as a junior officer in the Dutch West India Company, and, within two years, he was an independent merchant in the lucrative fur and tobacco trades. By 1663, he had married into the powerful Dutch family of Govert Loockermans, when he took the hand of the widow Elsie Tymens in marriage, giving him further access to the growing port city's booming economy, and eventually providing him with many influential English connections. By the mid-1680s, he had worked his way upward to become one of the wealthier merchants in the City, building a vast trading network extending from New York to Suriname, Amsterdam, and London. He lived with his wife, Elsie, and their seven children in a resplendent waterfront mansion on Pearl Street overlooking the East River estuary.[29]

Thus, while Leisler's Rebellion was a combined populist ethnic Dutch and Calvinist religious revolt against "elitism" and "papism," the leader of the rebellion came from well-to-do European lineage and was an affluent, anglicized member of New York. He regularly wore a powdered periwig and carried a walking cane. Yet, despite his upper-middle-class origins and prosperity since emigrating to New York, he reserved his greatest animosity for New York's Anglo-Dutch elite that included Frederick Philipse and Peter Schuyler, whom he believed unfairly controlled the levers of political and economic power in the City and throughout the province. A combative personality and religious fanatic, Leisler had had several run-ins over the years with Schuyler and the magistrates and church leaders of Dutch Albany, as well as numerous others in New York Province, which had earned him a reputation for intolerance and pugnacity.[30]

The Leislerians' goal was to simultaneously root out all "Jacobites" and "papists" and level the economic playing field for their followers—mostly disenfranchised Dutch men and women from the lower and middle classes, who had not fared well under English rule. They were also at odds with leaders of New York's Dutch Reformed Church, who refused to cast aside Dominion officeholders and openly back Leisler and his rebellion. However, for Leisler, effectively administering the office of royal governor proved daunting since he was burdened with a money-draining war with France, a depressed economy, a poorly defended Albany frontier, and widespread feelings of uncertainty throughout much of the province.[31]

As the chaotic summer of 1689 unfolded and the myriad problems confronting the province began to overwhelm him, Leisler became more undemocratic and arbitrary, especially as his foes dug in their heels and fled from the City to escape his roundups. He continued to desperately seek the stamp of approval for his actions from the Crown and the support of the entire province, not merely a sizable faction in New York City and in a few smaller pockets. But garnering the endorsement of William and Mary and the backing of the majority of New Yorkers, Albanians, Long Islanders, and other holdouts, who refused to recognize his legitimacy, continued to prove elusive.[32]

And his most formidable adversary happened to be one of the wealthiest and most well-connected denizens of New York and the greatest friend and protector of the Iroquois—the American-born frontiersman Peter Schuyler.

2
THE GATHERING STORM

The stunning news that England had declared war on France in May 1689 in the name of the Glorious Revolution did not reach New York Province until early August. King William's War, as it would become known in English America, would soon turn into a global contest fought for the next nine years in Europe, West Africa, the East and West Indies, and English and French North America. In England, the conflict was known as the "War of the League of Augsburg," while in France and the Dutch Republic it was referred to as the "War of the Grand Alliance."[1]

The timing of the war declaration could not have been worse for Jacob Leisler, for by midsummer he was not only deeply unpopular in New York City and on Long Island but far up the Hudson River in Albany. Peter Schuyler, the anglicized Dutch mayor of Albany, who doubled as major of the militia, and his fellow officials firmly rejected Leisler's authority from the very beginning. To maintain their political independence, preserve their valuable fur-trading monopoly, and protect their long-standing alliance with the Five Nations of the Iroquois, Schuyler and his fellow Albanians created a Convention in early August composed of local civil and military leaders. Declaring themselves loyal to William and Mary and the Glorious Revolution while awaiting the arrival of Governor Nicholson's Crown-appointed replacement, they rebuffed Leisler's aggressive attempts to bring the community under his control.[2]

No town in 17th-century America was more traditionally Dutch than Albany—or more resistant to outsiders meddling in its economic affairs and peaceful relations with the Iroquois. In 1689, the original Dutch West

India Company settlement founded in 1652 was a small village of around seven hundred people, protected from attack by a wooden stockade with five blockhouses. The town had only two streets, which crossed one another at right angles in the configuration of a wishbone. Haendeler's Straat, or Trader's Street, ran roughly north and south parallel to the river, while oriented generally east and west and partially up a steep hill was Yonkheer's Straat, or Gentleman's Street, known today as State Street. Clustered along Haendeler's and Yonkheer's streets in the stockaded village were over 150 houses crowded close together next to the Hudson River. Because the two dirt thoroughfares pinched together at the ends in a pattern that reminded early visitors of a fishnet, the town center had been known since Albany's inception as the *fuyck*, the Dutch term for a fishnet or deer trap.[3] Between Haendeler's Street and the Hudson lay the original Dutch fort, Fort Orange, which had been abandoned shortly after the English takeover of New Netherland in 1664 and replaced by a new fort, Fort Frederick, located at the top of the high hill above the town and farther from the river.[4]

The earliest and staunchest resistance to Leisler's regime came not from New York City or Long Island but from Dutch Albany. Withholding their support from Leisler, Mayor Peter Schuyler and the Convention preferred to govern themselves. However, this meant that they had to shoulder the burden in King William's War against Count de Frontenac and his potent French and Indian army gathering strength in New France.[5] Throughout the summer, the Albanians had organized the region's defenses and directed public affairs, but in early September when they learned from the young Mohawk war captain Lawrence and other Anglophile Iroquois scouts that French invasion was imminent, they swallowed their pride and asked Leisler for one hundred men to help protect their fur-trading outpost on the Hudson. But Leisler refused any aid until the Convention officially recognized his authority and dissolved itself.[6]

Disappointed yet determined to protect the Albany frontier, Schuyler and the Convention collected a special war provision tax and turned to neighboring Connecticut to loan them a company of soldiers to defend themselves against the rumored French invasion. When the New Englanders generously agreed, Leisler became enraged and a bitter feud arose between his government and Connecticut's leaders. Outmaneuvered by Schuyler and the Convention, the outraged Leisler sent a militia force of heavily armed soldiers upriver in early November 1689 under his second-in-command, Jacob Milborne.[7] Leisler sought not only the surrender of the Albany Convention and recognition of his legitimacy, but to ensure that his government in New York City retained control of the entire province and all its political and business affairs, including conducting negotiations with the League Iroquois allied with the English.[8]

But Schuyler, his fellow Albanians, and their powerful Iroquois allies stood in Leisler and Milborne's way.

Leisler recognized early in his seizure of power that while New York City was the strategic center of the mainland English American colonies, the upriver fur-trading outpost of Albany was just as vital to the province and his own success. In the late 17th century, the two cities were closely connected politically, militarily, culturally, and commercially, with Albany essentially a satellite of the larger metropole to the south. Not only did the two trading centers form the northern and southern extremities of the Hudson River's vital inland waterway transport system, Albany served as the supply depot and launching point of English attacks on French Canada. Moreover, New York's royal governors routinely made trips to Albany to conduct diplomatic councils with delegations of the powerful Five Nations of the Iroquois, or Haudenosaunee, the "People of the Longhouse."[9]

The Iroquois League, or Five Nations as the Confederation was known, included the Mohawks, Oneidas, Onondagas, Cayugas, and Senecas, living in what is today the Albany-Schenectady region and most of New York State, northern Pennsylvania, and the eastern Great Lakes region. The Iroquois viewed the Confederation as a metaphorical Longhouse extending in a rectangular, east-to-west corridor from the Hudson River Valley to southeastern Lake Ontario. The Mohawks—the Kanien'kehá:ka or "People of the Flint" as they called themselves—were the Keepers of the Eastern Door of the Five Nations' symbolic Longhouse, while the Senecas were the Keepers of the Western Door. The Onondagas in the middle of the metaphorical Longhouse were the Keepers of the Central Council Fire and Wampum. More precious than gold or silver to the Native Iroquois and Algonquin tribes as trade currency and known for its sociopolitical and ceremonial power, wampumpeag (wampum) consisted of woven strings or belts of small, symmetrical white and purple beads made from shallow marine quahog and whelk shells. Wampum was the shell currency used by all five of the Iroquois Nations in the fur trade, and wampum belts consisted of beads of polished shells strung in belts used by various North American Indian tribes in making ceremonial pledges. The Mohawks, Senecas, and Onondagas were the "elder brothers" of the Longhouse and played a prominent role in New York's diplomatic and military affairs in the late 17th century.[10]

Since the inception of the Dutch colony of New Netherland, the Haudenosaunee had controlled the fate of not only the Dutch Hudson River Valley settlements but New York City far to the south. Though the Dutch had by 1625 set up beaver-trading stockades at New Amsterdam on Manhattan Island and Fort Orange near present-day Albany, and by 1662, had added Beverwyck and Wiltwyck (later Esopus) to their commercial network, they did so only through the consent of the powerful Iroquois. By 1689, the People of the Longhouse were not only a critical trading partner but a protective shield for both the Hudson River Valley settlements and New York City in fending off attack by Frontenac's professional French soldiers and Canadian militia, as well as his Wendat (Huron), Odawa (Ottawa), and Laurentian Iroquois allies from the Montreal and western Great Lakes regions.[11]

Throughout the fall of 1689, New York's officials fretted that Frontenac would secretly muster his forces at Montreal and launch a major land-based assault upon Albany and even New York City itself, while a French war fleet simultaneously sailed down from Quebec to roll up the entire colony in a joint land-sea operation.[12] Due to its "strategic importance,"[13] Albany was regarded by King William III and English officials on both sides of the Atlantic as "the only bulwark and safeguard of all their Majesty's Plantations on the Main of America," since the French would have to attack from Canada by land and not just by sea.[14]

However, the Albany borderlands only served as a "bulwark" against French and Indian attack due to the strong Anglophile-Iroquois presence in the region. The Five Nations had long understood the power they wielded over their Euro-American allies—whom they referred to as "Christians" or "Brethren"—when it came to the defense of Albany, the Mohawk and Hudson River valleys, and the bustling port town perched on the southern tip of Manhattan Island. Their villages in Iroquoia were referred to by the Dutch and English as "castles" because they were formidable defensive bastions to protect against French and Indian attacks from New France and the Great Lakes region. In the late 17th century, Iroquois "castles" were enclosed by stout wooden palisades consisting of double rows of tall, sharpened logs standing side by side to form walls that protected the residents from attack. In addition to having inner and outer stockades encircling the villages, the fortifications had interlocking diamond patterns, protected galleries, and watchtowers to fend off attack.[15]

Having grown up in Albany, Peter Schuyler fully appreciated both the military might wielded by the Iroquois and Albany's strategic importance. Born in 1657 in Beverwyck, New Netherlands, into a powerful Dutch immigrant family of humble beginnings, Schuyler was not only Albany's preeminent government official but the most trusted and beloved diplomat for the Five Iroquois Nations.[16] He was the second son of Philip Pieterse Schuyler (1628–1683), a simple gunstock-maker who went on to become a leading government official and fur-trader; and Margarita van Slichtenhorst (1628–1711), daughter of the resident director of Rensselaerswyck, one of the founding Dutch settlements near Albany. Young Peter spent much of his youth not only ice skating upon the frozen Hudson and racing down hillsides on sleds made of rope and white pine, but exploring the wilds among the Mohawks, Mahicans, and other Indigenous tribes. Like Hawkeye in *The Last of the Mohicans*, he learned to hunt and track at an early age and to speak in the Mohawk tongue, in addition to mastering Dutch and English. He also learned early on to patiently listen to Indigenous peoples, to understand and appreciate their rituals, and to sympathize with them as human beings. Though the Dutch were aggressive mercantilists with a nose for profit, their approach to the New World was far different from the bellicose and imperialistic English, French, and Spanish. Due to their belief in strong trade partnerships, the Dutch of the Albany frontier advocated for fair treatment in political and commercial dealings with Native Americans, placed a high premium on maintaining peace with them, and helped mediate between rival Native factions to reduce conflict.[17]

Because of his unique frontier Dutch-American upbringing, Schuyler not only had important connections to the Dutch of Albany and New York City, where his father, Captain Philip Schuyler, had owned property and had held business interests, but to the Indigenous peoples of the Five Nations. His father had long been friendly and traded with the Iroquois as well as served as an interpreter in councils—and Peter Schuyler continued the family tradition. By 1685, the twenty-eight-year-old frontiersman was married to the affluent Angelica van Schaick, served the Albany community as an Indian agent and the treasurer of the Dutch Reformed Church, and had risen to a lieutenant of cavalry in the Albany militia and judge of the Court of Oyer and Terminer. Distinguishing himself as a good listener and natural leader—"ever temperate in his views and just to others"—in 1686 he became Albany's first mayor and ex officio chairman of the Board of the Commissioners for Indian Affairs when the fur-trading center was incorporated as a city. In the ensuing years, he would rise to the rank of colonel of the Albany militia, the highest grade ever granted to a native New Yorker by the Crown.[18]

As mayor of Albany and a leader in Indian affairs, he conducted all negotiations with the Five Nations and other Native American tribes of New York and was the top government official in negotiations in the absence of the colonial governor. All news of the French or their Indian allies in Canada was first communicated to him in Albany, and he, in turn, transmitted this information to the Crown-appointed governor in New York City. As the most prominent leader in borderlands Indian diplomacy during the early colonial era, Schuyler served as both liaison and protector of the League Iroquois. Because of his dedicated public service toward the Five Nations, the Iroquois bestowed upon him the honorable moniker "Brother Quider," the council title for the government of Albany based on a Mohawk pronunciation of Schuyler's given name, "Peter."[19]

The formal alliance between the Five Tribes of the Iroquois Nation and English America in the 17th and 18th centuries was known as the Covenant Chain. Initiated in 1677, the political arrangement established a series of treaties to stabilize relations with the Haudenosaunee by engaging in peaceful trading and community building within New York and bordering colonies. With the governments of New York, Massachusetts, Maryland, and Virginia signing on to the treaties, the Covenant Chain alliance ensured cooperation and peace between the Iroquois and the four English colonies, and between the Iroquois and their traditional enemies, which included the Mahicans, Schaghticokes, Susquehannocks, and other Algonquins.[20]

For the Five Nations, the synergistic arrangement with the Protestant English gave rise to a lengthy period of dominance in the northeast, making the Haudenosaunee the "first among equals by virtue of their ability to serve as brokers between English governments and Indian nations."[21] The League Iroquois benefitted by acquiring security on their eastern and southern borders and by gaining direct and safe access to the Albany fur market, where, according to Frontenac himself, beaver pelts sold at favorable prices typically one-third higher than in New France. The Albany nexus also provided the Iroquois with a steady supply of muskets, powder, ammunition, and cooking wares that were critical to their continued success against the Great Lakes nations of the *Pays d'en haut* (Upper Country or Western tribes), Canadian Algonquins, and the French.[22]

For the English provinces, the Covenant Chain helped protect New York City and other coastal townships from French and Indian attack. The Crown's close ties to the League Iroquois pacified the Mahicans and other Algonquian-speaking tribes, since they had no choice but to collaborate with the most powerful northeastern Indigenous confederacy and to move to the margins of Iroquoia as a security buffer.[23] The alliance also provided New York with a ready supply of veteran allied warriors to launch attacks and combat the French throughout the continental interior and into Canada.[24]

Schuyler and his fellow Albany officials went to great lengths to preserve the Covenant Chain and nurture their close diplomatic, economic, and military alliance with the Iroquois. During his long career as mayor of Albany, Indian Affairs liaison, and commanding officer of armed forces fighting the French, Schuyler worked hand in hand with the young Mohawk war leader and diplomat Lawrence to achieve peace and prosperity for both Euro-American New Yorkers and the Iroquois.[25]

But in the fall of 1689, the diplomatic skills of Schuyler and Lawrence were put to the test when they were forced to take on Jacob Milborne and the Leisler regime.

On November 8, 1689, Milborne and his band of fifty-one New York militiamen dispatched by Leisler disembarked from three sloops anchored in the Hudson and tromped into Dutch Albany with beating war drums and primed muskets. The hotheaded lieutenant was determined to bring Schuyler and the Albany Convention to their knees by seizing control of the military garrison and reinforcing it with his own officers and troops. An Englishman by birth, Milborne had been an indentured servant in Barbados and Connecticut before immigrating to New York in 1668. Following his term of bondage, he had served as a bookkeeper in the City until 1672 and became known for his fanatical Protestant beliefs and combativeness.[26]

Not happy with the situation but wanting to avoid bloodshed, Schuyler and the town's leaders extended an olive branch to Milborne by inviting him to address the Convention at the *Stadhuis*—City Hall. However, Leisler's second-in-command refused to read the proclamation from his commander in chief in front of Schuyler and the Convention and instead addressed the townspeople directly. He claimed that he and his troops were here to rescue the province from Catholic tyranny, popery, and the unlawful rule of James II and Albany's civil and military officeholders of the Convention. But Milborne was rejected not only by the mayor and Convention but by a substantial number of Albany's townspeople, as well as Lawrence and the Iroquois, who were keeping a close eye on the proceedings.[27]

Despite the rebuff, a vocal minority of Albanians and Schenectadians came out in support of Leisler and Milborne.[28] Schenectady at this time was a remote village twenty miles northwest of Albany on the edge of Mohawk country. Leisler had sent a letter to the settlers of Schenectady the week before dispatching Milborne, inviting them to show their support by coming to Albany and enticing them with the promise of breaking Albany's fur trade monopoly to their benefit. While some of the local farmers and tradesmen hurried to "Albany in all speed to receive privileges and liberties," most of the citizens of Schenectady, many of whom had kinship ties to the Iroquois through marriage, refused to make the journey. They forcefully maintained that "great disquiet" would arise among the Mohawks and their other Haudenosaunee allies in the region. Those who made the trip to Albany, however, were rabid Leislerians, and they came out in vociferous support of Milborne.[29]

Over two days of tense meetings, the Convention delegates and majority of the citizens reaffirmed their loyalty to William and Mary and commitment to the Glorious Revolution. But they refused to surrender the Albany Convention until a royal governor was appointed by the rightful king and queen. The town's government officials also made it clear that Schuyler, as major in the Albany militia, would remain the commander of the town's garrison over Milborne and that, until explicit orders were received from their new sovereigns, they would continue to coordinate the war against New France on their own and conduct negotiations with the Five Nations without outside interference.[30] Milborne countered by offering an inducement: he would leave behind his militia company to reinforce the fort at Crown expense if the Convention submitted. This offer was rejected, too, since the Albanians had already secured the promise of one hundred troops from Connecticut and had no need for the New York City militia.[31] Schuyler, who by this time had mustered his forces inside Fort Frederick and refused to give his militiamen up to Milborne, knew that Leisler's offer was nothing more than a ploy to seize the garrison and take over Albany's lawful government and militia.[32]

The debate went on for five more days without resolution, while Schuyler went back and forth between the garrison and City Hall to meet with the increasingly frustrated and belligerent Milborne. The Convention had no intention of allowing Leisler to dictate the region's economic or military policies, or to put their Crown-approved fur-trading monopoly at risk.[33] After multiple rejections, Milborne turned to violence to achieve his aims.[34] One week after his arrival to Albany, on November 15, he marched his band of more than fifty heavily armed Manhattan militiamen aggressively up Gentleman's Street to Fort Frederick at the top of the hill overlooking the town.[35]

Watching the unfolding showdown from the adjacent hill, the twenty-six-year-old war leader Lawrence and a force of some eight hundred Iroquois warriors, mostly Mohawks, had other ideas. They did not take kindly to threats against their "Brother Quider" and their "Brethren" of Albany with whom they held a sacred and binding Covenant Chain.[36]

Lawrence the Mohawk, as the war captain and peace envoy was known by Schuyler and the White Euro-Americans of Albany and Schenectady, stood as a towering figure in the 1690s. Unfortunately, his Native name is lost to history, and he is known only by his anglicized Christian name "Lawrence," given to him in the late 1680s during his baptism by the French Jesuits at the Kahnawake Iroquois mission outside Montreal. His baptismal name was likely in tribute to Saint Lawrence, one of the seven deacons of Rome under Pope Sixtus II, who were martyred in the persecution of the Christians ordered by the Roman emperor Valerian in 258 A.D. Allied with Schuyler and the Albanians throughout much of his life, Lawrence of the Five Nations came from a prominent family of the Mohawk Wolf Clan and had proven himself in battle against imperial French, Algonquin, and other Native American enemies on many occasions. Although he and his wife Maria had been baptized in Canada by the Jesuits, they had recently rejected the French up north and now lived at Tionnontoguen, the westernmost "principal" Mohawk settlement near present-day Palatine, New York. It was referred to as the "Upper Castle" in the late 17th century due to its position as the farthest upstream Iroquois village on the Mohawk River. Maria was the daughter of the powerful Turtle Clan matriarch Karanondo (Lifter). Because the Iroquois matrilineal kinship system placed prime importance on the mother's kin, Lawrence and Maria were a young married couple of great social prominence among the Mohawks and the two had been kindly received in Albany by both Mayor Peter Schuyler and the Dutch dominie Father Godfredius Dellius, spiritual leader of Albany's Protestant Dutch Reformed Church.[37]

Emigrating in 1683 from the Netherlands to take the pulpit at Albany, the staunch anti-Leislerian Dellius had allied himself early on with the anglicized Schuyler faction and the English Crown. The thirty-year-old clergyman quickly became popular with Albany's Dutch residents, and earned the acceptance of Lawrence, Maria, and other anti-French League Iroquois, who were open to Christianity but feared the political power that the Canadian Jesuit missionaries exercised among the Five Nations. By the fall of 1689, Dellius had achieved success in cultivating several Iroquois religious and political allies by instructing, converting, and baptizing them as Protestant Christians. For both Dellius and Lawrence, politics and conversion went hand in hand to strengthen personal ties between the Five Nations and English.[38]

Upon reaching the fort's gate, Milborne demanded that he and his men be admitted so they could take command of Fort Frederick on behalf of the rightful government of Jacob Leisler. From the wooden rampart, Major Peter Schuyler told him once again that he was holding the fort on behalf of William and Mary and would not relinquish it until he received express orders from the Crown. As head of the Albany militia, he commanded Milborne and his armed soldiers to leave town as what they were doing was a clear act of sedition. After delivering an angry retort, Milborne managed to push his way through the gate and stick one foot inside the stockade; however, he was beaten back by several of Schuyler's militia until the gate was reclosed.[39]

But he was not finished.

Ordering his men into battle formation, he had them give an about-face and marched them a short distance from the fort, where they deployed into an orderly line, presented the king's flag, and primed their muskets. From the parapet, Schuyler reiterated to Milborne that he and his Albanians held the fort for the Crown and that the lieutenant and his seditious troops would be held responsible for any bloodshed should the two sides come to blows. In response, Milborne began angrily reading an ultimatum.[40]

Meanwhile, Lawrence and his League Iroquois warriors, watching the hostile exchange from the knobby hill north of the fort, were becoming agitated. Having already formed up into a two-deep battle line to make a show of strength on behalf of their Albany allies, the Haudenosaunee were armed to the teeth and resplendently attired in full Iroquois war regalia. They had every intention of defending their "Christian" friends and allies against an attack by an enemy that seemed every bit as hostile as the French.[41]

At the sight of Lawrence and his braves blanketing the hill, Milborne's men began to bunch up nervously outside the gates of the fort. Most of the Dutchmen, Walloons (French-speaking Protestants from southern Netherlands), Englishmen, and Scots making up Milborne's militia force were city-dwelling artisans or rural farmers who had never seen so many Indigenous tribesmen in one place or witnessed such an awesome military display. They were rattled by the menacing-looking Lawrence and his 800 Haudenosaunee warriors, many of whom bore heavy tattoos decorated with animal symbols representing their Mohawk Turtle, Wolf, or Bear Clans.

Having conducted trade with Euro-American fur trappers and settlers for three generations now, Lawrence and his warriors donned a mixture of Native and European clothing and carried the weaponry of both cultures. Most wore traditional hand-sewn buckskin leggings and shirts, short trade-blanket or deerskin breechclouts, and an outer coat made of deerskin or a blanket woven of bison hair or animal fur, such as a bearskin, draped over their shoulders. Their deerskin shirts and leggings were decorated with fringes or ribbons, but some wore European-style cloth shirts to which they had added colorful beads and ribbons as embellishments. Many of the warriors had fastened animal-bone necklaces made of bear claws or cougar fangs about their necks. For footwear, they wore soft-soled, ornately beaded moccasins made of deerskin or bison hide.[42]

Though Lawrence and his warriors maintained their own individuality in dress, warpaint, and tattoos, they all wore their hair in the traditional Iroquois manner, with all the hair plucked out except for a three-inch tuft on the back crown of the head and three short braids as a decoration. Their head coverings consisted of wedges of animal fur to which they attached several lengthy golden-eagle or turkey feathers and some dyed porcupine quills. These headpieces were attached into the patches of hair left on the rear crown of the head after the remaining hair was pulled out with porcupine-quill pincers.[43]

Their weapons were just as multifarious as their clothing. Most of the warriors carried smoothbore, muzzle-loading flintlock trade muskets, though many were armed with bows and arrows. Their deerskin arrow quivers and bow cases were slung over their shoulders along with their gun ammunition bags. They also bore flintlock pistols, steel tomahawks, scalping knives, and heavy war clubs. Consisting of a large wooden ball at one end of a slightly curved wooden shaft carved from a single piece of wood, the traditional Iroquois war club was powerful enough to split or crush a human skull to a pulp in one or two devastating blows.[44]

Flintlock muskets had first become available to the Iroquois in the early 1630s and were their weapon of choice. With an accuracy of fifty to one hundred yards and delivering six times the kinetic energy of an arrow, flintlocks took nearly a minute to load and fire. Lawrence and the Native northeastern warriors of the late 17th century did not use trade muskets in open-field, pitched battles but as a close-range, surprise-and-ambush weapon. In skirmishes with rival Native American or European foes, the Indians would first deliver a volley of musket fire to mow down and destabilize enemy combatants and then rush in to finish them off with hand-to-hand combat weapons.[45]

The Mohawks were particularly skilled musketeers since they were among the first of the eastern tribes to gain possession of state-of-the-art European firearms on a massive scale. Within a decade of the Dutch founding of Fort Orange at Albany in 1626, the Mohawks built up an arsenal of four hundred muskets and plenty of ammunition, while the overall Five Nations boasted more than twice as many guns. The Mohawks and other Iroquois Nations used this weaponry to wipe out rivals in the fur trade and seize enemy prisoners from the Wendat (Huron), Odawa (Ottawa), Erie, and other competing tribes. During these raids, they would often take large numbers of captives to replenish their tribal ranks with strong young warriors and child-bearing women who would be assimilated into the Confederation.[46]

Having been briefed daily on the Albany Convention's ongoing negotiations with Milborne, Lawrence and his warriors had grown increasingly concerned about the standoff. The reports were delivered by Hilletie van Olinda, a forty-three-year-old biracial woman of Mohawk and Dutch heritage fluent in both languages and who spoke passable pidgin English. An important figure in early New York history, she served as an interpreter and messenger between Schuyler, Father Dellius, and the Convention and the League Iroquois allied with the English. With Milborne haranguing the major and his men positioned threateningly outside the fort, Lawrence and the Iroquois headmen sent word via Hilletie that they would open fire upon Milborne and his troops if they attempted to take over the military garrison by force.[47]

Milborne knew all about Hilletie and Dellius, whom he considered threats to the Leislerian cause just like Peter Schuyler and Frederick Philipse. The truculent lieutenant was bitter about the Albany-Iroquois alliance, since it tilted the power structure in favor of the Convention and the Albanians. Furthermore, the last thing he wanted was to have to return to New York City having failed in his mission. It particularly irked him that the Indians looked to their "Brother Quider" as their diplomatic leader and champion far more than their "Brother Corlaer," the generic name the Iroquois used for the royal governors of New York Province and the current name they used for Jacob Leisler.[48] Consequently, Milborne rudely dismissed Hilletie's warning of the dire consequences that would befall him and his men if they attempted to seize the fort.

With the tension at Fort Frederick's eastern gate mounting, Hilletie repeated the warning to Milborne so there would be no misunderstanding. The Iroquois were "very much dissatisfied" to see their Brother Quider and the other magistrates threatened, she said, since "they were in a firm Covenant Chain" with the Albany Convention. "Seeing that the People of New York came in a hostile manner to disturb their Brethren," she further explained, the Iroquois were determined to see Milborne "withdraw" his soldiers or "they would fire upon him."[49]

The negotiations between Schuyler and Milborne went back and forth for nearly an hour, with neither side backing down. At some point, the Dutch-American major became worried about what would happen if the Iroquois followed through with their threat. An assault on Milborne resulting in the killing of some of his troops would likely precipitate an open civil war between Albany and New York City. The dispute might lead to a rift with the Five Nations, further divide the province, and weaken Albany's defenses against French and Indian invasion. Schuyler also knew that the blame would fall on him and the Convention for failing to negotiate a peaceful solution to the impasse and that Leisler would send an even larger force to seize Albany. He, therefore, took Reverend Dellius aside and told him that he and Hilletie van Olinda must go to Lawrence and the warriors and "pacify" them.[50]

With Hilletie acting as interpreter, Dellius met with Lawrence and the Iroquois leaders to calm the situation. However, by this point, the Haudenosaunee were deeply affronted by Milborne's actions and believed he constituted an existential threat not only to Brother Quider and the Convention but to their own people. Therefore, they once again issued a warning for Milborne that they would "fire upon him" if he tried to seize the fort by force, and that his company would be killed to the last man if he continued to refuse to stand down and evacuate Albany. The Dutch minister and Hilletie now hurried down the hill to deliver the message to the English lieutenant. But this time as the message was delivered, the Iroquois warriors, to "emphasize" their point, began priming and loading their trade muskets and pistols. This robust display of force was too much for even the combative Milborne. Making "no further attempt to go to ye fort," wrote Schuyler and the Convention, he ordered the formation to make an about turn and "marched down ye town and dismissed his men."[51]

But before leaving Albany in disgrace the next day, November 16, he fired one last parting shot by leaving behind a detachment of troops under the command of Captain Joachim Staats. However, the Convention still refused to recognize Leisler's authority and insisted that Milborne's troops serve under the command of Schuyler until official word came from London.[52] In the end, the eight-day drama that played out at Albany proved humiliating for Leisler, who still had no official recognition of his governmental authority. Although Milborne left twenty soldiers quartered in private homes before skulking back down the Hudson in his three sloops, the Convention had stood firm and kept both Albany and Schenectady free from Leislerian control, at least for the time being.[53]

On November 25, 1689, Captain Jonathan Bull at the head of eighty-seven militiamen with "flying colors" reached Albany from Connecticut and was greeted warmly by Mayor Peter Schuyler and the townspeople.[54] Four days later, Schuyler sent Lieutenant Enos Talmadge to Schenectady with a detachment of twenty-four men. The New England soldiers were to be paid by the people of Albany and Schenectady, but in a compromise arrangement, they were to be under the joint command of the Albany Convention and Joachim Staats, the militia captain left behind by Milborne. This was an impossible situation since the Convention's force and Milborne's militia were rivals and could not agree on a plan to protect the region.[55]

Meanwhile, Captain Jacob Sanders Glen, the head of the Schenectady militia, refused to recognize Leisler's authority. In response, the Leislerians refused to acknowledge Glen's lawful commission and forbade him from entering the stockade. Cooperation with the garrison of Connecticut soldiers now dissolved since Talmadge and his militia were banned in Schenectady for their loyalty to anti-Leislerian Albany. Despite being outcasts in the community, Glen and Talmadge warned the town's pro-Leisler officials to post sentinels and keep a vigilant eye out for enemy war parties, but the Leislerians stubbornly refused to institute any precautionary measures.[56]

In December and January, Schuyler, Glen, and the other anti-Leislerian leaders of Albany and Schenectady stepped up their warnings to be vigilant. Especially since Lawrence and his Mohawk scouts had heard fresh whispers of an impending French attack from their fellow Kahnawake Iroquois tribesmen up north near Montreal, many of whom were blood relatives. But the Leislerians, still smarting over Milborne's humiliation at Albany, continued to ignore the warnings.[57] As a result, as February approached, the town of Schenectady was in a state of paralysis, with no one able to agree on how to protect the town "if the enemy should come."[58]

As fate would have it, the internal dissension and foot-dragging would prove enormously costly to both New York and the Iroquois.

3
THE ATTACK ON SCHENECTADY

Before the stroke of midnight on February 8, 1690, the Francophile Chief Togouiroui, known as the Great Mohawk, stood at the edge of the woods reconnoitering the preternaturally still and quiet township of Schenectady that the Indigenous tribes referred to as "Corlaer's Fort." The French war party's 220-mile southward march from Montreal to Schenectady in the depth of winter—tromping through waist-high drifts on snowshoes and dragging their provisions on Indian-blanket sledges—had been a grueling ordeal, but Togouiroui and his warriors now stood at the gates of the frontier outpost poised to vanquish their sworn Anglo-Dutch enemies.[1]

The French commander of the expedition, Lieutenant Jacques le Moyne de Sainte-Hélène, had wanted to postpone the attack until two o'clock in the morning to ensure the element of surprise. But with the temperature dropping well below freezing and a snowy blizzard upon them, he and his shivering French officers decided to move up the timetable and launch the assault in the next few minutes. Like a pack of stalking wolves overlooking a herd of unsuspecting deer, the marauding force was anxious to get on with the fight. Frontenac's dispatched army consisted of 114 battle-hardened French soldiers and French-Canadian bushfighters known as *coureurs des bois* (runners of the woods), eighty non-League Mohawks from the Kahnawake and La Montagne missions near Montreal, and sixteen Canadian Algonquins. The war party looked forward to taking many scalps, seizing prodigious war plunder, and capturing dozens of prisoners.[2]

In his early forties, Chief Togouiroui had received his Christian first name Joseph upon his baptism by French Jesuits and was known by Peter Schuyler and the Dutch of Albany as Kryn. A veteran of many great battles against Native foes, the Laurentian Mohawk headman had led two bands of Mohawks containing forty family members and friends from the Mohawk River Valley to live in Kahnawake in French Canada in the mid-1670s, where he "converted" to Catholicism at his baptized wife's insistence and became a venerated war leader and councilman. As a young warrior, Lawrence had fought alongside the veteran war chief against rival tribes in the 1680s before the Mohawk war captain and his wife Maria had rejected the Jesuits and returned from Kahnawake to the Mohawk River Valley. Despite his battle prowess, Togouiroui was known as an effective peacemaker by both the disaffected Laurentian Mohawks transplanted to the St. Lawrence River Valley, the so-called "praying Indians" who had been converted to Catholicism by French Jesuit priests and who supported the French in Canada; and the small but growing minority of Protestant Christian Mohawks like Lawrence, who fought alongside the English in colonial America. Despite their internal differences and varying allegiance, the Mohawks were overall more allied with the English than the French and were more firmly Anglophile than the Oneidas, Onondagas, Cayugas, and Senecas.[3]

The Great Mohawk—*Kaneakowa* in the Mohawk language and *Le Grand Agnié* in French—was highly regarded not only by his fellow Canadian tribesmen and the French but also the Anglo-Dutch of Albany and his Indigenous brothers and sisters of the Mohawk River Valley that he had left behind two decades earlier. He was "without contradiction the most considerable of his tribe," praised one French government official, "as full of spirit, prudence and generosity as it is possible, and capable at the same time of the grandest undertakings." He was also an inspirational orator. Hours earlier, he had delivered a stirring speech exhorting his warriors "to perform their duty," to forget about their "fatigue," and to take "ample revenge for the injuries they had received from the Iroquois at the solicitation of the English."[4]

In preparation for battle, Togouiroui and his "praying" Mohawk and Algonquin warriors wore blankets as hoods over their heads to fend off the snow and keep warm. They carried flintlock muskets in their mittened hands and bore freshly sharpened scalping knives, tomahawks, war clubs, and tobacco pouches at their belts, as well as lightened packs on their shoulders for the food and plunder to come. The air was so frigid it hurt to breathe and many of their French and Canadian counterparts, less adapted to the elements than their Native allies, had already contracted frostbite during the long, arduous southward journey over the frozen surfaces of Lake Champlain and Lake George. With chattering teeth and water vapor steaming from their nostrils, the battle-hardened Togouiroui and others from his Indigenous war party were impatient for Sainte-Hélène and his second-in-command, Lieutenant Nicolas d'Ailleboust de Manthet, to give the order to attack.[5]

The stretch of snow-covered forest and pastureland upon which Togouiroui and the war party now stood anxiously awaiting battle was called *skahnéhtati* by the Mohawks, meaning "beyond the open pines," which the 17th-century Dutch translated into "Schenectady."[6] It was about to be transformed into a scene of horrific carnage and fiery destruction in the very first major battle of King William's War on the North American continent.

Togouiroui continued to study the fortifications as the attackers conducted their final weapons check. Situated in a rectangular township on the floodplain south of the Mohawk River, the village of Schenectady was enclosed by a ten-foot-high palisade of sharp-pointed wooden logs. In February 1690, it was home to the biracial Mohawk-Dutch woman Hilletie van Olinda, her Dutch husband, Peter Danielse van Olinda, and some 250 European settlers, most of Dutch extraction. On this historic night, there were also thirty League Mohawks inside the fort on a trading visit. Earlier in the evening, the Dutch occupying the town and their Mohawk guests had celebrated a festivity, but it was long since over and the entire village lay in peaceful slumber.[7]

The town's stockade bore two gates, one on the north facing the Mohawk River and awaiting war party, the other on the south that led to the King's

Road to Albany. Although the walls of the stockade were barely visible in the whiteout of falling snow and Togouiroui had been unable to locate the south gate during his reconnaissance around the town's perimeter with Lieutenant Manthet, the Mohawk war chief had been able to identify the north gate, portions of the enclosing stockade, and the fortified blockhouse. Most important, he could see that the Anglo-Dutch citadel was unguarded, with not a single sentinel posted. Unbeknownst to him and the other attackers, the stout blockhouse in the northwest corner of the stockade near the north gate was occupied by nine Connecticut militiamen under Lieutenant Enos Talmadge. The small wooden fortification was equipped with loopholes to allow defenders to engage in small-arms fire in various directions, but it bore no cannon and the troops on the night of February 8 were fast asleep.[8]

In returning to New France for a second term as governor-general of New France in October 1689, Louis de Buade, Comte de Frontenac had brought with him a grandiose vision of striking a decisive blow against the English colonies and Five Iroquois Nations. His original plan had consisted of launching coordinated attacks by French and Indian land parties upon New York and the New England colonies in conjunction with an all-out naval assault upon New York City. The French offensive was in reprisal for the devastating attack upon Lachine, Quebec, on July 26, 1689, by a force of nearly 1,500 League Iroquois warriors, which had resulted in the killing, ritualized torturing, and burning of more than 200 French-settler men, women, and children and the capture of 120 more. The French royal governor also sought revenge against the Iroquois for having forced the abandonment of Fort Frontenac, the stockade and supply depot he had built in his name in 1673 at Cataraqui near the headwaters of the St. Lawrence River to profit from the fur trade. His ambitious military plan was for French land forces to raid the Hudson River Valley and New England settlements, while La Caffinière, the commander of the French naval squadron, would attack towns up and down the New England and Long Island coasts, seize New York Harbor, and take Manhattan Island by force.[9] However, lacking the resources for a massive land-sea operation, the count had been forced to scale back his strategy to three hit-and-run borderland raids.[10]

In the French governor's reconstituted and more realistic battle plan, the main land force was to launch a surprise attack on Albany and northern New York Province from Montreal, while the two smaller land forces, one based at Three Rivers and the other at Quebec, would be directed at New Hampshire and Maine.[11] However, when Sainte-Hélène informed Togouiroui during the southward march of the French plan to raid Albany and nearby Fort Frederick, the pragmatic war chief and his warriors refused to take part in an attack on the larger and more heavily defended stronghold of Albany, which contained around 700 settlers and troops to Schenectady's 250. Instead, they insisted that the French lieutenant divert the expeditionary force from Albany to smaller and less well-defended Schenectady, which would still provide a devastating blow to their mutual English enemies. Not wanting to jeopardize losing his invaluable and hard-fighting Laurentian Mohawk auxiliaries, Sainte-Hélène and his officers had no choice but to concur.[12]

The French now gave the signal to commence the attack from the north. With great stealth, the war party of 210 French soldiers, Canadian *coureur de bois* bushwhackers, Laurentian Mohawks, and Algonquins began pushing forward on their snowshoes from the stand of pine trees northeast of the fort. Though they moved quickly, their legs were stiff and cold in their frozen buckskins. Having endured a brutal, seventeen-day march from Montreal through deep snowdrifts, the war party had only two hours earlier made the difficult crossing of the iced-over Mohawk River north of the fort and town.[13]

As they stepped into the snow-blanketed clearing, with their shoulders hunched against the cold northerly wind and their muskets, tomahawks, war clubs, and pistols at the ready, the Great Mohawk felt the tension in the air. But the war chief wasn't worried. Earlier that afternoon, he and his scouts had gained valuable intelligence when they had stumbled across a women's menstrual hut a short distance from Schenectady. While warming themselves at the fire, they learned from the four Mohawk women inside the hut of the unsuspecting town's circumstances. Not only did the English seldom post a guard at night, Togouiroui discovered, but they appeared not to follow through with even the most rudimentary precautions for their safety against enemy attacks. Furthermore, a League Mohawk scouting party had recently been sent north to Lake George and was no longer at hand, leaving the town even more unprotected than usual.[14]

A short distance from the north gate, Sainte-Hélène called a halt. After ordering the men to quietly remove their snowshoes, he and Manthet formed into two separate companies for the attack. The gate was wide open and, according to New York legend, the only visible forms were a pair of children's snowmen standing passively beside the unguarded entrance. After forming up, the two French forces passed in dead silence through the ajar gate with its "blind and dumb" sentinels of snow, their snowshoes now strapped onto their backs or left outside the gate. With Sainte-Hélène's company turning to the right and Manthet's to the left, they filed around the village between the interior walls of the wooden palisade and log houses. The two French officers and their freezing cold and anxious fighters strung themselves along the inner wooden palisade until the lead elements rejoined at the southern end of the compound. The assault force was now positioned between the stockade and the houses with four to seven attackers per dwelling.[15]

Amazingly, the Great Mohawk and his raiding party had trekked 220 miles through enemy territory on snowshoes and achieved total surprise. There was not a single human stirring or yap of a dog and the doomed Anglo-Dutch village was surrounded. For the war chief, the opportunity for retaliation was personal following the crushing League attack upon Lachine in Quebec back in July. It is for this reason that Le Grand Agnié had vociferously rallied his Laurentian Mohawk and Algonquin followers at 4:00 P.M. "to wash out their wrongs in blood" for the massacre of more than 200 of their French allies.[16]

Lieutenant Sainte-Hélène now gave the signal to attack. With piercing war cries and crackling musket fire, the French troops and Native warriors burst through the log house doors and fell upon the peacefully sleeping inhabitants like a hurricane. Roused by the spine-chilling war whoops, musket fire, and smashing doors, some of the villagers leaped from their beds to defend themselves, but most were overwhelmed so quickly they were unable to put up effective resistance. As the screaming French soldiers and Indians attacked the settlers, they set fire to their log-cabin homes with their torches.[17]

Adam Vrooman, one of the Dutch villagers, fought so bravely that the attackers promised him his life, but not until after he had lost his wife and child, the latter smashed against the doorposts by the Native combatants and brains spilling out. Though orders had been given by Sainte-Hélène and his French officers to spare the town's minister, Petrus Tassemaker, he was hacked to pieces in the opening frenzy and his house burned to the ground as the carnage spread all around. At the blockhouse, Lieutenant Talmadge and his Connecticut militiamen put up stout resistance to a considerable enemy force led by Lieutenant de Manthet. But the heavy wooden doors were eventually battered down and most of the defenders were quickly dispatched with muskets, battle axes, tomahawks, and war clubs, as the tinderbox log fortress was put to the torch.[18]

With Frenchmen and Indigenous warriors pouring through front doors like floodwaters breaching a dam, only a few were able to crack off a shot with their preloaded muskets, or snatch up a sword or knife to grapple hand to hand like Adam Vrooman. Some awoke only to catch a terrifying glimpse of a swooshing Iroquois war club, a falling French hatchet, or the muzzle flash of a European trade musket. Others were dragged from their wooden abodes and slain on the snow-covered streets that crisscrossed the sleepy village. Still others perished in the leaping flames spreading through Schenectady like an inferno. Although most were cut down no sooner than they had jumped up from their beds, in all the fire, smoke, and confusion a surprising number were able to flee either unscathed or lightly wounded from the open gates of the stockade into the nearby woods.[19]

The interpreter Hilletie van Olinda and her extended van Olinda and van Slyck family members were among those who survived the initial onslaught, and whose lives and wooden-log homes inside the stockade were spared by the Great Mohawk and his Laurentian Iroquois warriors. Because Haudenosaunee descent was reckoned matrilineally, Schenectady families with Mohawk mothers or close ties by blood or marriage to such mothers were spared. Since Hilletie had been raised by her Haudenosaunee mother, Ots-Toch, in the Great Mohawk "castle" at Tionnontoguen and since she knew Togouiroui and several of the other Canadian Iroquois attackers personally, she and her Dutch husband, the tailor Peter Danielse van Olinda, and their three biracial sons, Daniel, Jacob, and the nonspeaking or nonverbal Matthew, their youngest, were not killed. At the same time, they may have received minor wounds in the initial onslaught. Hilletie's eldest brother Jacques Cornelissen van Slyck, her youngest sister Lea van Coppernol, and Lea's Dutch husband, Claes Willemsen van Coppernol, also managed to survive due to their Mohawk kinship ties. But most Schenectadians weren't so lucky, as the French and Indian war party swept through the unsuspecting village in a flurry of bloodcurdling war whoops, stormed the log buildings, cut down the settlers, and dragged the terrified captives from the burning cabins and through the blood-streaked snow.[20]

Disappearing into the raging snowstorm and thick forest, several of the townspeople who miraculously survived the opening maelstrom managed to wade their way through the waist-deep snow for twenty miles along the King's Road and to take refuge in Albany. One of these survivors was the Leislerian Dutch trader Symon Schermerhorn, who was able to fight his way through the enemy during the initial attack, while his son and three enslaved Black men were killed before his eyes. Mounting his horse, Schermerhorn rode out of the stockade amid a hailstorm of lead musket shot, one of which caught him in the thigh and another that wounded his terrified horse. Ploughing through snowdrifts, Schermerhorn rode along the River Road to Niskayuna, warning English settlers along the way. After covering thirty miles in a six-hour ride, he reached the gates of Albany just as his horse crumpled from exhaustion and he fainted from blood loss from his leg wound. Soon thereafter, he was revived and delivered the first full account of the "slaughter" to Mayor Peter Schuyler and Albany's stunned colonial officials.[21]

The attacking, pillaging, and burning of Schenectady lasted for two full hours, with the greatest number of casualties in the two houses just inside the south gate, where a large festive gathering had taken place earlier in the night and many people were sleeping. The surviving prisoners like Hilletie van Olinda and her extended family were then secured, sentinels posted, and the invaders ordered by Sainte-Hélène to eat and rest before the long journey back to Montreal. The sheer violence witnessed by Hilletie must have been shocking to her, even though she had witnessed frontier warfare up close many times before as a young Mohawk girl growing up in Tionnontoguen. The stunned survivors reported that pregnant women were "ripped up" and "children alive thrown into ye flames" and their "heads dashed in pieces against the doors and windows."[22]

By morning, fifty-six of the approximately 250 residents of Schenectady had been killed outright, died of their wounds, or passed away from exposure during the night, and only a handful of the eighty houses remained unburned and standing. In the wintry-white and blood-red-stained landscape, many of the fallen were captured in death poses like marble statues. The bitter cold had turned the skin a purplish claret color from the blood in the capillaries freezing upon death. The town had been so caught off guard that only one Laurentian Mohawk and one French soldier were killed in the raid and a single French officer severely wounded.[23]

In the aftermath, the leaders of Albany and Schenectady put together a list of the "killed and destroyed" in the fight, identifying every one of the fifty-six victims. Although most of those who perished were Dutch like Hilletie's and her sister Lea's surviving husbands, the dead included English, Scottish, African, Mohawk, and French men, women, and children.[24] The list consisted of "twenty-two adult white men [seven of whom were 'burnt' by the French and allied Laurentians], seven adult white women [one 'burnt' and another scalped], fourteen white children [one female and one male 'burnt'], eleven 'Negroes' [whose gender was not specified, two of whom were 'burnt'], one 'French girl prisoner among ye Mohawks' [evidently not a Schenectady resident], and one 'Mohawk Indian.'"[25]

Peter Schuyler and the Dutch *handlaers* of Albany and Schenectady had long feared just such a well-coordinated attack along the Hudson corridor and the mass pandemonium that would ensue. "The cruelties committed at said place no pen can write nor tongue express," wrote Schuyler in the aftermath of the bloody ordeal.[26] The attack would forever be etched into the American consciousness as the "Schenectady Massacre" or the "Burning of Schenectady." But in reality, it was a typical 17th-century North American frontier military raid involving allied European and Native American combatants. Such swift, stunningly violent, and sanguinary assaults, often conducted in reprisal for a previous enemy attack, were the norm not the exception.

At the same time, the French officers and Chief Togouiroui went out of their way to spare several notable Dutch and biracial Native-Dutch colonists, in addition to Hilletie van Olinda and her extended family, during the attack. The Great Mohawk also went to great lengths to spare all thirty of the League Mohawks present in the lodgings inside the stockade. Due to the war chief's stern warnings, only one Five Nations' Mohawk and his captive, the lone French girl, were killed by the invaders during the assault, and even these deaths were accidental.[27] "The thirty Mohawks in the town were treated with great kindness by the victors," wrote one 19th-century historian, "who declared that they had no quarrel with them, but only with the Dutch and English."[28] Furthermore, only two European Schenectady residents with established ties of marriage or kinship to neighboring Mohawk communities were among the battle casualties. Thus, even as Togouiroui and his Canadian Mohawks raided deeply into English territory and Iroquoia, they made a concerted effort to shield both their southern kin and colonists married to Mohawks, like the husbands of Hilletie and her sister Lea, both those living inside and outside the stockade.[29]

Hilletie and the men, women, and children of the van Olinda and van Slyck families were also not among the captives who would make the northward trek to French Canada. Their preservation was not only due to their matrilineal kinship ties to the Laurentian raiders, but because they hailed from a prominent Mohawk-Dutch family of the Hudson and Mohawk River Valley region. Born in 1646, Hilletie van Slyck was the fourth child of the matriarch Ots-Toch of the venerable Mohawk Wolf Clan and the peripatetic Dutch pioneer Cornelis Antonisen van Slyck. Her father, Cornelis, born in 1604 in Breuckelen in Holland's Utrecht Province, had lived and traded in the lower Mohawk River Valley by 1641. He was one of the first Europeans to put down peaceful roots alongside the Mohawks in the region.[30] Historians refer to Hilletie's father as one of "the most interesting and important figures in early Mohawk Valley history"—and the colorful Hilletie followed in his footsteps as a cross-cultural bridge and facilitator immersed in, and sympathetic to, both Native and European cultures.[31]

In the second half of the 17th century, Hilletie and her three siblings, Jacques, Martin, and Lea, had grown up in the Iroquois village of Tionnontoguen, while making frequent trading visits to Schenectady where their Dutch father maintained a residence and earned the bulk of his income. Prior to his death in the Mohawk River Valley in 1676, Cornelis Antonisen van Slyck served not only as a skilled carpenter and mason but as an important trader, interpreter, community leader, and trusted cross-cultural liaison in securing peace and prisoner exchanges for more than thirty years. Both Hilletie and her fifty-year-old brother Jacques had served as important translators and liaisons to the Mohawks since their father's death. Their skills as cross-cultural interpreters and diplomats made them invaluable in the eyes of their Native kin, and their prominent status on both their matrilineal-Mohawk-mother's side and their pioneer-trader-father's Dutch side, combined with their bilingual capabilities, ensured their continued importance to both the Iroquois and English. It was also for this reason that their lives and wooden-log homes were spared during the Schenectady raid and they were not taken as prisoners back to Montreal along with the other captives.[32]

Captain Jacob Sanders Glen and his family, too, were protected from attack during the bloody raid. Not only were the Glens early residents of the Mohawk River Valley and proprietors of Schenectady like the van Olindas and van Slycks, they had given medical treatment to seven wounded French soldiers left behind during a 1666 war expedition commanded by Daniel de Rémy de Courcelle, the governor-general of New France at the time. Because Glen and his wife had taken in and cared for the enemy frontiersmen during their rehabilitation, Frontenac gave specific orders that they be protected during the invasion. In the end, Sainte-Hélène and the Great Mohawk not only spared their lives and safeguarded their house for their prior humane treatment, but protected many of Glen's relatives and their houses.[33] However, once the Indigenous raiders saw how many people claimed to be family of the Dutch captain, they grumbled that Glen's kinsfolk were impossibly numerous and "that everybody seemed to be his relation."[34] But the resolute and venerated war leader and peacemaker Togouiroui kept his grousing warriors in line.

By noon of February 9, with most of the town in smoldering ruins, the war party withdrew, having suffered only two casualties. They left behind in Schenectady some sixty uninjured but freezing and ill-equipped old men, women, and children. Setting off across the frozen Mohawk River, they took with them twenty-seven men and older boys as prisoners, including five enslaved African Americans identified as "Negroes" in the historical records. They also carried with them considerable war booty, including more than fifty horses and several ice spurs and skates that they would use as horse-driven sledges to expedite their return over frozen Lake Champlain.[35]

The day after wounded Dutchman Symon Schermerhorn staggered into Albany and relayed the story of the "massacre" to town officials, the Albany authorities sent Captain Jonathan Bull, the commander of the Connecticut troops in Albany, to Schenectady with a company of troops. Bull and his men were to "bury ye dead," give "succor and relief to ye poor people left alive," and swiftly raise a retaliatory Anglo-Native force to "pursue and follow after the French and Indian enemy" and "use all means imaginable to rescue ye prisoners which they have carried along with them."[36]

The Mohawk war captain Lawrence and other League Iroquois from the Mohawk River Valley visiting Albany at the time were as stunned as their Anglo-Dutch counterparts at the slaughter and destruction done by the enemy in just a few hours. "The work of thirty years of human industry went blazing skyward and the night of that far off midwinter Sunday closed over the blackened ruin of what had once been the busy, thriving and comfortable little village of Schenectady."[37]

Horrified by the tragedy suffered by their New York compatriots, eight Mohawk headmen traveled to Albany to meet with Mayor Peter Schuyler and the Albany magistrates and perform a formal Iroquois mourning ceremony in honor of those who had perished and to condole the beleaguered survivors. The sachems included the non-Christian traditionalist speaker Sanonguirese of the esteemed Bear Clan, a friend of Lawrence and Peter

Schuyler, and two leading members of the Mohawk Turtle Clan. The translation of the highly emotional ceremony that had brought the region's war-traumatized settlers and the Iroquois together under the Covenant Chain in a time of mutual tragedy was performed by Hilletie van Olinda. Having grown up in the Mohawk Wolf Clan of her mother, Ots-Toch, until her late teens, she had long engaged in such sacred ceremonies along with her eldest brother Jacques, whose Indigenous name was Itsychoquachka, and her sister Lea.[38]

But unlike the Iroquois headmen and European settlers of Albany, Lawrence had retribution and prisoner recovery, not condolence, on his mind. Before the grieving ceremony, he swiftly rounded up a war party of eighty Mohawks and Mahicans to chase down the retreating French and Indian force before it reached the protection of Montreal.[39] Saddened by the sight of so much "blood shed," he vowed to chase the French invaders all the way to French Canada and to bring the "prisoners back again either by force or by stratagem." By this, the bold Iroquois war captain meant that he would recover the captives either by killing the enemy outright, or through clever diplomacy by conducting ransom negotiations with his kindred Laurentian Mohawks or the French officers.[40]

4
A MOST FRAGILE UNITY

True to his word, Lawrence and his fast-moving war party set out on February 12, 1690, in pursuit of Sainte-Hélène and Togouiroui's retreating force. Major Peter Schuyler and his Albany magistrates provided Lawrence and his warriors with extra muskets, powder, food, and supplies for the hard journey. Soon after his departure, the young Mohawk war leader came across a straggling Canadian warrior who had taken part in the Schenectady attack and took him prisoner. The unlucky "praying" captive was sent back to Schuyler and promptly confessed that when he had left Montreal to make war upon the English, he had been part of an overall invasion force of "600 men" tasked with sacking Albany and wreaking havoc in New England. This invaluable intelligence was the first indication that the "massacre" at Schenectady had been merely the first phase of a much larger and more ambitious invasion of the English colonies.[1]

Following the questioning, the prisoner was sent to Lawrence's fortified Mohawk village at Tionnontoguen, where he was first ritualistically tortured in the traditional Iroquois manner before being delivered to the sachems to replace their recent losses. In accordance with formal Iroquois mourning-war custom, the headmen gave the prisoner to a Mohawk woman as a condolence ritual to make up for the recent death of her warrior husband. Meanwhile, the determined Lawrence and his war party continued north to Lake Champlain.[2]

Equipped with snowshoes and heavy winter clothing, they moved at a furious pace to catch the retreating column before it reached Montreal. Due to the inclement weather and tough sledding, Sainte-Hélène and

Togouiroui's column was straggled out for miles and running low on food. While Togouiroui's hardy warriors and the French-Canadian bushwhackers were acclimated to harsh winter conditions and had no problem tromping through the deep snow with scant resources, many of Sainte-Hélène's French troops were seriously ill and on the verge of collapse from exhaustion as they waded through the snowdrifts of modern-day Saratoga County and upstate New York.[3]

As he pressed northward, Lawrence soon learned just how imperiled the enemy was and sent a messenger back to Albany. He informed Schuyler and Albany's officials that "he was within a day's journey" of the enemy and to send the agreed-upon reinforcements "to come up with all speed," so he could defeat the much larger French and Indian force and recover the prisoners. Although the major sent his younger cousin Ensign Abraham Schuyler in command of a small detachment of Mohawks and Mahicans and "nine whites," they were unable to catch up to the column in the heavy snow. Soon thereafter, reported the Albany council, "ye Christians came back and ye Indians went on."[4]

By February 22, the Dutchmen Symon van Ness and Andries Barents returned to Albany to report that when they had reached Crown Point on Lake Champlain, they had discovered that the French and Indian war party had made use of the horses, skates, and ice spurs seized at Schenectady. At that point, the two men had decided to turn back since the enemy could make such fast time over the smooth ice "that our People could gain nothing upon them."[5] Lawrence, however, was undeterred. He and his remaining stalwarts double-timed it and pushed on through the waist-deep snow with renewed vigor, for their time was running out. As van Ness and Barents reported, "Lawrence ye Maquase & about 140 Mohawks & River Indians are gone in pursuit of them & will follow them quite to Canada."[6]

Sanonguirese and the other Iroquois headmen, anxiously awaiting the outcome of the pursuit in Albany with Peter Schuyler and the City leaders, knew just how bold and determined Lawrence was, and they were every bit as optimistic of success as their Anglo-Dutch brethren. On February 25, during the condolence ceremony for the tragedy at Schenectady, the speaker Sanonguirese proclaimed, "We hope to be revenged. There is one hundred of our young men out still who will pursue them to their doors at Canada, nay ye French shall not be able to cut a stick of wood we will lay so close siege to them."[7]

The words of the Mohawk Bear Clan leader proved prophetic, for at that very moment Lawrence and his warriors were closing in fast on Sainte-Hélène's rear.

Though the French commander's plan had been to use the horses with the ice spurs and skates taken at Schenectady to move speedily across frozen Lake Champlain, he did not have sufficient food supplies for his men and the captives, or enough grain for the captured horses, to make the final leg of the return journey. He and his men were forced to eat thirty-four of the fifty horses en route to Montreal just to survive. The provisions grew so scarce that Sainte-Hélène dispatched two men "upon skates" to travel the remaining hundred miles to Montreal to obtain provisions and return to the bedraggled party.[8]

Lawrence and his determined Mohawk and Mahican warriors caught up to the rear of Sainte-Hélène's retreating column north of Lake Champlain within three days of Montreal. Despite the "extreme snow above knee deep" and the enemy's nearly four-day head start, the Mohawk war captain avenged Schenectady less than a fortnight after leaving Albany. With trade muskets, tomahawks, war clubs, and scalping knives, he and his braves pitched ferociously into the French soldiers lagging far behind their commander and the bulk of the withdrawing army. With fourteen or fifteen warriors, Lawrence personally led an attack on one party of Frenchmen that made a stand in the woods and cut six of them down, whooping in triumph as they waved the enemy's bloody scalps in the gelid winter air. At the same time, they showed mercy to Chief Togouiroui's Laurentian Mohawk auxiliaries, their Iroquois kin, whom they left unharmed throughout the pursuit.[9]

When it was all over, Lawrence and his warriors dispatched and scalped twenty of the enemy, sixteen of whom were Frenchmen, while taking nineteen French soldiers and one Laurentian Mohawk as prisoners. However, they failed to recover any of the captured Schenectady townspeople, who had been under close guard far ahead of the stragglers with Sainte-Hélène, Togouiroui, and the main column. In the hard winter fighting, Lawrence lost four of his fellow League warriors in the skirmishing near Lake Champlain. With their bound enemy captives, he and his exhausted war party trudged back more than 150 miles to Albany in their snowshoes and heavy animal-fur coats, arriving in early March.[10]

Viewed through 21st-century eyes, the expedition would seem to have been an extraordinary success. But by the Iroquois standards of the age and from the contemporaneous perspective of the settlers of Albany and Schenectady, it was more a modest win. In wiping out twenty of the enemy and taking twenty prisoners, Lawrence and his fellow warriors had achieved one of the chief aims of Iroquois' mourning wars on behalf of the grieving Schenectady survivors and their Mohawk allies, but they had failed to recover the English captives and lost four good warriors.[11]

For Lawrence and his fellow tribesmen, war was less about killing as many enemy combatants as possible, seizing territory, or gaining plunder in the European fashion and primarily a means for young men to gain military experience and combat honors, as well as a sacred "mourning ritual" to replace deceased tribal members by procuring captives to adopt, ritually torture and execute, or trade in prisoner exchanges.[12] While many Euro-Americans of the age admired the martial skill of the Iroquois and understood how vitally important war-making was to their culture, most utterly failed to grasp that the Iroquois waged war for far different but no less rational reasons than Europeans.[13] As historian Daniel Richter reminds us, war for the Five Nations was largely a foundation of male identity, a population sustainability measure, and a grief management tool:

> Participation in a war party was a benchmark episode in an Iroquois youth's development. [His] prospects for an advantageous marriage, his chances for recognition as a village leader, and his hopes for eventual selection to a sachemship depended [on] his skill on the warpath. . . . Warfare [was also] a means to

> increase the group's numbers [and] the Iroquois conceptualized the process of population maintenance in terms of individual and collective spiritual power. When a person died, the power of his or her lineage, clan, and nation was diminished in proportion to his or her individual spiritual strength. To replenish the depleted power the Iroquois conducted "requickening" ceremonies at which the deceased's name—and with it the social role and duties it represented—was transferred to a [war-captive] successor. Vacant positions in Iroquois families and villages were thus both literally and symbolically filled, and the continuity of Iroquois society was confirmed.[14]

During the return journey, Lawrence was angry with himself for having lost four warriors in the running fight near Lake Champlain. While Europeans considered perishing in combat acceptable and even honorable, the Iroquois regarded death in battle as disastrous. "A war party that, by European standards, seemed on the brink of triumph could be expected to retreat sorrowfully homeward if it suffered a few fatalities. For the Indians, such a campaign was no victory; casualties would subvert the purpose of warfare as a means of restocking the population."[15] Making matters worse for Lawrence and his war party, when the lone captured Native combatant was brought back to Albany, he soon thereafter escaped and returned to Canada instead of replenishing the ranks of the local Mohawks.[16]

For several of the Albany magistrates, the lack of success of Lawrence and his Mohawk and Mahican pursuit party was not on account of the sustained casualties, but because of the failure to recover any of the twenty-seven war captives taken at Schenectady. It was inconceivable to them that the war party had taken twenty French and Indian prisoners but failed to rescue even one of hostages. Bitter at being caught flat-footed during the surprise attack on February 8, New York officials badly needed a scapegoat, but the last participants they should have been blaming were Lawrence and his fast-moving warriors, who had made a herculean effort to chase down the enemy and recover the captives before they reached Montreal.[17]

As usual, Peter Schuyler was far more understanding than most of his Anglo-Dutch compatriots. Though he, too, remained angry and distraught over the horrible fate that had befallen the people of Schenectady and the failure to recapture the prisoners, he acknowledged the fortitude and tenacity of Lawrence and his braves and appreciated why they were reluctant to kill their "kindred" and "relations" among the "praying Mohawks" in Canada.[18] Meanwhile, Frontenac and his French government officials believed that Lawrence's party had not killed the Laurentian Mohawks, or taken them captive during the pursuit, because Sainte-Hélène and Togouiroui "had spared the lives" of the thirty Mohawks at Schenectady "when it was burnt by our Frenchmen and Indians."[19]

Hilletie van Olinda also made it clear to the Iroquois and settlers of Albany and Schenectady that her fellow Mohawk Lawrence and his warriors had done everything humanly possible to recover the prisoners. Like Schuyler, she was deeply sympathetic to the Iroquois with whom she had lived, traded, and interacted her entire life. Though she had eventually assimilated into her father's and husband's Dutch world at Schenectady, she was intimately familiar with Iroquois war customs and mourning rituals from the first two decades of her life living among her Mohawk mother Ots-Toch's people in Tionnontoguen.

Raised in a matrilineal Mohawk society in which women exercised control over everyday village life, the appointment and removal of political leaders, the right to demand mourning-war retribution for lost lives, child rearing, horticulture, providing hospitality to outside visitors, and other communal powers, she had been born and raised in a Native world in accordance with Indigenous—not European—customs, rituals, and notions of female roles. It was only by her late teens that she had begun to show an interest in the White European world beyond her village. By the age of seventeen, she became intrigued with the French Jesuit priests that traveled to Tionnontoguen and with whom she conversed during her trips to other Iroquois settlements. Over the next year, she became impressed with the teachings of the Holy Bible and the lofty words of the ministering priests. However, she was ridiculed and beaten for her interest in Christianity by her traditionalist mother, some of her Mohawk kin, and other tribal members.[20]

In 1663, she moved to Schenectady at the age of eighteen to escape the abuse, became a household servant, was taught to read and write Dutch, received the sacrament of baptism in the Dutch Reformed Church, and eventually married the Dutch-born tailor and property owner Peter Danielse van Olinda. In the early 1680s, she became one of only a handful of Native Americans to receive baptism at Albany before the arrival of Father Dellius in 1683. Soon thereafter, Albany's magistrates and Dellius began making use of her bicultural background and linguistic expertise, since the Dutch reverend had not mastered the Iroquoian language and required a full-time interpreter.[21]

Although some Mohawks and Euro-Americans still held her gender and biracial Native-European status against her and refused to accept her, Hilletie played a pivotal role in conferences between the Anglo-Dutch of Albany and Schenectady and Iroquois Anglophiles. For the past several years, she had served as Dellius's official translator and his loyal partner in his effort to peacefully bring Dutch Reformed Christianity to the Mohawks, and she remained critical in helping her Native people and the settlers of Albany better understand and negotiate with one another. Upon the return of Lawrence and his war party after their perilous three-hundred-plus-mile roundtrip journey in the dead of winter, Hilletie vigorously defended them before their critics, most of whom were Leislerians who had been caught totally unprepared at Schenectady from their own negligence.[22]

At this opening salvo in King William's War on the North American frontier, the finger-pointing for the disaster at Schenectady was only just beginning. When news of the horrific carnage reached New York City in mid-February, the opposing Leislerian and anti-Leislerian factions each tried to place the blame upon the other. In Albany, Peter Schuyler and his Scottish brother-in-law Robert Livingston, the town clerk and a fellow Indian Affairs secretary, maintained that Schenectady's Leislerians had ignored multiple warnings by the civil and military leadership to be vigilant with their sentinels and patrols. Because the Leislerians had failed to take proper precautionary measures, argued Schuyler and Livingston, the French and "praying" Laurentian Mohawks had been able to walk right through the unguarded gate and take the town completely by surprise.[23]

News of the "massacre" was quickly broadcast to other colonies by Schuyler and Livingston, as well as by Leisler and his supporters in New York City.[24] Word of the tragedy along the sleepy banks of the Mohawk River provided Leisler with an opportunity to neutralize his opponents in New York City, Albany, and elsewhere, while simultaneously unifying New York Province and the New England colonies for an all-out invasion of French Canada.[25]

Though Leisler's star was fading by the winter of 1690, the attack at Schenectady not only breathed new life into his regime but greatly strengthened his hand by uniting the English colonies. Having spurned Leisler's emissaries twice before, in the wake of the bloody raid the members of the Albany Convention reluctantly decided to extend an olive branch to Leisler by formally recognizing his authority. Having learned firsthand the perils of internal discord and knowing that Albany alone would be unable to resist a concerted French attack, Mayor Peter Schuyler and the town's leaders sent delegates to New York City to make peace with Leisler and his second-in-command, Jacob Milborne. In return for recognizing Leisler's authority as acting lieutenant governor and accepting his military reinforcements, Schuyler and several Albany magistrates were able to maintain their positions of authority, albeit with their power reduced. At this time, Schuyler and the Albany leadership also briefed Leisler on the plan they had put forward to Massachusetts Bay Colony, Plymouth, and Connecticut for a combined land-sea assault on Frontenac and New France.[26]

In response, the German-born strongman sent a three-man commission led by Milborne to Albany to bring the fur-trading town under his control, dissolve the Convention, and make plans for a massive summer invasion of French Canada. Though Schuyler chafed at being under the thumb of the incompetent, overbearing, and hotheaded Milborne, he kept his feelings to himself and cooperated fully for the benefit of Albany and his Iroquois brethren.[27]

Toward the end of the previous year, Leisler had begun to consolidate his power, knowing that his only hope for legitimacy in the eyes of the Crown was to deliver a lethal blow to Frontenac and New France. On December 10, 1689, a letter from the Privy Council in London had arrived to New York, bearing royal instructions directed to New York's governor Francis Nicholson, or in his absence whoever was responsible "for preserving the Peace and administering the Laws in their Majesty's Province of New York."[28] Seizing the letter from the messenger despite the objections of civic leaders, Leisler announced that the Crown had officially recognized him as lieutenant governor. He swiftly converted his supporters into a royal council, issued writs for a new Assembly, and gave orders to the militia. With these acts, he sought to administer the province, obtain funding for the colony's defense, and issue new commissions for justices of the peace as though he had the full backing of Whitehall, the seat of English governmental power in London.[29]

While King Louis XIV and Count Frontenac harbored grandiose visions of the conquest of New York and the Five Iroquois Nations, Leisler had long held just as ambitious plans for conquering New France—that "rookery of evil" as he and New England's Puritans called the Catholic French possession. Though he appears to have possessed genuine concern for the safety of New York Province's northern settlements, Leisler's foremost priority was to ensure that Albany was strong enough to repel an all-out French invasion, since its loss would endanger the rest of the colony all the way to Manhattan. He also recognized that New York lacked sufficient manpower to singlehandedly deal with the French in Canada. He therefore decided to host an intercolonial conference in New York City to garner the support of neighboring English colonies and to develop a comprehensive strategy to defeat the French.[30]

On April 2, 1690, eager to take the fight to Frontenac in King William's War, Leisler called for the conference to meet on May 1 and invited colonial governors from Massachusetts to Barbados to attend, or, alternatively, to provide troops, ships, or financial support for the planned offensive. However, the attendance did not meet expectations. Only the governors of Massachusetts, Plymouth, and Connecticut attended, and while they did promise to provide 355 total militiamen, this was far less than Leisler had hoped for. Furthermore, Massachusetts declared that her primary focus would be on a planned seaborne expedition to be led by Bostonian Sir William Phips against Port Royal in French-held Acadia.[31]

Though Maryland and Rhode Island did not send delegates, the governor of Maryland pledged one hundred men for the land expedition, while Rhode Island promised to raise £300 ($105,000 today). Because East Jersey had long been antagonistic toward Leisler and had served as a haven for persecuted New York exiles, the colony pointedly refused to aid her sworn enemy. Having been forced to flee New York City after being threatened by the Leislerian rebels a year earlier, Virginia's newly appointed colonial governor, Francis Nicholson, ignored the request for recruits altogether. William Penn's proprietary colony had no governor and its pacifistic Quakers cared little about military affairs, with the result that Pennsylvania, too, sent no delegates and offered no assistance.[32]

While most colonies rejected Leisler, the conference and follow-up negotiations concluded with an agreement for a two-pronged offensive: a land invasion of New France with New York in the lead role, and a naval assault with the responsibility falling to Massachusetts. The overland expedition would be conducted against Montreal from the military launching depot of Albany and rely heavily upon the Anglophile Iroquois, while the seaborne attack upon Quebec would be carried out by Phips and his New Englanders sailing out of Boston. In total, the supportive colonies agreed to raise 855 men, including 400 from New York.[33]

In the wake of Frontenac's raids on Salmon Falls, New Hampshire, on March 18 and Fort Loyal at Casco Bay, Maine, between May 16 and 20, 1690, Massachusetts withdrew from the land campaign to focus on protecting her own northeastern frontier and coastlines rather than fighting on foot far north of Albany in the Canadian hinterlands. The attack on Fort Loyal had been led by Chief Togouiroui following his successful return to the St. Lawrence region following the attack on Schenectady. The Great Mohawk had joined with more than four hundred French, Algonquin, and Abenaki fighters to capture the fort on June 4, killing more than two hundred English militia and settlers and generating a tidal wave of fear throughout the New England colonies. But on his way home to Canada from the Maine frontier following the attack, he was killed by friendly Abenakis, who mistook him for the enemy.[34]

During the conference, the delegates agreed that Leisler should be allowed to name the commander of the land expedition, but when he nominated his chief adviser, Milborne, he was rebuffed. The New England colonies had what amounted to veto power due to Leisler's desperate need for troops.[35] Robert Livingston, accused of treason by Leisler and now hiding out in Connecticut, had for the past two months been urging the New England colonies to conduct a major joint attack with Albany on New France, but not to accept either Leisler or Milborne as commander of the operation. A prominent anti-Leislerian fur-trader and government official, Livingston had immigrated to Albany in 1674 and was married to Schuyler's older sister Alida. Like Schuyler and Frederick Philipse, the affluent Livingston owned homes and performed business activities in both New York City and Albany.[36]

Based upon Livingston's advice, John Allyn, secretary of Connecticut, sent a letter to Leisler on May 25 declaring that Milborne was unqualified and too disliked by the troops of Albany and Connecticut to lead such an important expedition and strongly recommended that Major-General Fitz-John Winthrop of New Haven take his place. Winthrop, wrote Allyn, was a man of reputation who would command the instant respect of the troops.[37] Anxious for reprisal against the French and to resurrect his dwindling political fortunes, Leisler temporarily put aside his ambitions for his future son-in-law and withdrew Milborne's nomination. At the insistence of Connecticut and with the firm backing of Albany, the command of the land expedition was instead entrusted to Winthrop.[38]

Though the turnout and results of the intercolonial conference fell short of expectations, the meeting was a landmark achievement in colonial American history and a feather in Leisler's cap. Bringing together several colonies, without any direction from Mother England, to develop a detailed plan for a major counterattack by land and sea against the French was a spectacular executive accomplishment. It also reflected the growing maturity of the colonies, for in a time of political crisis and uncertainty,

Leisler and his fellow provincial war planners had put aside their differences and come up with a coherent military strategy in response to the attack on Schenectady.[39]

Throughout May and June, Leisler, Schuyler, and New York's government officials planned and outfitted the joint land-sea operation. The size of the land force for the first joint Anglo-Iroquois invasion of French Canada was optimistically pegged at "600 Christians" and 1,500 to 1,800 League Iroquois.[40] After arming their Indigenous allies and taking steps to refortify Albany and Schenectady, Schuyler and his militia officers were pleased that Five Nations' sentiment continued to remain hostile to "Yonondio"—the name the Iroquois bestowed upon Frontenac—and the French of New France. In fact, Lawrence and his fellow Iroquois braves could not wait to fill their "powder bags" and wage war against their Canadian enemies. But the mighty Iroquois were far from the Crown's lackeys: they would use the summer offensive for their young men to gain war honors, to take large numbers of captives to replace their ranks, and to further their own expansionist agenda.[41]

For Leisler, the stakes could not have been higher. The success or failure of the military operation was either going to make or break him politically. If he was triumphant over his opposite number Count Frontenac, he would secure his legitimacy as lieutenant governor and provincial commander in chief, fend off his critics, and be assured of remaining in power until the arrival of the Crown's handpicked governor of New York. And if he failed—well, that was a prospect too horrible to contemplate.

5

ROUNDUPS, GAUNTLETS, AND RIOTING IN THE STREETS

Back in mid-January 1690, on the eve of the French attack on Schenectady, Jacob Leisler had inadvertently opened the door for heavy criticism when he detained New York's public postmaster John Perry, ordered his mailbags to be searched, and discovered a packet of letters critical of his regime set to be sent to Boston for subsequent transshipment to Whitehall. Looking for a pretext to eliminate his most outspoken opponents, the embattled acting lieutenant governor seized upon the complaints regarding his arbitrary government by calling them treasonous acts. He promptly issued warrants for the arrest of all "papists," "disaffected persons," and those "popishly affected." Over the next two months, he conducted brutal citywide roundups to eliminate his most bitter rivals.[1]

His long list of undesirables included Peter Schuyler up in Albany and Schuyler's brother Brandt in New York City; former councilman Frederick Philipse; the Dutch merchant and former militia colonel Nicholas Bayard; the prominent English lawyer William Nicoll; the former mayor and governor's council member Stephanus van Cortlandt; and Robert Livingston, still hiding out in Connecticut. When the roundups began, many of the purged councilors and vocal opponents of Leisler fled New York City for Albany, East Jersey, Connecticut, Pennsylvania, and Maryland to avoid imprisonment. However, several residents were taken into custody and imprisoned for orchestrating a "popish plot" to incinerate the City and for other fabricated charges. While Stephanus van Cortlandt and several others managed to find safe havens in neighboring colonies, Nicholas Bayard and William Nicoll were not so lucky. They were arrested on January 20 on the trumped-up charge of fomenting a riot and would be confined in Fort William's dingy prison for the next fourteen months.[2]

By the end of March, Leisler had charged with conspiracy and locked up virtually everyone he regarded as an enemy of the state and even issued warrants to neighboring colonies to promptly hand over those who had fled the province. Through subtle coercion and open threats, he also forced around 150 officials to relinquish their civil or military commissions granted from Andros and Lieutenant Governor Nicholson. Having taken firm control of the government, he wanted to make sure he had eliminated the last of the "implacable and insulting enemies" who stood in his way before turning his full attention to his planned summer campaign against New France.[3]

Although Peter Schuyler was on the acting lieutenant governor's blacklist, he was too valuable as the lead liaison with the Iroquois, too popular as Albany's mayor and militia commander, and too knowledgeable about the borderland frontier to be removed from power. However, he was stripped of much of his governmental authority under Milborne, who assumed command over Albany's armed forces. Luckily for Schuyler, he and his fellow anti-Leislerians continued to find subtle ways to evade Leisler and Milborne's most ill-advised policies. Even the mayor's elderly widowed mother, the feisty Dutchwoman Margarita van Slichtenhorst Schuyler, resisted Leisler's efforts to reign over Dutch Albany through force.[4] Writing on May 19, 1690, to three of his loyal puppet commissioners he had installed in Albany, Leisler complained of the rumors he had heard that "ye widow Schuyler beat Captain Milborne, and that you all three were forced to fly out of ye towne and were gone to Esopus and Peter Schuyler was in ye fort."[5]

Though Schuyler's relationship with the Leislerians was uneasy, his evenhanded temperament, strong diplomatic skills, and collaborative nature continued to spare him from the wrath of Leisler and Milborne, even as he cleverly resisted their orders. Few characters in America's colonial history have shown greater diplomatic nimbleness or aplomb than Schuyler during Leisler's Rebellion and King William's War. Somehow, he was always able to bridge deep political and cultural divides, bring parties together productively, and achieve significant results under difficult circumstances. Even the heavy-handed Leisler was pragmatic enough to recognize how vital Schuyler was in maintaining the Covenant Chain with the Iroquois. Knowing that the frontier-savvy Schuyler would pay untold dividends for his planned summer invasion, he tolerated the Dutchman and his powerful family and, for the most part, left them alone. The Schuyler clan was far too well-connected from having planted deep roots in New Netherland two generations earlier and from having forged an unshakable alliance with the Iroquois.[6]

Although Leisler managed an uneasy truce with Schuyler, he had no such luck with the vast majority of the anti-Leislerian elite. His despotic leadership style, tax policies, and repressive trade regulations were so unpopular that by late April 1690 he had provoked ire among merchants and tradesmen who had previously supported or remained neutral toward him. Not only the colonial elite, but much of the middle-class was infuriated by his newly imposed, colony-wide wartime tax of threepence per pound and his undercutting of New York City's long-held, profitable monopolies on flour-bolting, baking, and transporting wheat.[7]

Since the attack at Schenectady, Leisler had been obsessed with winning the Crown a glorious victory against New France, which he knew was his only means of currying the favor of William and Mary. But waging war against the Roi du Soleil and his Grande Armée in Canada, he was fast discovering, cost vast sums of money. Because incoming revenues had come up short of defense requirements, he soon went beyond merely levying additional taxes and began seizing provisions from local merchants to meet war demands. On his orders, sheriffs broke into merchant warehouses, cellars, and outbuildings to seize whatever foodstuffs and other stores they could find of military value. Although the Leislerians insisted that exact records of the seized goods were being maintained and that the affected parties would be reimbursed by the government, the anti-Leislerians of New York City, Long Island, and Albany claimed they were being openly "plundered" to fund King William's War. They argued that the wealthy Crown and Parliament that had declared war on the French in the first place should be footing the bill, not financially strapped American colonists.[8]

In response to the growing list of offenses, on May 19 New York City's leading merchants and religious leaders sent a formal "Address" to Whitehall complaining that Leisler was illegally imprisoning his opponents, plundering their warehouses and homes, ruining trade, and abusing the dominies of the Dutch Reformed Church. Thirty-six New Yorkers appended their signatures to the petition, including Peter Schuyler's younger brother Brandt, deacon of the Dutch Reformed Church, and four prominent merchants who had previously supported or remained neutral toward Leisler: Abraham De Peyster, Stephen DeLancey, Gabriel Minvielle, and Charles Lodwick.[9]

As summer approached and Leisler prepared for the joint land-sea invasion of French Canada, New York City was on the brink of its own bloody war on the streets. It was during this anxious time that the leader of Leisler's Rebellion and his second-in-command received word of a new ploy by their archrival Frontenac in New France.

On May 27, 1690, Major Peter Schuyler was dispatched by Milborne to lead a delegation of prominent Albany leaders to Onondaga to meet with the League headmen, intervene against a French mission that had recently arrived at the village, and secure continued Iroquois loyalty in the war against imperial France. After having been rebuffed in his peace proposal to the Five Nations back in January, Frontenac had decided to send a second diplomatic legation to the seat of the Iroquois Confederation at Onondaga for follow-up negotiations to further French war aims and undermine his English adversaries. By reopening direct talks, he hoped to bring the Iroquois living west of the Mohawks—the Onondagas, Oneidas, Cayugas, and Senecas—over to the French side by appealing to the neutralists and Francophile-leaning sachems and war captains. By weakening the fragile Covenant Chain between the Five Nations and the English, he hoped to cleave away the Mohawks and other Anglophile Iroquois from the rest of the League.[10]

In the wake of the Schenectady attack and with the hotheaded Milborne in charge of military affairs on the Albany frontier, Schuyler was reluctant to leave his besieged military post and community. Milborne and his company of 160 troops had arrived at Albany on March 4 and Schuyler and his fellow magistrates had dissolved the Albany Convention and surrendered Fort Frederick on March 17. However, although the transfer of power went smoothly and many of Albany's public officials were retained in office, it was not easy for Schuyler to take orders from the despotic Leisler or Milborne, and he had mixed feelings about leaving Albany to the mercy of the Leislerians for a lengthy diplomatic mission to Indian country.[11]

He also had concerns over whether traveling to Onondaga to counter the French delegation might backfire. It was possible that all he and his Albanian envoys would accomplish would be to suffer the embarrassment of standing by as passive spectators while the Iroquois made peace with New France, weakened the Covenant Chain, and undermined England's tenuous grip in North America.[12] However, he considered such a drastic outcome unlikely given that the League Iroquois were winning the war against the French-allied tribes and, after Schenectady, had no reason to trust the French or make peace on Frontenac's terms. All the same, much was at stake and Schuyler knew there were tremendous risks in making the journey.[13]

In addition to Schuyler, the Albany delegation consisted of Robert Sanders, a Leislerian moderate and major fur trader with long-standing ties to the Mohawks, and four other Albanian leaders, at least one of whom spoke French.[14] Their marching orders from Milborne called upon them "to hasten with all possible speed, and animate the Indians to treat the French delegation as enemies." They were then to secure them as prisoners and transport them back to Albany, unless it was not "practicable so to do," in which case they were to "slay them outright."[15]

The honorable Schuyler, of course, had no intention of murdering official French emissaries in cold blood. However, he would push hard for the League headmen and war captains to reject Frontenac's recruitment efforts when the French had just slaughtered nearly sixty of the League's New York provincial allies and burned Schenectady to the ground. However, the Iroquois leaders might still refuse English demands that they not negotiate directly with the French in the absence of New York government officials.[16] During the recent negotiations with the Five Nations, the venerated Anglophile Onondaga sachem Sadekanaktie had declared, "We must stick to our Brother Quider and look on Yonondio as our enemy, for he is a cheat."[17] But that didn't mean he and his Iroquois brethren would roll over and be English America's lapdogs when it came to negotiations with the French and other Indigenous nations.

Many Iroquois had long recognized that Frontenac's strategy was to divide and rule the Five Nations through a combination of brute force, lavish gifts, and promised imperial protection, but despite the French courtier-governor's repeated treachery they wanted to keep their options open for diplomatic maneuvering between the two jostling superpowers. Furthermore, although they disliked being treated like rebellious children by the paternalistic and condescending count, who routinely used cajolery, threats, and coercion to compel "his Native subjects" to toe the line with the French Crown, they had no choice but to play both sides, given the uncertainty of their future in the European contest for North America.[18]

For the meeting at Onondaga, Count Frontenac's nine-man peace delegation had paddled down the ice-free St. Lawrence River in a pair of twenty-foot-long birchbark canoes. During their southward trek, the emissaries had stopped in the primary Oneida village to deliver wampum belts, rally political support for the French cause, and present letters to Pierre Millet, a French Jesuit missionary previously captured and adopted into the Iroquois Confederation. Father Millet was now an Oneida Bear Clan titleholder named Odatshedeh, though his political influence was limited by the tribal headmen. However, instead of being greeted as welcome dignitaries, the nine bearers of the peace offering were promptly taken as prisoners and the mail intended for Millet was seized by several angry Onondagas, who carried the emissaries to their own village. Because the Dutch interpreter Arnout Cornelisz Viele had been in Onondaga when the French delegation had arrived, he quickly sent messengers to Albany to report on Frontenac's diplomatic overture. The Onondaga sachem Sadekanaktie and the other leaders requested that Brother Quider and a New York delegation hurry to the planned Confederacy council in

Onondaga, where it would be decided what to do about the French outreach and the prisoners under the Covenant Chain.[19]

Thus, as Schuyler and his fellow envoys set out on horseback on their 300-mile round-trip journey, they knew who their French opposite numbers were and the goal of their diplomatic mission. Indeed, Frontenac had sent a formidable team to do his bidding. His top Indigenous war captain and diplomat, the Cayuga headman Ourehouare, was well respected by both sides. He had the unusual distinction of having helped prevent the purchase of Susquehanna lands by William Penn to preserve Cayuga territory and having served as a galley slave, along with fifty other captured Iroquois warriors, for two years aboard a French warship fighting the Barbary pirates in the Mediterranean. Paddling down the St. Lawrence and trekking overland with Ourehouare were four of his fellow liberated Iroquois *galériens* [galley slaves]; Chevalier Pierre d'Aux, a French half-pay officer, and the French interpreter Sieur Louis de Jolliet, both of whom had accompanied Frontenac, Ourehouare, and the thirteen surviving Iroquois *galériens* on their return voyage to New France from Europe; and two French-Canadian officers.[20]

Born in 1650, the forty-year-old Ourehouare was the lead envoy who had reached out to the Five Nations in January on the eve of the Schenectady raid. Although he had been unsuccessful and the League sachems Sadekanaktie and Sanonguirese had dismissed his entreaties on behalf of Frontenac, he was an accomplished orator, a respected statesman, and a veteran war leader with a considerable following among both the League and Laurentian Iroquois. He had served as one of the key headmen of the Cayuga villages established on the Bay of Quinte, Ontario, before the founding of Fort Frontenac at Cataraqui in 1673. In June 1687, the French governor who had replaced Frontenac following his first term, Brisay de Denonville, invaded the western League Iroquois, winning a victory and thereby preventing the English-backed Five Nations from wresting the western fur trade from French control. During the campaign, Ourehouare and fifty other Cayuga warriors were taken captive by the French, stripped naked, and tied to stakes in the compound of the fort, where they underwent torture at the hands of the French and their Wendat and Odawa allies. Upon the return of the French invaders to Montreal, the Cayuga chieftain and the other captives were transported down the St. Lawrence River to Quebec, leaving behind them 150 distraught women and children.[21]

At the request of the Sun King Louis XIV, Ourehouare and his fellow captives were shipped to France, where they were forced to serve as oarsmen in the king's galleys. However, the French treachery unleashed a wave of violence that culminated in the attack at Lachine, Quebec, on July 26, 1689, by a force of nearly 1,500 League Iroquois warriors, which had resulted in the killing, ritualized torturing, and burning of more than 200 French settlers and the capture of 120 more. Alarmed at the deteriorating situation overseas, Louis decided to return the well-respected Ourehouare and the other Iroquois captives to New France. He also replaced the much-disliked Governor de Denonville with Frontenac, who had served his first term as governor-general of New France from 1672–1682 and was now in his second stint as commander in chief of French Canada.[22]

When Frontenac sailed for Quebec for his second term in the fall of 1689, on the eve of Schenectady, he was accompanied by Ourehouare and thirteen Cayuga braves, the lone survivors of two years of enslavement in the king's galleys during France's war against the Mediterranean corsairs. On the lengthy voyage, Frontenac sought to gain the confidence and friendship of the powerful Cayuga headman, inviting him to dine with him and showering him with sumptuous gifts. In Quebec, Ourehouare was given a suite in the Château Saint-Louis, and was admitted to the governor's inner circle. As a result, he became a firm friend of Frontenac and now served as his top Indigenous envoy in King William's War.[23]

When Schuyler and his bedraggled Albany emissaries arrived in Onondaga after their lengthy 150-mile horseback journey, they met with the Anglophile Onondaga sachem Sadekanaktie and the other League headmen, the interpreter Arnout Viele, and Ourehouare. They wanted to make sure the French could not consolidate their military success at Schenectady with a diplomatic victory at the League capital. But to their surprise, they discovered that the Haudenosaunee leaders were in a much greater anti-French mood than anticipated. In fact, the League leaders staunchly refused even to speak with the French emissary Chevalier d'Aux, or any of the envoys except the venerated Ourehouare.[24]

That night, as the contemporary French writer and explorer Louis-Armand de Lom d'Arce de Lahontan noted, the "young Barbarians" and the "ancient Men" held a council with Schuyler and his Albany envoys on what to do with the French captives. It was decided that they would be dealt with in the traditional Iroquois manner by running a gauntlet and undergoing severe torture to determine their individual fates.[25] Depending on the courage displayed during their physical torment, the spectrum of possibilities that would follow ranged from being set free, undergoing assimilation as a mourning-war prisoner into one of the Five Nations, being exchanged for an enemy prisoner, or suffering a ceremonial burning to death at the stake.[26]

The veteran frontiersman Schuyler had observed many Iroquois, Mahican, and Lenape war rituals and condolence ceremonies, but this may have been the first time he witnessed the running of a gauntlet and violent follow-up rituals. The Onondaga villagers and Oneida and Seneca visitors lined up in two rows extending from the edge of the village into its center. Standing beside the Iroquois leaders Sadekanaktie and Ourehouare, the interpreter-traders Robert Sanders and Arnout Viele, and the other Albany envoys, Schuyler now watched as the French officer Chevalier Pierre d'Aux, the French interpreter Sieur Louis de Jolliet, and the two French-Canadian officers were forced to run the gauntlet.

To the taunts and jeers of the crowd, the prisoners, one at a time, began dashing through the opening between the two lines as the Iroquois warriors dealt them heavy blows with war clubs, the blunt end of battle axes, rifle butts, and other heavy objects. The young men delivered the stiffest wallops, while most of the old men, women, and children struck out with only modest force. The overall goal was to inflict considerable pain without causing serious injury. When the four Frenchmen had made it through to the other side of the gauntlet, they were winded, terrified, battered, and bloody but able to stand unsteadily on their own two feet.[27]

In the second phase of the ritual, they were stripped naked and led to a raised platform in the large open space inside the village, where old women led the Onondaga villagers in further physical abuse, tearing out fingernails and poking sensitive body parts with sticks and firebrands. The gauntlet and subsequent public humiliation and physical abuse of Pierre d'Aux and the other captives provided an opportunity for the entire community to hurl insults and seek retribution against enemy captives who had contributed to the killing of their people. It also served the secondary role of an adoption initiation rite for those fortunate enough not to be burned alive and instead taken into the Five Nations to be assimilated or ransomed. Following these ceremonial torments, the Frenchmen were allowed to rest and eat before having to dance before their captors and undergo more taunting and jeering. Meanwhile, their fate would be decided by the Iroquois leadership and grieving families, whose matriarchs played the key role in the decision of whether to adopt, execute, imprison, or barter the captives.[28]

In the end, two of the Frenchmen were spared and two were killed. The leader of Frontenac's ill-advised expedition, the half-pay officer d'Aux, was given to Arnout Viele to replace his son, also named Arnout, who had been captured at Schenectady. One of the French-Canadian officers was given as a condolence gift to the Oneidas, where he joined the Jesuit priest and Oneida Bear Clan titleholder Father Millet in captivity. Although the Oneidas allowed Millet to vote as a sachem in tribal councils while held prisoner, they did not fully trust him and used him as a pawn by having him correspond with Albany Dutch Reformed minister Godfredius Dellius, who vetted his Jesuit counterpart's correspondence and record-keeping to ensure that he acted in good faith to the Five Nations. Thus, Millet's adoption into the position of Odatshedeh provided a measure of security against threats to his life from hostile Oneidas and he would continue to serve as a key diplomatic bargaining chip and means of acquiring useful information. Familiar with Jesuit practices, the Oneidas knew that once reports of Millet and the new French-Canadian captive being held alive in Oneida country reached Frontenac, the royal governor would open up lines of communication with them through the Jesuits.[29]

The French-Canadian officer whose life was spared following his extended torture and was gifted to the Oneidas would now be assimilated into the Haudenosaunee. Having demonstrated bravery while enduring great suffering, he would now be a kinsman and his status as an adoptee would eventually be no different from that of the original member of the Oneidas he had replaced. Thus, he would no longer have his former European identity and would instead become a replacement for a lost warrior or loved one. In most cases, Europeans who were adopted chose to remain with their Iroquois families, and even those who eventually reentered colonial society still maintained close connections to the Five Nations by serving as cultural brokers, interpreters, and mediators, strengthening both Haudenosaunee and Anglo-Dutch communities and creating a multicultural northeastern American frontier.[30]

As historian Ned Blackhawk writes about the Iroquois adoption and assimilation process:

> They tormented captives ritually in order to break down their identities. To become a naturalized member of the Confederacy one had to disavow one's previous nation and accept, through violence, a new identity. . . . Family and clan leaders decided who would assume positions in Iroquois society. Captives were told the names, clans, and family positions of those who had perished. They were expected to assume these positions and names themselves. . . . To a surprising degree, such "ceremonial requickening" worked. Potentially as many as ten thousand were naturalized into Iroquois families in the half century following the epidemics of the 1630s.[31]

With Schuyler and the Albanians continuing to watch the unfolding spectacle, the unlucky French interpreter Sieur Louis de Jolliet was subjected to ramped-up torture and finally burned alive over a two-day period. Before being put to the torch, he was tied with a short rope to a stake, and the Iroquois villagers of both sexes and all ages took turns wielding firebrands and various red-hot objects to burn him systematically from the feet upward. Throughout the ritualistic torture, the Iroquois behaved with religious solemnity as the French-Canadian's screams rose into the air, he swooned into unconsciousness, and he was repeatedly revived and tormented. Eventually, when he was close to death, he was scalped and dispatched, likely with a tomahawk to the neck. Once dead, the flesh was stripped from his bones and thrown into cooking kettles and feasted upon by the entire village. The other captive French-Canadian officer who was not selected for requickening met a similar fate, but instead of being tortured and burned alive in Onondaga, he was sent to Seneca country to take part in the drawn-out death ritual in another village.[32]

Unfortunately, Schuyler did not leave behind his impressions of the mourning-war ceremonies he witnessed over the two-day period, but from his writings it is clear he was both intrigued and revolted by the gory rituals and cannibalism of his Iroquois brethren. For the Iroquois, writes historian Daniel Richter, the gauntlet, torture, and subsequent feasting upon a victim carried "great religious significance." However, despite the sound reasons behind these ceremonial wartime rituals, most European observers found them shocking and were unable to fully grasp their cultural importance to their Native hosts.[33]

Euro-Americans who witnessed the Iroquois in battle and their treatment of prisoners generally condemned their actions as "savage" or "barbarous." Missionaries and colonial officials on both sides of King William's War typically complained that Indians made war for sport or entertainment or out of uncontrollable bloodlust, and they sometimes reprimanded even their own allies for failing to pursue what they viewed as more noble and civilized war objectives such as conquering new territory, seizing plunder, and recovering captured women and children. While frontier European observers often noted that the Iroquois could be quite warm and caring to captives selected for adoption, they were mortified by the torture and cannibalism exhibited by the Five Nations and other tribes, attributing these actions to a "primitive" savagery lurking in the pagan souls of the Natives. The Iroquois, by contrast, saw violent warfare, ritualistic torture, intertribal adoption, and cannibalism as natural and necessary activities that bound their families and villages closer together, replenished their communities, preserved their culture, gave them powerful war medicine, and kept their people strong.[34]

To his credit, Schuyler was no ordinary European and understood better than most of his contemporaries why the Iroquois did what they did. Thus, while he may have been revolted on one level, he appreciated the ceremonial value the Iroquois attached to their actions. Throughout his life, he went out of his way to understand his Indian allies and enemies alike and maintained a high degree of empathy for his Native counterparts living in Iroquoia. Far more than the vast majority of his peers, he knew that the Iroquois had an important reason for ceremonially humiliating, torturing, and then killing or adopting their foes: these rituals were regenerative and allowed not only those who had recently lost loved ones but the entire community to participate directly in the defeat of the tribe's enemies and, in the process, they promoted group cohesion and demonstrated Iroquois superiority over the French and their Indigenous allies. Nonetheless, while Schuyler understood that his Iroquois brethren were not "bloodthirsty savages who waged war for mere sport," he had to have been unsettled by the unspeakable violence he witnessed up close at Onondaga.

Once the ceremonies were complete, Schuyler and his contingent made their way back on their 150-mile journey to Albany. Upon learning of the mission's success, Leisler was ecstatic that his archrival Frontenac had been foiled in his attempts "to seduce" the Five Nations away from their English brethren with money and presents and that the Iroquois had treated the four Frenchmen in a "barbarous manner."[35] But before he could celebrate his victory and turn his full attention to his land-sea campaign against New France, he had to first quell his own people rising up in open rebellion against him.

On June 6, 1690, a group of Leisler-appointed government officials read a proclamation before sixty to seventy angry citizens from the steps of New York's City Hall. The topics were the maintenance of the town watch, the defenses of Fort William, and the military preparedness of the City in the event of French attack. However, the irate townspeople, fed up with Leisler and his draconian policies, weren't listening.[36]

On April 23, the New York Assembly had passed the new wartime surtax of threepence per pound sterling value of all real and personal property, and the whole town remained up in arms about the new duties being levied against them. But what those gathered on the steps of City Hall found most galling was the continued imprisonment, without due process, of their friends and family members, whose only crime had been refusing to recognize the authority of Leisler and his political cronies. When the town's citizens had lobbied to have the prisoners released, the Leislerians had promised that if those incarcerated in Fort William "would sign a bond for their good behavior and acknowledge the authority of the Lieut. Governor and Council, they would be set free." But the offer of reconciliation was later revoked. Now several of the prominent merchants in the crowd began yelling that they would not allow the tax proclamation to be read until the prisoners were released.[37]

When Gerardus Beekman, the City's chief justice, and the other Leisler-appointed council members insisted on reading the orders, the angry citizens vigorously protested. The anti-Leislerians were led by Peter Schuyler's younger brother Brandt Schuyler and Balthazar Bayard. Brandt was not only a church deacon married to Cornelia van Cortlandt of the powerful van Cortlandt family, he had served as a New York militia captain and was a strident anti-Leislerian who had previously been arrested under false pretext during the recent roundups and held in custody overnight. Balthazar Bayard was the older brother of Colonel Nicholas Bayard, still locked up in chains in the fort along with lawyer William Nicoll.[38]

Once again, Brandt Schuyler and Balthazar Bayard, who had both signed the May 19 petition against Leisler, demanded that their friends and loved ones locked up in the Fort William prison be released, as previously promised. But again, Chief Justice Gerardus Beekman and the other Leislerian councilors refused, drawing fierce protests from the crowd. To restore order, the high constable commanded his deputy, the Englishman Edward Buckmaster "to keep the King's peace," but Buckmaster suddenly produced a club and "joined with the opposers." The high constable then instructed Abraham Gouverneur, the city clerk, to "read on" but a scuffle ensued, with one of the anti-Leislerians threatening to strike Abraham Brasher, ensign of the foot soldiers, with a walking cane.[39]

At this point, several of the officers drew their swords. With this aggressive move, Schuyler and the anti-Leislerians backed down and allowed Gouverneur to read the tax order without interruption. But they insisted that Justice Gerardus Beekman and the other officials escort them to Fort William and release the prisoners. When the council members again refused, another shouting match ensued and the irate citizens roared that they would go "fetch their guns" and liberate the prisoners themselves.[40]

But somehow, impossibly, cooler heads prevailed. Brandt Schuyler and the other outraged citizens "said they would speak to Leisler himself" and "ask his consent" to release the prisoners. At the time, the acting lieutenant governor was known to be visiting the home of Mayor Peter Delanoy just down the street near Fort William. After some back and forth, this was agreed to and the townspeople gave "two or three huzzahs" and "went from the City Hall toward the Fort." Escorted by the sword-carrying councilors, the crowd of disgruntled New Yorkers that had grown to nearly a hundred strong, proceeded southwest along Dock Street, promptly located Leisler near Delanoy's house, and somehow persuaded him to release the prisoners "on bail" after they signed a bond.[41]

The large party then set off again, this time heading northwest up Broad Way for the fort. With a frisson of danger in the air and an angry mob surrounding him, Leisler may have merely been stalling for time. But as the group started up the street, the two opposing sides were unable to control their tempers.[42] The anti-Leislerians "demanded to have the prisoners at once, saying that they would immediately sign the bond." More townspeople came rushing up to see what all the commotion was about. It is at this point that the streets of colonial New York City, just west of the Great Dock in the Dock Ward and at the northeast corner of the intersection of present-day Whitehall and Pearl Streets, turned into a violent street riot "as soldiers were summoned from the fort."[43]

Fearful for his father's life with the mob growing larger and more uncontrollable, Leisler's son, Jacob Jr., "drew his sword and began to hack right and left, but the people got hold of him and took the sword out of his hand and broke it in two." Now surrounded on all sides, Leisler Sr.

lashed out against his attackers with his cane. He was struck by another cane from one of the anti-Leislerians, and a second attacker, the English cooper John Crooke, "struck him on the shoulder with his adze, so that there was much confusion."[44]

The soldiers summoned from Fort William now poured from the garrison and charged southeast down Broad Way. Emboldened by the troops rushing to his support, the former militia captain Leisler slipped from the crowd and joined the wave of onrushing soldiers. With armed troops arriving on the scene, Brandt Schuyler and many of the other anti-Leislerians scattered. Using naked swords, the butt ends of their muskets, and halberds, the soldiers now pitched into the mostly unarmed crowd. A particularly lethal two-handed weapon used in hand-to-hand combat since the Middle Ages, the halberd consisted of an axe blade topped with a sharpened spike mounted on a six-foot-long shaft. With the crowd retreating southward toward the Weigh House next to the docks, one of the soldiers stabbed an Englishman, Captain Jeremy Tothill, with his halberd, who spun around and delivered "a heavy blow with his cane, and parried other blows with his cane, for he had no other weapon."[45]

With most of the protesters realizing that they were now overmatched and scrambling to get away from the soldiers, the fighting shifted northward up Dock Street in the direction of City Hall. The soldiers pursued the retreating townspeople two blocks to Long Mary's Corner, where the Dutchman Teunis de Key and several others formed up in a rearguard action.

De Key came forward with two pistols and a short cavalry musket, or carbine. Swiftly arming Tothill with a pistol and Dutchman Hendrick Jacobs with a carbine, the three men, and perhaps others, held the Dutch sergeant of the fort and a score of soldiers "at bay until the others got away." With the crowd dispersed, Leisler sounded a general alarm by having one of the Fort William cannons fired and placed the town under martial law.[46]

According to one contemporary account, the Leislerian roundups and retribution in the aftermath of what became known as the "New York Riot of 1690" were swift and brutal:

> The soldiers, with naked swords in their hands, ran like madmen through the streets and those who happened to be about and were not of their party were at once taken to the fort, thrown in chains and put on bread and water. . . . The following day, the drum was beaten again and all the farmers and burghers were once more under arms. About noon, a proclamation was read which sounded as if the people who were opposed to him [Leisler] intended to commit treason and had tried to murder him, and he gave orders to seize [many others], whether they were guilty or not. . . . They had stationed soldiers in some houses against which they were embittered, about 9 or 10 in each house. These remained there until evening [making] a good deal of trouble.[47]

Eventually, Leisler stepped in to rein in his men but his actions proved too little, too late. The plundering and brutality by scores of angry, mostly Dutch Leislerians from the City and up-island farms and towns drew the censure of most New Yorkers and alienated many of those who had previously been sympathetic to his cause.[48]

By June 8, 1690, two days after the riot, Leisler had rounded up Brandt Schuyler and more than thirty other New Yorkers and locked them up in Fort William. Here they joined Nicholas Bayard, William Nicoll, and the other "traitors and papists" already incarcerated. The newly arrested and imprisoned English, Scottish, Dutch, French Huguenot, and African citizens came from all social classes and occupations, from leading merchants to stonemasons to house servants.[49] Many of those arrested had simply been advocating for the release of their family members held in confinement, had stepped out onto the street at the wrong moment, or had refused to allow the soldiers to ransack their homes.[50]

Soon thereafter, Leisler renewed his threats against New York's rebellious religious community, which had close ties to Peter Schuyler and other anti-Leislerians. On June 8, he harassed and publicly humiliated Dutch Reformed minister Henricus Selyns as he was delivering his Sunday sermon, and over the next two days he continued his reign of martial law and intimidation.[51] Using the prospect of an invasion by James II's army in Ireland as a pretext, he forced everyone in the City to sign an oath to defend Fort William. On Monday and Tuesday, June 9 and 10, the drum was beaten once again and a new proclamation was read commanding all townspeople to come to the fort and sign a pledge of loyalty, or be declared "enemies to His Majesty and country." Meanwhile, the manhunt for more than a dozen wanted anti-Leislerians, including Teunis de Key, Jeremy Tothill, and John Crooke, who had fought against Leisler and the soldiers before escaping, continued as Manhattan remained a police state.[52]

Still angry and bitter, Leisler continued to harass Henricus Selyns and the other dominies of the Dutch Reformed Church for months following the riot. He made life miserable for Dominie Rudolphus Varick of Long Island and Peter Schuyler's, Hilletie van Olinda's, and Lawrence's friend Godfredius Dellius in Albany, whom Leisler detested for continuing to refuse to recognize his authority.[53] In addition to continuing to wage war against the Dutch Reformed Church, Leisler confiscated church property in both New York City and Albany[54] and forcibly "stripped" English merchants "of their goods in the name of the King."[55]

Within two weeks following the June 6 riot, twelve of the thirty-odd prisoners were released after paying a hefty fine and signing a bond guaranteeing future good behavior. But it hardly mattered. From this point on, far more citizens in the City and outlying areas opposed Leisler than supported him. Meanwhile, New Yorkers continued their exodus to the sanctuary of East Jersey, where they joined a growing number of refugees. Even the merchant captains, sailors, and passengers of ships arriving to New York Harbor underwent interrogation by "Leisler's Men," with several arrested for treason.[56]

The June 1690 Riot was the first instance of an open insurrection against Leisler's authority in New York Province. Rising to meet the opposition, he swiftly put down all resistance. However, in winning the short-term battle, he made it impossible to win the long-term war against the gathering forces opposing him.

But the acting lieutenant governor—whom New Yorkers now referred to as "that tyrant and usurper Leisler"[57]—soon had more pressing problems than the riot and its controversial aftermath. For Count Frontenac and his powerful frontier army loomed to the north fresh off their triumphs at Schenectady, Salmon Falls, and Fort Loyal.

6
THE INVASION OF NEW FRANCE

On July 11, 1690, shortly before setting out for the garrison at Saratoga to rendezvous with General Fitz-John Winthrop of Connecticut and his English-Iroquois land force, the Mohawk war captain Lawrence and his wife Maria brought their adopted twelve-year-old son to be baptized at the Dutch Reformed Church in North Albany. The ceremony was performed by Father Dellius and Hilletie van Olinda, who were personal friends of the young but prominent war leader and his wife, the daughter of the powerful Mohawk Turtle Clan matriarch Karanondo (Lifter). The Albany church was where the anti-Leislerian Dutch dominie ministered regularly to the Schuyler, Philipse, van Olinda, and other Euro- and Native-American families living in and around Albany.[1]

During the ceremony, three Mohawk men, three women, and four children were baptized, or had their faith renewed through Protestant communion, by Father Dellius and Hilletie. Maria's mother, Karanondo, was one of those who received baptism, taking the Christian name Lydia, while Lawrence's good friend and fellow Wolf Clan member Tejonihokarawa, who would by the close of the decade become an important Mohawk sachem, took the baptismal name Hendrick. Those who took part in the ritual were all part of Karanondo's (Lydia's) extended Turtle Clan family group, with Lawrence and the other Wolf Clan males having married outside their group since Mohawk clans were exogamous. Because this interrelated family group connecting the matriarch Karanondo's Turtle Clan with Lawrence's and Hilletie's Wolf Clan was one of great influence among the Mohawks, the baptisms represented a significant triumph not only for Father Dellius but for Hilletie van Olinda. The Mohawks' respect for Hilletie's cross-cultural skill is demonstrated by the fact that one of the baptized women, Karehojenda, took "Hilletie" as her formal baptismal name during the sacred ceremony.[2]

Lawrence and Maria's adopted son Sagonorasse (Fastener), whose parents had been killed by a rival Indigenous war party, was baptized as Adam. Because the Mohawk war captain and his wife had previously been baptized by the French Jesuits, they were not baptized at this time but were admitted to Protestant communion in the church by Dellius and Hilletie. In being admitted "to the Lord's holy and high-worthy supper," Lawrence and Maria wanted their adopted son "educated in the doctrines of Christ." Lawrence and his fellow Mohawks had chosen to seek communion in the Protestant faith to give their people strength in the coming battle against the French, to help them resist the Old-World contagions that were ravaging their villages, and to reaffirm their commitment to their Albany brethren and the Covenant Chain that they hoped would protect them from their many enemies in Iroquoia and French Canada.[3]

Following the baptismal ceremony, a revitalized Lawrence returned with Maria and their newly adopted son Sagonorasse, now baptized Adam, to their village of Tionnontoguen, up the Mohawk River. On August 2, Lawrence and a small party of Mohawks that included Hendrick (Tejonihokarawa) rendezvoused at the old Dutch garrison in Saratoga with a contingent of Anglophile League warriors and English military officers and troops. The officers included Major General Fitz-John Winthrop of Connecticut, the commanding general selected to lead the 1690 Canadian land campaign; Major Peter Schuyler of Albany; and his youngest brother, Lieutenant Johannes Schuyler.[4]

An experienced outdoorsman and soldier, the fifty-three-year-old Winthrop was the product of a distinguished Massachusetts family as the grandson of the legendary Puritan John Winthrop, founding governor of Massachusetts Bay Colony. The commanding general of the land expedition would go on to serve as governor of Connecticut from 1696 until his death in 1707. When Winthrop and his troops had first arrived in Albany from Connecticut, Major Peter Schuyler had allowed them to camp in the grassy fields and woods of Schuyler Flatts. Named originally after the Dutch *DeVlackte* or *Flats*, the major's sprawling farm was located on the west bank of the Hudson River four miles south of Albany and Fort Frederick.[5]

During the war conference held soon after his arrival to Saratoga, Lawrence was surprised that Winthrop's English force for the land attack on Montreal consisted of only 150 New York provincials. This was a far cry from the 850 militia from New York, New England, and Maryland Leisler had promised the Five Nations back in May to coordinate with the Boston-based assault on Quebec by sea. Unfortunately, Massachusetts Bay and Plymouth had withdrawn their promise of men following the French attacks on Salmon Falls, New Hampshire, and Fort Loyal in Maine, and a smallpox epidemic had "much disabled" Winthrop's militia force by the time it had completed its northward trek to Saratoga. Winthrop and his Connecticut troops had brought the pox along with them when they had marched into Albany for Schuyler Flatts on July 21 and the infectious disease was already spreading into Iroquoia.[6]

When he learned of the smallpox epidemic, Lawrence was angry at the New Englanders' disregard for the welfare of the Haudenosaunee. The "running face sickness" was the greatest of the White man's curses upon him and his people. He worried for the safety of his young wife Maria and their adopted son at Tionnontoguen.

But there was more bad news. Not only was there a severe shortage of healthy troops, there were insufficient canoes to transport the war party northward and inadequate provisions to sustain the joint Anglo-Indian army for the expedition to Montreal and back. Despite these setbacks, Winthrop and his army pushed on to Wood Creek, the final assembly point a hundred miles north of Albany at the headwaters of Lake Champlain. Here they were met by several dozen Mohawk, Oneida, Mahican, and Schaghticoke volunteers; however, the numbers were still far below the expected 1,500 to 1,800 warriors promised by the Five Nations for the land attack. Upon learning that the Albany smallpox outbreak had reached Onondaga country to the northwest, the Onondaga, Cayuga, and Seneca warriors to the west of Tionnontoguen had refused to take part in the expedition, not wanting to risk their peoples' lives. Without the full force of League warriors, many of whom were veterans of the July 1689 Lachine raid, General Winthrop realized that his land campaign was doomed before his army had made it halfway to Canada.[7]

Making matters worse, Winthrop and his New England officers inadvertently insulted their Native American allies by refusing to make use of the elm-bark canoes recently constructed by the Mohawks and Oneidas. To make up for Winthrop's faux pas, Schuyler took Lawrence and a small detachment down Lake Champlain in search of better-suited birchbark materials to quickly construct sufficient canoes for the invasion force. However, in mid-August the season was so far along that bark could no longer peel from the trees, thus preventing the construction of more canoes.[8]

After waiting in vain at Wood Creek for six days for the fresh provisions and supply of canoes to arrive, Winthrop held a war council with Major Peter Schuyler, Lawrence, and the other officers. Given their limited supplies and manpower, the group decided to dispatch a small but potent war party to wreak havoc upon the enemy and thereby salvage something positive from the campaign. The plan was to wage a Schenectady-like hit-and-run attack on Fort Chambly on the Chambly (present-day Richelieu) River, or on Fort La Prairie de la Madeleine on the south bank of the St. Lawrence River, keeping a safe distance from the well-protected bastion of Montreal.[9]

Twenty-one-year-old Johannes Schuyler volunteered to lead the war party. A rising member of the Albany community, Schuyler had been a governing delegate of the Albany Convention that opposed Leisler and Milborne. Fluent in English, Dutch, and basic Mohawk like his eldest brother Peter, he had learned much about Indian affairs and frontier military matters under the tutelage of the wise and experienced Brother Quider.[10] When other frontier officers "of more age and experience held back, he volunteered to lead a company into the enemy's country and do all the damage possible."[11]

Winthrop commissioned him captain, supplied him with a fleet of canoes, muskets, powder, and food stores, and sent him off with twenty-nine soldiers and 120 Mohawk, Oneida, Mahican, and Schaghticoke volunteers. The New Englander then returned to Albany with Major Peter

Schuyler and the remainder of the force. As he had in leading the reprisal party following the Schenectady attack, Lawrence volunteered to serve as one of the key League war captains on the expedition.[12] Quider was both relieved and pleased, for he knew that his youngest brother Johannes was in good hands with the veteran Mohawk war leader.

Leaving the Wood Creek encampment on August 13, Captain Johannes Schuyler and Lawrence soon encountered Captain Jacob Sanders Glen, survivor of Schenectady, and a scouting detachment near Ticonderoga. Schuyler recruited him and his thirteen Dutch militiamen and five Iroquois scouts to join the expedition, augmenting his small but fast-moving force. For eight days, the war party paddled north up Lake Champlain and the Chambly River until reaching a point several miles south of Fort Chambly. To maintain surprise, they camped for much of the day and canoed mostly at night.[13]

During the journey, Schuyler called a war council with Lawrence and the other war commanders, where by democratic vote it was decided to launch the attack at Fort La Prairie rather than Fort Chambly.[14] Wampum belts were then passed between the Mohawk, Oneida, Mahican, and Schaghticoke headmen "to ratify the decision and to stand by each other," and the Native warriors voted for Lawrence and two other prominent war captains to lead the attack. With the battle plan worked out, the council concluded with vigorous "hand-shaking all around among Christians and Indians."[15]

Schuyler's flotilla consisted of more than a dozen twenty-foot-long canoes, each able to hold more than a dozen passengers and up to a half ton of supplies. Most Iroquois canoes were constructed of birchbark, but those used by Schuyler and Lawrence were fashioned of both birch and elm bark and waterproofed along the seams with hot spruce and pine resin. In the 17th and 18th centuries, these lightweight but long and sturdy vessels that had originated with the northeastern Indigenous tribes allowed war parties and traders alike to move fast over great distances, while keeping military stores and trade goods dry even when carrying heavy loads. When emptied, they could be portaged around waterfalls, rapids, and other obstacles by two to four able-bodied men.[16]

On August 21, the war party stowed away their canoes and a store of provisions in the brush along the western bank of the Chambly (Richelieu) River a mile south of Fort Chambly. Over the past two days, Schuyler had sent out Lawrence and his scouts to ensure they remained undetected in enemy territory. The Mohawk war captain and his scouting party quickly discovered several previously occupied French and Indian campsites bearing prisoner palisades along the western shore. These were the relics of Frontenac and Togouiroui's war parties that had returned with captives from the raids on Casco Bay and Fort Loyal, Maine. But there was no sign of any prowling Frenchmen or Native enemy scouting patrols.[17]

With the coast clear, Schuyler and the attack force of just under 170 men began marching westward across the thickly forested floodplain toward La Prairie de la Madeleine and its stockade built of sharpened logs and timber planks. The French settlement near Kahnawake lay twenty miles northwest on the south bank of the St. Lawrence, upstream of Montreal.[18] In his journal of the expedition, the young captain reported on their stealthy approach to Fort La Prairie during the final leg of his harrowing nineteen-day, 220-mile northward journey that had begun in Albany:

> We pursued our journey by land and traveled that day close under La Prairie—the road being very difficult on account of the softness of the clay, over which we had to travel, so that two of our Christians returned to our canoes. Coming through the clay we heard much firing of musketry, of which we were astonished what it might be.[19]

The musket fire was a blessing in disguise, for neither Frontenac nor the French governor's Wendat (Huron), Odawa (Ottawa), or Laurentian Iroquois allies were aware of the English war party closing in on La Prairie. Although Frontenac's scouts had two weeks earlier detected the original Winthrop column near the headwaters of Lake Champlain, the Laurentian Iroquois scouting parties sent out in mid-August had learned from League Iroquois hunters captured near the lake that the bulk of Winthrop's army had abandoned plans for the assault and turned back to Albany.[20] When Frontenac had first learned of the large army of English and Iroquois assembling at Lake Champlain, he had held a war council with a "Grand Feast" for his Laurentian and upper Great Lakes nation allies of the Pays d'en haut. For the ceremony, he had his French cooks slow-roast "two oxen" and "six large dogs" with "some prunes" for his guests, and he also lavished them with "two barrels of wine" and plenty of "tobacco to smoke." After assuring his allies that he intended to aggressively prosecute the war against the English until they sued for peace, the sixty-eight-year-old French courtier had exhorted them by waving a tomahawk about his head, singing and dancing in the Indian manner, and enjoining them to wage war "unremittingly" against their mutual enemies to the south who would soon knock at the gates of Montreal.[21]

Following the war ceremony, he mustered his French troops, the local militia, and the "praying" Laurentian Iroquois to repulse the impending attack, while inviting the up-country Wendat, Odawa, and other Great Lakes tribesmen to join in the fighting. After assembling an army of eight hundred French soldiers and four hundred Indian auxiliaries, on August 19 Frontenac marched his muscular force across the St. Lawrence River, made his way southward to La Prairie de la Magdelaine, and camped near the fort for three days. Additional French and Indian scouting parties were sent out to scour the area, but they could find no trace of the reported smaller Anglo-Iroquois detachment that had broken off from Winthrop and was advancing northward. On August 22, with still no sign of the enemy, Frontenac withdrew his 800 French troops along with his Indigenous allies, who celebrated by firing a volley from their trade muskets as Johannes Schuyler's still-undetected enemy detachment neared the area.[22]

Thus, it was only by a stroke of luck that Peter Schuyler's youngest brother did not face the formidable Louis de Buade, Comte de Frontenac and his full force of twelve hundred enemy fighters at La Prairie. A product of the ancient French nobility of the pen and sword and something of an autocrat, the count was not only experienced in combat and unafraid to take strategic risks but as comfortable "with the company of kings" in the halls of Versailles as he was "woodland warriors." He had served as a military man since 1635, when at the tender age of thirteen he signed on to serve under the Prince of Orange in Holland. Fighting in several campaigns in the Thirty Years' War, he rose to the lofty rank of *maître de camp* (colonel) before his twenty-first birthday in 1643, and he was badly wounded in the arm while commanding his Normandie regiment at the siege of Orbetello, Italy, in 1646. In reward for his dash and daring, the French Crown promoted him to the rank of *maréchal-de-camp*, or brigadier general. Frontenac's value to King Louis as a brave warrior and strong colonial administrator had been demonstrated by his recent recall for a second term as governor-general of French Canada, after having served previously in the role from 1672–1682.[23]

As Schuyler neared Fort La Prairie, he sent Lawrence and his Mohawk scouts forward to reconnoiter the stockade and surrounding area. Soon Lawrence returned to report that the French soldiers and farmers were leaving the safety of the fort to gather the late summer wheat harvest. More important, there were less than ten armed troops and only a handful of the yeomen carried muskets. After performing a quick reconnaissance from the edge of the forest, young Schuyler held a war council. We "resolved in what manner we should hinder them to obtain the fort again," he wrote in his journal, "and agreed to do so by intercepting them."[24]

Guarding the St. Lawrence floodplain, Fort La Prairie stood a mere thirty paces from the south bank of the river. Hoping to kill or capture the entire party, Schuyler directed his forces to take up a position between the stockade and fields. He knew he had the element of surprise and numerical advantage on his side: the French officer commanding the garrison had not bothered to post sentries, nor did he have a full company of armed militia standing by in reserve in the event of an attack. But even more fortuitously, Frontenac's large body of French regulars and Indian scouts had vacated the area and most of those who remained were unarmed militiamen-farmers preoccupied with harvesting their crops.[25]

But as the war party took the attack position, one of the young, overeager warriors gave a battle cry and prematurely charged the enemy. Bristling to fight, several other braves and English troops suddenly jumped up from their concealed positions to join him. Though the mass of attackers descended quickly upon the startled French soldiers and settlers in a tumult of war whoops, the enemy had been alerted and were now too widely scattered in the tall wheat fields to be rolled up in one fell swoop, which infuriated Schuyler.[26]

While several of the French regulars and farmers stood their ground to offer resistance, most of the enemy attempted to flee to the safety of Fort La Prairie or hide among the wheat stalks. Those who managed to put up a fight swiftly became gripped in frenzied hand-to-hand combat with the onrushing Anglo-Iroquois attackers. Whizzing, whooshing, and thumping sounds reverberated up and down the wheat rows as musket balls, arrows, and tomahawks whirled through the air and drove into flesh and bone. While their French comrades made a mad dash for the fort, those who stood and fought took aim with their trade muskets, or wrestled away weapons and turned them on the invaders. However, only a scant few were able to put up effective resistance as the hot, gnarly lead balls began to fly.[27]

After firing an initial volley with their muskets, Lawrence and his Native attackers cut down some of the Frenchmen by the short-distance throwing of European-style axes made from forged steel. But they mostly cracked open skulls and slashed away at exposed shoulders at close range with their tomahawks, wooden-ball-headed war clubs, and huge stone-headed war mallets bearing hickory, ash, or maple wood handles. Screams of startlement and terror in the French tongue filled the air along with the terrifying, high-pitched, animalistic battle cry of the Mohawk, Oneida, Mahican, and Schaghticoke warriors that European settlers called the "Indian war whoop" and that would one day be imitated by Confederate soldiers in the Civil War. Mingling with the truculent, undulating roar of the Native combatants were the bloodthirsty vows of reprisal from the Anglo-Dutch soldiers intent on avenging Schenectady.[28]

The fight lasted perhaps fifteen minutes, with most of the French able to escape back into Fort La Prairie. In the wheat field next to the fort, Lawrence likely made swift work of several enemy militiamen with his wooden ball-headed war club. As he was a member of the Mohawk Wolf

Clan, the heavy wooden ball of his club was tightly clenched in the jaws of a symbolic wolf fashioned from the curved, three-foot-long wooden handle or shaft. A cluster of eagle feathers was customarily tied through the hole above the wooden grip on such lethal weapons to enhance their war medicine.

When it was all over, twelve French soldiers and harvesters lay dead, around the same number had been wounded but had managed to make it safely into the fort, and fifteen men and four women had been captured alive. Meanwhile, six League warriors had died in the attack. Schuyler was irate that his Indigenous allies and some of his own troops had raised "the war-whoop" and prematurely "rushed" the enemy, prohibiting him from "capturing the whole party." But the fight was still an English and Five Nations' victory: not only had Schuyler evaded an enemy army of twelve hundred men, he had brought terror to Frontenac's doorstep and paid him back in kind for his "massacre" at Schenectady.[29]

Once the prisoners were secured, Schuyler had them questioned by his French-speaking interpreter, and possibly Lawrence, who was conversant in basic English and French. The captured Frenchmen informed their captors that Frontenac had withdrawn his eight hundred soldiers only the day before, after his Native scouts had reported no sign of the English force. Meanwhile, the French militia fired off several rounds from Fort La Prairie's alarm cannons, which were promptly answered from Montreal and Chambly. Knowing from the newly acquired intelligence that he had at most two hours before he would be under attack by a Montreal relief column, Schuyler ordered his men to quickly destroy everything outside the fort, including houses, barns, sheds, haystacks, draft animals, grain supplies, and the unharvested wheat and other crops in the fields.[30] The invaders shot to death with muskets and stabbed with knives, tomahawks, and axes "nearly 150 head of oxen and cows," wrote Schuyler, "and then we set fire to all their houses and barns which we found in the fields, their hay, and everything else which would take fire."[31]

With leaping flames engulfing the area and their blood running hot, he and his officers seem to have become overconfident, as they now proposed launching a second attack and seizing the fort. But Lawrence and the other

League war captains deemed the risk too great, as they had already lost six good men in the initial assault and intended to properly mourn their deaths. Unable to secure the "consent" of his Native allies to support the attack on the fort and being safe for the moment with no enemy in sight, Schuyler allowed the men to take a few minutes to eat their rations in the woods before setting out with the tightly bound prisoners on the grueling return journey to Albany. Like his eldest brother Peter, Johannes treated the Iroquois, Mahican, and other Native American tribesmen he fought alongside with respect and dignity, even if he didn't fully embrace their methods of waging war or mourning-war rituals.[32] "[W]e sat down to eat and thanked the Governor of Canada for his salute of heavy cannon during our meal," wrote Schuyler with a hint of cockiness, which "they fired from the morning till 2 o'clock in the afternoon from all three of the forts."[33]

Before setting out, the League warriors dispatched and scalped two of the badly wounded French prisoners, whom they believed would slow up the retreating column. The war party then marched seven miles eastward to "the music of the great guns," reaching by early afternoon the canoes stashed in the forest next to the river above Fort Chambly. After safely reaching the canoes, Schuyler and his Anglo-Iroquois force paddled upriver more than one hundred miles against the current, arriving to Albany on August 30. By the time they set foot in the fur-trading outpost, the Five Nations had raided several other isolated settlements up north, killing at least twenty-eight French settlers and soldiers, including two of Frontenac's trusted officers.[34]

Despite the significant punishment inflicted by Johannes Schuyler and Lawrence upon the French, Major-General Fitz-John Winthrop's land expedition to vanquish Montreal was deemed an overall failure. On the positive side, the young captain from Albany had exacted revenge not only for Schenectady but Salmon Falls and Casco Bay. More important, he had spread dread and panic throughout the Montreal region, thereby salvaging something positive from "the first colonial expedition against Canada."[35] Frontenac himself was so "galled" by the attack on his doorstep that "he made no mention of it in his dispatches to the court" and was forced to defend his actions to his superiors in Paris and the distressed French settlers.[36]

All the same, the raid did not match the sheer terror of Schenectady. Even worse, it failed to coincide with the planned maritime assault on Quebec. Which meant that the wily old French courtier who had staved off disaster could now dance a real war dance by concentrating his forces on the New Englanders approaching by sea—thereby snatching victory from the jaws of defeat.[37]

On October 6, 1690, the Boston invasion fleet of 34 gunships and 2,300 Massachusetts militiamen sailed up the St. Lawrence River and dropped anchor three miles east of Quebec City, the capital of New France. Standing on the quarterdeck of his forty-two-gun flagship, *Six Friends*, just outside the range of the French garrison's heavy cannons, Sir William Phips, the expedition's swashbuckling commander, stared wolfishly at the prize he hoped to soon claim on behalf of his English king. In May, he and his force of seven hundred men had easily taken Port Royal in French Acadia (present-day Nova Scotia) and he was confident that his massive army standing by on his flotilla of frigates, brigantines, and ketches were on the cusp of victory and that he would return to Boston once again as a conquering hero.[38]

All he had to do was formally demand Frontenac's surrender as he had done with the French governor at Port Royal—and all of Quebec Province would be his. After all, from two captured French prisoners he had learned that not only were Frontenac's twelve cannons dismounted but he had less than two hundred troops total to defend Quebec City. Furthermore, Phips was certain the French-Canadian people would gladly renounce despotism under the rule of the Sun King for freedom under the Protestant English flag.[39]

Described as a tall and powerful "New England buccaneer," William Phips was one of the more colorful and rascally figures of the early colonial era. Born in 1651 on a "plantation on the River of the Kennebeck," a farming, fishing, and Indian-trading community far off the beaten path in Maine, he grew up in humble circumstances as a wild, energetic, and illiterate frontier boy who enjoyed fisticuffs and a good cuss word. In 1673, he moved to the burgeoning Puritan seaport of Boston, married the widow of a well-to-do local merchant, soon became a reputable shipbuilder, and began to make trading and wrecking (treasure-salvaging) voyages to the Bahamas and West Indies on behalf of Boston investors.[40] But he had higher aspirations. In 1687, he led a London-backed salvaging expedition to the Bahamas, recovering £210,000 ($73,500,000 today) worth of silver treasure from a sunken Spanish galleon. He promptly carried the vast sum to England and the court of James II. After the king claimed his royal "tenth" of £21,000 sterling ($7,350,000 today) and Phips received his £11,000 ($3,850,000 today) cut of the proceeds, James knighted Phips in June 1687, making "Sir" William the first native-born New Englander to receive the coveted honor.[41]

Upon his return to Massachusetts as the Crown-appointed provost marshal of the Dominion of New England, second only to the governor in authority, he purchased a fine brick mansion near the North Church, where the legendary Puritan ministerial father-son tandem of Increase and Cotton Mather preached their sermons. He was not only celebrated by the Mathers and Boston's civic leaders, he was compared to "Jason fetching the Golden Fleece" at the 1688 Harvard College commencement for his wildly successful treasure-hunting expedition.[42] With his newfound wealth, prestige, and seafaring credentials, the rough-hewn and potty-mouthed adventurer was the overwhelming choice to lead the seaborne attack on Port Royal, Acadia. After recapturing the French stronghold in May 1690, Phips allowed his rowdy New Englanders to collect their pay by plundering the town, and he took the French governor and entire garrison to New England as prisoners of war, treating them harshly.[43] However, Boston's pious Puritans saw nothing wrong with piratical pillaging and roughing-up Catholic Frenchmen in the name of profit, so Phips was once again received as a conquering hero. Upon his triumphant return to port "with ye Governor of Port Royal, two priests, & about sixty soldiers with their great guns & stores of war & other plunder," it was a fait accompli that he would lead the late-summer amphibious expedition up the Saint Lawrence River to Quebec.[44]

On the morning following his arrival to Quebec City, October 7, 1690, Phips dispatched Major Thomas Savage under flag of truce to obtain Frontenac's surrender. After being blindfolded, the English envoy was led by a steep, circuitous route meant to disorient and unnerve him to an august hall in the Château St. Louis. With his blindfold removed, he found Frontenac standing there to greet him along with a courtly entourage of officers, including Lieutenant Jacques le Moyne de Sainte-Hélène, who had led the attack on Schenectady. Bedecked in "the martial foppery" in which the French took particular delight, the receiving party wore "gold and silver lace, ribands and plumed hats." Their hair was "powdered and curled" and their expressions were "anything but those of men who feared what events might bring."[45] Both surprised and duly impressed by the show of aplomb in the face of a massive enemy war fleet, the English major handed Frontenac his commander's ultimatum demanding the unconditional surrender of the town, its forts, food stores, and military ordnance—within one hour. If the governor refused, warned Phips in his letter, "I am come provided and am resolved by the help of God" and "by force of arms" to "bring you under subjection to the Crown of England."[46]

Unimpressed by Sir William's braggadocio, Frontenac proceeded to diss Phips, declare William III a usurper to the Crown, and inform Savage that he most certainly did not need an hour to make his decision, for his mind was already made up. The major asked the sumptuously attired French count if he wouldn't mind putting his reply in writing. "No, the only answer I can give your General will be from the mouth of my cannon and musketry," shot back Frontenac frostily, "that he may learn it is not in such a style that a person of my rank is summoned. Let him do his best as I will do mine!"[47] Stunned by the rejection, Savage was again blindfolded, escorted back over the barricades, and rowed out to the flagship of the impatiently waiting Sir William Phips, to whom he delivered the terrible news.[48]

Taken aback by Frontenac's unexpected tenacity but firmly resolved to give the French a good spanking, Phips held an immediate war council. With the concurrence of his officers, he decided to launch a combined land assault and naval bombardment upon the city. However, if he was going to take Quebec, he had to move quickly before Frontenac summoned reinforcements and winter set in, since it was already late in the season and the St. Lawrence would soon be impassable due to accumulating ice. The last thing he could afford was a protracted siege. The French had only to hold him at bay for two or three weeks before he would be forced to turn around and sail back to New England, or run the risk of being trapped in French Canada and battered by lethal winter storms. He was also desperately short of gunpowder, since the military ordnance he had requested from London had never arrived in Boston before his departure, which further limited his options.[49]

The final plan called for his second-in-command, Major John Walley, and an amphibious force of thirteen hundred militia to seize and occupy the north shore at Beauport where the Saint-Charles River emptied, just below and east of Quebec. Meanwhile, Phips would advance upriver with his fleet of four gunships and draw off a substantial portion of the defending forces by bombarding the battlements. However, due to a combination of bad luck and unforeseen difficulties, the operation failed miserably. The night before the attack, Louis-Hector de Callière, an experienced French military officer and the governor of Montreal, reached Quebec with six hundred soldiers and Algonquin and Laurentian Iroquois warriors, reinforcing Frontenac in the nick of time. Making matters worse, the marshlands at Beauport flats turned out to be boggier than expected and covered with dense brush, making it difficult for Phips to deploy his landing forces in the oarboats. But the inclement weather and a deadly smallpox outbreak turned out to be the decisive factors. On the morning of the attack, with the temperature plummeting to below freezing and crashing waves pummeling the boat landing sites, Phips's men aboard the gunships and Walley's troops taking part in the land attack began falling sick with the dreaded pox.[50]

After a week of hard fighting, Major Walley and his force of thirteen hundred men had still not made it across the well-defended Saint-Charles River, while Phips's naval bombardment failed because his cannons could not penetrate the city's lofty stone battlements and he ran out of ammunition. Throughout the battle, Frontenac wisely kept his main force on the

Quebec side of the Saint-Charles, unleashing a galling fire whenever the New Englanders attempted to ford the river and harassing them with hit-and-run attacks with small squadrons of foot soldiers and Native warriors. Whenever Walley's troops attempted to move to higher ground, they came under withering musket and cannon fire from the well-fortified Canadians. Meanwhile, Phips and his waterborne forces were forced to break off from the artillery duel when his warships began receiving direct hits from the French 18- and 24-pounders.[51]

On the third day of the battle, when Phips's mainmast and admiral's flagstaff took a cannonball from one of the booming enemy guns, his Cross of St. George tumbled into the river and was fished out by nose-thumbing French soldiers. With iron shot raining down upon his flagship like hailstones, he was forced to cut his anchor cable and retire from the action, while two of his remaining large gunships continued a desultory fire before withdrawing to safety. Although Major Walley kept up a brisk fire and sent out companies to clear the French out of the marshes and thickets near his main forces, he and his trapped men were eventually forced to surrender their position. They were rescued by oarboats under heavy sniper fire and ferried to the waiting ships. Realizing that he now faced virtually the entire military strength of New France, by the third day of the struggle the "New England buccaneer" had no alternative but to regroup for a concerted attack or return to Boston.[52]

On Wednesday, October 15, with a heavy gale blowing in and thick ice beginning to form, Phips decided that he and his men had endured quite enough punishment from Count Frontenac and the stalwart defenders of Quebec. Following the fortuitous capture of an enemy barkentine carrying a cargo of flour, pork, and salt and a multi-prisoner exchange, he and his defeated fleet raised sail and headed downriver toward the Gulf of St. Lawrence. Before setting out, the ever-boastful Sir William, the pride of Puritan Boston, issued a hollow parting threat that he would return next spring to lay waste to Quebec City.[53]

Though he had lost only around thirty English soldiers and sailors to death, more than four hundred suffered from mild to severe battle wounds, noncombat injuries, frostbite, and smallpox during the seven days of brisk fighting.[54] Frontenac believed the total English killed, wounded, and missing might have been as high as 500 men, while one of his officers "calculated" the "killed or wounded" at 450.[55] According to Major Thomas Savage, more than thirty French troops were killed by Walley's land forces alone during the bout, making the total French and Indian casualties upward of this number.[56] The French killed included the commander of the attack on Schenectady, Lieutenant Sainte-Hélène.[57]

Ultimately, smallpox and the sea elements exacted the heaviest toll on Phips's vanquished armed force as it withdrew southward from Canada on the return journey to Boston. During the grueling voyage, the fleet ran into a series of deadly North Atlantic storms that blew several of the ships perilously off course and shipwrecked one of the vessels against the rocks. Phips himself did not reach Boston until November 19, 1690, with sixty-five out of 120 of the men aboard his flagship afflicted by smallpox and fever.[58] One by one, the rest of the fleet came straggling into Boston Harbor after him, but at least three vessels became lost at sea and never made it home. In the end, as many as nine hundred soldiers and sailors out of the twenty-three hundred that had set sail from Boston Harbor on August 9 perished during and immediately following the disastrous campaign from battle wounds, smallpox, fever, exposure, drowning, and other shipborne accidents.[59]

For Massachusetts Bay and the other contributing New England colonies, the invasion of New France proved to be not only a massive military failure but a financial disaster. With "not a penny in the Treasury," the humiliating loss swamped the Massachusetts government with "extreme debts" from the soldiers' wages and bills for the expedition's victuals and military supplies.[60] On the cusp of insolvency, the post-Andros Massachusetts government came up with a novel solution: the authorities simply printed the necessary funds on paper. To pay the soldiers and settle the colony's debts, the government issued "the first paper money in the Western world" by authorizing the printing of £40,000 ($14,000,000 today) in paper bills in denominations ranging from two shillings to ten pounds.[61]

In New York, the failure of the joint land-sea invasion was nearly as calamitous for Jacob Leisler. A successful two-pronged invasion of French Canada by Winthrop and Phips would have given New York and New

England the unity of victory, demonstrated their firm loyalty to William and Mary, and ensured Leisler's continued grip on interim power. But with the mission an abysmal failure—with the exception of Captain Johannes Schuyler's small but successful La Prairie raid—the acting lieutenant governor squandered his best opportunity to win over his fellow New Yorkers. Instead, the military disaster brought out an even greater authoritarian streak in the orthodox Calvinist, who viewed all opposition to his policies as treason and a nefarious plot to destroy him and the Protestant cause.[62]

As the winter of 1690–1691 approached, Jacob Leisler was a desperate man barely clinging to power and holed up in the military fort of a fractious, war-torn, and financially depressed city. And his situation was about to get much worse.

7
THE BLASPHEMOUS PRIVATEER

On November 29, 1690, Colonel Henry Sloughter set sail from London on the HMS *Archangel* to replace Leisler as the official royal governor of New York. He had been appointed over a year earlier on September 25, 1689, but because he had been commanding troops on the Isle of Wight, he took an inordinately long time to recruit soldiers for the New York City garrison, settle his affairs in London, and prepare for the lengthy transatlantic voyage. Having been briefed by Nicholson and other Dominion officials, he was no friend of the Leislerians and believed New York was a province in total chaos, governed by a "rabble," and threatened by French invasion.[1]

The lengthy time that Sloughter took to reach his post played a key role in Leisler's fate. The HMS *Archangel* was blown off course en route from England, ran aground in Bermuda, and would not reach New York City until mid-March of 1691. Meanwhile, Major Richard Ingoldsby, commander of the new garrison and the governor's advance guard of troops, sailed on to New York without the newly commissioned military commander in chief of New York Province.[2]

On January 30, Ingoldsby arrived in New York Harbor, bringing with him two companies of Redcoats, "an imperiousness which matched Leisler's," and a firm belief that the interim government was "a usurpation."[3] Unwilling to wait for the arrival of Sloughter, he informed Leisler that he was the incoming royal governor's military commander, issued a proclamation protecting all New Yorkers loyal to William and Mary, and demanded that the acting lieutenant governor immediately surrender Fort William. Convinced that Ingoldsby was a "papist" who had come to seize New York

Province in the name of the deposed Catholic King James II, Leisler flatly refused to withdraw from the garrison until he was presented with a royal commission bearing the stamp of the king. Unfortunately, Ingoldsby did not carry Sloughter's official commission with him, which remained behind with the governor in Bermuda.[4]

A tense standoff ensued, with both sides calling up reinforcements and preparing for a long-term siege. At this stage of the rebellion, Leisler's ranks had plummeted to a mere three to four hundred hardcore followers. With the firm backing of Frederick Philipse and the deposed councilmen, as well as the City's merchants, clergy, seamen, and the English of Long Island, Ingoldsby was able to muster a larger force than Leisler of four to five hundred militia to augment his two companies of English regulars.[5]

Over the next six weeks, there were vicious written and verbal exchanges, running skirmishes, and blood spilled in the streets. The escalating conflict continued to tear New York apart and would not be settled until the return of a salty English-American privateer and Caribbean war hero.

On March 5, 1691, as Captain William Kidd passed through the narrow neck between Staten Island and Brooklyn into the Upper Bay, he was excited about his return to his home port of New York City and getting back on his feet again. After his roguish West Indian privateering crew had mutinied and stolen his Crown-licensed gunship, the *Blessed William*, and his life savings of £2,000 ($700,000 today) because he refused to commit piracy, he had been left penniless overnight except for his several New York real estate properties. Fortunately, Christopher Codrington, the English governor-general of the Caribbean Leeward Islands, had so valued his military service in King William's War that in December 1690 he rewarded him with his own sixteen-gun ship, the *Antigua*, to replace the *Blessed William* after Kidd had captured the French barkentine in battle. After more than a year and a half of fighting in the Caribbean, Kidd had fulfilled his military obligation to Codrington and was returning home as a sea captain in command of his own privateering and merchant vessel, with the goal of recouping his lost fortune and making a fresh start.[6]

Tall, robustly built, and thirty-four years of age, William Kidd was an educated man who could read and write and trace his roots to a humble and upstanding Protestant Christian family hailing from Soham Parish, Cambridgeshire, England.[7] However, he was also a restless and adventurous soul, who had gone away at an early age to sea as a cabin boy from the port town of Dundee, Scotland, and knew only the life of a mariner. Considering himself as much a Scotsman and colonial American as an Englishman, he had spent the last two decades roving the Caribbean aboard privateers and merchant vessels, before making New York his home in 1688 and purchasing several prime properties overlooking the pristine East River.[8]

William Kidd could afford properties near the Schuylers, Philipses, van Cortlandts, and other wealthy New York City families—properties that today comprise some of the most valuable real estate holdings in the entire world—because he had made a bundle of silver coinage as a respectable privateer and occasional merchant officer throughout the 1680s. As a private commerce raider taking richly laden enemy ships as prizes, he had earned far more than the average overworked and downtrodden Royal Navy or merchant deck hand, who typically netted a paltry £16 to £25 ($5,600 to $8,750 today) per annum.[9] Because he was a duly commissioned privateer and not an outlaw pirate taking the ships of all nations, his plundering activities were lawfully sanctioned by government officials through a "letter of marque," a license authorizing him to legally attack, capture, and plunder valuable enemy vessels in wartime—or merely in the name of "empire-building."[10]

Trained in mathematics and navigation, he had sailed extensively to and from the Caribbean, the American colonies, and the metropole of London. In the 1670s and 1680s, he had fought as a licensed buccaneer in the West Indies, patriotically sticking it to the Spanish as a militant vanguard of Protestant English expansion and to weaken Spain's grip in the New World.[11] A mere scrap of paper may have separated a licensed buccaneer or privateer from a pirate or freebooter, but for seamen like William Kidd the distinction was paramount. The key difference was that privateers received official government sanction and recognition from the court system when taking a ship as a prize, which granted them rightful ownership of the seized vessel and all captured goods on board and shielded them from legal action—a privilege pirates lacked.[12] Privateering ships and the privateersmen who manned them (both are referred to as "privateers") not only strengthened the royal navies and provided coast guard protection during King William's War but severely disrupted the enemy's trade.[13]

Captain Kidd skillfully navigated the *Antigua* on a northeasterly course through the Narrows—the *Hoofden* as the Dutch called it—where even experienced mariners ran their ships aground on dangerous shoals and sandbars. All warships and trading vessels sailing into New York Harbor from the south had to pass through this mile-wide choke point between Staten Island and Long Island. After tacking his way through the treacherous narrow passage, he steered through the choppy Upper Bay and anchored in New York Harbor.

In his hold, he carried a shipment of sugar, molasses, rum, indigo, linen, and spices to sell in the City. However, he was barely given time to sell his West Indian goods and settle into his comfortable lodgings overlooking the East River, for soon after his arrival he was recruited by Major Richard Ingoldsby, reinstated council member Frederick Philipse, and the City's merchant elite in a plan to dislodge the embattled Leisler and his band of holdouts from Fort William.[14] The architect of Leisler's Rebellion continued to maintain that Ingoldsby and his troops were Catholic conspirators who were attempting to seize the fort and hold New York Province for the deposed James II.[15] Kidd also learned that the newly appointed royal governor, Henry Sloughter, had been blown off course during his transatlantic voyage from England, had run aground in Bermuda, and was only now making his way to the City to take office.[16]

Though politically Kidd was a progressive Whig and not a pro-monarchy Tory, he agreed to fight on behalf of the Crown and the incoming Tory governor Sloughter as a licensed privateer to help take down Leisler and put an end to his rebellion. He recognized that Leisler was a poor horse to back for anyone with aspirations for a future in New York and that his chances for patronage and rapid advancement lay with the English establishment.[17]

On March 17, 1691, Major Richard Ingoldsby, his English regulars, and the New York militia encircled the fort to force Leisler and his men to surrender. Jacob Milborne, who was now Leisler's son-in-law after recently marrying his daughter Mary, issued false declarations in Dutch that the English troops were secretly working with Catholic sympathizers and enslaved Africans to overthrow William and Mary. Stirred up by the propaganda, Leisler's rebel force opened fire from the blockhouse on Ingoldsby. Unfortunately, many curious bystanders stood on Broad Way and other throughfares watching the unfolding drama and they took the brunt of the flying lead musket balls. When the smoke cleared, one White soldier and a Black man had been killed, seventeen townspeople lay wounded, and "a good deal of property" had been destroyed.[18]

Immediately following the firefight, Major Ingoldsby, along with Frederick Philipse, Stephanus van Cortlandt, and several of the City's other wealthy merchants—representing the government in exile—summoned Captain Kidd for a war conference. They wanted him to lead a coordinated seaborne attack on the Fort William blockhouse inside the stockade, while Ingoldsby assaulted once again by land to force Leisler to give up the blockhouse. Governor Sloughter, they informed him, was expected to arrive any day now from his circuitous voyage from London by way of Bermuda, and they hoped Kidd would help them clear the way for the royal governor. Not only did Captain Kidd readily agree, he came up with a bold plan to bombard the blockhouse from the Hudson River.[19] However, although he had an ample supply of cannonballs, the manpower, and the ship, he needed gunpowder and some additional supplies. Philipse and the merchants provided him with two hundred pounds of powder and other military ordnance to force the capitulation of Leisler and his holdouts.[20]

Three hours later, the newly commissioned privateer had loaded up with victuals and gunpowder in New York Harbor, sailed westward around the southern tip of Manhattan, anchored a quarter mile up the Hudson, and prepared to open fire upon the blockhouse with his 12-pound cannons.[21] However, with the violent storm that had struck early that morning picking up in intensity, the *Antigua* pitched and rolled in the rough seas and was driven back by the frothing waves despite her heavy bow and stern anchors. From the heaving quarterdeck, Kidd pointed his spyglass at the wood-and-earthen palisades and stout blockhouse of Fort William, where Leisler and his holdouts were holed up. With ice-cold sleet pelting his face, he struggled to maintain his balance as several of the *Antigua's* larboard gun ports slowly opened. Shouting over the howling wind, Kidd gave his chief gunner the order to prepare to fire on the blockhouse.[22]

But with the roiling tidewaters frothing with foam and colossal waves crashing against the barkentine's hull and swamping her decks with frigid seawater, he wasn't sure if he would be able to control his fire enough to avoid striking houses or taking civilian casualties.[23] He had his chief gunner dutifully sight and resight the cannons in the raging seas and gale-force winds, hoping to bombard the blockhouse without risking collateral damage. However, after more than two hours the cannoneers still didn't have a clean shot and the surf inside New York Harbor had turned even more precarious.[24]

Eventually, Kidd decided to navigate the *Antigua* into shallower water to cannonade the blockhouse and force Leisler's surrender. Unfortunately, the choppy seas still proved too strong and his gunners were unable to sight the target with the barkentine bucking and swaying like a wild horse.[25] But just as he was about to pack it in, he saw through his spyglass some twenty militiamen making a mad dash through the slush from the blockhouse to the protection of Fort William. A rousing cheer of huzzahs went up from the crew of the *Antigua*, who had emerged victorious in the battle without firing a single shot or losing a single man to the enemy. Leisler, oblivious to the challenges Kidd faced in aligning his cannons in the storm, had issued orders from the fort to abandon the blockhouse rather than square off against Captain Kidd and his formidable 12-pounders.[26]

Kidd was already on Leisler's blacklist for taking up arms against him, but the rebel leader now fulminated as the scales were tipped heavily against him in the battle for New York City. Only the day before, Leisler had complained in writing about the "Blasphemous Privateer" who had joined forces with the "papists" Ingoldsby and Philipse, but now Kidd had forced him to evacuate the blockhouse, thereby sealing his fate.[27]

The next day, March 18, Governor Sloughter and the HMS *Archangel* appeared on the horizon. But with the storm still raging, the strong contrary winds made it impossible for his frigate to navigate the final leg into New York Harbor. Once again Johnny-on-the-spot, the skilled mariner Captain Kidd sailed several leagues downwind on March 19 in the direction of Sandy Hook and personally ferried the new royal governor ashore in the *Antigua*'s pinnace.[28]

Joined by Captain Kidd, Sloughter headed to City Hall, where Ingoldsby and his men were stationed, proclaimed his Crown appointment as governor, and made three requests for Leisler to surrender Fort William. But Leisler insisted on holding on to the fort until he received a directive from the king personally addressed to him. After more back and forth, Leisler around midnight dispatched his son-in-law Jacob Milborne, council member Peter Delanoy, and others to arrange terms for handing over the fort. However, they stubbornly insisted that it was against the rules of military conduct to surrender a garrison at night so they refused to hand over the fort until the following day.[29] Growing impatient and angry, Sloughter arrested Milborne and his messengers—but not until after Captain Kidd, ticked off by the lack of respect shown the incoming governor, roughed up one of Leisler's confederates whom he found particularly irksome.[30]

In the morning, Leisler sent a conciliatory letter to Sloughter, disclaiming any wish to further withhold Fort William from him. But he continued to stall by asking for clarification on certain points. Fed up, Sloughter ordered Kidd to once again sail around the tip of Manhattan and train his guns on the backside of the fort. As the privateer commander sailed into position for a second attack, the governor sent Ingoldsby and his foot soldiers to order the fort's garrison to ground arms and march out, promising full pardons to everyone except Leisler and his councilmen. With the pugnacious Captain Kidd again threatening his rear with his big carriage guns, Leisler and his holdouts were forced to surrender. The leader of the two-year rebellion and his councilors were promptly arrested and tossed into the fort's gaol.[31]

Two hours later, Kidd arrived at City Hall to celebrate with the victors. Governor Sloughter and New York's glitterati toasted him and Ingoldsby as the heroes of the hour. Frederick Philipse, lawyer James Emott, former mayor Stephanus van Cortlandt, and other bigwigs held up their glasses in tribute to the saviors of the City. Also present were Colonel Nicholas Bayard and lawyer William Nicoll, freshly released from Fort William thanks to Kidd and Ingoldsby.[32] To officially usher in his new administration, New York's ninth royal governor since the 1664 English takeover now swore in his Crown-picked council that included Peter Schuyler (in absentia), Philipse, van Cortlandt, and Nicoll. Schuyler, Sloughter would write days later to London, was a man "of approved loyalty and integrity" who would no doubt show his readiness in service to William and Mary.[33]

Just like New York's new war hero Captain Kidd, who would soon become friends with Schuyler and his brother-in-law Robert Livingston.

On March 26, a Grand Jury brought charges against Leisler, Milborne, and eight of their ranking followers for bringing "great terror, ruin, and destruction of their Majesties faithful and allegiant subjects."[34] By April 8, the verdict was in and Peter Schuyler had a front-row seat along with Captain Kidd, Frederick Philipse, and Schuyler's younger brothers Brandt and Philip. Like everyone else in the courtroom, the mayor of Albany and newly appointed New York governor's council member was gripped with anticipation as he awaited the final decision. The Leisler treason trial had been going on for eight days and Chief Judge Joseph Dudley and the panel of nine judges of oyer and terminer had reached their verdict, which would now be delivered before the court.[35]

Leisler, Milborne, and the other eight defendants looked on nervously as they awaited their judgment. Near them sat the chief prosecutors, New York's attorney general, and the committee for preparing the prosecution that included Schuyler's friends Colonel Nicholas Bayard and Stephanus van Cortlandt.[36] With the courtroom hushed, the bewigged Judge Dudley laid out the indictments against the ten accused men. There was no mercy for Leisler and Milborne: both the ringleader and his second-in-command were found guilty of murder and treason. Six other defendants were also found guilty, while Mayor Peter Delanoy and another man were acquitted.[37]

Dudley then moved to the portion of the trial that Schuyler and the others had been breathlessly anticipating: the sentencing. In a stentorian voice, the judge declared that the convicted men were to be "carried to the place from whence they came, and from thence to the place of execution, that there they shall be severally hanged by the neck, and being alive their bodies be cut down to the earth, that their bowels be taken out, and they being alive burnt before their faces, that their heads shall be struck off and their bodies cut in four parts, and which shall be disposed of as their Majesties shall assign."[38]

The courtroom gave an audible gasp. Elsie Leisler and the wives of the other condemned men began to weep and moan, while the anti-Leislerians, who had been solemn and reflective to this point, cheered the decision.

Pious and well-mannered Peter Schuyler was not among those who gloated. Instead, he likely quietly thanked his Protestant Christian God that justice had been served and Leisler's Rebellion was finally over.

8
THE DANCE OF DEATH

On May 16, 1691, a misty and damp Saturday afternoon, Peter Schuyler and more than two thousand men, women, and children turned out to witness the long-anticipated execution of the leader of Leisler's Rebellion and his son-in-law Jacob Milborne. The hanging site stood a third of a mile outside the stockaded wall on the eastern edge of the Common, which today is City Hall Park. A public hanging was not only grand theater but a public holiday, and at least half the free citizens of the City and many of the enslaved Blacks and White indentured servants had made their way through the two city gates, or from the northern Manhattan countryside, to watch the violent spectacle. Some had taken the old Lenape pathway that ran along Pearl Street, walked through the Water Gate of the wooden palisade on the corner of Wall and Pearl Streets, and then followed the footpath northward along the City Wall, passing green fields of grazing horses, cattle, and pigs and dozens of Dutch-style homes, many of which doubled as informal taverns. Others had come from the north along Broad Way—Brede Wegh as the Dutch called it—and then followed the dirt walking trail southward that ran parallel to the Wall to the Common where the scaffold was erected.[1]

While Manhattanites made up the vast majority of those present, some had traveled all the way from Long Island or New Jersey and a few, like Schuyler, had come from as far away as Albany or Connecticut. Taking a position near the front row, Schuyler looked up with grim foreboding at the gallows, along with a multiethnic assortment of people of Dutch, English, Scottish, French, German, Swedish, Jewish, and African extraction. He knew many of these people from the City and upriver personally. They included outspoken Leislerians like New York's future Dutch mayor Abraham De Peyster; Schuyler's reputable English friends William and Sarah Kidd who had been married only that morning; prominent anti-Leislerians like his Scottish brother-in-law Robert Livingston; and his fellow governor's council members Frederick Philipse and Stephanus van Cortlandt, as well as their families. Amid this diverse sea of colonial-era humanity, two companies of scarlet-jacketed soldiers clutching muskets with rain-flecked bayonets, stood guard to keep the Leislerians in line, their faces grim and wary. Shouts from the street hawkers selling food and drink filled the air, along with a rumble of conversation from the spectators and the grinding of oxcarts, horse-drawn wagons, and carriages shuttling people in for the event.[2]

The "hanging tree," as the execution scaffold was called, was constructed from timbers that had been set aside to shore up the walls of Fort William, and a pair of nooses dangled from the heavy wooden crossbeam.[3] Although Governor Sloughter had denied a petition for mercy on behalf of Leisler and Milborne with eighteen hundred signatures from New York Province attached to it, a substantial percentage of the population in a colony of around ten thousand total free and enslaved adults, he had bowed to public sentiment by reprieving the other six convicted men.[4] He had also nixed the grisly drawing and quartering components of the sentence, so that the two condemned men would only be hanged and beheaded without being diced up like poultry.[5]

Following the trial, Sloughter had initially been hesitant to order the execution of Leisler and the other convicted insurrectionists. After all, they had been the first in the City to raise the standard of Protestant William and Mary, and to cover his back from his Leislerian critics the governor had sought instructions from Whitehall. But Frederick Philipse, William Nicoll, Nicholas Bayard, Stephanus van Cortlandt, and the other leading members of the anti-Leisler faction and restored governor's council—as well as their assertive wives—didn't want to wait for the Crown authorities in London to give their blessing. For the past month, they had been engaged in a relentless campaign to convince Sloughter to sign the death warrants.[6]

Eventually, Schuyler's friend Philipse and the leading merchants were able to extract a promise from the governor not to reprieve those convicted without consent of the council, and they continued to demand their pound of flesh. Colonel Bayard and other strident anti-Leislerians, many of whom had been shackled in chains or singled out for special abuse, claimed that without the execution of Leisler and his chief lieutenants, no one was safe and the government could not be considered secure.[7] Under heavy pressure, Sloughter finally caved in and signed the death warrants.[8]

Soon Leisler and Milborne were transported to the gallows on a "sledge" by the sheriff and a squadron of Redcoats.[9] In the spring drizzle, Schuyler watched the spectacle with morbid fascination along with everyone else. The sheriff, the file of bayonet-clutching soldiers, and the two prisoners slowly parted their way through the crowd standing in front of the hanging scaffold.[10]

Weeping people thronged about the two condemned men as they stoically threaded their way through the crowd. While some of the passionate observers jeered those who were about to deprive them of their leader, other spectators cursed and spat upon Leisler and Milborne. A moment later, the two condemned men began climbing the separate wooden ladders leaning against the gallows.

After being guided to the upper rungs, the nooses dangling from the crossbeam of the wooden gallows were placed around their necks by the executioner. Leisler and Milborne would be pushed—or "turned off"—simultaneously from their designated heights on their ladders, left to hang and die by slow asphyxiation while kicking and spasming with their hands tied behind their backs, rather than from broken necks. No stranger to death, Schuyler had seen outlaws swinging from the gallows before. Instead of an instant and somewhat merciful death, he knew, Leisler and Milborne would take an excruciatingly long time to die in a grisly and dehumanizing fashion that New Yorkers called "the dance of death."

Once the high sheriff had laid out the crimes for which the two doomed men had been convicted, he asked Leisler if he had any last words. The gathered throng became quiet as they awaited his address. The hope from the Crown authorities at such public executions was that the convicted felons would stand penitently before the crowd, admit their guilt, warn those in attendance of the evils of their crimes, ask for forgiveness, and acknowledge the justice of the proceedings against them. But what many observers looked forward to most were a few unrepentant remarks or antisocial defiance at the end to spark controversy and take down the high and mighty.

Leisler now commenced his final sermon from the gallows: "Gentlemen and fellow brethren, all hope in the grace and fear of the Lord Jesus," he opened with, and then, over the next ten minutes, he publicly declared that he had forgiven his enemies, proclaimed his loyalty to William and Mary, and argued that all along he had done what he genuinely believed was in the best interest of New York Province. He declared that all he had ever wanted was to protect Protestantism and the rightful Crown. He admitted that he had fallen short of his goal, leaving behind "great and weighty matters of state affairs requiring at such a helm more wise, cunning, and powerful pilots than either of us was." He concluded with a call for his wife, Elsie, and family members to be treated respectfully once his execution was carried out.[11]

It was as honorable and conciliatory a speech as a condemned man could make from the gallows, and Peter Schuyler, despite his struggles over the past two years with the dictatorial leader and his incorrigible son-in-law, could not help but be moved.

"Are you ready now?" the sheriff asked Leisler.

"Yes," he replied, lifting his eyes in prayer. He then implored Governor Sloughter and his council to act in a Christianly manner and deliver his body to his wife upon his death.[12]

The sheriff now turned and asked Jacob Milborne if he had anything to say before his sentence was carried out. To Schuyler's surprise, the former indentured servant and son of a tailor proceeded to glare down at his nearby brother-in-law Robert Livingston, married to his older sister Alida, standing in the front row. Three years older than Schuyler, the ruddy-cheeked and periwigged First Lord of Livingston Manor had only recently returned to New York City after hiding out from Leisler for the past year in Connecticut. Like Schuyler, Livingston spent more time in Albany than New York City, but the wealthy merchant and part-time government agent kept a home in the City to attend to his affairs in the lucrative fur trade and other oceangoing commerce.[13]

In a booming voice filled with rage, Milborne now shouted down from the gallows at Livingston, who stood a mere ten feet from him.

"I forgive the governor and my judges, but I shall never forgive you, Robert Livingston! For it is you who have caused my death!"

The crowd gave an audible gasp and a number of people cheered as Milborne continued to glare down at the Scotsman. The rain drizzled down from the mercury-colored sky as Schuyler saw his stunned brother-in-law go ghostly pale.

"You are the one who hath caused the king that I must now die!" cried Milborne. "But before God's tribunal, I will implead you for the same!"[14]

Some of the Leislerians in the crowd booed and hissed Livingston, who looked aghast as all eyes riveted upon him. While Schuyler had put aside his pride the past year and worked with the Leislerians to protect the Albany frontier, his brother-in-law had continued to be Leisler and Milborne's most formidable opponent. In response, Leisler had canceled Livingston's cozy government contracts up north as clerk of Albany and victualler of the English troops, as well as forced Livingston to take refuge in Connecticut.[15]

Milborne now turned away from Livingston and looked at his father-in-law. "We are thoroughly wet with rain," he said to Leisler, "but in a little while we shall be rained through with the Holy Spirit."

"Will you not bless the King and Queen?" the sheriff then asked Milborne.

"Aye," said Milborne. "It is for the King and Queen I die, and the Protestant religion to which I was born and bred. I am ready, I am ready, Father. Into thy hands I recommend my soul."

"I hope these eyes of mine shall see our Lord Jesus Christ in heaven," pronounced Leisler. "I am ready, I am ready."[16]

The sheriff tied handkerchiefs over the eyes of each of the condemned men. When finished, he moved into position from the scaffold to push Leisler and Milborne off their ladders.

The execution site now turned totally silent.

With the rain picking up and wind gusting in from the harbor, the executioner shoved the ladders out from under each convicted man. In stepping out into eternity, the two Jacobs dropped less than two feet. With the fall not enough to break their necks, they hung suspended in midair, suffocating as they twitched and struggled. For a moment, the crowd stood there gawking in shock and disbelief. And then, in the drenching rain, Schuyler saw mothers and daughters fainting and heard the lugubrious keening of the Dutch women and the terrible "shrieks" of the crowd rumbling like a storm.[17]

Suddenly, fights broke out between the Leislerians and their avowed enemies. More women fainted, some "taken in labor."[18]

After a few minutes, the kicking and convulsing stopped.

The executioner cut down the limp bodies. With the Leislerian men and women both now openly wailing and soldiers breaking up the fights between the young men, a hooded axman stepped up to behead the corpses. To his credit, the strong-armed executioner did his job well, delivering a pair of clean blows that brought more anguished cries from the passionate crowd. Roughly one half of those present believed Jacob Leisler a loyal governor and servant of God, while the other half considered him a brutal Caesar.[19]

Once the prisoners were beheaded, their garments were cut into individual pieces by family members and strands of Leisler's hair were doled out as the precious relics of a martyr. The men's separated heads and bodies were then buried next to the gallows in the unconsecrated ground of a pair of unmarked graves.[20]

When the grim spectacle was over, Leisler's supporters began to sing Psalm 79 in unison.[21] As a faithful follower of the Protestant Christian faith and important member of Albany's Dutch Reformed Church, Schuyler was quite familiar with the biblical story of the heathens' destruction of Jerusalem, the tale of Jacob's martyrdom, and the looming threat of God's wrath. The mourners of Leisler and Milborne appeared to be signaling that God would surely deliver justice upon Governor Sloughter and the English party for the wrongs they had committed against the City's fallen Calvinist hero.[22]

As the mass singing of Psalm 79 rose into the drizzly air, people began to move off solemnly in small groups. As an in-your-face backdrop to the bloody execution, the English victory flag at Schuyler's friend Nicholas Bayard's mansion, hoisted two days earlier, fluttered in the sea breeze that had kicked up from the harbor.[23]

As he headed back into the port city south of Wall Street, Schuyler was just relieved that the Leislerian turmoil was finally over and he could focus on his family and fighting the French.

9

PEACE OFFERINGS AND WAR DRUMS

In the spring of 1691—while Leisler received his long-awaited comeuppance and Schuyler continued to secure the borderlands from French and Indian attacks—Lawrence and many of his fellow League Iroquois were having second thoughts about their commitment to King William's War. Neither the English nor the Five Nations were satisfied with the results of the 1690 campaign against French Canada and both parties felt victimized in the aftermath. The Iroquois were especially bitter at General Fitz-John Winthrop of Connecticut and his New Englanders for disregarding their welfare by introducing a smallpox epidemic into their villages. Estimates at the time put the losses between one hundred and five hundred Iroquois, a disproportionate number of whom were elders, including many influential sachems.[1]

Upon their return to Albany following Johannes Schuyler's small but successful La Prairie raid, the Mohawks and Oneidas were hungry and exhausted. But more important, they were so "incensed" at the pain and suffering brought on by the smallpox contagion that they destroyed much of the colonists' grain around Albany and killed dozens of livestock. In fact, Lawrence and his fellow Mohawks were so distraught over the recent losses to their kinsmen that they refused to cooperate with the English in any joint war operations for the foreseeable future. That was quite a turnaround for the Anglophile war captain, who loathed Frontenac and the French and had been extraordinarily loyal to his English brethren over the years.[2]

Following the massive July 1689 League Iroquois attack at Lachine in which some 200 French settlers were killed and 120 taken captive, Lawrence had accused French officials of forcing the Kahnawake Iroquois to live inside Montreal in a makeshift village because "the French were jealous of the praying Indians."[3] By this, he meant that New France's imperial authorities feared a mass Kahnawake defection to the League Iroquois of the Mohawk River Valley, which would deplete France's ability to wage war against the English and their Indian allies. It was this incident that had caused the Jesuit-baptized Mohawk warrior to abandon the Laurentian Iroquois community and seek solace with the Confederation and Father Dellius and his Dutch Reformed Church in Albany. But now Lawrence the Mohawk, the sobriquet of veneration bestowed upon him by his Albany allies, was nearly as disenchanted with the English as he was his sworn French enemies.[4]

Frontenac and his officials were just as disappointed with the results of the 1690 invasion, despite having suffered modest casualties at Montreal and having turned back Phips's ill-fated siege of Quebec that nearly bankrupted Massachusetts. The French complained about the "negligence" of their own Laurentian Iroquois scouts, whose premature withdrawal from La Prairie, they claimed, had ensured that Schuyler and Lawrence's force made it to the outskirts of Montreal undetected.[5] Though New France had survived, Frontenac and his military commanders could not rest easy as the Five Nations continued to send small raiding parties into the Montreal region. Furthermore, Frontenac could not claim a great victory at Quebec since Phips's forces had been defeated more by smallpox, the elements, and their commander's ineptitude than by the French governor's clever strategy or tactics.[6]

By the spring of 1691, Lawrence and many among the League Iroquois were committed to reestablishing peace and trade with their Laurentian kinfolk at Kahnawake and other missions in French Canada. Though both the League and Laurentian warriors had outright refused, or at least blunted, attacks upon their fellow Iroquois during the various engagements of 1689 and 1690, the two sides sustained battlefield casualties that amplified the reductions in numbers due to disease. Although the Anglo-Iroquois alliance remained strong despite a few hiccups, many of the older sachems and rising younger leaders of the Mohawks and other Four Nations were alarmed by the severe losses to their ranks and intended to reverse them.[7]

In late March, Lawrence and a hunting party of forty Mohawks came across a small party of Canadian Indian hunters south of Fort Chambly on the Chambly (Richelieu) River. After disarming the dozen or so hunters without a fight, Lawrence and his warriors peacefully escorted them as nominal "prisoners" back to their new, adopted hometown of Kahnawake outside Montreal. It was here in the Laurentian Iroquois community where Lawrence and his Mohawk wife Maria had previously lived among the Jesuit priests and the late Chief Togouiroui, the Great Mohawk, who had led the Native contingent in the attack on Schenectady.[8]

Lawrence and Onnonouagaren, the Mohawks' chief speaker, advised their Iroquois brothers of their interest in restoring peace and security to the Lake Champlain-Chambly River corridor. If the Laurentians would continue to withhold large-scale military support from Yonondio—Count Frontenac—and smoke instead "in peace on their mats," Lawrence and Onnonouagaren promised that they would obtain a similar peace initiative with their English allies in Albany.[9] As reported by the French Jesuits, the two up-and-coming Mohawk leaders represented a "renegade" faction that sought to attain peace "on their own account, and not through the Elders."[10]

While the Kahnawake Iroquois formally presented the visitors with belts of wampum so that their words were binding, Lawrence and Onnonouagaren could not offer diplomatic belts in their peace talks. Because they did not have the official sanction of their League tribal headmen, they could only conduct a preliminary overture and were not allowed to make a formal ceremonial pledge by offering one of the elaborate belts strung with the beads of polished marine shells. The reason they did not "consult" the sachems about their peace initiative, the two young Mohawks explained, was because these men were "not always very sincere" and most of those "who had sense are dead."[11] Lawrence and his cohorts knew they faced a crisis of leadership from the depopulation of the Mohawks and other Four Nations through disease, captivity, combat death, and famine.[12]

The olive-branch offering was, thus, spearheaded by the twenty-seven-year-old Lawrence and Onnonouagaren, two young but rising Mohawk leaders who in the aftermath of the smallpox epidemic and failed 1690 invasion knew that the first step in preserving the lives of their people was to reach out to their Laurentian kinfolk and reaffirm a stronger, mutually beneficial alliance. Because League policy relied on broad consensus, Lawrence and Onnonouagaren were attempting to put forward new initiatives for the benefit of their people, who continued to be trapped between the English and French in King William's War while being decimated from battle and disease.[13]

Prior to leaving Kahnawake, Lawrence also informed his Indigenous hosts of an eight hundred–man League Iroquois army preparing to raid Canada. He told them if they wanted to preserve Iroquois' lives, they should stay out of the fight to avoid killing their own kin. As a sign of good faith, he and Onnonouagaren left behind two of their fellow League warriors at Kahnawake, pending an answer to the proposed peace initiative from Albany.[14]

Unfortunately, the French had no intention of allowing their Laurentian Iroquois allies, or the Great Lakes tribes of the Pays d'en haut, to do anything but prosecute the war to the fullest to promote the Sun King's imperial interests in the New World. Though Frontenac doubted that the League would follow through with the peace proposal of Lawrence and his Mohawk faction, he feared that if it did gain traction with the sachems, it would lead to a large-scale Laurentian exodus from New France to the Mohawk River Valley, removing an important protective buffer.[15] Therefore, soon after learning of the peace overture, he issued a bounty of thirty-three livres (*dix écus*, $825 today) to the French-allied tribes for Iroquois "enemy" scalps.[16] His goal with the sanguinary financial incentive was not only to bolster Laurentian Iroquois support for New France but to undermine the recent council with the "two influential Iroquois of the Mohawk tribe."[17]

With their diplomatic mission complete, Lawrence and his Mohawk party returned to Albany for a conference with the League headmen, New York's new royal governor, and Albany's Indian Affairs commission. Fresh off sending Leisler and Milborne to the gallows, the hard-drinking "country" Englishman and new "Brother Corlaer" Henry Sloughter arrived in Albany on May 26 to conduct the annual meeting with the Five Nations. Like his predecessors, Sloughter had been coached by Mayor Peter Schuyler, Hilletie van Olinda, and other Albany officials on the importance of respecting Iroquois diplomatic protocols, which revolved around the principles of reciprocal gift-giving, a respect for rhetoric, and the exchange of wampum belts.[18] Like his predecessor, the governor hoped to reaffirm the Covenant Chain and put an end to French imperial claims in North America once and for all.[19]

Held at Albany City Hall over the course of eleven days, the conference included Lawrence and more than thirty League Iroquois headmen and war chieftains; most of Sloughter's New York council, including Frederick Philipse and Stephanus van Cortlandt; and an Albany contingent that included Schuyler as lead Indian affairs commissioner, Hilletie as official interpreter, Robert Livingston as recorder, and Father Dellius as spiritual advisor.[20]

With Hilletie translating, Lawrence and Onnonouagaren delivered a wampum-belt peace offering from the Kahnawakes and briefed Sloughter and the League representatives on their recent diplomatic council outside Montreal. As a sign of Kahnawakes' good faith, they said, the Laurentians had relinquished two prisoners captured at Schenectady the year before. One of these men was Joseph Marks, a land proprietor from Brookfield, Massachusetts, who had enlisted in Lieutenant Enos Talmadge's military detachment sent to aid Schenectady. After handing over the much-relieved Marks to Schuyler and his officials, the Mohawk emissaries offered to build upon their preliminary negotiations with the Kahnawakes into a comprehensive Iroquois-brokered peace between the English and French and to attempt to bring more of the Schenectady prisoners safely home to their families.[21]

During the multiday conference that followed, the Anglophile sachem Sanonguirese, the Mohawk spokesman for the council meeting, emphasized what an outstanding job the two young, idealistic Iroquois diplomats had done in laying the groundwater for peaceful negotiations by sparing the lives of the Canadian Iroquois hunting party. "The Governor of Canada," stated Sanonguirese, "was glad to see them there in his country. It was even as if the sun shined upon him when he saw his Children there and gave them one belt of wampum for all the Five Nations and thanked Lawrence the Maquase and his company for sparing of his Children the praying Indians."[22]

Unfortunately for Lawrence and Onnonouagaren, Sloughter was no more interested in extending olive branches to the Native opposition than Frontenac. The new royal governor not only reiterated the English demand that the League Iroquois not make any separate treaty with the French "without particular orders" from himself, he rejected the Mohawk peace proposal out of hand.[23] The "massacre" at Schenectady, he argued, had revealed that the Laurentian Iroquois were "as much enemies to the brethren as the French" for they had "burnt our houses and destroyed our people." He, therefore, proposed prosecuting "the war with all speed and violence, till they be rooted out of the world." To the shock and dismay of Lawrence and the other Mohawk leaders, he then demanded to know "what number of men" could be spared "to join with a party of Christians" he intended "to dispatch within 14 days."[24]

Sloughter and his governor's council weren't the only ones out for blood. The leaders of the other Four Nations of Haudenosaunee—the Oneidas, Onondagas, Cayugas, and Senecas—also rejected the proposed Mohawk peace initiative since they anticipated new raids from Canada. This agreed with Schuyler's intelligence that the French had received fresh reinforcements and supplies in preparation for an invasion of Onondaga country and perhaps even an attack on Albany.[25] The Oneida headman Ohede was emphatic in rejecting the peace offering, on the grounds that Frontenac and the Laurentians doing the French governor's bidding could never be trusted. He vowed that he and his people would "prosecute the war as long as we live." To underscore his message, he tossed the wampum belt angrily upon the ground of the courthouse yard of the Albany City Hall.[26]

In the end, Lawrence and the Mohawks submitted to the demands of Sloughter and their Iroquois brothers by agreeing to support a second English invasion of Montreal, which the governor claimed would be fully supported by William III's powerful navy. To demonstrate the commitment of their English Father across the Great Water, he then distributed £100 ($35,000 today) in Crown "presents" to his Iroquois allies that included

"1,000 guilders white-strung wampum, 400 pounds powder, 600 pounds lead, 679 pounds tobacco, 120 shirts, 30 runlets rum, 15 guns, 10 dozen stockings." To further gain the trust of the Iroquois and rekindle their spirits, Sloughter informed the leaders that the military expedition would be led by none other than their trusty friend Brother Quider. Furthermore, no more than two hundred warriors would be required to join Schuyler's invasion force of "Christians," since the governor expected militia and additional aid from New England, Virginia, and Maryland.[27]

Although the Iroquois representatives agreed to lend their support to the invasion, the headmen refused to commit to a specific number of warriors or a definitive timetable.[28] Furthermore, in return for their support, they requested that Sloughter ensure cheaper prices for ammunition and supplies in Albany, send skilled gunsmiths to Onondaga, and overlook the killing of the cattle and hogs outside Schenectady and Albany the previous summer by the returning League war parties. Lawrence and his warriors had been tired, hungry, and angry after their grueling journey to Canada, explained the sachems, and from discovering that many of their tribal headmen had died from the "running face sickness" brought on by Winthrop's troops. Because the warriors had been performing a great service on behalf of their English king in striking a blow against New France, the Five Nations should not be on the hook for reparations.[29]

By the end of the conference, it was agreed that a combined Anglo-Indian force of 130 New York provincials and 300 Mohawks and Mahicans, under the command of Schuyler and the war captains Lawrence and Onnonouagaren, would paddle to Lake Champlain and the Chambly River and rendezvous with a separate body of 500 warriors from the western League Nations for the attack on the Montreal region.[30] The new collaborative summer 1691 Anglo-Iroquois expedition would preempt the rumored French invasion of Iroquoia and be a repeat of the 1690 pincer movement, but would have the benefit of the lessons learned from the prior offensive.[31]

During the council, the Mohawk headman Sanonguirese and Onondaga sachem Sadekanaktie made a special point of honoring Hilletie van Olinda for her significant contributions to Anglo-Iroquois negotiations. Because of her "good service for the public" and being the "mouth and ears" of the

Five Nations, they urged the governor to "take her as the daughter, and provide for her that she may not want since she is so serviceable both to us and to you." To show their respect for the Mohawk-Dutch woman abused and exiled by her own mother, Ots-Toch, and other Mohawk Wolf Clan family members for her early interest in Christianity, the chiefs presented her with four valuable beaver pelts in Sloughter's presence.[32]

As assistant to Father Dellius and provincial interpreter for New York, Hilletie received a salary of £20 ($7,000 today) per year, but the kind words and presents publicly bestowed upon her by the Iroquois sachems meant far more to her. In an age when women were seldom acknowledged for their accomplishments, the praise and presents from the esteemed Iroquois headmen represented a tremendous gift and sign of veneration for her diplomatic skills. Aware of the difficulties she had faced growing up in Tionnontoguen and during her early transitional years in Schenectady when she was ridiculed by vulgar Dutchmen, the leaders were also compensating her for the ill treatment she had long endured in both worlds for being a mixed-blooded Native and Dutch-European. However, despite having earned the respect of the sachems and many Albanians, the biracial Hilletie continued to be ostracized by some members of the Mohawk community and a smattering of Dutch settlers in Albany and Schenectady, who were envious of her "literacy, income, status, and privilege."[33]

Throughout her government employment as an interpreter from 1690–1707, she remained close to her fellow Mohawk Sanonguirese, the Onondaga leader Sadekanaktie, and other League Iroquois peace chiefs, who greatly valued her as a cross-cultural liaison and translator. With a strong personality and astute mind, she also retained a good relationship with Peter Schuyler and Father Dellius; Lawrence and Maria; Hendrick, his wife Catherine, and many other baptized Christian Mohawks; and the Dutch settlers who belonged to Albany's and Schenectady's Dutch Reformed Churches. Like the respected Iroquois sachems and the female leaders of the matrilineal Mohawk Turtle, Wolf, and Bear Clan family groups, the powerful Schuyler, Philipse, Livingston, and van Cortlandt families of Albany and New York City all recognized her importance to mutually beneficial negotiations with the Iroquois and combating the French during King William's War.[34]

During the conference, the Mohawks also requested that Sloughter send Protestant ministers to Tionnontoguen and the other two "castles" in the Mohawk River Valley to teach their people English and Christian ways. Many of the Iroquois, they reported, had been "drawn out" of their country "to the French by their Priests," and they wanted their English allies to "instruct" them in the "true" Protestant Christian religion "as the French send Priests to instruct their Indians."[35]

Lawrence, his wife Maria, and the other Christian Mohawks embraced Protestantism not to supplant their traditional culture but to find a middle ground between European and Iroquois religious custom, as a form of self-preservation in an increasingly dangerous, European-dominated world. They looked upon Christianity mostly as a means of protecting themselves and their people; bridging the gap between Europeans and Native Americans; and bringing a lasting peace between their people and their Anglo-Dutch neighbors, whose numbers were visibly growing.[36] As historian William Hart writes:

> During the tumultuous times of King William's War, many of the Mohawks who aligned themselves with Europeans changed some aspects of their cultural habits: Christian rituals supplemented or replaced Haudenosaunee sacred practices [and] fabric garb augmented or replaced animal hides and furs. . . . Invoking the Haudenosaunee principle of reciprocity, the engine that powered all interpersonal and international relations, they insinuated themselves into the other's faith community and sought to turn outsiders into insiders.[37]

On June 5, the meeting ended on a positive note with a firm commitment to the joint Anglo-Iroquois invasion of New France. Sloughter's liberal disbursement of muskets, lead, and powder played no small role in winning over Native "affections." Though Lawrence and his Mohawk diplomatic party had attempted to broker peace between the League and Laurentian Iroquois, they had been vetoed by Sloughter and the Oneidas, Onondagas, Cayugas, and Senecas. Meanwhile, as Robert Livingston would inform Sloughter shortly after the council meeting, the French in Canada still expected "an answer of Lawrence" regarding "his treaty with them in the Spring, for which they are very impatient and seem hugely concerned." However, with the minds of the governor and other Four Nations made up, there was now no stopping the war drums that would reverberate once again along the northern frontier and gates of Montreal.[38]

Knowing how critical Lawrence was for the planned invasion, the new Brother Corlaer went out of his way following the conference to show his support for the Mohawk war captain and his wife Maria. On July 5, 1691, a month after the conference, Sloughter sponsored Lawrence in absentia and his wife Maria in a ceremony at the First Dutch Church in Albany by becoming the godfather of their newborn baptized son, Henry, who was named after the royal governor. Because Lawrence was up north on his way to fight the French by this time, it is likely that he was notified by Sloughter of the planned sponsorship before he set out on the expedition and that the governor's serving as godfather to Lawrence and Maria's soon-to-be born child was recommended by Schuyler, Dellius, and Hilletie. For His Majesty King William III's handpicked royal governor of New York—a typical Crown representative of rigidly hierarchal England—to serve as godfather of the child of an Iroquois "savage" and his Indigenous wife shows the high esteem Sloughter, Schuyler, and the New York authorities held for the Mohawk war captain.[39]

But even with Lawrence on board, Schuyler knew he still had his work cut out for him if he wanted the invasion of French Canada to be a success this time around.

Two and a half weeks later, on June 22, 1691, with a furious northerly wind whipping the canvas tent flaps, Major Peter Schuyler welcomed Lawrence and his allied Native war party to his camp along the northern shore of Lake Champlain. Lawrence and his fellow war captains presented Brother Quider with "a bundle of ninety-two sticks," representing the total number of Mohawk warriors who had agreed to join the expedition from their three "castles" on the Mohawk River. With the fresh recruits added to his current forces, Schuyler now had 120 New Yorkers, 80 League Mohawks, and 66 Mahicans for a total of 266 men for the assault on New France.[40]

Though he had hoped for a thousand "Christians" and Native auxiliaries total, he was relieved to have finally assembled a formidable army for the invasion. While building his fleet of canoes and paddling his way northward over a two-week period, he had been waiting anxiously for the bulk of his Native force to arrive. Up until today, he had only managed to recruit 15 Mohawk warriors and around 60 Mahicans. The reason for the lower-than-expected turnout, he discovered, was because the venerated Mohawk sachem Tahiadoris had recently passed away. The peace chief's entire village was mourning his death and the residents refused to release any warriors for the expedition until their ceremonies were completed.[41]

With Lawrence and his large force of Mohawks having finally arrived, Schuyler held a war conference. Lawrence, Onnonouagaren, Garistatsi, and three other veteran fighters were democratically voted by their fellow Mohawk tribesmen as the official League Iroquois war leaders for the invasion of New France. The Anglophile Mahican Etowaucum, who had been baptized as Nicholas by Father Dellius and Hilletie van Olinda, and three other Mahicans were also elected as war captains by their fellow warriors to represent the "River Indians."[42]

Though Lawrence and Onnonouagaren had worked hard to bring about peace for their fellow Mohawks during the previous spring's negotiations at Kahnawake, they now felt no qualms about waging war after having been outvoted at Albany by their Anglo-Dutch allies and the other Four Nations. But while the two young war captains were willing to lead their warriors in battle, they did so only after having already sent scouts to warn their Laurentian Iroquois kin of their impending attack and to stay out of the fighting unless they wanted to die for the treacherous Yonondio. Furthermore, Lawrence and his warriors would soon go to great lengths to limit Iroquois battlefield casualties up north. After all, they were driving for Montreal to kill Frenchmen, not their own Native people.[43]

As Schuyler prepared to strike north and wage war as commander of the expedition, he had little actual control over his Mohawk and Mahican allies, who fought on their own terms. When it came to his Indian auxiliaries, his role was more as a motivational leader and intercultural negotiator than field general. He, his officers, and the French commanders against whom he battled "enjoyed no coercive authority over the warriors whom they accompanied; at the most, they could hope to earn the respect and deference given to war chiefs through demonstrations of bravery, ability, and generosity." Thus, Schuyler and other European military officers of the North American frontier could only shape the course of a campaign by ensuring that colonial and Native goals overlapped and through their own "inspiration, persuasion, and negotiation."[44]

On June 23, Schuyler dispatched a small scouting party to advance down the Chambly River and then followed with over 250 men in his fleet of freshly built canoes. The Anglo-Native war party followed the same route his youngest brother Johannes had taken during the previous summer's campaign. Six days later, as the reunited flotilla approached within ten miles of Fort Chambly, located eighteen miles southeast of Montreal, Schuyler's advanced scouting party was fired upon by a French patrol consisting of Canadian militia and Francophile Algonquin warriors. Three of the four Mohawks were badly wounded in their canoes and forced to make a hasty retreat back upriver to Schuyler's advancing war party.[45] "When we came up to them," reported the major in his expedition journal, "we carried them on shore, and dressed them and encamped over them that night within . . . 26 miles from La Prairie."[46]

Having been discovered, Schuyler held a war council that night with Lawrence, the other Mohawk and Mahican leaders, and his New York officers. Though they had earlier in the day made the decision to attack once again at La Prairie de la Madeleine, on the south bank of the St. Lawrence River southwest of Montreal, they decided to protect their canoes, provisions, and the wounded with a stronger rear guard. This would keep their escape route up the Chambly River open for an orderly tactical withdrawal following the battle.[47]

The following morning, while building a wood-and-brush fortification to protect the rearguard company, they heard alarm-cannons firing from Fort Chambly to the north and Fort La Prairie to the west. With heavy rain in the afternoon that turned torrential that night, they reinforced the bastion and set out after daybreak for La Prairie. Schuyler left behind a force of twenty men, including the expedition's surgeons, to guard the makeshift stockade containing the canoes, food provisions, and wounded Indian scouts.[48]

Having sent out several scouting parties in the past week, Captain Louis-Hector de Callière, the French governor of Montreal who had saved the day at Quebec the year before with his timely reinforcements, was aware of the approaching war party. But he didn't know its precise location. He had at his disposal a total force of more than a thousand French soldiers, Canadian militia, and Native auxiliaries, including Algonquins, Wendats, Odawas, and Kahnawake Iroquois. After posting approximately 760 French troops and Indians at his encampment at La Prairie, he sent his experienced subordinate, Philippe Clément Du Vuault de Valrennes, and a reconnaissance party of over three hundred men to guard the road leading to Chambly in case the enemy should attempt to capture its fort or attack the nearby settlements. For three nerve-wracking days, while suffering through a debilitating fever brought on by gout, the chevalier Callière awaited word of the whereabouts of the mysteriously vanished Anglo-Iroquois army he knew was advancing upon New France.[49]

Meanwhile, Schuyler, after leaving his small force behind at the riverbank, made his way overland toward La Prairie. After marching through eleven miles of dense forest, he came across a trail "where a considerable party of men had lately passed." This was the well-traveled foot trail connecting Fort La Prairie to Fort Chambly. In his first stroke of good fortune, Schuyler had missed—by mere hours—Valrennes and his large reconnaissance party on their way to Fort Chambly. After holding a conference with Lawrence and his other war captains, he detached seven men to return to the party left behind at the river "to acquaint them of our approach to the French, and to be on their guard." Resuming the march, he and his reduced force of 239 men proceeded several more miles before making camp on the evening of July 31 next to a marsh two miles from Fort La Prairie.[50]

The attack was set for dawn.

10

THE BATTLES OF LA PRAIRIE

Two hours before sunup on August 1, 1691, Major Peter Schuyler and his troops made their Protestant Christian prayers while Lawrence and his fellow Mohawks paid tribute to their Great Spirit, Hawenneyu, and asked for protection in the coming fight. The Mohawks and Mahicans then fastened white ribbons, strips of linen, and tree bark to their hair so they could be distinguished from the enemy warriors in the heat of battle. After checking their weapons and making sure their powder was dry, the Anglo-Indian war party set off to the west at the quick step toward La Prairie. Less than one mile from the fort, still immersed in inky predawn blackness, the men removed their knapsacks so they could move forward swiftly and unimpeded for the assault on the fort and adjacent encampment.[1]

Perched on the overbank of the St. Lawrence, Fort La Prairie served as Captain Louis-Hector de Callière's headquarters. The French commander's Canadian militia and Algonquin, Wendat, and Odawa warriors were bivouacked on the east side of the fort, on the gently sloping floodplain near the river's edge between the fort and a small stream with a nearby windmill that served as a lookout post. His French regulars from the vaunted Troupes de la Marine (Free Companies of the Marine), trained by seasoned officers, were encamped farther away on a small hill on the grassy plain, on the west side of the stockade. After being in a heightened state of alert and on the lookout for Schuyler's column for several days without any sighting of the enemy, the French soldiers and militia had warning fatigue and their guard was down.[2]

The night of July 31–August 1 was also unusually dark and rainy, which gave Schuyler an added advantage. With still no word on the whereabouts of the enemy, many of the French regulars and Canadian militia had taken shelter inside the fort, and the officers had failed to post sufficient sentinels. Moreover, the men were well supplied with brandy, which during the cold and wet night they had indulged in "freely." Further undermining their combat readiness, their experienced commander Callière remained bedridden with fever inside the fort and was in no condition to rally his men if attacked.[3]

On silent boots and moccasins, Schuyler and his assault force moved stealthily through the cornfields east of the fort, paralleling the burbling St. Lawrence, before angling into the streambed a quarter of a mile from the fort. An hour before daybreak, as they pushed down the incised alluvial channel, a French sentry posted at the windmill spotted vague figures coming toward him.[4] "Qui vive?" he demanded.[5] When he received no answer, he quickly signaled the fort by igniting a preprepared warning fire, squeezed off a round with his loaded musket that took the life of a Mohawk warrior, and shouted "To arms!" as he attempted to reload his musket.[6]

But before he could crack off a second round, he was killed by one of the New York militiamen and his body was left hanging "half in and half out of the window."[7] Though he had put up a valiant effort to alert his comrades, his warning proved too late to make a difference as Lawrence and his Mohawks in the vanguard swarmed into the riverside encampment of the Canadian militia and Indigenous allies, with Schuyler's New Yorkers and Etowaucum and his Mahicans right on their heels. Already on top of the enemy when the warning signal was given, Lawrence and his lead element of warriors rushed in with muskets, tomahawks, and war clubs, screaming at the top of their lungs and catching the enemy completely by surprise.[8]

As Schuyler's muscular force swarmed in a body upon Callière's French Canadians and Indian allies, they quickly dispatched more than a dozen of the enemy with muskets and hand-to-hand weaponry. With most of the enemy warriors sleeping under their canoes to shelter themselves from the drizzling rain, six of the unfortunates mowed down early in the bout included members of an Odawa trade convoy encamped on the nearby strand. Running for their lives, the surviving Canadian militiamen, Algonquins, Wendats, and Odawas made a mad dash for the French regulars and the safety of the fort.[9]

By this time, the French infantrymen on the west side of Fort La Prairie, roused by the battle cries and thunderous musket fire, sprang to arms and quick-marched toward the overrun encampment. With Callière still gravely ill and confined to his bed inside the fort, the troops were led by Captain Jean Louis Jadon de Saint-Cirque, an old war horse who had commanded a battalion in Sicily and fought all along the Canadian frontier. Although Saint-Cirque and his professional foot soldiers marched to the rescue in good military order, in the still-faint predawn light they were unable to make out whether the hazy silhouettes before them were the English enemy or their own men. Not wanting to incur collateral damage, they hesitated for several minutes by forming up instead of charging forward to drive off the attackers.[10]

Their indecisiveness would prove costly as Schuyler quickly commanded his non-regular backwoods New Yorkers, Mohawks, and Mahicans to form an orderly firing line. They swiftly unleashed a furious volley that made the vaunted Free Companies of the Marine wish they had undergone more extensive drilling by their officers, dropping fifty Frenchmen to the ground like stringless marionettes. Among them was Saint-Cirque, who was mortally wounded by a piping-hot lead musket ball that struck his thigh and severed an artery. Along with him, four of his senior officers were instantly killed or mortally wounded, including Captains Desquérat and d'Hosta, also veterans of European campaigns. Suffering heavy losses and now dangerously short of experienced officers, the French fell back in disorder. But unbeknownst to Schuyler, the enemy outnumbered him more than two to one and the reeling survivors were able to quickly recover from the blistering fusillade and countercharge en masse.[11]

Now it was Schuyler and Lawrence who were forced to take flight and reform in the more favorable terrain of the streambed to make a stand. In his journal account of the battle, Schuyler captures the frantic back-and-forth attacks and counterattacks as the first streaks of sunlight pierced the overhanging cloud cover:

> [There were] 420 men lying outside the Fort ready to receive us, [and] they charged us so hard to force a retreat of 150 yards, where there happened a ditch [the streambed], which our men possessed themselves of. The French advancing so far in their full body were well received, and lost many of their men. We drove them back but they rallied and advanced a second time toward the ditch and fired upon us, but did us no damage. Instantly our people rose up and discharged upon their whole body, and killed a great many; nevertheless, they rallied the third time, but to avoid the ditch, they drove their men toward the East and thought to divide our people; then we left the ditch, fell into their rear, and then in a full body engaged them in the plain ground and fought them fairly, until we drove them into their Fort in great disorder and took three French prisoners.[12]

By the time the desperate seesaw battle along the banks of the St. Lawrence River wound down, it was full daylight and the two opposing sides could see each other clearly. After Schuyler's force had abandoned the streambed, shifted position farther uphill and away from the river, and taken protective cover along the edge of the woods, Lawrence and the victorious Mohawk warriors and the Mahicans waved their smoothbore trade muskets triumphantly in the air and verbally taunted the enemy. "Uttering frightful howls," they shouted to the French that "they were not men, but dogs."[13] Having won the day and inflicted significant casualties, Schuyler had his men recover their knapsacks and withdrew his army in orderly fashion, while hacking down and burning the corn and hay in the fields. However, the corn was still green and soaked with rain and proved difficult to put to the torch.[14]

As his men struggled to fire the fields, Schuyler took the opportunity to interrogate the three captured French prisoners. Under the threat of torture, they swiftly provided invaluable intelligence on the disposition of Callière's army. The French forces consisted of 460 men total at La Prairie, the prisoners said, 40 in the fort with "the governor" and 420 outside the stockade.

When questioned about the large force that had marched to Fort Chambly, the Frenchmen divulged that the trail had been made by some 300 French soldiers and 40 Francophile Native allies. This was the reconnaissance party Callière had dispatched three days earlier under the command of Captain Philippe Clément Du Vuault de Valrennes.[15]

For the first time, Schuyler realized just how badly he was outnumbered. Though he was pleased to have inflicted heavy enemy losses at little cost to his command, he had not anticipated encountering more than three times his own strength in his Canadian foray. Moreover, although he had suffered only a handful of casualties, he had more than a dozen wounded and had been forced to leave behind twenty-seven good fighting men at the Chambly River to guard the canoes and provisions. Thus, he quickly "resolved" to make "all haste" for the river and ordered his men to double-time it lest they be trapped in a pincer movement by two converging armies.[16]

However, unbeknownst to Schuyler and his trusted Native American war captains Lawrence, Onnonouagaren, Garistatsi, and Etowaucum, a trap was already being set for them and their retreating invasion force.

Like his bedridden commander Callière, Captain Valrennes had lost track of Schuyler's column during the past three days. But by eight o'clock on the morning of August 1, he and his force of three hundred French soldiers and forty allied Wendat, Algonquin, and non-League Iroquois warriors marched quickly to the sound of the guns to cut off the withdrawing enemy. His written orders called for him to "defend" Fort Chambly in case of enemy attack, but if the English "marched against La Prairie," he was "to follow and attack them in the rear whilst those remaining in the Camp would oppose them in front."[17]

The forty-four-year-old Valrennes was a tough, seasoned field officer. After committing manslaughter against a man under suspicious circumstances at the tender age of fourteen, he had managed to escape punishment, join the French army, and serve thirteen years as an officer in Normandy before crossing the Atlantic and taking his post along the Canadian frontier in 1685. Now Johnny-on-the-spot in yet another bloody backwoods engagement, he ordered his men into defensive formation on the rutted trail eight miles from La Prairie, roughly midway between the two forts.[18]

Around nine o'clock, Lawrence and his advance Mohawk scouts came upon the French and Indian party. Valrennes had already formed up in a half-moon-shaped defensive position on a thickly forested ridge to prevent the English withdrawal. His main force was deployed in a three-deep firing line behind two huge fallen tree trunks along the crest of the hill. Flanking him on either side were Canadian militia and his Indigenous allies, who together with a smattering of French regulars occupied the dense woodlands blocking the trailhead.[19]

Standing near Valrennes were his two top Native war leaders: the Cayuga Iroquois headman Ourehouare, the favorite of Frontenac who had served as a galley slave for two years aboard a French warship fighting the Barbary pirates; and Paul, one of the few Kahnawake Iroquois fighting alongside the French. Following Lawrence and Onnonouagaren's peace overture the previous spring, the Kahnawakes had held back the majority of their warriors from joining Frontenac's forces outside Montreal to protect members of their own kindred Iroquois Nation.[20]

Crouching behind their timber "retrenchment" and the thick stand of trees, the French foot soldiers and their Wendat, Algonquin, and Laurentian Iroquois allies not only blocked Schuyler's path to the river but possessed both the better defensive position and superior numbers. For Schuyler and Lawrence, the only consolation was the two sides were more evenly matched than at Fort La Prairie.[21]

At the sight of the advance guard, Valrennes's westernmost scouts opened up with their muskets on Lawrence and his warriors, who returned a brisk fire and retreated without serious loss to Schuyler coming up from behind. When the major reached the site of what is known today as the Second Battle of La Prairie, he had his men once again discard their knapsacks and performed a quick reconnaissance. He concluded that he had no choice but to push straight through the French line if he wanted to reach his canoes, for the enemy's objective was clearly to delay his retreat and drive him back toward the superior force at Fort La Prairie, thereby trapping him between the two armies.[22]

Assembling his New York officers and Lawrence, Onnonouagaren, Garistatsi, and Etowaucum, he bluntly told them that "there was no other choice, fight or die they must, the enemy being between us and our canoes."[23] With his hearty New Yorkers giving a rousing battle cry and his Indian allies thunderous war whoops, they charged "briskly" toward Valrennes and the French "half-moon," unleashing their muskets as they dashed up the gentle hill and through the thick underbrush and trees.[24]

But the battle-tested Valrennes remained cool under fire and ordered his sharpshooters to hold their musket volley until the enemy approached within pistol range, or twenty-five yards. Though several French foot soldiers were wounded due to the suppression of their fire until the last second, Schuyler and his men were cut to pieces by the first close-range fusillade. Thirty men fell in the initial salvo, and the survivors were sent reeling backward through the rain-soaked underbrush.[25]

Despite the heavy losses, they quickly regrouped for a second frontal assault. However, the Mahicans had already seen enough carnage for one morning. While Etowaucum and two-thirds of his fellow warriors would keep fighting, the rest of the Mahicans withdrew hastily from the field after the charge, leaving Schuyler and his colonials and Lawrence and his League Mohawks to do the bulk of the fighting for the remainder of the battle. Yelling at the top of their lungs, the Albanians, Mohawks, and Etowaucum's remaining Mahicans pressed forward once again through the pall of powder smoke, receiving a second measured "volley of shot" at close quarters.[26] Onnonouagaren, Lawrence's fellow Mohawk war captain, friend, and peace diplomat, was cut down during this desperate attempt to break the French line.[27] According to Schuyler, most of the casualties of the two Battles of La Prairie were sustained during the first two frontal attacks against Valrennes's strong position, with the felled trees and dense woods protecting the French officer and his men.[28]

With the second charge, the French line bent but did not break. However, Schuyler's Anglo-Dutch New Yorkers and Lawrence, Garistatsi, and their stalwart Mohawks regrouped and swept in again, with support provided by the Mahicans—and this time they were able to infiltrate the enemy line and "dislodge the French from their ambuscade."[29] The assault was so well-coordinated that dozens of the French Canadians, most of them young lads "who had never smelled powder before," turned tail and ran like jackrabbits, abandoning their strong defensive position despite having inflicted devastating casualties and possessing superior numbers.[30] However, their commander, Jean-Vincent Le Ber Du Chesne, quickly rallied them and they returned to the fray. But the line was broken and, despite the inspiring leadership of Valrennes and Du Chesne, as well as their Native war captains Ourehouare and Paul, the seemingly impregnable French position was overrun. Now some of the Algonquins on the French side abandoned the field along with the terror-stricken Canadians.[31]

The battle now turned into a close-quarters frontier melee. For Schuyler, Lawrence, Garistatsi, and Etowaucum on the English side, and Valrennes, Ourehouare, and Paul on the French, there was fierce hand-to-hand fighting in every direction as a cacophony of battle cries reverberated through the dense woodlands. Men screamed, charged, wheeled, fell, fought breast to breast, and shot their pistols and muskets at such close range that they scorched the shirts of their enemies by the flash of their guns. Smoothbores, battle axes, and heavy war clubs swooshed through the air and made pulp of human heads. Musket balls flew past like swarms of locusts. The combatants on both sides materialized from the smoke like phantoms one instant only to disappear the next. Wounded men crumpled over logs and tumbled into brush, while those with mortal wounds cried for their mothers and crawled away to die. Ground would open for a moment and then close like a beating heart. It was a bloody, smoky, tangled mess.[32]

The hand-to-hand fighting would involve multiple charges and counter-charges and would last for over an hour. Frontenac himself—no shrinking violet when it came to gory combat—would later declare the Second Battle of La Prairie "the most obstinate battle that has ever been fought in Canada since the foundation of the colony."[33] Indeed, it proved to be not only one of the fiercest military engagements fought between England and France and their respective Native American allies in the 17th century, but one of the bloodiest engagements of the four French and Indian Wars fought on North American soil between 1689 and 1762.[34]

It was precisely because the musketry was so deafening, the violence so visceral, and the casualties on both sides so extreme that some of the Native American warriors, as well as the green French-Canadian soldiers, abandoned the field in the heat of battle. English and French observers at the time, and even 19th-century historians like Francis Parkman, considered the French-allied Algonquins and the English-led Mahicans who abandoned the field to be guilty of cowardice. However, today we recognize that, unlike the young French Canadians who ran away out of pure "flight response," the Indians were simply observing the northeastern Native American custom of refusing to take unacceptable battlefield casualties.[35] As historian Daniel Richter soberingly reminds us:

> In contrast to European beliefs that to perish in combat was acceptable and even honorable, Iroquois beliefs made death in battle a frightful prospect. . . . Slain warriors [were] said to be excluded from the villages of the dead, doomed to spend a roving eternity seeking vengeance. As a result, their bodies were not interred in village cemeteries, lest their angry souls disturb the repose of others. Both in burial and in the afterlife, a warrior who fell in combat faced separation from his family and friends. . . . Efforts to minimize fatalities accordingly underlay several tactics that contemporary Euro-Americans considered cowardly: fondness for ambushes and surprise attacks; unwillingness to fight when outnumbered; and avoidance of frontal assaults on fortified places. Defensive tactics showed a similar emphasis on precluding loss of life.[36]

Taking into account the Native American wartime customs of the late 17th century, what is remarkable is that Lawrence and his Mohawks charged repeatedly in the high-mortality-rate European manner at both the First and Second Battles of La Prairie—and were reportedly the *most redoubtable* fighters of the day. "The Mohawks, upon no occasion, yielded an inch of ground, till the English first gave way," wrote Cadwallader Colden, who would in the early 18th century serve as a representative to the Iroquois as colonial governor of New York.[37] Along with Lawrence and his Mohawks, the French-allied war chiefs Ourehouare and Paul and their Canadian Iroquois and Wendat braves on the French side were recognized for their courage under enemy fire. Like Lawrence's comrade Onnonouagaren, killed during the initial English frontal assault, the Laurentian Iroquois Paul died from injuries sustained during the battle. He was heralded by Frontenac and the French officers in their post-battle reports for his bravery in "encouraging all by word and example" during the fight. However, in the aftermath of the battle, Onnonouagaren's and Paul's Indigenous loved ones saw their deaths in a far different light, as they deeply mourned their losses in the traditional Iroquois manner from their respective villages.[38]

In his journal, Schuyler captured the frantic hand-to-hand fighting and English breakthrough during the second battle that morning:

> We fought stoutly one whole hour. A French captain [Valrennes] hearing me encourage our men to fight for the honor of our King and the Protestant religion, said aloud, I am here ready to answer you, but our men being resolute, fell in upon them, broke thro' the middle of their body, until we got into their rear trampling upon their dead, then faced about upon them and fought them a pretty while close, until we made them give way, then drove them by strength of arms 400 paces before us, and to say the truth we were all glad to see them retreat.[39]

Having driven Valrennes and what remained of his three-hundred-man French and Indian army from the field, Schuyler and his men withdrew in good order and carried their gravely wounded to the rendezvous point on the Chambly River. Because they were still deep in enemy territory and outnumbered three to one by Callière's and Valrennes's combined forces, they had no choice but to leave more than thirty dead behind them, an English battle flag, and most of their knapsacks, which they had thrown off at the beginning of the second contest. Upon reaching the small English fortification along the banks of the Chambly, they found the rearguard company, their canoes, and their provisions secure. Here Schuyler waited five full hours for stragglers, which enabled an additional handful of men to reach the river before the war party disembarked for the return trip to Albany.[40]

French battlefield reports later claimed that Valrennes's forces were too exhausted to pursue the English and that the veteran infantry captain, who had demonstrated such "calm confidence" that "his orders put heart into everyone," had barely enough strength to tend to his own wounded.[41] No doubt he and his brave men were battered and fatigued, but certainly far less than Schuyler and his force, who had marched and paddled their canoes more than 230 total miles, fought two desperate battles against two separate armies that together outnumbered them more than three to one, and then marched, with all their wounded and without losing a single man, ten miles back to the river.[42] "Nothing saved them from destruction," writes Francis Parkman, "but the failure of the French at La Prairie to follow their retreat and thus enclose them between two fires."[43]

Overall, Schuyler and Lawrence's Canadian foray was a joint English-League Iroquois victory due to possession of the field and greater inflicted casualties at both the First and Second Battles of La Prairie, but it came at a steep price. Schuyler reported thirty-seven killed and thirty-one wounded out of a total force of 239 men, which excluded the small force left behind at the Chambly River that did not take part in the fighting. His original estimated dead consisted of twenty-one Englishmen, sixteen Mohawks, and six Mahicans, but six of the presumed dead were merely missing and eventually hobbled back to Albany. For the French forces, contemporary observer Sieur Benac reported forty-five killed, including two captains, six lieutenants, and five ensigns, and sixty wounded. The casualty rates for the English and French for the two battles combined were, thus, 28 percent and 13 percent, respectively.[44] But this disparity is expected given that Schuyler commanded the smaller force and was on the offensive deep in enemy territory. All the same, he lost more than a quarter of his troops to death or injury, and he narrowly avoided being completely wiped out by a far more formidable French army.[45]

After bagging five large elk to "refresh the whole company" on the way home, the major and his exhausted men staggered into Albany eight days later on August 9, having covered 450 miles by foot and canoe in the past three weeks.[46] As had happened following the invasion of Canada the year before, the finger-pointing began as soon as they set foot back in town.

On August 24, 1691, Schuyler arrived in New York City by sloop to present his report of his "expedition against Canada" to the governor and council and to collect the prodigious sum of money the penny-pinching Crown owed him for his wartime expenses.[47] Governor Sloughter was not there to receive him. He had died suddenly on July 23—less than three weeks after becoming the godfather of Lawrence and Maria's baptized son Henry. Some said he had died from a "drunken debauch," others from pneumonia, but the only certainty was that New York was once again without clear-cut leadership.[48]

With Sloughter's death, New York's new commander in chief, Major Richard Ingoldsby, had been voted by Frederick Philipse and the council to serve as New York's de facto executive officer "until Their Majesty's pleasure should be further known." With the existential threat of French invasion, military expediency was the ostensible reason for installing the lifelong English soldier as commander in chief of the province. But like Leisler, Ingoldsby was merely an "interim" leader without definitive Crown authority.[49]

At the military conference, Schuyler presented a detailed action report on the Canadian campaign, making sure to give Lawrence and his Mohawks ample praise for their courage under heavy fire. While Ingoldsby, Philipse, and the others applauded the major and his men for their fortitude, they were still unsatisfied with the outcome. In their eyes, the invasion was only slightly more successful than the previous year's disastrous joint land-sea operation against La Prairie and Quebec. Ingoldsby and his councilors were also vexed by the continuing problem of League warriors supplying advance intelligence to their Laurentian Iroquois kin of English military columns driving northward into the St. Lawrence River Valley. Once again, Iroquois field communications and battlefield actions had ensured that the English and French imperial powers, not the Iroquois, sustained most of the casualties in the two battles at La Prairie.[50]

At the same time, there was a silver lining to the Iroquois policy of protecting their fellow kinsmen. Following the battles at La Prairie, the Laurentians at Kahnawake had withheld the bulk of their warriors from either fighting or engaging in pursuit, thereby greatly reducing the killing of members of their "own nation." Soon after the end of the second battle, with Callière and Valrennes unwilling (but not unable) to combine their forces and pursue the enemy, 120 Laurentian warriors mounted a sufficiently slow pursuit of the retreating Mohawk and Mahican force to allow Schuyler and his men to return "unmolested" to Albany eight days later.[51]

Ultimately, there was little Ingoldsby or Frontenac could do about the Iroquois practice of fighting alongside New York and New France while limiting Iroquois losses. But what irked New York's government officials most was that the promised five-hundred-man League Iroquois army had never showed up to augment Schuyler's Albany-based offensive, since most of the young warriors had gone on hunting expeditions to the Great Lakes country.[52] Frontenac was even more perturbed with his Indigenous allies, so much so that he attempted in September 1691 to relocate the entire community of Kahnawake within Montreal's palisade. However, the Canadian Iroquois resisted his power play.[53] What Frontenac found particularly frustrating was that French settlers and soldiers had to remain in and around Montreal and Quebec for their own safety, while the Kahnawake and other Laurentian Iroquois moved about the Canadian frontier and Iroquoia unimpeded—and even protected—by their fellow kinsmen allied with the English.[54]

If Schuyler and his fellow New York officials had known just how much damage they had inflicted upon the enemy's psyche in the second invasion of French Canada in two years, they would have been far more thrilled with the outcome of the expedition. Prior to the attack, Frontenac had wanted to invade Albany with a large army, but after Schuyler and Lawrence's foray, he was forced to shelve his plans for a military offensive.[55] In fact, the situation for the French in Canada had become desperate, though Frontenac could not bring himself to admit to the king or his superiors in Paris "the grievous losses the colony had suffered."[56]

Since the beginning of King William's War, the French had lost, according to their own reports, over two thousand total people, of whom more than five hundred were soldiers. Provisions were so low that Frontenac could no longer support his own troops in garrison and they had to be quartered with local farmers, who had scarcely enough for their own families. The ships arriving to Quebec from France were too infrequent to provide sufficient supplies or troops, forcing him to remain on the defensive throughout 1691 and 1692.[57]

Just as onerous for the French, the performance of Schuyler and his provincials had made a favorable impression on Lawrence and the Five Nations. With two successful attacks on La Prairie led by the Schuyler brothers, the English had struck terror into the French, and the Iroquois were now convinced that their allies could defeat their mutual enemies and were more willing to risk their own lives to achieve that victory. They may not have trusted the Crown officials in New York City, or the Indian-killing Puritans of New England waging "holy war" against the "heathens," but they believed in their Brother Quider, his brother Johannes, and the rugged Anglo-Dutch frontiersmen with whom they had fought alongside in battle twice at La Prairie.[58]

"Amid warfare and political rebellion," writes Daniel Richter, "Quider and his fellow magistrates . . . proved loyal allies." Schuyler and his youngest brother did so by commanding from the front in the 1690 and 1691 attacks on La Prairie, where they led by example and demonstrated that they would lay down their lives alongside their intrepid Iroquois compatriots in the name of freedom from French rule.[59]

11
BORDERLAND KILLING FIELDS

Three months later, on December 6, 1691, Major Peter Schuyler was stunned to learn of the killing of the Mohawk war captain Garistatsi and a party of League Iroquois in a bloody battle against Frontenac's Canadian Indian allies near Lake George. With Hilletie van Olinda interpreting, he and his fellow Albany magistrates learned about the disaster from two bedraggled Mohawk warriors who had returned to Albany that afternoon, as well as from two more survivors who limped into town eight days later.[1]

Along with Garistatsi and his fellow Mohawk war captain and brother Kaakhare (Gaxari in Onondaga), twenty-nine Mohawk and Oneida warriors had been pursued, surrounded, and attacked by a large force of forty "French North Indians and Praying Indians." Garistatsi—the chief sachem of Tionnontoguen who had fought bravely alongside Lawrence and the late Onnonouagaren at the Battles of La Prairie—and his Anglophile League party had five days earlier attacked thirteen Laurentian Iroquois braves hunting south of the French Fort Chambly. Garistatsi and Kaakhare had sought to avenge the death of their and Lawrence's good friend Onnonouagaren and the other Mohawks who had perished during the Battles of La Prairie. The Laurentian hunting party had two "Christian boys taken at Schenectady" with them as captives. In the ensuing engagement, the Anglophile Mohawks and Oneidas killed four Laurentian men, captured six men and ten women, and liberated the two Schenectady captives. But on their southward journey following the successful skirmish, Garistatsi and Kaakhare met with disaster.[2]

The two war captains and at least fifteen of their braves were caught and killed by the pursuing forty-man war party, with eleven warriors being taken captive and only four managing to escape. Schuyler and Hilletie were shocked and crestfallen by the losses, as they personally knew Lawrence's good friend and fellow war leader Garistatsi and many of those who had perished. Indeed, Schuyler had supped with several of them at his dinner table at Schuyler Flatts. Not only had the Wolf Clan leader Garistatsi fallen, but both his brother Kaakhare, a bold veteran fighter, and his promising son Ianodathe, poised to become a headman, had been killed during the bloody fracas.[3] The fatalities brought the total manpower losses of the Mohawks and Oneidas to ninety men during the two previous years of King William's War. Even more disturbing to Schuyler and Hilletie, the deaths left the three primary Mohawk "castles" with only around 130 warriors, while the smaller Oneida Nation could now only field half as many braves.[4]

The incident revealed how the struggle between England and France had escalated the conflict between the Anglophile Five Nations and the Francophile Laurentian Iroquois. Over the past two years, both sides had grappled mightily to spare the lives of their kinfolk at Schenectady, La Prairie, and various other engagements, but with the rising violence between the two European superpowers, Lawrence's League Iroquois and their Laurentian kinfolk were showing less and less restraint.[5] The Natives on both sides were now killing and capturing "one another with an intensity that was . . . unprecedented."[6] The rise in the hostile encounters and resultant internecine killing were a consequence of both the increasing violence of King William's War and the ramping up of family- and clan-level conflicts due to the increased wartime strain. Many of these intra-Iroquois quarrels were over the recovery and repatriation of adoptees and relatives captured in the many skirmishes in Iroquoia since the commencement of imperial warfare, with both sides desperate for the return of their friends and family members to their original villages.[7]

To condole the beleaguered Mohawks and Oneidas and honor their Covenant Chain obligations, Schuyler and his fellow Albany officials immediately fed and clothed the four surviving warriors and consoled the League headmen and family members. They also made arrangements to deliver a ceremonial mourning gift of "1000 or 1200 guilders in white strung wampum" in the annual summer council meeting to the family members and friends of the deceased to help their Iroquois allies "wipe off their tears."[8] Schuyler also dispatched scouting parties to Lake George to obtain the physical details of the battle, since the four warriors who had escaped had been separated from the main party during the battle. Two of the braves had merely "heard the fight," while the other two survivors had caught only glimpses of the bout since they had been hiding behind rocky outcrops a short distance from the large enemy war party.[9]

Following the disaster, Schuyler wrote Ingoldsby on December 30 to brief him on the battle, the crisis in Iroquoia, and the desperate military situation on the Albany frontier. The four survivors had overheard that the French were preparing for an attack on the Mohawk River Valley and Albany region as soon as the ice was strong enough to enable river crossings. Schuyler knew he didn't have sufficient troops, fighting settlers, or Native warriors to defend against a concentrated attack like Schenectady, and he told Ingoldsby as much.[10] The Mohawks were "loath to go out upon any occasion," he wrote, for "this great loss of their men hath struck such a terror in them that they are quite out of heart." Meanwhile, the settlers could not be counted on to defend the region, he wrote glumly, unless they were properly paid for their military service. All in all, he reported, he and his fellow Albany officials were "so bare of money that we cannot do those things which are requisite and necessary for the safety of the King's interest here."[11]

In the fourth year of a grueling war that would last nine, the people of Albany, the quartered troops, and the League Iroquois were weak and dispirited. With the beaver trade severely disrupted from the ongoing hostilities and the neglect of hunting, trapping, and farming, the Albany region was gripped in an economic depression, with farmers, brokers, and tradesmen leaving in droves rather than eking out an existence while having to rebuild Schenectady and other hard-hit settler communities. Meanwhile, Lawrence and the League leaders were growing tired of their erstwhile allies' failure to deliver on their promises of muskets, powder, axes, knives, food, clothing, and other critical supplies.[12] How were the Haudenosaunee supposed to hunt, feed their families, and wage war when firearms and gunpowder were scarce and expensive, they warned Schuyler, and when the promised gunsmiths for their villages were nowhere to be found? If the situation continued, they might have no choice but to put aside the "Tree of Prosperity and ye Covenant" with their "Brethren" and send out peace feelers to Yonondio and the French.[13]

Schuyler was just as angry about the deteriorating situation as his Indigenous allies. He and Ingoldsby had been pleading for months for London to provide more weapons, powder, and supplies to their hard-fighting Iroquois allies, to provide more regular troops, and to distribute funds for a Protestant minister for the westernmost Mohawk "castle" of Tionnontoguen, which lay fifty-six miles up the Mohawk River Valley from Albany. However, their requests continued to go unanswered, which only added to the despair among both the Anglo-Dutch settlers and Five Nations. With the failure of the Crown to provide adequate troops and defend the region, the insufficient supply of guns and ammunition for the Iroquois, the low prices for animal furs, and the debilitating losses from battlefield casualties, seized captives, and smallpox, virtually everyone living along the Albany frontier and in Iroquoia had reached an all-time nadir. All Schuyler knew was the situation had to be rectified—quickly—which is why he decided to sail downriver to New York City to address Ingoldsby and the governor's council in person.[14]

On June 30, 1692, Schuyler walked along Broad Street in the South Ward and headed west toward Fort William, where he was scheduled to address the governor and council on the current state of the war in the borderlands. Wanting to look his best, he wore a freshly powdered periwig, a dark blue Dutch-made linen jacket, waistcoat, and breeches, white silk stockings, and silver-buckled leather shoes. His razor-sharp forged-steel sword in the lengthy scabbard bobbing at his hip lent him the appropriate martial spirit.[15]

At this stage of his adventurous life spent mostly on the Indian frontier but also part-time in New York City, the thirty-four-year-old mayor of

Albany and militia major had experienced more than his fair share of personal tragedy to go along with his political and military triumphs. After losing his son Philip in 1684, his beloved first wife, Angelica van Schaick Schuyler, had passed away during childbirth in August 1689, and he lost his daughter Gertruj to disease that same year. After a two-year mourning period following his first wife Angelica's death, he had rebounded in the summer of 1691 when he took Maria van Rensselaer of the powerful Dutch van Rensselaer and van Cortlandt families as his second wife. A month ago, in May 1692, she had given birth to their first daughter, which the couple named Maria after their mother and grandmother. With his wife Maria still recovering from childbirth, Schuyler had left her and their newborn daughter behind in Albany under the care and support of his mother and extended family. He also still had two young daughters from his first marriage, Margarita and Anna, who lived with him and his second wife, Maria, in Albany. But he was still a husband and father who had suffered significant loss in the past eight years, which is an important reason why he was so sympathetic to the Iroquois for their mourning-war grieving and condolence rituals.[16]

He began walking southwest along Stone Street, passing the resplendent homes of Stephanus van Cortlandt, married to his older sister Gertrude, and Frederick Philipse, who like Schuyler had recently lost his first wife and was married to the wealthy widow Catherine van Cortlandt Derval, the younger sister of Stephanus van Cortlandt. During Schuyler's last visit to the City following the La Prairie campaign, he had been amazed at how much more cosmopolitan, bustling, and energetic New York City was than war-ravaged Albany—and he could not help but notice it once again. To his left and right on Stone Street were affluent three-story houses of red, yellow, and brown Holland brick with fancy glass windows and high peaked gabled roofs that dwarfed his simple Dutch frontier-style home on Gentleman's Street (today State Street) in Albany. To the north was the Stadt Huys, or City Hall, located on Dock Street a stone's throw from the Great Dock, New York Harbor, and the brick and stone shorefront mansions and warehouses along the ebbing and flowing East River. Nearby rose the marketplace the original Dutch inhabitants called Het Markvelt, which always seemed to be busy with people buying, selling, and unloading goods.[17]

Although Schuyler and his family spent most of their time upriver in Albany, he often attended the gala functions of Manhattan's Anglo-Dutch elite during his trips to the port city. At the lavish parties held at the colonial governor's mansion inside Fort William and in the private homes of New York's leading magistrates and merchants, Schuyler, his first wife, Angelica, until her death, and his second wife, Maria, hobnobbed with his younger brothers Brandt and Philip and their families and the Philipses, van Cortlandts, Bayards, Emotts, Grahams, Nicolls, and other Manhattan mover-and-shaker families that included the war hero and successful merchant captain William Kidd and his socialite wife, Sarah. At these fashionable New York parties, many of the men dressed in silk waistcoats with jeweled buttons, full wigs, and lace cuffs, while the women often wore the latest fashions from London—narrow-waisted, floor-length, bright-colored dresses of silk or satin, with a slight décolletage in the front and padded bustles that plumped out the backside. Though Schuyler and his wife Maria dressed smartly for these social events, they never wore gaudy or pretentious clothing or the latest fashions from London or Paris because of their humble Dutch backgrounds. Unlike the foppish English, French, and Spanish, the Dutch of late 17th-century New York frowned upon public displays of social status, extravagant clothing, and overt ambition.[18]

Schuyler now began crossing what would one day be America's most famous street, Broadway. In the 1620s, New Amsterdam's Dutch residents had originally named the broad thoroughfare Heeren Wegh—Gentlemen's Way—echoing the name of a similar street in Amsterdam called "High Street" or "the Highway," as it was the major artery into the City. But when the English took over the City in 1664 and renamed it after the Duke of York, the street was significantly widened and its name changed to Broad Way, or Breede Wegh as the Dutch called it.[19]

The streets were packed all the way to the Great Dock with an eclectic mixture of merchants, mariners, shipwrights, stevedores, shopkeepers, farmers, carpenters, mechanics, bakers, hatters, tailors, coopers, fishmongers, wagon haulers, and glaziers. Ethnically, the City had a completely different look than homogenous Dutch Albany, Puritan Boston, or Quaker Philadelphia. The original Dutch settlement of New Amsterdam had grown into the most diverse English colony in America and was home not only to a large number of Dutch and English but French, French-speaking Belgian Protestants called Walloons, Scots, Irish, Germans, Swedes, Norwegians, Portuguese, Jews, as well as hundreds of enslaved Africans and some freedmen.[20]

When he reached Fort William, he also noticed how much more impressive the star-shaped fort at the southern tip of the island was compared to Albany's dilapidated Fort Frederick. Brandishing twenty-foot-high walls built of hard-packed earth and rubble instead of stone to absorb cannon fire, the fort was four-sided with a palisade at each corner and nearly four dozen heavy cannons commanding the sea to fend off French naval attacks. He could only hope that military funding for Albany would soon be provided by the Crown, before Frontenac and his Indian allies sacked the frontier outpost and swept all the way down the Hudson to Manhattan.[21]

At Fort William, he was greeted by Ingoldsby, his brother-in-law Stephanus van Cortlandt, Frederick Philipse, and the other civil and military leaders. After being officially sworn in by the council, he stepped up to the podium with a sheaf of papers to deliver his report. The painted royal coat of arms of the King of England hung on the wall behind him, above a magisterial bench covered with stuffed red cushions, a handsomely carved nutwood chest, and a pair of leather fire-buckets ready for use as he launched into his speech.[22]

Having met with the Iroquois three weeks earlier in Albany with Hilletie acting as interpreter, he first recapped the council. He and Ingoldsby had offered their condolences for the deaths of Garistatsi and the other Iroquois warriors killed at the tragedy at Lake George and distributed presents of white strung wampum for each of the fallen braves and for those killed in action since the battle.[23] Ingoldsby also delivered an "animating speech upon carrying on the war against the French," while urging the sachems to seek rapprochement with the upper Great Lakes tribes to weaken Frontenac's grip over them.[24]

After summarizing the condolence ceremony, Schuyler read his prepared statement regarding the conditions on the borderlands. He did not hold back, forcefully telling the council just how devastating the Crown's neglect of her troops, the Iroquois, Fort Frederick, and the entire region continued to be and what it was going to take to properly defend Albany, protect the Hudson River corridor, and maintain the fidelity of the Iroquois under the Covenant Chain.[25] "We are reduced to great extremity by the long war, so much so that of 550 men that we had four years ago, we have but 290," he said. But that wasn't the worst of it. "The French had such success last year among the Indians, destroying many of their leading men and warriors, that the Indians are discouraged, complaining that they are fighting for our sakes, that we provide no force to secure ourselves and destroy our enemies, and that all the burden of war falls on them." All they want, he said, is for us to do "our share."[26]

He then described the embarrassing state of Fort Frederick. "The stockades and fortifications were decayed, and required a large expenditure for repairs," he said. "They were all of wood, and at their best a poor protection to the inhabitants against such an enemy as the French." Furthermore, the garrison was regrettably "in a starving condition and on the point of mutiny" and he "had exhausted his own private stock of grain to supply their wants."[27] Though there was ample wheat in the region ready for the harvest, the recent attacks on the outlying farms by the hostile tribes prevented the farmers of Albany and Schenectady from reaping their crops without the protection of large numbers of armed men. The settlers had suffered as much as the Iroquois since the war's inception, he said.[28] They "were too poor to provide for their own security and the safety of the frontiers" and could barely provide "for their own subsistence."[29]

He proposed six specific remedies that he believed would help restore stability and military security to the region and bring hope to the settlers, the troops, and their Native allies. His top priority was to increase the number of soldiers in the region to four hundred men, with two hundred posted at Fort Frederick in Albany and fifty each at the stockades at Schenectady, Half Moon, and Canastagione. The remaining fifty men would serve as roving scouts to help promote better mutual understanding and cooperation between the English and the Iroquois in fighting the French and their Native allies. He recommended that one hundred League Indians join with the detachment of fifty soldiers to engage in routine patrols to protect the region.[30] He also proposed that Fort Frederick be refurbished and strengthened, which he estimated would cost around £500 ($175,000 today). To augment the patrols by the English troops and Iroquois scouts, he wanted sixty of the youth of the city and surrounding country who knew the backwoods to be "kept in constant pay, for they are so impoverished that they must be maintained."[31]

In his summation, he warned that even if all his recommendations were implemented, New York would still remain at risk from Frontenac and the French if the New England and other neighboring colonies continued to refuse to lend financial assistance and troops to the Albany frontier. The struggle against New France could not be won without their support. It was an effective way to end his speech, for nothing had been more frustrating to New York's officials than the lack of support from Massachusetts, East and West Jersey, Pennsylvania, Maryland, and Virginia.[32]

Schuyler's plea for financial and military aid made an impression on the governor and council and they swiftly approved his plan.[33] As he had done on the battlefields at La Prairie and in the longhouse at Onondaga, he had once again won the day, this time in the New York governor's council chamber. Despite all the losses he had suffered, both personally and professionally, over the past several years, and despite the wretched state of the Albany frontier, he felt a renewed sense of hope. He also had a new baby girl, Maria, to love, hold, and watch grow up—and it was largely for her and his other two daughters that he sought to secure a safe future for both New York and the Five Nations.

In the late seventeenth century, the upper Hudson River Valley and future State of New York were controlled by the Five Iroquois Nations (*Haudenosaunee*). The Iroquois League consisted of the Mohawks, Oneidas, Onondagas, Cayugas, and Senecas, who viewed the Confederacy as a metaphorical longhouse extending from the Hudson Valley to Lake Ontario. *Indian Rescue*, by Asher Brown Durand, 1846, oil on canvas. *The American Museum of Western Art, Anschutz Collection.*

The Seneca Discover the French by Thomas Hart Benton, 1956. From the perspective of the Iroquois, who met with the French explorer Jacques Cartier during his 1535 voyage up the St. Lawrence River. *Courtesy of the New York State Museum, New York State Education Department. Photo by Samuel Marquis.*

In 1688, the Dutch Prince of Orange became King William III (1650–1702) by seizing the English throne occupied by the Catholic King James II in the Protestant Glorious Revolution. Soon thereafter, William launched England into the global War of the League of Augsburg against imperial France, which in English America was known as King William's War (1689–1697). *Godfrey Kneller, National Galleries of Scotland, Wikimedia Commons.*

Colonel Peter Schuyler (1657–1724) was the Dutch-American mayor of Albany, Indian Affairs commissioner, and commander of New York's militia in the 1690s. Considered the George Washington of the early colonial era, he led joint English-Iroquois military expeditions against French Canada during King William's War and was venerated by the Five Iroquois Nations, who fought alongside him and referred to him as "Brother Quider" based on the pronunciation of his given name, "Peter." *New York Public Library.*

Jacob Leisler (1640–1691), a German-born merchant, militant Calvinist Protestant, and New York City militia officer, took control of New York in 1689 in the name of the Glorious Revolution, in what became known as Leisler's Rebellion. *The trainbands signing Leisler's declaration, New York Public Library Digital Collections.*

The Mohawk River Valley is a natural passageway connecting the Atlantic Ocean to the North American interior via the Hudson River. The *Haudenosaunee* (Iroquois) were the principal people living throughout the east-west trending river valley in the late seventeenth century, with the Mohawks living close to Albany and the other Four Nations living further west. The Mohawk war captain Lawrence and Mohawk-Dutch interpreter Hilletie van Olinda grew up in the majestic valley and spent considerable time there throughout their lives. *Photo by Samuel Marquis.*

In the seventeenth century, the Haudenosaunee forged alliances and concluded treaties by exchanging belts made of wampumpeag, or wampum. More precious than gold to the Iroquois and Algonquin tribes, wampum consisted of woven strings or belts of beads made from shallow marine quahog and whelk shells. Wampum was the shell currency used by the Five Nations in the fur trade and wampum belts were used by various tribes in making ceremonial pledges. *Hiawatha Belt, unknown artist and date, owned and maintained by The Onondaga Nation, Nedrow, NY.*

The "Schenectady Massacre" of February 8, 1690. The French attack on the English stockade was led by Lieutenant Jacques le Moyne de Sainte-Hélène and the Francophile Chief Togouiroui, known as the Great Mohawk. The marauding force of 210 French soldiers, French-Canadian bushfighters, non-League Mohawks from Montreal, and Canadian Algonquins caught the village totally by surprise. During the raid, fifty-six of the town's 250 residents were killed, twenty-seven male prisoners taken, and most log houses burned down. *Originally from Bryant, William Cullen and Syndey Howard Gay,* A Popular History of the United States *(New York: Charles Scribner's Sons, 1890).*

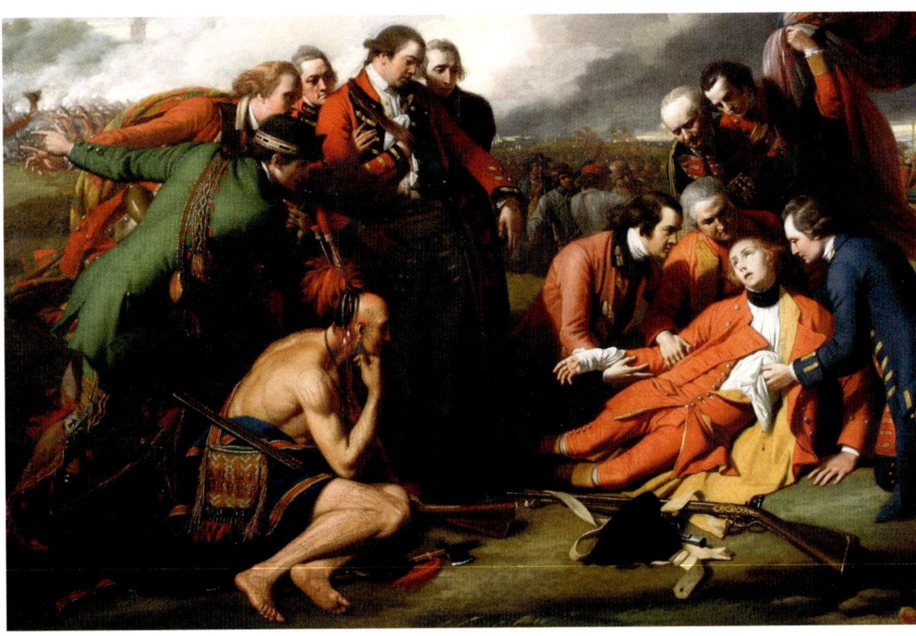

Accurate depiction of a Mohawk warrior on the North American frontier of the seventeenth and eighteenth centuries. *The Death of General Wolfe*, by Benjamin West, 1770. *National Gallery of Canada, Ottawa. Gift of the 2nd Duke of Westminster to the Canadian War Memorials, 1918; transferred 1921.*

Born around 1663 into the Mohawk Wolf Clan in Tiononderoge in the Mohawk River Valley, the English-allied war captain and peace negotiator Lawrence led the League Iroquois in several important expeditions against the French during King William's War, fighting alongside Colonel Peter Schuyler and his brothers. In honor of his achievements and leadership during the pursuit of the retreating French and Indian war party following the 1690 attack at Schenectady, the statue *Lawrence the Indian*, erected in 1887, still stands today near the original raid site. Refurbished in 2012, this statue, while not an historically accurate rendition, continues to be a cultural attraction for the people of the region, who consider Lawrence a source of profound historical inspiration. *Photo by Samuel Marquis.*

Hilletie van Olinda (1646-1707) was a biracial and multilingual Mohawk-Dutch woman who grew up in the Mohawk River Valley and later lived in Schenectady. She was an important council interpreter during King William's War, as well as a Protestant Christian religious text translator and messenger between the Iroquois and New York Indian Affairs officials. *Schenectady County Historical Society.*

An inaccurate but vivid depiction of Captain William Kidd aboard the *Adventure Galley* in 1696 in New York Harbor looking onto Fort William and southern Manhattan. The former Caribbean buccaneer, wealthy New York gentleman, and civic leader became a war hero serving as a Crown privateer against the French during King William's War and played a pivotal role in the capture of Jacob Leisler and ending Leisler's Rebellion. *Arrival of Captain Kidd in New York Harbor, 1696, by J.L.G Ferris, circa 1920, oil on canvas, Independence Hall, Philadelphia.*

During King William's War, New York City had a population of 4,500 people and Fort William at the southern tip of Manhattan protected New York province from French attack. Pictured above is Captain William and Sarah Kidd's three-story, Dutch-style home at 119–121 Pearl Street (large white house) and the stockaded Wall with an entry gate (background) from which Wall Street is named. In the 1690s, colonial elites like the Schuyler brothers, Frederick Philipse, and Robert Livingston had residences near Captain Kidd's prime waterfront property overlooking the East River and close to the fort, where Governors Sloughter, Fletcher, and Bellomont lived. *Gothamhistory.*

Benjamin Fletcher (1640-1703, right) served as the Tory royal governor and commander in chief of New York province during King William's War. An able administrator, he promoted oceanic commerce (both legal and illegal) and was respected by the League Iroquois, who called him *Cayenquiragoe* (Great Swift Arrow). However, he became the target of his successor Lord Bellomont and English officials by condoning New York's lucrative Madagascar pirate trade and lining his own pockets. *Artist Howard Pyle's illustration of Governor Fletcher chatting with the "gentleman pirate" Thomas Tew. Originally published in Janvier, Thomas, "Sea Robbers of New York." Harper's Magazine, November 1894.*

Richard Coote, the First Earl of Bellomont (1636–1701), was an Irish-born Whig nobleman and pro-Leislerian governor of New York, Massachusetts Bay, and New Hampshire. Ousting his predecessor Benjamin Fletcher to become governor of New York in 1698, he led an anti-piracy crusade after coercing Captain Kidd into commanding an ill-conceived 1696–1699 expedition to the Indian Ocean to hunt down pirates. Disliked by New Yorkers and the Iroquois, he was an enemy of Peter Schuyler, Hilletie van Olinda, and Captain Kidd. *Etched engraving of Richard Coote, first Earl of Bellomont, by Samuel Smith Kilburn, n.d. The Miriam and Ira D. Wallach Division of Art, Prints and Photographs: Print Collection, The New York Public Library. New York Public Library Digital Collections.*

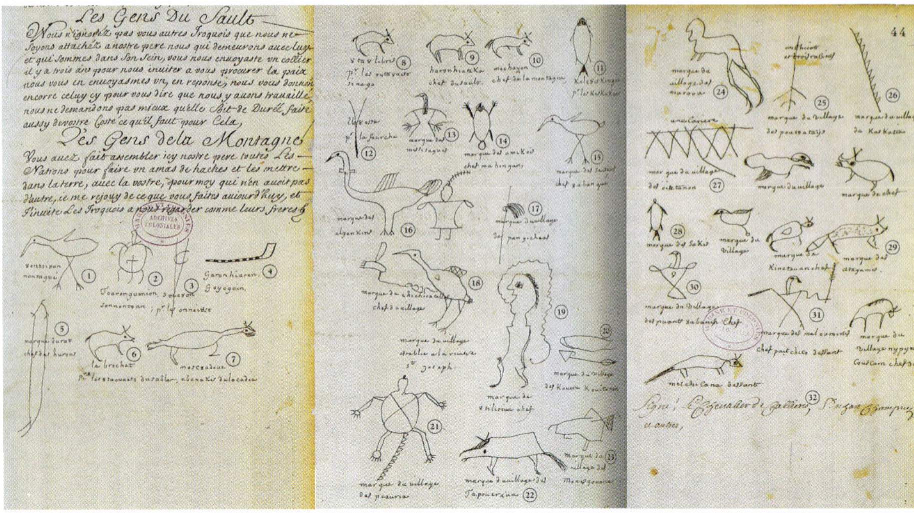

Les Gens Du Sault

Nous n'ignorez pas vous autres Iroquois que nous ne Soyons attachéz a nostre pere nous qui demeurons auec luy et qui Sommes dans Son Sein, vous nous enuoyaste vn collier il y a trois ans pour nous inuiter a vous procurer la paix nous vous en enuoyasmes vn, en reponse, nous vous donnons encorre celuy cy pour vous dire que nous y auons trauaillé, nous ne demandons pas mieux quelle Soit de Durée faite aussy devostre Costé ce qu'il faut pour Cela,

Les Gens dela Montagne

Vous auez fait assembler icy nostre pere toutes Les Nations pour faire vn amas de haches et les mettre dans la terre, auec la vostre, pour moy qui n'en auoit pas d'autre, ie me rejouy de ce que vous faites auiourd'huy, et J'inuite Les Iroquois a nous regarder comme leurs freres

The Great Peace Treaty of Montreal of 1701, with the hand-drawn animal pictograms of the Iroquois and other Native signatories representing thirty-nine northeastern tribes. Under the terms of the "Grand Settlement of 1701," the parallel treaties signed in Montreal and in Albany with Colonel Peter Schuyler and Hilletie van Olinda present allowed the Five Nations freedom of movement in Iroquoia, provided neutrality in future conflicts between England and France, and secured improved trading status with both European powers. *Library and Archives Canada, MIKAN 3050235, folio 44. Archives nationales d'outre-mer (France), CIIA, 19/fol. 41–44.*

The Anglophile Mahican war captain Etowaucum, who fought with Colonel Peter Schuyler and the Mohawk war leader Lawrence in the joint English-Iroquois raids upon French Canada in the 1690s. Like Lawrence and Lawrence's wife Maria, he was baptized at Albany in the Protestant Christian faith by Father Dellius and Hilletie van Olinda. Etowaucum (baptized Nicholas) was one of the "Four Indian Kings of Iroquoia" who traveled with Schuyler to London in 1710 to persuade Queen Anne to support a renewed invasion of French Canada during Queen Anne's War, the second French and Indian war. *Etowaucum (Christianized Nicholas, Mahican), John Verelst, 1710. Oil. National Archives of Canada.*

12
THE RECKONING

On August 10, 1692, Schuyler learned from his scouts that Lawrence and a force of 350 Iroquois warriors were encamped at Schenectady in preparation for a major attack on French Canada. He immediately met with Robert Livingston and other Albany officials about how they could best lend material aid to the war party for the offensive expedition deep into enemy territory.[1] To support the planned raid, they quickly ordered several wagons loaded with ammunition and other supplies worth just under £55 ($19,250 today). Unlike La Prairie, it would be a purely Iroquois mission similar to the devastating attack at Lachine, Quebec, in July 1689 at the beginning of King William's War.[2]

The next day, he headed northwest with Robert Livingston and a platoon of New York militia along the King's Road from Albany to Schenectady, used by those who had fled in the freezing cold during the surprise attack two and a half years earlier. Reaching the still-rebuilding frontier outpost early that evening, they greeted the Mohawk headman Rode, the Mohawk war captain Lawrence, and several other prominent sachems and war leaders, then went to see Hilletie van Olinda to secure her services for the next day's planned council with the Iroquois. Hilletie and her Dutch husband, Peter Danielse van Olinda, lived with their unmarried youngest son Matthew in a handsome Amsterdam-style home on their 600-by-1,100-foot property on Union Street between Church and Ferry Streets. One of the few houses that had not been burned to the ground during the 1690 attack, their home inside the wooden stockade looked out onto the fast-flowing Mohawk River and its floodplain.[3]

The war captain Lawrence and his fellow Mohawks had played a crucial role in the rebuilding of Schenectady since the disaster. According to historian Susan Staffa, the small village might not have even been rebuilt "were it not for the entreaties of Lawrence and other Mohawks. Between helping to rebuild and protect the village, to the condolence ceremonies and the burnishing of their symbolic silver chain, the Mohawks made it known that they were true allies." Hilletie van Olinda and her fellow Schenectadians reciprocated the "Two Row Wampum Belt agreement" by constructing two Mohawk longhouses in the revitalized village. With this symbolic exchange in the wake of a tragedy that had dramatically affected both peoples, no longer were the Mohawks and Anglo-Dutch of *skahnéhtati*—the beautiful place beyond the open pines—sailing separately down the river of life. Now they were "a united, amalgamated community."[4]

Since the raid, Hilletie's extended clan and most of the other Schenectady families had received governmental relief in the form of food, clothing, linens, and other supplies. However, the surprise attack on the settlement and execution of Jacob Leisler and his son-in-law Milborne continued to divide the community into Leislerian and anti-Leislerian factions. Though the German-born strongman had become a martyr to many Schenectadians and others in the colony, Hilletie and her family remained in the anti-Leislerian camp along with the Schuyler, Philipse, and Livingston families of Albany.[5]

For Hilletie, the friction between her family and the Schenectady faction that sided with Leisler went back more than two decades, well before Leisler's Rebellion. As members of the Dutch van Slyck clan through their Dutch carpenter-mason-trader father, Cornelis Antonisen van Slyck, who died in 1676, Hilletie and her siblings were in competition with the future Leislerians at an early age, and the friction continued throughout the 1690s. The animosity was over economic and social status. Most of the Leislerians of Schenectady were late arrivals to the region, lesser landholders, and generally poorer than the early Dutch immigrants like the van Olindas and van Slycks, who, although only a generation removed from the middling ranks of society, were now reasonably affluent and prominent in commercial enterprise and politics, especially with the anti-Leislerian faction restored to power.[6]

In the wake of the Schenectady raid and with the town's recovery still a work in progress, the Leislerians continued to threaten Hilletie and her extended van Olinda and van Slyck families because they believed their elevated economic position was due to preferred treatment by the Mohawks and English officials. While Hilletie, her husband Peter, the extended van Slyck and van Olinda families, and other prominent Schenectady anti-Leislerians were all early proprietors, or the descendants of proprietors, who owned land and material wealth, the Leislerians of the region were somewhat younger than their opponents and included individuals who had arrived at Schenectady after its first decade of settlement, or under circumstances less favorable than their rivals. Like Hilletie, her late eldest brother Jacques had been of biracial Mohawk and Dutch ancestry and had served as an important interpreter and diplomatic envoy from 1663 until his death in 1690 at age fifty. The Leislerians resented that she and her family members had acquired valuable land from the Iroquois due to their favored biracial Indigenous-European status. Hilletie, her husband Peter, her late Mohawk-Dutch brother Jacques, and her youngest sister Lea married to the Dutchman Claes Willemsen van Coppernol had all received properties from the Mohawks due to their connection to the tribe, through their Native matriarch Ots-Toch and Dutch patriarch Cornelis van Slyck.[7]

When Schuyler met with Hilletie at her log home on Union Street, she agreed to serve as official government interpreter for the council. In her vital role as a bridge between the Indigenous world of her Mohawk Wolf Clan mother and the European world of her Dutch father and husband, she continued to win the respect and admiration of both parties due to her linguistic capabilities. She was successful due to her ability to draw upon her own personal experiences in both cultures and religious spheres. In deciphering and translating the words of her Indigenous people and the Anglo-Dutch of New York in complex diplomatic negotiations, she was not only invaluable in councils through her ability to effectively communicate, she was able to follow up with important explanations and clarifications to ensure that there was no misunderstanding. Furthermore, due to her detailed understanding of frontier warfare and the languages and traditions on both sides, she was able to carefully explain what each side hoped to gain from negotiations. In the process, she time and again succeeded in bringing each side to a better understanding of the other, when other interpreters often struggled just to translate the verbal exchanges.[8]

It is for these important reasons that at the end of the council held between the League Iroquois and New York officials back in early June, Hilletie had once again been publicly honored. The Oneida headman Ohede praised her in front of all those present. Not only did he insist that she receive adequate compensation from Ingoldsby and the English for her services, he gave her two fine beaver pelts in recognition of her invaluable contributions as a translator:

> Brother Corlaer, we desire you to take care of our Interpreter, that she may have a sufficient maintenance. She is our mouth and takes great care to give you the true sense of our meaning, for if we should want her, it would cause a great confusion.[99]

The following morning, August 12, Schuyler, Hilletie, and Livingston met with the assembled headmen. Schuyler's principal goal was to rally the old sage Rode, Lawrence, and the other sachems and war leaders for the coming fight. He wanted the Iroquois to unleash holy terror upon the French military outposts and Canadian Indian villages north of Lake Champlain, including the settlements of their Laurentian Iroquois kinfolk who had taken part in the slaughter at Schenectady, the killing of Garistatsi and Kaakhare's war party, and the brutal attacks in western Iroquoia led by Ourehouare. The Cayuga Iroquois headman and Frontenac favorite Ourehouare had Oneida and Onondaga blood on his hands, was under French pay and collecting bounties on League scalps under Frontenac's payment policy, and continued to provoke intra-Iroquois aggression.[10]

With the all-important Hilletie ensuring an accurate translation and Robert Livingston scratching out the council minutes that would eventually be documented in both Dutch and English, Schuyler began the meeting by thanking his "Brethren" for prosecuting the war against their mutual enemies the French "so vigorously" and wished the war party "good success." He then reminded them that the "French Praying Indians," the Laurentian Iroquois, had done the League and the settlers of Albany significant harm over the years and must not be spared in the coming fight. "I do, therefore, recommend ye Brethren to lay their principal design against them in which you must be more wary and cunning than formerly when ye Brethren were out with Lawrence, who let them escape after they were in their hands."[11]

Schuyler was not trying to humiliate his indispensable Mohawk war captain with whom he had fought alongside, entertained at his dinner table at Schuyler Flatts, and prayed next to at Father Dellius's house of worship. Nor did he want to offend the Iroquois headmen present. Instead, his purpose was to call attention to one of the Crown's biggest sore points: the continuing military threat posed by the Laurentian Iroquois striking from the Kahnawake and La Montagne missions outside Montreal. With their fellow settlers being massacred, taken hostage, and abandoning the region, Schuyler and the English authorities continued to find problematic the lukewarm loyalty of their Native allies and the mutual nonaggression pact between the Iroquois of Canada and New York.[12] Because the "French Praying Indians" had wreaked bloody death and destruction all across the Albany frontier, Schuyler considered it a personal slap in the face and a violation of the Covenant Chain for his League Iroquois brothers to protect the Laurentians—before, during, and following engagements—in the name of advancing kinship interests.[13]

Frontenac and the French didn't like the cozy relationship between the League and Laurentian Iroquois any more than their English counterparts. In the view of the courtier-governor and his officials, it was unacceptable that his French soldiers and provincials had to remain close to Montreal and Quebec for their own safety, while the Kahnawake and other Laurentians moved about the Canadian frontier and Iroquoia unimpeded and were protected by their fellow kinsmen. Although the internecine violence from family and clan-level disputes had ramped up between the League Iroquois and their Laurentian kinfolk in the past several months, these conflicts appeared to have reached a peak with the battle near Lake George, which is why Frontenac and Schuyler continued to believe they were being manipulated by the Iroquois. But the freedom of movement of the Haudenosaunee posed a far greater threat to the French than the English. Unlike the Iroquois warriors who traveled overland with efficiency, French troops and settlers struggled to travel safely and speedily through the northeastern frontier and had to confront countless "impediments" to their travel through seemingly ubiquitous Native hunting and war parties with ties to the English.[14]

As Schuyler laid out the government's position through Hilletie's carefully worded translation, he made it clear that not only did he want Lawrence and his warriors to take the fight to the French and the Laurentians and to destroy their corn crops before the fall harvest, he wanted them to recruit their wayward Iroquois kin to rejoin them in their traditional homeland of the Mohawk River Valley:

> You must dally no more with them [Canadian Iroquois] but give them a blow at once and destroy their Indian corn and then come to talk with them. Their necessity then and no hopes of recovery will be ye best argument to cause the residue to come along with you, whom you may assure shall be well treated here and looked upon by this government as ye rest of ye Brethren. . . . Neither shall they want food for their wives and children when they come, we having plenty of corn this not being so barren a country as Canada.[15]

Schuyler concluded his speech by requesting that his Iroquois allies stop raiding farms and settlements around Albany and Schenectady when the war parties set out and returned from northern raids. He had recently heard many complaints of young warriors killing horses and cattle, destroying corn, and burning fences, which he said was "insufferable since we have furnished you with what necessaries you wanted and granted ye request in every respect."[16] He then presented the much-anticipated gifts. "Here is now powder and ball to annoy your enemies," he said, but please "have a care in your march out and home to do no more harm to your friends." Though he had not been able to get his hands on any muskets on such short notice, the supplies doled out were substantial and consisted of "15 bags powder, 200 lb lead, 2 barrels pork and beef, 12 shepl of peas, 4 quarters of beef, 400 flints, 30 loaves of bread."[17]

Upon receiving the gifts, Lawrence, Rode, and the other headmen and warriors, 350 men strong, "made a great shout and returned thanks." At their request, they were also given a male dog, a pistol, a sword, silver coinage, and two sheets of paper. They promptly killed the dog and sang songs over the fallen creature as a sacrifice to the spirit world, seeking not only the sacred blessings of the animal but guidance and protection for the upcoming battle.[18] Having witnessed the practice before, the frontier-savvy Schuyler recognized that the Iroquois ritual was rooted in their beliefs about spiritual reciprocity. Lawrence and his warriors were honoring the slain animal, seeking the creature's spiritual assistance, and preparing themselves mentally for the great battle to come.

Two days later, on August 14, the council resumed after the Iroquois had undertaken their war celebrations and prepared their response to Schuyler's introductory speech. Once again, the spokesman for all the Five Nations was the seventy-six-year-old Mohawk sachem Rode. Born in 1615, a decade before the arrival of Dutchmen to the shores of Manhattan, he had witnessed incredible changes in Iroquoia over his lifetime. In his younger years, he had been a great war captain and had fought only with war clubs and bows and arrows against northeastern Mahican, Lenape, and other Algonquin enemies, since Dutch flintlock muskets did not become widely available to the Mohawks until the mid-1630s. Now he didn't go anywhere without a trusty European trade musket.[19]

Rode gave Schuyler and the commissioners "hearty thanks" for traveling all the way to Schenectady to encourage him and his people and to provide them with "provisions and ammunition" to wage war against their mutual enemies. He and the headmen had reached a consensus to follow the major's recommendation regarding the Laurentian Iroquois who fought under Frontenac and the French. "We can assure you of nothing but of our design and inclination which is to spoil and annoy ye enemy," he said, and "we will use all means imaginable to put ye Praying Indians out of a capacity of ever doing you or us any more harm. We will spare them no longer."[20]

As always, the Iroquois had grievances of their own and Rode now brought these to the attention of Schuyler, with Hilletie translating and Livingston, as the official recorder, struggling to keep up with his ink pen and parchment. They were the same complaints Rode and the other spokesmen had lodged back in June: New England and New York's other "neighbors" under the Covenant Chain needed to join the fight in King William's War by ponying up troops and supplies; and the League required many more muskets if its war parties were to be an effective fighting force going forward. The New Englanders "all stay at home and set us on to do ye work," he complained, "and yet when ye least harm is done to your cattle or corn you chide us severely for it." He hoped Schuyler and the commissioners could overlook these unfortunate incidents, which could not "be helped in these times." He reminded the major and Livingston that the Iroquois were going into battle all alone on behalf of their English allies, without Schuyler and his New York militia joining them, and they would be augmented by 380 more warriors when they rendezvoused in Canada. "We doubt not but shall do some good exploit before we come back," he said, giving a belt of wampum and three pelts.[21]

To his credit, Schuyler apologized for coming across so sharply the first day of the council. However, he told the Iroquois not to take it personally that he had "reproved" them for killing the horses and cattle and ravaging the settlers' farms. "You tell us we must maintain our post and not desert Schenectady, but our people cannot live here if you destroy their cattle and corn," he said firmly but respectfully. "Therefore, let me hear no more complaints."[22]

To make sure that the council ended on a positive note, Adogaounwa, a tall Oneida war captain, stood up on behalf of all Five Nations to give his parting thoughts. He thanked Schuyler for his "provision of ammunition" and stated that he and the warriors would make "good use of it." During the conference, both Adogaounwa and Rode addressed Schuyler as "Corlaer." Thus, the Iroquois viewed him—not Governor Ingoldsby—as the true principal-in-charge of Indian Affairs in New York Province and English America.[23]

The council ended there. Before Schuyler, Hilletie, and Livingston returned to Albany, they spoke with an adopted Iroquois war leader,

"Captain Canochquonnie," who confided to Schuyler that Lawrence and the other warriors had no plans for a direct assault on the Laurentian settlements outside Montreal. Instead, they would escort Canochquonnie to the outskirts of the Kahnawake mission and have him deliver League wampum belts to open peace negotiations with Frontenac's Laurentian Indian allies. Their goal was to initiate an Iroquois prisoner exchange program and to persuade the Laurentians to withhold military assistance from the French. Having learned that his Iroquois brethren had misled him about the true nature of their expedition to Canada, Schuyler didn't get angry. Instead, he tried to outmaneuver his Iroquois allies at their own game.[24]

He advised Canochquonnie not to trust either the French or the Kahnawake Iroquois and to encourage the Laurentians to join their Native kinfolk to the south in the Mohawk River Valley. As a sign of English good faith, Schuyler gave him two wampum belts to seal the agreement in the traditional Iroquois manner. "They shall have a minister and land to plant upon and provisions for ye first year," he assured the messenger, and they would be "looked upon as ye rest of our Brethren without any distinction, neither shall they be forced to go out to war against ye French but live peaceably and quietly in ye government the place of their nativity."[25]

Schuyler was, in effect, acting as a New York recruitment officer to bring back the Mohawks that had moved north to Canada. In the mid-1670s, the Great Mohawk Togouiroui and forty Iroquois had left the Mohawk River Valley to live at the Kahnawake mission near Montreal, and since that time many others had gone north to live under the ostensible protection of the French. Like his League Iroquois brethren, Schuyler wanted them to return to their homeland and help repopulate and rebuild their devastated Five Nations communities in the Mohawk River Valley.

That same day, Schuyler returned to Albany with Hilletie and Livingston and soon thereafter the war party struck north to attack French Canada.

In late August, after having traveled north in two separate military columns, Lawrence and the Iroquois army that now numbered 800 braves assembled southwest of Montreal. There was not a single English soldier or bushfighter in the Indigenous war party. As Schuyler had discovered, the expedition combined military and diplomatic objectives. While waging ferocious war against Frontenac and the French, the League warriors hoped to simultaneously seek rapprochement with the Francophile Laurentian Iroquois of the St. Lawrence River Valley to secure peace and limit the Indian casualties that had exploded in the last year.[26]

The Iroquois fighters were bedecked in a mixture of clothing from both Native and European cultures. They wore traditional buckskin leggings, moccasins, and animal-bone necklaces made of bear claws or cougar fangs, while their breechclouts and shirts were fashioned of European trade-cloth, the latter to which many had added colorful beads and ribbons as embellishments. Many of the Iroquois warriors had intricate animal tattoos representing their clans painted on their faces and bodies, and most of them wore the traditional Iroquois scalp lock. Their weaponry consisted primarily of English- and Dutch-manufactured trade muskets, wooden ball-headed war clubs, and freshly sharpened trade hatchets. Several of the warriors had adorned their muskets and war clubs with fresh enemy scalps taken during the northward advance.

By the time the League war party gathered along the southern bank of Lake Saint-Louis west of Montreal, Frontenac had received reports of the approaching warriors. One of these came from a Francophile Iroquois woman from La Montagne, who had recently escaped after two years of Mohawk captivity at Tionnontoguen, the westernmost and largest of the League settlements on the Mohawk River. The woman reported that eight hundred Iroquois were on the way to Canada and they intended "to draw out the greatest number of the Indians possible under plea of a negotiation, and to bind them or knock them on the head."[27] Thus, she corroborated Rode's description of the League plan to camp near Kahnawake and reach out to their Laurentian kinfolk regarding a peace agreement and prisoner exchanges. However, she claimed that it was merely a ruse to draw out the Laurentians and either capture them to replenish League ranks or outright kill them. The woman also reported that one of the objectives of the raid was for the Mohawks and Oneidas to avenge the deaths of Garistatsi,

Kaakhare, and their fifteen warriors killed at Lake George and to secure the release of the survivors still being held in captivity.[28]

Unsure of the true intentions of the Five Nations army, the Laurentian headmen were wary and cautious. Fearing reprisal for last winter's Lake George attack and previous incursions into Iroquoia, they refused to either meet with or open up communications with their kinfolk from the south.[29] Meanwhile, the governor of Montreal, Louis-Hector de Callière, dispatched several companies of French troops to reinforce the garrison at Kahnawake and "ordered everyone to retire into the forts." With only half as many men on hand as the Iroquois, he dared not march "openly against the enemy," especially since he didn't know from "what quarter they would attack." He also sent a garrison to abandoned Fort Sorel north of Montreal and commanded officers away in distant Quebec to return quickly to their posts.[30]

At midday in early September, Lawrence and a large body of Iroquois warriors encountered several companies of French troops and a party of Laurentians on Lake Saint-Louis. The Mohawk war captain and his braves appear to have been attempting to reach out peacefully to the Laurentians, as Lawrence and Onnonouagaren had done on their March 1691 diplomatic visit to the Montreal region. However, the French troops at Kahnawake had no interest in permitting any negotiations to take place between the Anglophile and Francophile Iroquois and gunfire was soon exchanged.[31] The French soldiers drove off the "would-be Iroquois diplomats"[32] with several volleys of musket fire, but "there was no great loss on either side."[33] Thus, the dual war-maker and peace-negotiator Lawrence and his fellow Anglophile war captains were likely trying to execute their plan for "Captain Canochquonnie" to deliver the League wampum belts and open peace negotiations, but the French had other plans and the Laurentians did not want to risk their lives unnecessarily in case of treachery by the League.

With their diplomatic outreach having been rebuffed by the French and with no communication lines open between the League and Canadian Indians, Lawrence and his warriors withdrew in the evening and headed for Lake Saint Francis. From there, the eight-hundred-warrior force broke up into several smaller raiding parties to attack French settlers, and also to hunt. Throughout September and October, Lawrence and his Mohawks and the Oneidas, Onondagas, Cayugas, and Senecas wreaked death and destruction across the St. Lawrence River Valley, keeping Frontenac, Callière, and their French troops on high alert.[34]

With the Iroquois having dispersed into more than a dozen small but wide-ranging parties that still boasted eight hundred warriors total, Callière chose not to send out any large detachments to pursue the enemy. "The number of persons that could be mustered," maintained one French official, did not equal "half their force."[35] Eventually, six companies and fifty Canadian Indian scouts were sent to Fort Chambly, but the patrols failed to catch any enemy warriors and the French continued to receive only half-hearted assistance from their Laurentian Iroquois allies. Though Frontenac and Callière had enjoyed significant Laurentian auxiliary support against the Five Nations for much of the previous year, they now had to face these aggressors almost completely on their own. Only a handful of Laurentians took part in the pursuit parties against their southern kinfolk in September and October 1692, leaving Lawrence and his warriors free to prowl the area without fear of large-scale counterattack.[36]

Most of the French farmers of the region were able to get their crops in, but they paid a heavy price as many were killed by the enemy raiders sweeping through the Canadian countryside with hit-and-run attacks.[37] "Youthful members of one French family managed a famous defense against the Iroquois at the Verchères seigneury north of Montreal in October 1692," writes historian Jon Parmenter, "but many other Canadian settlers were not so fortunate."[38] During the attack, the League Iroquois party killed several settlers, took a number of prisoners, and drove the cattle into the woods, and they later "scalped a soldier at Saint-Ours."[39]

Taking many scalps and war prisoners, the Mohawks continued to earn their reputation as the most feared warriors of the Five Nations in the eyes of Frontenac and his French commanders. At this stage of King William's War, raiding for Lawrence and his fellow warriors was less a means to prove themselves in battle or to fight off their fur-trading competition than to humiliate Yonondio and the French and to replenish their communities ravaged by three years of warfare, disease, internal strife, and out-migration.

To sustain their population, the Iroquois had no choice but to adopt their vanquished foes in large numbers to make up for their losses from war casualties as well as smallpox and other diseases. Adopted captives made up more than half of some Haudenosaunee villages and most estimates place the number of Indigenous captives taken by the Five Nations in the 17th century at between six and ten thousand individuals.[40]

As a war captain, Lawrence played a central role in the mourning-war rituals of the Five Nations. He was often being prodded by Wolf Clan matrons and other bereaved family members to lead war parties and to bring back captives who could be adopted to replace lost kin. For Lawrence, the goal was to seek out the traditional enemies of the Iroquois and secure prisoners while incurring minimal casualties to the warriors he led into action. He likely also felt the need to avenge the death of his two deceased friends and fellow war leaders, Onnonouagaren and Garistatsi, with whom he had fought alongside at the First and Second Battles of La Prairie.

While Iroquois warfare was highly destructive to both European and Indigenous communities, it continued to provide the traditional means for young warriors to demonstrate their valor, helped restock the population, and allowed communities to heal and undergo restoration through mourning rituals and much-needed victories over their hated enemies. But on the negative side of the ledger, the constant warfare resulted in too many casualties and excessive emotional trauma, and forced warriors to spend considerable time away from their villages and families, which made Iroquoia even more vulnerable to reprisal attacks.[41] For Lawrence, the Anglo-French struggle for control of the continent had turned his Haudenosaunee homeland into a dangerous place for him and his wife Maria to live and raise their two sons.

The fall 1692 Iroquois offensive spread panic among the French and their Indigenous allies from the Great Lakes region to Quebec. Although they faced negligible resistance and rampaged through the Canadian hinterlands virtually uncontested, Lawrence and the war parties did come to blows with the enemy and sustain casualties. Furthermore, several of the scouting parties dispatched by Callière from Montreal and nearby stockades managed to wreak havoc upon English and Iroquois settlements through hit-and-run attacks. Slipping stealthily in and out of enemy territory, they probed the distant communities in search of prisoners and intelligence.[42]

"The French Indians" were "wolves" who "lay so close, no man can discover them," complained one English colonial official. "The parties I send daily out, they let pass—lurking close—but if a naked [unarmed] man, woman or child pass they kill them or take them. Our Indians act the same part and with greater success on the French plantations."[43] The Wendats and Odawas also inflicted damage, taking forty-two scalps and bringing the League death toll to 102 warriors by the end of the year. They also captured forty-four prisoners, thirty of whom were men and the rest women and children.[44]

The Indigenous tribesmen on both sides continued to collect bounties for enemy scalps. Frontenac and the French paid bounties of 60 livres ($1,500 today) for male prisoners, 30 livres ($750 today) for female prisoners and White male scalps, and 33 livres ($825 today) for League Iroquois scalps. Meanwhile, Ingoldsby and New York paid £6 ($2,100 today) for every Frenchman or French Indian killed within three miles of the frontier, while Massachusetts paid £12 ($4,200 today) for every enemy killed or taken prisoner.[45]

While the French and their Indian allies had some minor successes in the fall of 1692, Lawrence and his League warriors inflicted far heavier casualties and wreaked greater destruction. By the time they returned to Gandagaro, Caughnawaga, and Tionnontoguen on the Mohawk River and their other settlements farther west, Count Frontenac was beside himself with outrage over the enemy's reign of terror through French Canada.[46] His Laurentian Iroquois allies, too, had taken a severe beating from the several independent war parties that had swept through their country like a hurricane. "Nearly the half of them have perished fighting, like brave men, against the English and against the Iroquois, their relatives, and other Indians, our enemies," a French report lamented.[47]

Like their League kin to the south and the settlers on both sides of the conflict, the Laurentian Iroquois, as well as the Canadian Algonquins living in the St. Lawrence River Valley, had been ground down from four years of battlefield losses, disease, losing family members, repeated false alarms of enemy attacks, and cyclical drops in fur prices. As the French authorities wrote:

> Our Indians who are daily perishing in our service on the frontier of the Colony, are weary of the war, perceiving that the enemy are continually attacking our settlements, without our daring to go, either in detachments or with an army, to their country for want of people; contenting ourselves with acting on the defensive. The enemy is, consequently, sapping and destroying us little by little.[48]

Following the League attacks throughout the northern borderlands, Frontenac's officials urged him that the time had come to reclaim the offensive by invading the western Five Nations settlements and destroying them. Because the Iroquois usually only made war "when the leaves were on the trees," he wanted to send a strong force to attack the three "castles" of the Mohawk River Valley. The goal would be to annihilate the Mohawks, push all the way to Albany, and destroy the English outpost as he had done at Schenectady three years earlier.[49]

The last thing he wanted was for the Mohawks and other Nations to build on their success by persuading their Laurentian relatives to withhold military assistance to the French and relocate to the Mohawk River Valley.[50] It irritated him that the League "omitted no effort to seduce the greatest number possible of our Indians" and that they conducted "frequent negotiations" and "secret communications" with the Laurentians "very much to our prejudice." To put a stop to the collaboration between the League and Laurentian Iroquois, he believed he had no choice but "to obtain by force what our Indians could not effect by their negotiations."[51]

In November 1692, Count Frontenac began his preparations for an expedition into Mohawk country in consultation with Iroquois leaders he identified as the "oldest and best heads" of Kahnawake and La Montagne.[52] Once again, he would strike terror in northern New York Province and Iroquoia.

Only this time, he vowed to bring both the English and their Mohawk allies to their knees.

13
BENJAMIN FLETCHER

On August 30, 1692, as Lawrence and the League Iroquois waged war on French Canada and Frontenac plotted his revenge, New York's new royal governor, Colonel Benjamin Fletcher, disembarked from the HMS *Wolf* in New York Harbor and was welcomed ashore at the Great Dock by several hundred Manhattanites. New York governor's council member Peter Schuyler was not there to greet him, but Frederick Philipse and the other councilors stood with their families at the wharf to meet the incoming governor, along with Mayor Abraham De Peyster and his wife. They were joined by leading citizens Captain William and Sarah Kidd, two score of aldermen and City officials, and the New York militia brandishing fluttering English colors and full regalia. Following his reception at the dock, the Tory governor was escorted by the welcoming committee and soldiers under arms to Fort William. Here his commission was read aloud and posted in the council chamber and subsequently at City Hall, accompanied by great "acclamations and firing" from the fort's cannons. Thus began the six-year governorship of one of the most controversial yet effective Crown-appointed administrators in the history of New York.[1]

Fifty-two years old, tall, and ruddy-faced, Benjamin Fletcher was the son of a London linen draper and homemaker and a lifelong soldier. With his father dying when he was five, young Benjamin had no choice but to fend for himself at an early age. Joining the English army in his teens, he served as an infantry and cavalry officer in Ireland from 1663 to 1685 in the Duke of Ormonde's forces, distinguishing himself in combat and rising from cornet to captain. By the mid-1680s, he had transferred to England and joined the Princess Anne of Denmark's Regiment of Foot, an outfit noted for its Protestant esprit de corps, and he soon thereafter allied himself with William and Mary during their early rise to power. After once again receiving battle honors in Ireland for his actions at Carrickfergus (1689), Boyne (1690), and the sieges of Cork, Kinsale, and Limerick (1690), he continued to distinguish himself. He rose to lieutenant-colonel but suffered a serious financial setback when his property in County Westmeath was destroyed by Irish Catholic forces.[2]

As a reward for his military exploits and to help him recoup his fortunes after the destruction of his "small patrimony," he was recommended to the Crown by Sir William Blathwayt, King William III's secretary of war and to the Privy Council, the cabinet charged with colonial funding and administration. It was from his association with the influential Blathwayt that Fletcher became the king's personal choice to direct the war in New York.[3] Because the royal colony was the fulcrum of colonial defense against imperial France, Fletcher was the military commander of a vast disputed war zone that included not only New York Province but Pennsylvania, East and West Jersey, Connecticut, and Rhode Island.[4] He was also vice-admiral of "all the seas and coasts" in his jurisdiction.[5] Despite his impressive authority, the incoming governor soon discovered that he had inherited an "impoverished, divided, contentious" colony that would be difficult to unite and govern, especially with the still-simmering discontent over the Leisler affair and ongoing costly war with France.[6]

Within a week of Fletcher taking office, Schuyler, Philipse, and other leaders wrote him a lengthy letter apologizing for the province's endless list of problems he now had to address:

> We are sorry that the bright day of your arrival should be clouded by the gloomy condition of the Colony. We are engaged in an expensive war, the revenue is exhausted, the country in debt, the soldiers unpaid, the people much impoverished by the late disorders, and many so disloyal to the Government that they are a disturbance rather than a help.[7]

His two most critical challenges were how to maintain the unity, loyalty, and support of his fellow New Yorkers, the Five Iroquois Nations, and the neighboring English colonies to defend the vital Hudson River corridor; and how to administer and generate revenue for New York when it continued to be deeply divided from Leisler's Rebellion. Despite the long odds of success, the military man rolled up his shirt sleeves and plunged into his new role, for which he had scant training, with alacrity.[8]

Within the first six months of his administration, Fletcher would call a new Assembly and enact several important statutes to bring New York Province safety and prosperity. He refurbished Fort William and other fortifications in the City and at Albany; made sure the troops were properly fed and clothed and that the victuallers were paid; created a post office; reaffirmed the Covenant Chain with the powerful Iroquois; properly outfitted the New York militia; and posted a provincial agent in London as a lobbyist to advocate on New York's behalf before the Crown and Parliament.[9]

Because his governor's council of Schuyler, Philipse, Stephanus van Cortlandt, William Nicoll, Nicholas Bayard, and others hostile to the Leisler regime had been appointed by the Crown before he had set sail for America, he had no choice but to ally himself with the anti-Leislerian faction and distance himself from the insurgents.[10] However, while he had to ingratiate himself with the political and merchant elite since he could never hope to administer the colony without their support, he was troubled by New York's factionalism.[11] To resolve the ongoing conflict, he attempted to reach out with several olive branches to placate Leisler's followers. He reappointed as mayor Abraham De Peyster, a former outspoken Leisler supporter from a wealthy New York Dutch family, who would serve in the post for three terms through 1694. He also swiftly released Leisler's top lieutenants convicted of treason still imprisoned at Fort William. Although he threatened to revoke their parole if they again caused unrest, his attempts to bury the hatchet and unite the colony did not go unnoticed by the more reasonable Leislerians.[12] Thus, at least initially, his policies of appeasement brought more "calm in the city's politics" than his predecessors.[13]

Upon taking office, Fletcher continued the pattern of America's royal colonies by serving as a powerful Crown-appointed governor and commander in chief who administered the colony with the advice of his council and attorney-general. With a robust Executive and the merchant class once again the locus of power, Schuyler, Philipse, and Attorney-General James Graham were positioned to remain at the top of New York politics for years to come.[14] At the same time, to keep the governor and his handpicked council in check and ensure the rights of the citizenry, the New York Assembly begun in 1691 in the aftermath of Leisler's Rebellion continued to promulgate an impressive bill of rights. The Assembly became an important economic tool whereby Schuyler's Dutch Albany and Anglo-Dutch Long Island stripped New York City of its longtime flour-bolting and other prohibitive monopolies.[15] Thus, one positive outcome of Leisler's insurgency was that it helped lead to the formation of the New York Assembly, which "made the government more amenable to the will of the people."[16]

However, the Leislerians still remained a disruptive force in New York City, Long Island, Albany, and Schenectady. Despite Fletcher's evenhanded approach and his strenuous efforts to restore law and order, the province continued to remain politically polarized into the "Black" (Leislerian) and "White" (anti-Leislerian) camps grappling for a share of the government.[17] As the Anglican cleric John Miller, who moved to New York City in 1692, wrote, "These injuries done by either side to their opposites have made a most unhappy division and breach among them which will hardly of a long time admit a cure."[18]

The new royal government with its strong Executive that was held in check by the Assembly provided the battleground for the new power struggle between the Leislerians and anti-Leislerians. In this ongoing struggle, the Schuylers, Philipses, and New York's other anglicized Dutch first families not only reestablished their preeminence, but were able to expand their power and influence and would go on to dominate life in New York throughout much of the 18th century.[19] In contrast, the mostly Dutch, working class Calvinist Leislerians who had lost the contest now saw their economic opportunity and political power plummet in the new English order. Bitter over having to relinquish their two-year run of political dominance, they continued to be a combative faction that would seek retribution whenever possible and aggressively battle for votes and influence.[20]

Unfortunately, the ongoing political strife made it virtually impossible to properly govern New York or to protect the Albany frontier and Iroquoia from French attack.

While the battle between the Leislerians and anti-Leislerians continued to grip New York during Fletcher's administration, the most pressing issue in the colony was still maintaining the alliance with the League Iroquois and waging King William's War.[21] Desperate to shore up the defenses at Albany, renew the Covenant Chain with the Five Nations, and rally support for the defense of New York from French invasion, the new governor sailed upriver to the fur-trading outpost on September 28, 1692. According to two captured prisoners of war, Frontenac had recently been reinforced with "2,000 men from France with all necessaries for war in fourteen ships."[22] Fletcher hoped that "the news of his arrival at Albany with guns and ammunition might reach the enemy and deter them from attack."[23] But if the French had already committed to an all-out invasion, he vowed to give Count Frontenac "warm entertainment, if the people here will be persuaded to unite."[24]

Arriving in Albany in early October, he met with Peter Schuyler, who continued to wear four different hats as a New York governor's council member, the mayor of Albany, the lead commissioner of Indian Affairs, and the commander of the Albany militia. Schuyler briefed the new governor and commander in chief on the military situation of the Albany frontier and Iroquoia by leading him on an inspection tour of Fort Frederick, still-rebuilding Schenectady, and the nearby smaller settlements. The soft-spoken Dutch-American frontiersman and tall, opinionated English military man got along well and saw eye to eye from the very beginning—which is surprising considering that the two men couldn't have been more different.

What made Schuyler unique for the early Age of Enlightenment is that he did not inhabit merely one colonial American world but straddled three separate worlds: Dutch Albany, English New York, and Iroquoia.

While serving in his multifarious roles as Albany's mayor, militia leader, and largest landowner, he was a faithful servant of the Mother Country's imperial order, but he was still first and foremost a Dutch frontiersman and New York's principal political liaison to the Five Nations and superintendent for Indian Affairs. Having been raised on the frontier since his birth in Beverwyck in 1657, he grew up immersed in the Dutch cultural values that defined the community, while at the same time interacting closely with the Iroquois and Mahican tribes in positive ways that made him sensitive and appreciative of their culture. In the process, he benefitted both the settlers of New York Province and the Indigenous Peoples of the Mohawk and Hudson River Valleys through his ability to navigate between the two very different worlds and bridge the gap between them.[25]

Steeped in Dutch social and familial culture, mercantilism, tolerance, and independent-minded thinking, he disliked England's stringent Navigation Acts and believed that New York's merchants had every right to trade furs and other products in the colonies, West Indies, and Europe without interference from the English Crown. The Acts of Trade and Navigation, as they were known, restricted colonial trade to English ships and ports and forced New York and other colonies to pay heavy customs duties, thereby ensuring England's commercial dominance by squeezing the economic vitality out of the colonies and by keeping them fiscally underdeveloped. Circumventing the Navigation Acts was one way in which Dutch New Yorkers like Schuyler could quietly thumb their noses at the English invaders who had conquered them in 1664.[26]

Unlike the rigidly hierarchal English, Schuyler believed in traditional Dutch values that held that property holdings were a private matter and public displays of status and social ambition were distasteful. He also believed that the way the Puritans of Massachusetts treated and negotiated with the League Iroquois and other Native tribes made no sense from a business or military standpoint—and was most definitely not neighborly. Unlike Schuyler and the Dutch of New York, many Puritans believed the Iroquois and other Native American tribes were godless, sexually licentious heathens and bloodthirsty "savages," who disrespected the Sabbath by worshiping animal spirits and should be exterminated just like satanic Catholics and Muslims. Schuyler, more attuned to emerging Age of Enlightenment values, firmly rejected such puritanical nonsense.[27]

Thus, although Schuyler worked hard on behalf of and supported the policies of the English government, he never fully embraced English culture or commercial practices, and he always kept a distance from the hardcore English Puritans, except when it came to joint military operations. Furthermore, he openly violated English trade laws by stocking his house with Dutch household furniture and other items banned under the Navigation Acts, including Dutch smoking pipes, blankets, high-quality flintlock muskets, kettles, knives, axes, awls, glass beads, and furniture.[28]

Because Schuyler spent considerable time living and working among the anglicized movers and shakers of both Albany and New York City, some historians have made him out to be "British inside and out" and no different than Benjamin Fletcher, Richard Ingoldsby, Henry Sloughter, Charles Lodwick, Robert Livingston, William Nicoll, James Graham, and other members of the colony's English-Scottish elite. But as archaeologist and historian James Bradley writes, the material evidence unearthed from the ground at Schuyler Flatts reveals that the frontier-American-born Dutchman, who had spent his youth running through the backwoods of Iroquoia, was a far more nuanced and complex individual:[29]

> Like many of the Albany Dutch, Schuyler was able to balance his public appearance with the needs of his personal life. One could be a good servant of the empire, yet true to the values of one's upbringing and community. This view of Schuyler is entirely consistent with the archaeological evidence from the Flatts. The ability to live successfully in two different worlds is . . . reflected in Schuyler's surviving personal possessions. These include stylish furniture such as a William and Mary tea table . . . side chairs imported from Boston [and] a [Hollandia-style] cast iron fireback from the Flatts farm . . . dated 1665, the year after the English "conquest."[30]

Though Peter Schuyler's core values were unquestionably derived from the Netherlands and not England despite that New York had been an English colony since he was seven years old, he was still an amalgamation of all three cultures—Dutch, English, and Iroquois—that had been shaping the wild Albany frontier since he was born. As Bradley writes, Schuyler had evolved by the late 1680s into "something new" that we can begin to recognize as uniquely "American."[31]

But it is his respect for Native American culture that shines through most of all, making him a man way ahead of his time. Throughout his life, he would share his family's principal country estate at Schuyler Flatts with sachems, matrons, warriors, and their extended families—inviting them to dinner at his table with his wife and children, allowing them to camp in his woods and fields, and providing a long-term safe refuge after the French burned their villages to the ground or they were forced to flee due to stressful internal conflict.[32] The now thirty-five-year-old Schuyler's deep sympathy for his Iroquois brethren was rooted in the significant personal losses he had endured in his life with the deaths of his father, Philip Pieterse Schuyler, in 1683, his son Philip in 1684, and his daughter Gertruj from the fever and his first wife, Angelica van Schaick Schuyler, during childbirth in 1689. Because of his own personal sufferings, he felt profoundly for the Mohawks and their mourning-war grieving and condolence rituals.[33]

During Fletcher's military inspection tour, Schuyler showed the new governor the continuing deteriorated condition of Fort Frederick despite the promises made by the Crown and how "exposed and unprotected" the region was overall to French and Indian attack. Fletcher quickly realized that the local defenses would require significant improvements before winter to fend off a concerted invasion. After his one-year stint as interim governor, Ingoldsby was in overall command of the military forces stationed at Albany, and Fletcher made it the major's responsibility to repair the defenses and protect the Upper Hudson and Mohawk River Valleys from attack. Meanwhile, Schuyler remained in charge of the Albany militia and the key liaison with the League Iroquois.[34]

During the governor's visit to Albany, Fletcher and Schuyler met with the Iroquois headmen and Lawrence and the war captains to hear their concerns, obtain their support, and distribute the usual presents. Once again, Hilletie van Olinda acted in the important role of interpreter to bridge the cultural divide and promote unity in defeating the French. On October 11, Fletcher recognized her by renewing her annual fixed salary of £20 ($7,000 today) and making her an official New York government interpreter in his administration. Her salary was higher than the yearly earnings of many New York dockworkers, artisans, schoolteachers, and seamen of the age, and half the £40 ($14,000 today) suffrage requirement to be a freeholder (a servant who outlived their indenture contract). More important, the "Mohawk interpretess" Hilletie stands today as one of the few women to be referenced on a regular basis in a professional working capacity in the New York colonial documents of the late 17th century.[35]

For Lawrence and the Iroquois, the tall and soldierly Fletcher presented a strong martial presence like their Brother Quider, who continued to share their hardships and fight bravely alongside them. All the same, they had grievances: The lack of support of the war effort by New England, Virginia, and Maryland continued to be a nagging issue, and trade muskets, powder, and lead shot continued to be insufficient and expensive and to arrive too late to be of consequence against the French.[36] Despite the complaints on both sides, which had been aired on September 6 in a preliminary meeting between Schuyler, Hilletie, and the Iroquois before Fletcher's arrival, the gifts doled out by the governor were well-received and the meeting ended harmoniously with a reaffirmation of Anglo-Iroquois unity.[37]

During the negotiations, Hilletie once again played a critical role in ensuring congenial Anglo-Iroquois relations, in ironing out differences, and in furthering mutual support of the war effort. At the same time, she did her best to protect her fellow Mohawks with whom she had spent the first eighteen years of her life, knowing that both the English and French were exploiting the Iroquois to further their own imperial ambitions in North America. However, at this stage of her life she saw the world more through a European lens than a Native one. Having married the Dutchman Peter Danielse van Olinda and raised their three biracial sons—Daniel, Jacob, and Matthew—as European Christians, she maintained strong Protestant religious beliefs and fully embraced European culture.[38]

However, throughout her adult life she did not fully trust White Europeans, whom she knew from hard experience could often not be trusted to do the right thing. While she believed that her fellow Mohawks could benefit from Protestant Christianity, this could only happen "if they were taught, as they seek to be, and had good examples set before them" by the English and Dutch and "were not so deceived and cheated by the Christians who ought to assist them." Having observed firsthand the corruption among the Jesuits of New France, she was well aware that some Christians could not be trusted to look after the interests of the Five Nations and that strong guardrails needed to be in place to prevent abuses of power.[39]

Thus, although both her late father and husband were of Dutch ancestry, she maintained a strong distrust of Euro-Americans, having witnessed firsthand their abuse, treachery, and bellicosity. While working as a housekeeper in the early 1680s before her second career as a translator, she had one day gently admonished some rough Dutchmen of Schenectady for their public drunkenness and foul language in her presence. In response, they bristled, "Well, how is this, there is a sow converted. Run boys, to the brewer's and bring some swill for a converted sow."[40] Unable to see her as an equal, the Dutch bullies refused to believe that the "half-breed" standing before them could have transformed herself into a practicing Christian of her own free will. Instead, they considered her the chattel of the Dutch, who "could be sustained as much by the slop from the distillery—swill, the waste product commonly fed to hogs—as by the teachings of Christ."[41]

Due to her mixed blood, she also continued to be rejected by some of her fellow Mohawks. Like her mother, Ots-Toch, who had beaten her for her interest in Christianity as a teenager, when she was merely trying to find meaning in a rapidly changing world, a minority of the Iroquois in Tionnontoguen and the other "castles" regarded her allegiance to her late Dutch father and husband's community as problematic. But her ability as a translator and strong Mohawk kinship ties ensured her a continuing strong "alliance in Haudenosaunee society" and the firm support of the tribal headmen.[42] Throughout her life, she was held in high regard by both the Iroquois and the Anglo-Dutch of Albany and Schenectady for her strong-willed but affable nature, quick mind, honesty, and unrivalled skills as a translator. In fact, despite "her twin handicaps as a woman and a métis," many people considered her to be a far better person than her Dutch tailor husband and believed that Peter Danielse van Olinda was fortunate to have married her.[43] "She spoke with such feeling and tenderness, such depth of love," wrote the Dutch traveler Jasper Danckaerts, "that I cannot describe it, and it affected me. . . . Her husband is not as good as she is, though he is not one of the worst; she sets a good example before him, and knows how to direct him."[44]

Throughout the mid-1690s, Hilletie, Lawrence, and other Christian Mohawks continued as "valuable informants" by passing along intelligence obtained from Kahnawake and the other mission communities in the St. Lawrence Valley.[45] The information provided by Hilletie, Lawrence, and other cross-cultural liaisons was used to support English incursions into Canada and defense against French invasion, but it was also used to sustain mutual nonaggression and promote peace between the kindred League and Canadian Iroquois. Their intelligence also directly benefited New York's new colonial governor, Benjamin Fletcher, upon whom the Iroquois would soon bestow their own special honorific.

Upon his return to New York City, Fletcher set about improving the province's defenses and appealing to other colonies for military aid. Whitehall recognized that heavily taxed New York continued to bear the brunt of the costs and manpower in King William's War and that coordination between the northeastern colonies was critical if the French were to be defeated.[46] In fact, Queen Mary herself had on October 11 written Sir William Phips in Massachusetts, as well as the governors of Connecticut, Rhode Island, Virginia, Maryland, and Pennsylvania, requesting that they send Fletcher immediate "aid and assistance" in militia, provisions, and money and institute a quota system for supplying provincial troops.[47]

During Fletcher's visit to Albany, Schuyler had warned him that there was a vast difference between royal prerogatives transmitted across an ocean and actual intercolonial cooperation. The governor would soon learn that lesson the hard way, as the New England colonies and New York's other neighbors continued to care more about protecting their charter and proprietary privileges, remaining economically independent, and resisting absorption into a larger New York dominion than cooperating in King William's War.[48]

Fletcher's spat with Sir William Phips and the witch-hanging Puritans of New England—with whom Peter Schuyler, as mayor of Albany, had long had troubles—was particularly acrimonious. A new charter had been issued in 1691 that united the colonies of Massachusetts Bay, Plymouth, and Maine as the Province of Massachusetts Bay, stretching all the way from the Canadian border to Connecticut. When requested by the Crown and Fletcher to send troops to protect the Albany frontier, Phips flew into a rage, fuming that "he would send neither a man nor a farthing of money to the assistance of New York."[49] Not only did the "New England buccaneer" resist the Crown's quota system and Fletcher's pleas for aid, he and his Massachusetts officials bombarded the Lords of Trade in London with endless written complaints and sent over their own lobbyists to justify their opposition to supporting the war effort.[50]

The battle between Fletcher and Phips and their colonies was exacerbated by the continuing partisan warfare over the legacy of Jacob Leisler.[51] The Puritans of Massachusetts were for the most part pro-Leislerian due to their strong anti-Catholic sentiments. But the principal conflict between Fletcher and Phips was due to Fletcher's protection of persecuted men and women fleeing the New England colonies over the Salem witch trials. Between February 1692 and May 1693, more than two hundred people were accused of witchcraft in Salem and thirty were found guilty. Many of those accused, and even some tried and found guilty, managed to escape to New York Province, which frowned upon the witch trials and eventually helped shut them down on humanitarian grounds. Of the thirty Massachusetts citizens found guilty of witchcraft, fourteen women and six men total were put to death—along with *two dogs*. One of the unfortunate men "was crushed to death by stones for refusing to enter a plea."[52]

An early proponent of the trials, Phips had pushed hard for the prosecutions of the alleged "witches" in his province. However, the fugitives in Massachusetts, and later Connecticut and Rhode Island, discovered that New York provided a safe haven and fled to the colony in droves. Not only did Fletcher disapprove of the hanging of innocent people for the unprovable crime of "witchery," the governor of liberal New York had little inclination to arrest the escapees and return them to Massachusetts when Phips was obstructing him from performing his job. Fletcher and his fellow New Yorkers did far more than merely ignore the law. They welcomed the purported "witches" with open arms, took them into their homes, and provided food and shelter until the hysteria blew over.[53] "His Excellency Benjamin Fletcher, Esq., Governor . . . was very courteous to us," wrote reputable Boston mariner Captain Nathaniel Cary, "and some others that had escaped their cruel hands."[54]

Peter Schuyler and his fellow Albanians also provided refuge for the falsely accused New Englanders due to the strong Dutch cultural influence. New York's Dutch population had always been skeptical of English New England's rigid and narrow-minded Puritans. Consequently, they played a huge role in mitigating the severity of witchcraft accusations throughout the province.

Unfortunately for both Schuyler and Fletcher, the tension between Fletcher and Phips, and between New York and her other neighboring provinces, would only harden. Massachusetts and the other Puritan colonies, as well as Quaker Pennsylvania, would continue to show little interest in helping New York defend the Albany frontier from French attack. In the end, the Mother Country's efforts to unite the northeastern colonies under one command would not result in intercolonial cooperation in King William's War, but instead lead to united political opposition to Fletcher himself.[55]

As New York had been three years earlier during Leisler's Rebellion, the colony was by late 1692 once again bickering, disunited, and vulnerable to attack from New France.[56] Thus, on the eve of the third anniversary of the Schenectady Massacre, the timing could not have been better for the opportunistic Count Frontenac to unleash his Franco-Indian legions for a long overdue counterstroke on poorly defended New York and Iroquoia.

14
THE 1693 FRONTENAC EXPEDITION

On January 15, 1693, an army of more than four hundred French regulars and Canadian militia and two hundred Native allies marched out of Montreal on the same southern route taken during the winter attack on Schenectady three years earlier. The French were led by Lieutenant Nicolas d'Ailleboust de Manthet, a veteran of Schenectady, and Lieutenants Augustin Le Gardeur de Courtemanche and Zacharie Robutel de La Noue, all three of whom were specifically requested by their Canadian Indian auxiliaries. The Indigenous force consisted of 120 Kahnawake Iroquois and 80 Wendats, Abenakis, Algonquins, and Sokokis from southern Canada and the Laurentian missions near Montreal.[1]

The orders of the war party were "to proceed against and destroy" the three easternmost Mohawk villages on the Mohawk River and "afterward to commit as great ravages as possible around Orange [Albany]."[2] Along with the complete destruction of the Mohawk stockades and the killing of all men "found under arms," the women and children were to be rounded up and taken prisoner "to populate" New France's Iroquois missions.[3] In capturing a large number of Mohawks, Frontenac wanted to punish the Anglophile Iroquois, bolster the numerical strength of his Canadian warrior population, and humiliate the new English royal governor of New York.[4]

Just as they had at Schenectady three years earlier, the Laurentian Kahnawake Iroquois would take part in a major French military offensive against the English and Five Nations. However, like Lawrence and their

Mohawk kin to the south and the Francophile Great Mohawk Togouiroui at Schenectady, they would "place Iroquois interests ahead of those of their European allies and sponsors," both during the battle and its immediate aftermath.[5]

For more than a year now, Frontenac had been anxious to avenge Schuyler and Lawrence's La Prairie attack and pummel the Iroquois Confederation into submission. Though the Mohawks were not the largest among the Five Nations, Frontenac continued to regard them as the fiercest fighters and wily diplomats who undercut his authority.[6] This made their "humiliation" a matter of great "importance" to him and his fellow French officials. He remained convinced that an invasion of Mohawk country would bring an end to the "frequent negotiations" and "secret communications" between the Five Nations and their Laurentian "brethren and relatives" up north, whom Frontenac patriarchally referred to as "our Indians."[7]

For three weeks, the snowshoe-clad, moose-skin-wrapped invasion force pushed southward over the ice of Lake Champlain and heavy snow of modern-day Saratoga County. Dragging their supplies on toboggans, the half-mile-long procession followed the same major north-south thoroughfare that would continue to be used by large Euro-Native war parties throughout all four French and Indian Wars, the American Revolution, and the War of 1812.[8]

At nightfall on February 8, the 625-man force arrived undetected at the two easternmost Mohawk "castles" of Gandagaro and Caughnawaga. The two fortified villages consisted of a series of wooden longhouses and smaller cabins surrounded by a rectangular stockade of sharpened logs and enclosed with strong gates. Here the veteran of Schenectady, Lieutenant Manthet, dispatched his Laurentian Native scouts and some French officers and Canadian voyageurs to reconnoiter the two "little Mohawk forts." The separate scouting parties soon returned to report that although there were no sentries posted at either stockade, the gates were locked and they heard Mohawk men, women, and children peacefully singing inside. The lieutenant and his officers decided to hold off from the attack "until the Indians should retire in order to surprise them whilst sleeping."[9]

It is at this critical juncture, as the war party lay anxiously waiting in the frigid cold for the singing voices to hush, that two young Dutchmen who had been captured three years earlier at Schenectady, Jan Baptist van Eps and Arnout Viele the Younger, either escaped or were quietly released by their Kahnawake Iroquois captors and dashed off into the dark night. After transporting them under guard back to their homeland, the Indians may have released them so they could give advanced warning and thus spare Iroquois lives, much as Lawrence had delivered the Indigenous captives to the Kahnawake Iroquois outside Montreal as a gesture of good faith in March 1691. Familiar with the local terrain, Eps and Viele pushed quickly eastward through the heavy snow drifts in the direction of nearby Schenectady to raise the alarm.[10]

Meanwhile, Manthet split his forces into two battalions for a simultaneous attack on the two stockades. He and Lieutenant Courtemanche led one column for the assault on Gandagaro, while Lieutenant La Noue remained behind with the second force to attack Caughnawaga. Once the singing stopped, the battalions surrounded the two villages, blocking the gates and other potential escape routes. A handful of Indian scouts, their faces darkened with soot and vermilion war paint, were then dispatched to scale the wooden bastions and stealthily open the gates for the attackers.[11]

The two forces, each more than 250-men strong, poured into the heavily fortified villages. But to their surprise, they found both Mohawk stockades virtually empty since most of the braves were out on a winter hunt. At Caughnawaga, Lieutenant La Noue found the village abandoned by all but five men and several women and children, whom they "experienced no difficulty in overpowering."[12] At Gandagaro, Lieutenants Manthet and Courtemanche "found still fewer people" and swiftly "became masters of all the cabins without resistance."[13] Despite Frontenac's explicit order not to give any quarter to the Mohawk men, not a single male was killed. With the two villages taken by surprise, the elder warriors and young boys remaining behind did not put up a fight, but the main reason they were spared was because the Laurentian Iroquois zealously protected both the male and female Indigenous captives, their kinfolk.[14]

After putting the torch to Caughnawaga and posting Courtemanche with a guard detail at Gandagaro to secure the twenty-odd Mohawk prisoners, Manthet set out the next morning with La Noue and a force of around six hundred men for Tionnontoguen. The westernmost, largest, and best-defended of the three Mohawk settlements, the stockaded town was home to 350 villagers.[15] Reaching the third Mohawk "castle" after darkness on February 10, the French and their Native allies "were surprised to hear great uproar and war songs." At first, they were worried that they had been discovered, "but it turned out to be some forty warriors who were about to join a large party that was organizing at Oneida." Shivering in the frigid winter air, the French war party waited until the singing stopped before sneaking in "to open the gates of the fort into which an entrance was easily effected."[16]

Manthet and his four hundred French Troupes de la Marine and Canadian militia and 200 Indigenous warriors poured through the open gates unopposed. Screaming at the tops of their lungs, they busted open the longhouse doors, fired their muskets and pistols, and hacked away with swords, tomahawks, battle axes, and war clubs at the terrified villagers, few of whom had time to snatch their weapons and mount resistance. Outnumbering the League Mohawk men more than two to one, the raiders carried the town in less than fifteen minutes, losing only one French soldier killed and a single warrior wounded.[17]

Once the smoke cleared and the final tally was in, the French war party had killed some twenty-five Tionnontoguen Mohawk men and a handful of women and taken more than three hundred men, women, and children prisoner. Meanwhile, a dozen or so had managed to escape into the woods and strike out for Schenectady to warn their English allies. Two days later, after drinking themselves into a stupor on a discovered cache of rum, the victors burned Tionnontoguen to the ground and retreated to Gandagaro with the prisoners, who would replenish the ranks of the war-depleted Laurentian Iroquois communities outside Montreal. Here Manthet and his French officers tried to convince their Native allies to push on to Albany with them, burn Fort Frederick to the ground, and kill as many settlers as possible before the English could mount a rescue and reprisal party.[18]

But unbeknownst to the French, their fate was already sealed. At 2:00 P.M. on Wednesday, February 8, the same day that the first two Mohawk forts were attacked, Major Richard Ingoldsby and Major Peter Schuyler were notified in Albany of Frontenac's invasion of Mohawk country. Acutely aware of his military obligations under the Covenant Chain, Brother Quider wanted to take swift and decisive action on behalf of his Iroquois brethren and their traumatized families. But unfortunately, the glacially slow and by-the-book Ingoldsby stood in his way.[19]

Both cautious and bombastic by nature, the English major who had defeated Leisler and retaken Fort William on Manhattan with the help of Captain Kidd refused to allow Schuyler to engage the French until he had assembled all the available troops from Albany, Esopus, and New York City. However, by February 13, Schuyler could stand no more of Ingoldsby's foot-dragging and proceeded without orders to pursue, counterattack, and recover the captives from the retreating enemy force. With the English-allied Iroquois furious with Ingoldsby and close to desertion, the colonial American backwoodsman and major of the New York militia could wait no longer for the dillydallying Crown's man.[20]

Marching northward in defiance of the orders of his commanding officer, he sent word to the dispersed Mohawk hunting parties to join him and his Albany force in the pursuit. On February 16, three days after learning that the French and their Indian allies had burned all three Mohawk "castles" to the ground and were withdrawing for Montreal with the prisoners, he and his fast-moving army of 250 militiamen and 290 Mohawk "men and boys" that included his trusted war captain Lawrence caught up to the rear of the retreating enemy column.[21]

Schuyler immediately ordered a reconnaissance. The enemy had felled trees and constructed a strong defensive fortification, or abatis, to fend off attack and corral the prisoners. After surveying the French and Indian forces, Lawrence and his Mohawk scouts estimated the enemy's strength at six hundred to seven hundred men, which was in agreement with the report of the young escaped Dutchman Arnout Viele. The number of Mohawk prisoners still under French captivity was just over 150, Lawrence and his scouts reported, with just under half of the original 320 captives having already escaped due to lax guarding by their kindred Laurentian Iroquois, or from having been left behind because they were holding up the retreating column. With the fresh intelligence, Schuyler was confident that his battle odds were close to even, since the French would have to guard their prisoners during the fight. He then "sent an express to Major Ingoldsby to acquaint him that the enemy had built a fort and were resolved to fight us" and to send "supplies of provision, ammunition and men." Not only was Schuyler running low on food, but some of his Mohawk allies had no muskets and were armed with only bows and arrows.[22]

On Friday, February 17, 1693, after reconnoitering Manthet's improvised fortifications and troop deployments, Schuyler assembled his officers and commanded them "to take their posts and make ready to engage." There would be no parley with the French holding 150 Mohawk men, women, and children captive. The French responded by giving three loud huzzahs, which Schuyler and his men "answered" heartily by making "the woods ring."[23] As the two sides prepared to wage war in the frontier fashion, the League Mohawks and New York militiamen went quickly to work gathering fallen logs, chopping down trees, and constructing their own makeshift fortification to counter the enemy's "retrenchment."[24]

Not wanting the English and their Native allies to barricade "themselves behind a large abatis of trees," Manthet gave the command for an all-out attack on Schuyler's position, leaving behind only enough men to guard the Mohawk prisoners.[25] "The forest rang with war whoops," as several hundred Frenchmen and Kahnawake Iroquois, Wendat, Abenaki, Algonquin, and Sokoki warriors charged forward to "dislodge" the enemy. "The attack was fierce, and the resistance equally so. Both sides lost ground by turns."[26] During this initial charge, the French and English both lost eight or more men. But it was Manthet's French regulars, Canadian militia, and Native allies who were forced to retreat back "into their fort" under a withering volley of musketry from the Albanian militiamen and Lawrence and his hardy Mohawk sharpshooters.[27]

With the enemy repelled, Schuyler's force worked frenetically to pile up more fallen trees and brush to reinforce their defensive works. But there wasn't sufficient time to erect a full barricade, or tend to the wounded, as the French and Indian war party quickly regrouped and made a second frontal assault on the English position. "The enemy sallied out with all their strength," wrote Schuyler in his battlefield report, "encouraging their men, crying as they ran, we will cut them all off and get their provisions. We received them briskly and beat them back into their fort with the loss of several of their men."[28]

After regrouping, Manthet ordered a third concerted attack on Schuyler's position, which was becoming more impregnable by the minute as the Albany militiamen and Mohawk warriors scrambled to pile up more felled trees and brush. At this point, many of the French-allied Algonquins and Kahnawake Iroquois had seen enough bloodshed and were content to let Lieutenant Manthet and his Frenchmen drive off the Anglo-Iroquois attackers on their own.[29] Refusing to take part in any more frontal assaults, they remained behind in the improvised stockade to guard the Mohawk prisoners rather than die in the mind-bogglingly deadly European manner they considered dishonorable compared to their Indigenous way of fighting.[30]

The enemy was "repulsed" once again, wrote Schuyler. But this time, they were beaten "back into their fort with considerable loss" and the triumphant Mohawks carried "several of their heads and scalps into our fort."[31] The third attack on "the enemy's retrenchments was very vigorous," wrote a French observer. "[We would] have succeeded in driving them altogether from their position had not many of the French been occupied in removing the dead and the wounded, and had not several Indians remained in the fort, doing nothing."[32]

Once the smoke cleared, the French broke off the engagement to lick their wounds and Schuyler held the field, just as he had at the two Battles of La Prairie. In the three unsuccessful attacks to dislodge the English, Manthet had lost thirty-three men killed, including two officers, and twenty-six seriously wounded. Given his heavy casualties and the unwillingness of his Native allies to sacrifice their lives for nothing in a European-style suicide mission, he dared not risk another bloody charge.[33]

But the English and their Mohawk allies were just as tired, hungry, and battered, having "lost four private soldiers and 4 Indians" and "two officers and 12 Christians and Indians wounded." While the Albany militiamen and Mohawks worked furiously to build up their makeshift timber fortress to fend off further attack, Schuyler sent a dispatch to Ingoldsby briefing him on the battle and "praying him to hasten our recruits with provisions and ammunition for the greatest part of the men had not had any provision in 2 days' time." He sent out scouts throughout the night to probe Manthet's position and keep an eye on his movements, as the exhausted New Yorkers and Mohawks struggled to keep warm "in the extreme bad cold snowy weather."[34]

The next morning, February 18, the French packed up and withdrew in good military order, carrying their wounded on litters, or improvised stretchers, their retreat aided by a blinding snowstorm. When Lawrence and his Mohawk scouts reported the French on the move, Schuyler commanded his officers "to pursue them to hinder their retreat, till men and provisions came up." However, his cold and hungry troops insisted upon waiting for the supplies to arrive and "refused to march."[35]

Schuyler would have none of it. In a fiery oration, he reminded them that the Mohawk men, women, and children were counting on them for their liberation and that they must continue to harass the enemy. Shamed into compliance, sixty provincials and one hundred Mohawks quickly assembled and pursued the enemy to its next fortified campsite, where a smaller force was dispatched to closely monitor "their motion." Unbeknownst to Schuyler, the French were themselves running perilously short of food and close to the breaking point in the freezing cold, with the League captives barely guarded by their Kahnawake Iroquois brethren and a handful sneaking away every day.[36]

When the convoy carrying the provisions arrived the following morning, Schuyler quickly ordered the men to fall into line to receive their ration of five biscuits per man. After the first eighty men were fed, he dispatched them under his younger brother, Captain Arent Schuyler, and another officer to pursue the retreating French column. By four that afternoon, they had caught up to the fleeing enemy once again. Upon learning that the French were less than a mile away, the major consulted with Lawrence and his League allies. Schuyler wanted them to join him and his advance party and "fall upon" the enemy's rear while the rest of the force "came up, sending in the meantime to our people to march in all haste."[37]

But the Mohawks refused to allow any attack to be undertaken. The French had by this time released several Mohawk prisoners, who informed Lawrence and his scouts that Lieutenant Manthet and the French had threatened to kill the remaining captives if the English attacked the retreating column. The three days prior to the winter storm, a thaw had set in, and as Manthet had neared the Hudson, he had realized that with the ice breaking up and difficult to traverse, he needed to delay his pursuers to allow him and his men to secure a crossing with their gravely wounded troops having to be carried on the cumbersome litters. His solution was to send back a handful of the captives to warn their kin of the consequences of an English assault. Whether the French commander intended to follow through with his dire threat or not, it proved to be a clever tactic. Schuyler was forced to back off from an all-out attack and hold a lengthy council with his Indian allies, costing him critical time and threatening to undermine his fragile alliance with the Mohawks.[38]

Late on February 18, the French and their Indigenous allies were able to cross the Hudson where a large sheet of ice had become wedged at a turn in the river to form a temporary bridge.[39] Though Schuyler and his vanguard "marched with all speed thinking to overtake the enemy before they got to the river's side," they were too late and forced to camp beside the Hudson that night. The next morning, the frustrated major "resolved to march over the river to pursue the enemy, ordering the officers to get their men ready for that purpose." But with his men exhausted from ten straight days of marching through deep winter snow and "their shoes quite worn out and provisions scarce," they were unable "to make any further pursuit." Furthermore, with the Mohawks still reluctant "to fall upon the enemy because of their wives and children," Schuyler had no choice but to abandon the chase and return to Albany.[40]

On the way home, Lawrence and the Mohawks sifted through the burnt blankets, baggage, and kettles left behind and the enemy bodies lying semi-frozen on the field. Some of the dead Frenchmen the hungry warriors cut up into pieces, roasted or boiled in a soup, and consumed in a ritualized act that bestowed upon them their vanquished enemy's spiritual power. When Brother Quider was invited to share some broth with a group of his Mohawk friends, he sat down with them and consumed a bowl, but when they dipped the ladle into the kettle to refill his bowl and a Frenchman's hand appeared, that "put an end to his appetite."[41]

At the Hudson, the French had gained a reprieve but the worst was not yet behind them. When the retreating party reached Lake George in late February, the melting ice would not bear their weight and they were forced to scrabble over the rocky shoreline and local hillocks, navigating their way through slushy snow and matted thickets. At this still-desperate stage, many of the Laurentian Iroquois and other warriors parted company with the beleaguered French column to hunt. Since the Indians "alone were masters of the prisoners" and did not guard them "very strictly," wrote one French official, many of the prisoners "escaped" at this time, thus undermining one of the key objectives of the expedition: replenishing the ranks of the Laurentian Iroquois settlements outside Montreal.[42]

The situation worsened two days later when Manthet reached the shores of Lake Champlain. Not only did he now retain a mere fifty-eight Mohawks out of the 320 originally captured, his critical food stores cached along the far shore for the return journey to Montreal had spoiled.[43] He and his men were still more than one hundred miles from Montreal, "with no food and the wounded to transport through the wet, clinging snow which made the mere lifting of a snowshoed foot hard work."[44]

The French commander dispatched four tribesmen and a Canadian coureur de bois to push for Montreal, notify Callière of their terrible plight, and obtain food and supplies for those left behind. By this point, the men had been totally abandoned by their Native allies and were reduced to boiling their moccasins for broth and scraping away the snow to find hickory and beech nuts. While Lieutenant Manthet and those still able to walk had struggled onward a few miles, two of his officers, all of his wounded men, and 120 men who were too weak to move had been left behind on the shore of Lake Champlain. Although Callière immediately sent 150 men with supplies to feed and clothe the stranded army, by the time the relief column arrived days later several men had died of famine and exposure.[45]

Nineteen days after the skirmish with Schuyler and two weeks after being deserted by their Indigenous allies, Manthet and his cadaverous French soldiers staggered into Montreal, most having tossed away their muskets, blankets, and fur cloaks to lighten their loads.[46] "Everyone reached Montreal so exhausted by the fatigue of the march and by hunger," wrote Monseignat, Frontenac's secretary, "that only those who saw them could understand what they had been through."[47] Having been abandoned by most of their Kahnawake Iroquois, Wendat, Algonquin, and other Indigenous auxiliaries, and with more than 250 League prisoners having liberated themselves from captivity during the return to Montreal, the French troopers and Canadian militiamen cursed what they viewed as the "false pity" of their Iroquois allies toward their kindred Mohawk prisoners, whom they had allowed to escape in droves.[48]

Back in November 1692, when Frontenac had first instituted a bounty policy for his Indian allies, he had offered them thirty-three livres ($825 today) per League Iroquois scalp or prisoner, with the reward doubled for each Iroquois prisoner handed over alive to French officials. Although a number of the Francophile Native allies collected bounty payments for the Mohawks captured from the three castles in February 1693, "no more than five Mohawk men and a handful of women and children ended up as prisoners in the Laurentian settlements."[49] In the end, Frontenac's ambitious expedition had failed miserably in its primary objective of restocking the Iroquois population around Montreal.

The total French losses upon the return of Manthet and his men to Canada were eighty men dead and thirty-three wounded, several of whom were in extremis and later died.[50] Despite the fact that the French survivors who straggled into Montreal "were so wasted by fatigue and hunger that they did not seem like human beings," and although they carried with them a mere 5 percent of the original 320 Indian prisoners taken,[51] Frontenac stubbornly declared the military mission "a glorious success."[52]

When word of the French invasion reached Manhattan on the night of February 12, Governor Benjamin Fletcher mustered 150 militia in less than forty-eight hours and embarked for Albany in eight sloops loaded with provisions and ammunition. Before leaving, he directed Frederick Philipse and the council to ship reinforcements upriver once he set sail and to send word of the attack to Massachusetts, Connecticut, and other colonies with renewed pleas for assistance. With the favorable winds, he was able to navigate through the floating icebergs 150 miles upriver and reach the fur-trading outpost in less than three days, an unprecedented feat.[53]

Upon his arrival to Albany on the morning of the seventeenth, the veteran English footslogger and cavalryman, itching to recapture the glory of battle, marched at the quick step with his troops to Schenectady, where they soon thereafter began crossing the partially iced-over Mohawk River on their way to join Schuyler's pursuing column. By this time, more than two hundred fresh troops had poured into Albany from New York City, Esopus, and Long Island. On February 21, Fletcher received word by messenger that the French had retreated to Montreal and Schuyler was returning after his successful chase. With the battle long since over, the commander in chief recalled his forces and sent them back home.[54] Though Fletcher was unhappy with Ingoldsby's performance in the campaign, he was effusive in his praise of Schuyler, recommending him for promotion to full captain in the regular English Army.[55]

Although Fletcher arrived too late to engage the enemy, his swift response to the crisis in Mohawk country and expeditious delivery of troops and war matériel were greatly appreciated by the Five Nations. They were still angry with Ingoldsby for not warning them of the invasion and for holding back their trusted Brother Quider from promptly pursuing the retreating column. But with the governor having rushed to their aid from Manhattan in the heart of winter with hundreds of men and ample provisions, the Iroquois could not help but be impressed, recognizing the difference between genuine effort and empty bluster.[56]

With the Albany frontier stabilized, Fletcher invited the League Iroquois headmen and war leaders who had accompanied Schuyler's rescue party to meet in a council at Albany. During the meeting with the tribal leaders, the two sides communicated as usual through Hilletie van Olinda, who informed the governor that his Native allies had bestowed upon him a new name as a supreme compliment. His furious 150-mile sprint under full sail upriver with "so many men for their relief when the enemy had fallen on the Castles" had earned him the title by which he would henceforth be known to the Five Nations: Cayenquiragoe, or "Great Swift Arrow." The Iroquois had chosen the venerable moniker not only because he had rushed to their aid but since his English surname meant "arrow-maker."[57]

In his speech translated by Hilletie, the old soldier was polite but direct. He apologized for having failed to bring presents in the usual Iroquois manner of reciprocal friendship, but he had come in "great haste," and he offered them his condolences for the loss of their beloved family members. He would soon have a shipment of corn for them and their trusted Quider would provide a safe refuge where they would live and be cared for until their stockaded villages could be rebuilt. However, while he condoled them for their losses, he confessed he was shocked that his "Brethren," the mighty Mohawks, the Keepers of the Eastern Door of the Longhouse of the Five Nations, could be "so supine and careless as to suffer the French and the Indians to enter their Castles without the least resistance." To avoid the calamity that had befallen them in the future, they needed to conduct improved scouting patrols and maintain constant alertness. He further urged them to join with their New York allies under the Covenant Chain in the near future for a large-scale attack on New France as a matter of "honor and reputation" and to exact "a severe revenge."[58]

As usual, the Iroquois tribal elders, well versed in the delicate art of diplomacy, pushed back with admonishments of their own. They had heard the same stern, patriarchal lecture about their cavalier scouting and shoddy defense from the past several "Brother Corlaers" and, even though they were in mourning, they were not the least bit intimidated by the Great Swift

Arrow's tough talk. They politely informed him that they were in no condition to undertake reprisal attacks any time soon, since they needed time for their communities to heal and to grieve for their dead.[59] Given their recent losses, they were also going to need more guns, powder, and ammunition if they were to take the fight to the French. "Some of our men," complained the Onondaga headman Aqueendara, "have guns but no powder and ball and some but bows and arrows . . . whereas the Governor of Canada supplies his Indians with all sorts of arms and ammunition, which we found when we engaged them."[60]

Despite the criticism on both sides, the two parties remained committed allies and the council ended on a positive note. Lawrence, his fellow Christian Mohawks, and the other Anglophile leaders recognized that the Great Swift Arrow was a no-nonsense soldier, who had rushed to their defense and was committed to providing them with critical food stores to get through the winter, as well as arms and ammunition to hunt and wage war. He had also offered to help them relocate their burned-down villages to safer locations on the south side of the Mohawk River and to provide them with a local gunsmith to repair their firearms so they could hunt and better defend themselves. In return for the Great Swift Arrow's generosity, the Five Nations' representatives agreed to resume the war against the French as soon as they had condoled their dead.[61]

But once again, it was Brother Quider upon whom they bestowed their most fulsome praise, for it was he who had come to the rescue of the Five Nations and dashed Frontenac's hopes of realizing a major victory. In disobeying Ingoldsby's orders and aggressively pursuing the retreating French and Indian attackers, Schuyler had succeeded in recovering more than 80 percent of the Mohawk men, women, and children still being held captive when he had first engaged the enemy, thus saving face for Ingoldsby's failings.[62] As one 1690s Iroquois leader later declared, "During the whole War, all the succor and relief that ever we had was from Colonel Peter Schuyler."[63]

By the summer of 1693, Lawrence and his League Mohawks had largely recovered from the French invasion of their homeland and the Great Swift Arrow made good on his pledge of generous gifts to help the Iroquois wipe away their tears for their losses. In June, the Mohawks were once again conducting retaliatory raids on French settlements, and by mid-August they had rebuilt their new and better-protected settlements. Though their fields had been devastated, their villages burned, and many of their bravest warriors slain in battle, they had not only regrouped but were gaining in strength.[64]

While a few Mohawks relocated to the Kahnawake mission outside Montreal shortly after Frontenac's invasion, most seized the opportunity to reorganize their Mohawk River Valley settlements. The Turtle Clan residents of Caughnawaga and Bear Clan residents of Gandagaro moved upriver from their preinvasion locations and formed the new Mohawk "Upper Castle" at Canajoharie. Meanwhile, Lawrence, his wife Maria and their two sons, and the other villagers of the westernmost Wolf Clan town of Tionnontoguen relocated to an eastern site overlooking Schoharie Creek that they named Tiononderoge and that now served as the "Lower Castle" of the Mohawks. The bellicose French and their Native allies had reduced the number of settlements of the Kanien'kehá:ka—the People of the Flint and Keepers of the Eastern Longhouse Door—in the Mohawk River Valley from four "castles" in 1680 to just two by 1693. But the Mohawks and other Four Iroquois Nations had proven that they were unusually resilient people in times of crisis.[65]

In early July, Fletcher met once again with the Iroquois at Albany to console the Mohawks for their losses and renew the Covenant Chain. During the conference, he distributed the Crown's gifts as he had promised five months earlier, while again warning the headmen to maintain their vigilance against French attack and to reject the false peace overtures from Frontenac and the French. This time, the Iroquois were far more impressed with his oration since it was accompanied by an unprecedentedly lavish distribution of presents, including 86 muskets, 800 pounds of powder, 800 bars of lead, 576 knives, 87 hatchets, 200 loaves of bread, 60 gallons of rum, and a large supply of brass kettles, coats, hats, shirts, tobacco, beer, salt, and other goods for individual headmen.[66] His diplomatic efforts "coincided nicely with Iroquois expectations about generous headmen and the ratification of political ties through ritual exchanges of gifts."[67]

On July 4, following the main conference, the Great Swift Arrow gave "two fat bulls" to the young warriors and then invited "several of the chief sachems and captains of most note and bravery on board their Majesty's ketch *Albrought*." With Schuyler and Hilletie acting as liaisons and interpreting, Fletcher treated Lawrence and the other leaders "to their extraordinary satisfaction," while recounting some of England's recent victories over the French in Europe and on the high seas. Having been wined and dined, Lawrence and his fellow chieftains renewed the Anglo-Iroquois alliance, sang war songs, and promised not to deal directly with the treacherous Yonondio and the French. They also agreed to send any messages intercepted from the French Jesuit priests of Canada to their trusted friend Cayenquiragoe in New York City. At the end of the festivities, Fletcher bade them good night with a five-gun salute, to which Lawrence and the other Iroquois leaders responded with vigorous war whoops.[68]

Although the two sides departed Albany outwardly satisfied, Fletcher, Schuyler, and Hilletie remained unaware that the Iroquois were already in the process of charting an altogether new and different path for their people. The Great Swift Arrow returned to New York City on July 14 to report to his council and London that the Covenant Chain was secure and the Five Nations remained firmly committed to Mother England and vanquishing the French. In appreciation of his skillful leadership during the crisis, the mayor and common council presented him with a gold cup. But the celebration was premature. By the end of the summer, Lawrence and many of his fellow sachems and military leaders would make the strategic decision to support English war aims only to the extent that they promoted the political and trade objectives of the Five Nations, thus preserving Iroquois lives and hegemony in the bitterly contested northeast. While the Confederation remained divided between Anglophile, neutralist, and Francophile factions, the heavy toll from five years of warfare and contagions unleashed by Old World pathogens had brought about a unified turning point in Iroquois diplomacy toward the English and French.[69]

Under the new unofficial Five Nations policy, they would continue minor raids on the French and their Indian enemies in return for English arms and ammunition, while patiently awaiting a general peace between the two European superpowers. From this point on, Lawrence and his League Iroquois aimed to prevent complete dependence upon any one power by keeping lines of communication and trade open to both the English and French, without forming exclusive alliances with either empire.[70] For they knew that only through neutrality and a "spirit of rapprochement" between all the Haudenosaunee could they ensure the survival of their people and their way of life.[71]

15
IMPERIAL WARFARE, IROQUOIS PEACE

On January 4, 1694, Major Peter Schuyler set out on horseback from Albany on a 240-mile round-trip journey to Oneida with the "Mohawk interpretess" Hilletie van Olinda and Albany's new mayor, the Dutch fur trader and longtime envoy to the Iroquois, Dirck Wessels. Having received news of a forthcoming conference between the Five Nations and New France to forge a peace agreement—which New York's officials believed would be conducted on Frontenac's terms and hostile to English interests—Governor Benjamin Fletcher had dispatched his two most trusted Indian Affairs liaisons and his top translator to address the situation. But in the middle of a savage winter, it was hard going for the thirty-six-year-old Schuyler, forty-seven-year-old Hilletie, and fifty-five-year-old Wessels as they plodded through the heavy snowdrifts and over the icy trails. Their first stop along their lengthy journey was the still-rebuilding frontier outpost of Schenectady, nestled in the snow-blanketed lower Mohawk River Valley.[1]

Schuyler and his fellow New York officials had long dreaded the possibility that the Iroquois might submit to one-sided peace terms or surrender outright to the French. This, they believed, would leave the Hudson River Valley open to attack by Frontenac's powerful legions all the way to Manhattan. Schuyler had also been hearing reports from Lawrence and his Iroquois scouts of enemy forays just north of Albany and military preparations at Montreal, which added to his consternation.[2] At this stage of

King William's War, with yet another French attack "expected" along the Albany frontier, Schuyler had been entrusted "with the main responsibility for Iroquois affairs," placing a heavy burden on his shoulders.[3]

Yet, his hands continued to be tied due to the paucity of Crown resources and the feeble military manpower at his disposal. Because of the embarrassing shortfalls in Mother England's support for her Indigenous allies, he had recently begun to despair of Iroquois fidelity nearly as much as Frontenac and Callière in Canada. The only reason the Iroquois didn't abandon the English cause after a half-decade of brutal and destructive warfare was because of his own strenuous efforts and prudent diplomacy.[4] In his letters to Fletcher and others, he continued to plead for firearms, powder, cooking utensils, food, and other supplies for the Five Nations and for more money to pay Indian scouts, couriers, and informants. However, since the beginning of the war, Parliament had never properly funded her American colonies, with the result that the English settlers and Native inhabitants on the front lines suffered the most.[5]

Despite the lack of resources, Schuyler continued to make the most of a difficult situation. He often paid the troops out of his own pocket, even though repayment by the Crown usually took several months, if it came at all.[6] Due to the difficulties raising money, he had to pay some of his scouts and noncommissioned officers an entire year of accumulated back pay out of his private funds. Despite the financial hardships imposed upon him and his frontier Dutch-American family, he declared to his superiors that he would "in all things and on all occasions whatsoever be very ready to discharge my duty for His Majesty's service & country's good."[7]

Shivering against the frigid cold, Schuyler and his party followed what we today call the Old Mohawk Turnpike, an originally Haudenosaunee hunting, trading, and war-making trail used frequently by the Mohawks and Oneidas, extending between modern-day Albany and Rome, New York. With temperatures hovering around zero, their teeth chattered as they pushed westward through heavy snowdrifts piled up along the trail, frequently dismounting to walk on foot on snowshoes and rest their exhausted horses. That night, after covering a rugged twenty miles, they stopped to rest in Schenectady before continuing westward the next morning on the only major link between the Hudson River Valley and Great Lakes, an unimproved dirt trail heaped with snow that would one day become an important national transportation connection.[8]

On January 5, they stopped overnight at the "Praying Mohawk Castle called Tiononderoge," relocated to a hill at the junction of Schoharie Creek and the Mohawk River, before setting out the following morning for "the last" Mohawk castle of Canajoharie. Here the envoys were received "kindly" by "all the Sachems and young Indians [who] were glad to see us," reported Schuyler. With Hilletie translating, they held a council and the Mohawk headmen made a lengthy speech about the long history of friendship and alliance between the English and Iroquois under the Covenant Chain. They spoke of the "former times" with a nostalgic glow but sounded melancholy about the present. "We lie amazed and discomfited upon our knees," they confided to Schuyler and his party, "and know not what we shall do."[9]

Gazing across the council fire at his brethren, after traveling more than forty miles in the frigid winter cold, Brother Quider saw the wisdom, strength, and resilience of the Five Iroquois Nations in the features of the crinkle-faced sachems and the heavily tattooed warriors he had fought alongside in battle. However, after five years of warfare, there was no question that the Mohawks and other Four Nations had fallen on hard times. At the same time, that didn't mean they weren't still the undisputed masters of the continental interior. After all, they still commanded a territory that stretched westward from the Hudson River Valley all the way to Lake Onondaga in modern-day western New York and was bounded to the north by Lake Ontario and to the south by southeastern Pennsylvania. Through a combination of military prowess and savvy diplomacy, they continued to control a trade network that extended throughout a vast swath of northeastern North America.[10]

Through Hilletie, Schuyler informed their hosts about their mission to the Iroquois seat of power at Oneida. In June 1693, an Oneida leader named Tarriha, closely connected to the captive Jesuit priest Father Millet, had traveled to Quebec to conduct peace talks with Frontenac.[11] The French royal governor had declared an informal cessation of hostilities and promised a settlement if the Oneida Francophiles could convince their compatriots of the Onondagas, Cayugas, and Senecas to send "two of the principal and most influential chiefs of each Nation" to meet with him at Quebec. However, if the headmen failed to appear, threatened Frontenac, he vowed to wage war until all Five Nations were "wholly exterminated."[12] Since meeting with the count, Tarriha had returned to Oneida country, and Schuyler informed the Mohawks that he, Hilletie, and Wessels were heading west to meet with the League sachems to decide a course of action regarding the outreach to Frontenac. He wanted a delegation of Mohawk leaders from the village to travel with him to Oneida. Having undertaken "this troublesome journey," he said, "I invite the Brethren to go along with me and help to consult."[13]

As always, Schuyler sought to influence the decisions of the Confederacy council in the English favor, with his goal this time to mitigate the growing influence of Millet and the Francophile faction among the western League Iroquois. This was no easy task given the deteriorating military situation in Iroquoia in the wake of Frontenac's scorched-earth campaign the past winter. But after two days of back-and-forth deliberations, the Mohawks agreed to have four prominent headmen accompany Schuyler and his party to Oneida to support his position before the council. Although they continued to be disappointed with Ingoldsby for his inexplicable failure to warn them and to engage the enemy, and although they complained about the insufficient material aid from the Great Father across the Atlantic, they knew what a herculean effort their Brother Quider, their trusted interpreter Hilletie, and the hardy Wessels had made to travel through knee-deep snow to reach their village. More importantly, they recognized the great lengths Schuyler had gone to chase down Frontenac's retreating force and recover their people the year before.[14]

However, Schuyler's dedication to their welfare and his battlefield exploits were not the only things that continued to endear him to the Iroquois. Six months earlier, in June 1693, the authorities in Springfield, Massachusetts, had imprisoned a young Mohawk man and a Schaghticoke on suspicion of committing murder against several settlers near Deerfield. Knowing the warriors personally and that they were innocent, Schuyler sent his younger brother Johannes, Wessels, and the young interpreter Jan Baptist van Eps to Massachusetts to secure dismissal of the charges against the two falsely accused men.[15] Schuyler's party managed to convince the magistrate John Pynchon to exonerate the prisoners by having van Eps swear out an affidavit that attributed the "marks and figures" on war clubs left at the scene to anonymous "French Indians."[16] Van Eps had been taken prisoner at age seventeen during the 1690 Schenectady raid but had escaped from Laurentian Iroquois captivity during Frontenac's 1693 campaign of total war in the Mohawk River Valley. In the end, the two Native prisoners didn't trust the New England authorities and in August escaped from the Springfield jail, but by then, because of Schuyler's intervention efforts, Pynchon had already decided to rule in favor of the accused Indians and had been about to set them free.[17]

Loaded with fresh provisions, Schuyler and his now seven-person party set off on horseback on the morning of January 9, reaching the charred skeleton of the original Mohawk fort of Tionnontoguen just before dark. Though the wooden stockade, towers, and most of the interior longhouses and cabins had been burned completely to the ground by Frontenac's troops and Indigenous allies the previous winter, they were able to take shelter for the night from the biting cold in the blackened ruins of the once-formidable fortress.[18]

The next day, with temperatures plummeting, they set off westward once again up the river valley, the water vapor steaming from their nostrils as they pushed their way over the hard, frozen ground and pockets of heavy windblown snow. All around them was an endless, wintry landscape of barren white without sightlines except the river and surrounding bluffs. Schuyler and the others could hear their own ragged breathing whenever they dismounted to rest the horses and fought their way on their snowshoes through what soon became waist-deep snow. After ten miles of guiding the horses through the thickening drifts and dismounting again to travel on foot by snowshoe, all seven members of the party were freezing cold and struggling in the heavy snow.[19]

Peering back through the mists of time, one cannot help but marvel at the toughness of the lone female on the dangerous winter expedition. Hilletie van Olinda was indeed one stalwart frontierswoman, this being not her first journey to the frozen, faraway Oneida and Onondaga country as a government liaison. Her granite foundation had been laid during the first two decades of her life growing up in her mother Ots-Toch's Mohawk Wolf Clan village at Tionnontoguen, where she and her siblings Itsychoquachka (Jacques), Martin, and Lea had spent considerable time in the cold rain and snow and backwoods country of what is today rugged western and upstate New York.

As a young Mohawk girl, she had become intimately familiar with the network of trails of the Mohawk River Valley from her frequent excursions with her mother not only to neighboring villages, but to trade in Schenectady and Albany, both located more than forty miles downriver from her Wolf Clan village of Tionnontoguen. She knew the Old Mohawk Turnpike that had been used by the Haudenosaunee for centuries better than even Schuyler and Wessels, as she had lived the past four decades in the wild and untamed borderlands of Indian country. As handy with a knife and musket as a sewing needle and broom, she was well equipped to travel in hard country under harsh winter conditions, keeping pace with men much stronger than herself without a whisper of complaint.

Hardy frontier women like Hilletie were the norm, not the exception, along the 17th-century Albany frontier and in Iroquoia—whether they were biracial Native-Euro-Americans or of Dutch, English, Scottish, French, African, or other stock. Peter Schuyler's widowed mother, Margarita van Slichtenhorst, his first and second wives Angelica van Schaick Schuyler and Maria van Rensselaer Schuyler, and his several daughters were all frontier-savvy women who were often away from "home" and out in the wilds "treating and bargaining and trading" with the various northeastern Native American tribes. Furthermore, they and many of their female contemporaries were noted for their ability in conversing in "the Indian languages." Like Hilletie, they were as handy with a trade musket, flintlock pistol, and the sharp "tube-knives" they carried on their person as they were in roasting haunches of venison in their great brick and Dutch ovens, preparing thick porridges of Indian corn, fire-searing and pickling pailfuls of Gowanus oysters, and baking cakes consisting of eggs, raisins, currants, brandy, and rum mixed in wooden washtubs.[20]

A mile later, the trail became nearly impassable. Even the doggedly determined Schuyler admitted in his journal that the deep snow "made me almost resolve to turn back, being impossible to perform the journey." It was at this critical juncture that the struggling party met with an Iroquois scout, who informed Schuyler and the group that they would not be able to proceed much farther due to the heavy snow. After a conference translated by Hilletie, Schuyler decided to turn back to Canajoharie and send two young Mohawk scouts forward on snowshoes with a belt of wampum to report to the Four Nations at Oneida about the diplomatic crisis and to "come with all speed to Albany" for a meeting of all the Nations. The headmen would be told "expressly" not to send emissaries to Canada until attending the meeting with the entire Confederation present.[21]

Schuyler and his party then started off to the east, retracing their steps back down the Mohawk River Valley. After resting a night at Canajoharie, they bid farewell to the four Mohawk leaders and made their way through the heavy snow back to Albany. They reached the fur-trading outpost on January 12. Although they had failed to make it even halfway to Oneida on their grueling, nine-day, one hundred–mile journey, at least Schuyler had called together a meeting of all the League Iroquois.[22]

The council sessions that began on February 2, 1694, were far more contentious than usual due to the enormous physical and emotional toll of King William's War and growing mistrust on both sides. For Schuyler and Lawrence, the conference revealed for the first time just how far the alliance between the English and Five Nations had slipped since the beginning of the war. Sharp and lively debates had always been part of Indian Affairs proceedings, but this time even the level-headed Schuyler appeared hot under the collar from the very beginning, perhaps because Governor Fletcher—Cayenquiragoe, the Great Swift Arrow—had not even bothered to show up.[23]

The speaker for the Five Nations at the historic conference held at Albany City Hall was a rising Onondaga orator named Teganissorens, the principal advocate for the neutralist faction who stood poised to become the leading Iroquois council spokesperson of his generation.[24] In 1694, he was already known for his "great fluency in speaking" and "graceful elocution."[25] With Hilletie once again serving in her critical but unheralded role as government interpreter, since she often had to wait months before receiving her pay just like Schuyler and the troops, Teganissorens delivered a forceful opening speech. He recounted the Oneida emissary Tarriha's negotiations with Frontenac, the status of the influential captive Jesuit priest Father Millet who continued to worry New York's authorities, and the general state of affairs in Iroquoia. Despite the factional disagreement within the Five Nations, he said, there was a consensus that they had reached the point where they had no choice but to negotiate a cessation of hostilities not only between the League and the French and between the Iroquois and their Indigenous rivals, including the Laurentians, but between the two competing European superpowers as well.[26]

With an exquisite combination of practical reasoning and lofty rhetoric, Teganissorens also tried to heal the growing mistrust between the League Iroquois and their English "Brethren." He openly acknowledged the growing friction between the longtime allies and hoped that the Great Swift Arrow, Brother Quider, and the English could move forward in harmony under the Covenant Chain. "Whatever misunderstandings have arisen between us occasioned by Jesuits' letters or otherwise," he said, "let them be buried in oblivion and our hearts reestablished in love and unity as formerly."[27]

It was a remarkable speech, signifying a huge paradigm shift in Five Nations' diplomacy, and the longtime Anglophile Lawrence, attending the council not as a headman but in his customary role as respected war captain from a prominent Iroquois hereditary family, had to have been deeply moved. Now in the sixth year of the war, Lawrence's political outlook hewed far closer to that of the neutralist Teganissorens than to the young, idealistic war leader he had been when he had chased down Sainte-Hélène and Togouiroui's retreating war party in February 1690, following the attack at Schenectady. Like the charismatic Onondaga orator Teganissorens, he recognized that the Five Nations had no choice but to rely on European trade; however, he hoped to preclude complete cultural capitulation by keeping lines of diplomatic negotiation and trade alliances open to both the English and French, while steering clear of exclusive partnerships with either side. Having undergone a transformation over the past two years, Lawrence understood that the only way for the Iroquois to survive was to remove themselves from the conflict without undercutting ties to either the English or French. There was no other course of action if the Haudenosaunee wanted to control their own destiny.

The day after Teganissorens made his heartfelt oration to open the proceedings and laid down "a Belt of Wampum" in the traditional ceremonial manner, Schuyler provided his "answer to the Five Nations." With Fletcher far down the Hudson in New York City, he unleashed a tirade rarely witnessed at the Albany council meetings. He could never have imagined, he growled to Teganissorens and the other sachems, "that you would be so treacherous to your own interest" as to have "called any meeting to consult" with Frontenac and the French. "None of the Brethren were to hearken in the least to that perfidious enemy," he complained, "but immediately to have sent their messenger and his letters and belt hither." Striking a one-sided deal with the hated French, he said, would "be a mark that you are in the wrong and bring you and posterity into perpetual infamy and slavery to the French forever."[28]

He considered it a personal affront that the Iroquois had conducted independent negotiations with the untrustworthy French when the English had always been there for them. "This Government hath been always true and steadfast to you and ready at all times to protect and defend you against the French, as when they came to hurt you in February last." By holding independent council with the French governor, he said, the Iroquois were deciding the fate of the settlers of New York to which they were linked in arms under the Covenant Chain and allowing Frontenac to turn them into his personal serfs. The treacherous Yonondio and the French had "always done the first mischief, even in time of peace" to the Iroquois, he pointed out to the headmen, which was precisely why they should be taking the "advice and directions" of "his Excellency the Great Swift Arrow" and not the untrustworthy Frontenac.[29]

Teganissorens, Lawrence, and the other Iroquois leaders were taken aback by the stinging rebuke. After all, they were only trying to extricate themselves from the two warring European superpowers to save their own people and preserve their autonomy. But the two sides managed to hash out a working agreement over the next week. Going forward, the League leadership agreed that any negotiations would not proceed without the consent of all Five Nations, that there would be no peace pact unless the English were included, and that the planned visit to Frontenac would be delayed until they had met with Governor Fletcher in "seventy days' time" for a scheduled League meeting.[30]

But in the end, all the careful deliberation and exhaustive diplomatic outreach by Teganissorens, Sadekanaktie, Lawrence, and the other headmen and war leaders on both sides of the conflict went for nought. The deeply divided Five Nations, their English allies, and the French were unable to reach a consensus on anything remotely resembling a peaceful and pragmatic solution to the crisis gripping Iroquoia. Not only did neither Cayenquiragoe nor Yonondio ever fully embrace Teganissorens's comprehensive neutralist peace plan, they were not even authorized, as mere provincial governors, to negotiate peace treaties on behalf of their respective kings. Furthermore, Fletcher could not openly support an Iroquois-brokered security agreement between New York and New France, since that would infuriate Massachusetts Bay and the other New England colonies, which continued to come under heavy attack from the Canadian Algonquin tribes allied with the French.[31]

While Fletcher, Schuyler, and New York's officials did eventually give their blessing to the separate Iroquois peace initiative, the wily Frontenac, ever distrustful of the English and Five Nations and always looking ahead in his imperial chess match for control of North America, used the drawn-out negotiations to regroup and prepare for another all-out invasion of Iroquoia. In mid-May, when Teganissorens appeared at Montreal with ten wampum belts to meet with Frontenac, a group of Jesuit priests, and representatives of the Wendats, Odawas, and Laurentian Iroquois,[32] "an effusion of bicultural ceremony and lofty rhetoric" accompanied the proceedings. However, little was accomplished.[33]

Going into the council, Teganissorens's most pressing concern was Frontenac's plan to reestablish the abandoned fort at Cataraqui that bore his name, and he also wanted to make sure the governor understood that New York would need to be included in any formal treaty negotiations.[34] Bedecked in a scarlet coat trimmed with gold braid and a glittering new beaver hat that he announced were cherished gifts given to him by his "Brother Corlaer," Governor Fletcher, the tall and stately Onondaga orator exchanged wampum belts with the courtier-governor and dined in sumptuous splendor alongside New France's leading dignitaries. But he received little give-and-take from his French counterpart, even after three days of tough bargaining. The only thing that Frontenac agreed to was an eighty-day ceasefire to allow the League to return with all French and French-allied Indigenous prisoners living in Iroquoia. Under the rules of European statecraft, explained Frontenac, he could not authorize a general peace between France, her Indian allies, New York, and the other English colonies, as that high-level approval could come only from the respective Crowns across the Great Water. In the end, all Teganissorens and the Iroquois gained was a brief respite from French assaults due to the prolongation of negotiations and a temporary ceasefire between the League and the Wendats, Odawas, Miamis, and other enemy tribes.[35]

In what was intended as a supreme compliment but today comes across as patriarchal and condescending, a French officer present at the multiday council described Teganissorens's speech as "enunciated with as perfect grace as is vouchsafed to an unpolished and uncivilized people."[36] But despite the Onondaga headman's regal bearing, fine oratory skills, and impressive sartorial accoutrements courtesy of the Great Swift Arrow, the French count refused to permanently abandon Fort Frontenac and continued to reject the idea of the Iroquois serving as mediators in the peace between New France and the English colonies. For Frontenac, diplomacy with the Five Nations was a zero-sum game with no room for compromise and with imperial France as the indisputable master.[37]

By the beginning of 1696, the royal governor had not only dispatched a large force of troops to Cataraqui and rebuilt Fort Frontenac, he was putting together plans for a major invasion of western Onondaga country.

Teganissorens, Sadekanaktie, and Lawrence and his Iroquois scouts had long warned Schuyler and the Albany leaders that the treacherous Yonondio would one day refortify Cataraqui and use it as a forward base to launch another scorched-earth campaign in Oneida, Onondaga, and Seneca country, as he had done in 1693 at the three eastern Mohawk "castles." They had pleaded with their English brethren to help them destroy the fort, but to no avail.[38] Which meant that with one final bold thrust, Frontenac stood poised to eliminate the Five Nations' threat to French imperial designs in North America and to deprive the English of their only significant military ally.[39]

The only remaining question was whether Major Peter Schuyler, his fellow New Yorkers, and the League Iroquois could stop him.

16
WIPING AWAY THE TEARS

On July 31, 1696, a mounted messenger galloped through the Land Gate at Broad Way and Wall Street in New York City and rumbled into Fort William. Carrying an urgent dispatch from up north, the rider promptly informed Governor Benjamin Fletcher that Frontenac was personally leading an attack in Onondaga and Oneida country with some seventeen hundred French Troupes de la Marine and Canadian militia and five hundred Indigenous allies. The enemy had forced the evacuation of the Onondaga stockade, burned the fortified village and corn stores at Oneida, and taken a large number of Confederation captives. The essential foods of Iroquoia were the "three sisters" of corn, beans, and squash—and with these critical resources destroyed, it would be a hard winter for the western Five Nations. But even worse, it appeared nothing could stop Frontenac's fast-moving French and Indian army from pushing all the way to Albany.[1]

For Benjamin Fletcher and the people of New York City, the military situation was equally frantic and alarming. Three weeks earlier, the governor had received intelligence of an impending French attack by sea upon the City. With the latest reports that Frontenac's forces were wreaking havoc in Onondaga and Oneida near modern-day Syracuse, it now appeared that Frontenac's coordinated invasion by both land and sea had finally begun. With the Five Nations pleading for help from their English allies under the Covenant Chain, Frederick Philipse and four of his fellow councilors stepped up with £200 ($70,000 today) in private funding to send a New York relief force to Iroquoia, since no public monies were currently available due to the Crown's neglect.[2]

Fearing that Frontenac, if left unchecked, would overrun Iroquoia while simultaneously sacking New York City by sea, the governor commanded the king's official printer, William Bradford, to issue a war proclamation at his shop, the Sign of the Bible. Bradford had been run out of Philadelphia in 1693 for printing materials in opposition to piracy, which was widely supported in New York and other American colonies provided the predations were committed against Catholic or Muslim nations, since commerce raiding and smuggling brought in significant gold bullion, silver specie, trade goods, weapons, and clothing into the major ports. Bradford had been quickly scooped up and made New York's official printer by Fletcher, who recognized "the benefits of having a printer closely aligned with the government."[3] Fletcher had Bradford declare the province in a state of emergency in preparation for "an anticipated attack by the French"[4] and commanded all New Yorkers "to have their arms in order" and "the militia to be called out."[5] Anyone who spotted three or more vessels upon the coast was required to report immediately to the authorities; and the next day, the city council directed that citizens at the highlands of Navesink were to be on the lookout for French warships.[6]

At this point, all of Manhattan was in a war panic. Not only were there rumors of an all-out French invasion, but the City was crippled by bread shortages due to war-profiteering merchants, who had exported most of the province's flour to line their own pockets. The scarcity had become so acute that the city council passed an ordinance on June 10 ordering that "no person or persons shall presume to bake bread, biscuit, or cookies of any sort or kind whatsoever within this city without entering their names with the mayor."[7]

As fate would have it, the sole protector of Manhattan Island from French seaborne attack in the summer of 1696 was none other than the legendary Captain William Kidd. The friend of Peter Schuyler and business partner of Schuyler's brother-in-law Robert Livingston, Kidd had recently returned from London to fill out his 150-man crew for his new thirty-four-cannon warship, the *Adventure Galley*. The privateer commander and successful merchant ship captain carried a pair of lofty Crown commissions, one to fight the French and the other to hunt down Red

Sea pirates. Though Schuyler and Kidd had known each other since 1691, they had become friends in the fall of 1694 when Kidd had served as a jury foreman in a court case involving a trading vessel owned by Schuyler and Livingston.[8] In the past five years, Captain Kidd had become one of New York's wealthiest gentlemen married to one of its most dazzling socialites, the well-liked and comely Englishwoman Sarah Kidd. Schuyler had originally been introduced to the captain and his wife through Livingston, who had purchased two lots at 90 and 92 Pearl Street from the Kidds in June 1693 and was currently a key investor in Kidd's Crown-sponsored voyage to the Indian Ocean.[9]

Concocted back in the fall of 1695 by the avaricious Livingston, who had been in London with Kidd at the time, the risky scheme called for Captain Kidd to hunt down pirates in the East Indies and legally seize their ill-gotten riches. These Kidd would keep for not only his sponsor and partner Livingston, himself, and his crew but for King William III, who was to receive a 10 percent cut of the profits; Livingston's friend Lord Bellomont, the soon-to-be royal governor of New York, Massachusetts, and New Hampshire; and four other well-heeled London financial backers that Livingston and Bellomont put in place. At the time, the Indian Ocean was infested with English and American pirates who preyed on the shipping of the Great Mughal of India, Emperor Aurangzeb Alamgir I.[10]

The goal was for Kidd to capture the pirates after they had raided the Great Mughal's treasure fleets and East Indian shipping. In addition to Livingston, Bellomont, and William III, he was backed by Lord John Somers, Lord Chancellor and Keeper of the Great Seal; Charles Talbot, the Duke of Shrewsbury, Secretary of State; Admiral Edward Russell, First Lord of the Admiralty and Treasurer of the Royal Navy; and Henry Sidney, the Earl of Romney, Master General of Ordnance. The four wealthy partners were some of the most powerful men in all of England and were all members of the Whig Junto that ran the English government.[11]

Initially, Kidd turned down the command of the dangerous venture. However, given the considerable time and money already invested in the enterprise, the huge stakes, and the highbrow investors, Bellomont threatened to have him arrested, to seize his privateering ship *Antigua*, and to "oppress" Kidd in New York when he took office as governor if he didn't agree to command the voyage.[12] Under pressure from both Bellomont and Livingston, Kidd decided to carry out the difficult mission rather than make enemies of Bellomont and the other powerful English noblemen, who offered him further assurances "of their support and his impunity from criminal prosecution."[13]

Now, with New York City in a war panic, Captain Kidd and his formidable new warship *Adventure Galley* were the only things standing in the way of French sea marauders sailing down from Quebec and seizing Manhattan. The City Council had taken the drastic step of passing an embargo forbidding Kidd's privateer and other vessels from sailing out of New York Harbor, which was to remain in effect through September 1. While Kidd and his scrappy sea dogs outfitted their gunship for the long voyage to the Indian Ocean, they remained on call twenty-four hours a day to protect the City from French attack. The French fleet was expected to invade from either Long Island Sound or from the Narrows between Staten Island and Long Island. The lone Royal Navy warship in New York Harbor, Captain John Evans's dry-rot-infested HMS *Richmond*, was in poor shape and in no position to actively patrol the coast, let alone fire repeated broadsides, so the fate of New York City was in Kidd's hands.[14]

On August 2, Fletcher began a five-day sail 150 miles upriver to Albany with a company of troops. His military objectives were to thwart Frontenac's advance through Iroquoia, to lend aid to the Onondagas and Oneidas, and to prevent the French and their Indian allies from not only seizing Albany and Schenectady but from continuing unchecked down the Hudson to New York City. There, it was feared, Frontenac and his victorious army would rendezvous with the French fleet.[15]

Arriving on August 7, Fletcher proposed leading an expedition of ninety troops to cover the Iroquois retreat. However, Schuyler informed him that the French were by this time withdrawing from the region and that pursuing Frontenac's two-thousand-plus-man force was ill-advised. The time would be better spent condoling their Iroquois brethren and helping them get back on their feet before winter. With Hilletie acting as interpreter, the Great Swift Arrow met with several Mohawk and Oneida headmen and war leaders, including Lawrence, to hear the full story of what had transpired at the Onondaga and Oneida villages.[16]

He quickly learned that the seat of the League Iroquois lay in smoldering ruins and had been turned into a barren wasteland. The Onondagas and Oneidas now joined the Mohawks, the Keepers of the Eastern Door of the Longhouse, in having their villages and critical food stores destroyed by the enemy raiders.[17] With a hard winter coming, the Five Nations once again questioned the commitment of their English allies and pondered their future. "The enemy has brought us to a very low condition and have destroyed five of our castles," reported the Anglophile orator and headman Sanonguirese of the Mohawk Bear Clan. Only one Mohawk settlement was "now left" in the Cayuga country, he said, "and if that be destroyed, we know not what to do; we know not what shall become of us next."[18]

Like Schuyler and Hilletie, Fletcher sympathized with the Iroquois, but he still believed they should have been more vigilant in their scouting patrols and protecting their fortified villages. However, confronted with yet another frontier disaster and Iroquois mourning period, all he could do was condole his allies for their terrible losses, provide for their present needs, encourage future military readiness, and promise to return soon with food, armaments, and necessities to help them make it through the winter.[19]

At the same time, the French victory was not as spectacular as Frontenac claimed to his superiors in Paris. While being carried about in a silk chair like an emperor by a royal guard detail throughout the campaign, the courtier-governor had hoped to be covered in glory and to reap substantial financial rewards, but he instead found "no enemy to fight" and "no fortifications to assault with cannon and mortars."[20] The Onondaga had burned down their own village and food stores to prevent their capture, and the Oneidas had managed to broker a deal with the Laurentian Iroquois warriors accompanying the French to spare their lives by promising not to put up resistance and to relocate to the Kahnawake mission outside Montreal. Some thirty-five League Iroquois would ultimately resettle in Canada with their kin.[21]

Though the Onondaga and Oneida still suffered horribly from the destruction of their villages, crops, and food stores, the success of the expedition was dampened by the decisive actions of the Iroquois that limited casualties to one person: an Onondaga headman too old and infirm to slip away from the invaders—and even he proudly defied his captors.[22] When the Canadian Indians slow-tortured the Onondaga elder, he "exhorted those who tormented him to remember his death" and to exhibit the same courage when confronted by the League avengers who would one day cut them down in reprisal. "Learn French dogs" how to take punishment with honor, he harangued the French officers, "and you Savages, their allies, who are dogs of dogs, remember what you have to do when you will occupy a position similar to mine."[23]

In his reports, Frontenac called the expedition a "considerable" victory over the Onondagas and Oneidas, who would now be "reduced to the necessity of perishing of hunger" or "accepting peace" on French terms.[24] But he proved a poor prognosticator. The resilient Onondagas would rebuild within months after the attack near the headwaters of the Susquehanna River, and the homeless Oneidas would find ample relief from Albany and their fellow Mohawks. Soon after his visit, Fletcher ordered corn to be supplied to the Onondagas and Oneidas at public expense, and he forbade its shipment down the Hudson to New York City until Iroquois needs were first met. The displaced villagers were, thus, well cared for during the winter of 1696–1697 through provisions provided by generous colonial New Yorkers.[25]

Before returning to New York City, Fletcher established an official Board of Commissioners for Indian Affairs to conduct negotiations with the Iroquois. Previously, Indian relations had been handled by Albany's public officials and English military officers, but the governor now created an independent board, consisting of Schuyler, Father Godfredius Dellius, and Mayor Dirck Wessels. Another Albany official would later be added, and the multilingual Hilletie van Olinda was retained as official government interpreter. With military security continuing to be the most vital issue of New York, the newly created board was supplied with an annual budget of £100 ($35,000 today) to pay for gifts, messengers, and other expenses. The first act of Schuyler and the Board was to supply the destitute Onondagas and Oneidas with food and to prohibit the exportation of corn from Albany so that it could be used to meet Iroquois needs.[26]

In creating the new Board of Commissioners for Indian Affairs, Fletcher and his governor's council stripped Schuyler's brother-in-law Robert Livingston of his office as secretary of Indian affairs and also removed him from his position as sub-collector of the excise and quit-rents. Livingston had become persona non grata because he had been overcharging the government for feeding the troops and because he continued to demand financial compensation for recording the Five Nations' council meetings even though funding was tight. Livingston had never been "sent on any public message or ever had any power of agency to treat with the Indians," pointed out the council, "having no knowledge of their language or influence on the Nations."[27] To save costs, Father Dellius would record the Iroquois conferences at Albany for the next year and a half, while Livingston would scramble to recover his outstanding claims at a hefty 8 percent interest.[28]

Although Schuyler did not take part in the meetings to remove Livingston, he appears to have merely tolerated his greedy brother-in-law and likely withheld his vote out of a sense of familial obligation to his older sister Alida. In contrast, Fletcher was anything but lukewarm regarding the "acquisitive" Scottish merchant of royal lineage.[29] The governor wrote to London that Livingston had amassed his great fortune by "never disbursing six pence but with the expectation of twelve pence, his beginning being a little book keeper who hath screwed himself [through his marriage to Alida Schuyler, the wealthy widow of Nicholas van Rensselaer] into one of the most considerable estates in the province." Even more tellingly, Fletcher would say of Schuyler's brother-in-law that "he had rather be called knave Livingston, than poor Livingston" and that "a man of such vile principles" should be prevented "from sucking any more the blood of the province, for he has been a very sponge to it."[30]

In mid-August, with the new Board of Commissioners for Indian Affairs in place and the frontier stabilized, Fletcher returned to New York City. While French invasion by sea was still greatly feared, the governor found himself under attack not by the French but by the resurgent Leislerians.

The pro-Leislerian coalition within the New York Assembly attacked Fletcher for raising taxes to support the military garrison at Albany and for transporting large detachments of militia upriver to fight the French. They also blamed him for the frightful condition and frequent desertion of the troops and for coddling Massachusetts, Pennsylvania, and the other English colonies that continued to stubbornly refuse to lend troops or money for the war effort.[31] In truth, with Schuyler's help, the governor had worked strenuously for four straight years to resolve these problems and it was the parsimonious Crown and New York's stingy neighbors that failed to provide adequate support to prosecute the war. But that meant little to the Leislerians, who were once again on the warpath.[32]

While Frontenac continued to deploy imperial regulars in battle, the English soldiers and New York's colonial militia were underpaid, malnourished, poorly equipped, and inadequately trained—despite Fletcher's and Schuyler's constant complaints to Crown officials about the lack of funding. Not only was combat readiness of the troops abysmal, but the "deplorable conditions under which the common soldiers were forced to serve further alienated them from their commanders and from the society at large."[33] Unwilling to put their lives on the line for nothing, many of the troops continued to desert to surrounding colonies. In a desperate attempt to halt the outflow, Fletcher issued a proclamation forbidding further desertion, but it proved futile.[34]

Unfortunately, the still-smarting Leislerians cared little that Fletcher was doing more to build up and safeguard their colony than *any* Crown-appointed colonial governor since the English takeover three decades earlier. To the dismay of Schuyler and the province's anti-Leislerian majority, all the Leislerians cared about was bringing him to his knees and removing him from power. However, unbeknownst to Fletcher, Schuyler, and the council, the Leislerians had already succeeded in their mission to topple him.

Back in April of 1695, Jacob Leisler Jr. and Abraham Gouverneur, the sons of the two leaders of Leisler's Rebellion, had arranged in London to have their fathers' names cleared and to regain their family estates, which had been attainted when Jacob Leisler Sr. and his council were convicted of treason in 1691.[35] On April 30, Parliament passed a bill reversing the attainders of several leading Leislerians.[36] But more importantly, with the Whigs back in power in England, the testimony of Leisler Jr. and Gouverneur played a huge role in undermining Fletcher and positioned Lord Bellomont to receive the appointment as royal governor of New York and to replace the tarnished Tory Fletcher.[37]

In the fall of 1695, after due deliberation in the chambers of the Lords of Trade, a verdict was reached with the recommendation that Fletcher be recalled to London to answer charges.[38] Accordingly, on September 11, 1695, an Order in Council was issued, followed eventually by a letter from the Duke of Shrewsbury that removed Fletcher from power.[39] Though he was technically recalled for administrative malfeasance and strong-arm election tactics, it was the taint of supporting and sponsoring the Red Sea pirates that eventually sealed his fate. The denunciations would come primarily from Bellomont, Livingston and Kidd's business partner in the Indian Ocean expedition, who would, due to various delays, not replace Fletcher as governor of New York until April 1698.[40]

On September 17, 1696—with French seaborne invasion having failed to materialize and Captain Kidd released from coastguard protection to pursue his Crown-backed voyage to the East Indies—Fletcher headed back upriver to Albany to inspect the garrison, meet with the Iroquois, and deliver "presents sent from His Majesty."[41] At a meeting on the 29th with the headmen, Schuyler, and Hilletie, the Great Swift Arrow presented two belts of wampum to help the Onondagas and Oneidas "wipe away their tears" for their recent losses. As part of the ceremony, the governor distributed goods valued at over £660 ($231,000 today) to help their communities heal.[42]

But the Iroquois were not to be won over so easily and once again aired their grievances. Their foremost complaint was that the English, despite their many promises, had been unable to coordinate a joint land-sea invasion of French Canada. Lawrence's friend, the Mohawk headman Sanonguirese, responded to the governor's condolence offering with a bundle of six beaver skins marked on the outside with a "map of the river of Canada with the chief places" indicated to show Fletcher how easily New France could be taken by sea. The Mohawk leader demanded that his map and the League's propositions be delivered in person to William III, so the king could see for himself how vulnerable New France was to invasion and would dispatch a large army and navy in the spring to "destroy Canada."[43]

The Five Nations, warned the Mohawk speaker through Hilletie, would not accept any more broken promises on this matter, and to ensure their message was delivered to the king they offered five beaver skins to pay for the necessary ink, pen, and paper. If they did not receive a positive answer by "the next time the trees grow green," they would make their own peace with Yonondio and the French.[44] Their position was clear: The invasions of Mohawk, Onondaga, and Oneida country in recent years had been catastrophic for the Five Nations and they could no longer continue to bear the brunt of the war alone. If the English were too incompetent or disunited to coordinate a major attack by land and sea to conquer Canada, the Iroquois had no choice but to make peace with their French enemies on the best possible terms. Fletcher protested that there was insufficient time to send the message all the way to London, make the necessary war preparations, and transmit the news back to America by spring, but the sachems remained unpersuaded.[45]

At the conclusion of the conference, the Covenant Chain was once again renewed, the governor agreed to write the king on behalf of the Five Nations, and he returned to New York City and sent the message to London as promised.[46] But at this stage of the war, the Anglo-Iroquois coalition was hanging on by a slender thread. Four of the five Nations of the Iroquois Confederacy—the Mohawks, Oneidas, Onondagas, and Senecas—had seen their fortified settlements and crops destroyed by French and Indian invaders, and they blamed English negligence and incompetence for a goodly portion of their suffering. They had been ravaged not merely by battlefield losses and disease but through the captivity of their warriors and child-bearing women, famine, and out-migration to Kahnawake and other Canadian settlements under Jesuit control. Those who left for a new life in French Canada could hardly be blamed: They sought cheaper goods, reliable supplies of food, clothing, and shelter, and ready access to the Christian priests that they had been demanding the English send to their western villages for the past three years, but had not been delivered by the Crown as promised.[47]

The only reason the Iroquois continued to support the English in the eighth year of what increasingly seemed like a never-ending war was because they knew they could count on Schuyler and his fellow Albanians, while it continued to be widely believed that Frontenac and the French could not be trusted. With their Brother Quider, Sanonguirese, Sadekanaktie, and the other League headmen all knew where they stood, but Frontenac's divide-and-rule strategy and duplicity toward the Five Nations continued to make him a risky bet. "We must stick to our Brother Quider," Sadekanaktie had warned his fellow Iroquois on more than one occasion, "and look on Yonondio as our enemy, for he is a cheat."[48]

Father Dellius and Hilletie, too, remained in high standing among the Iroquois for their diplomatic efforts. With Livingston having been removed from military and Indian affairs by Fletcher for milking the government, Dellius now served as the chief council recorder and an influential voice in treaty sessions with League ambassadors, with Hilletie acting as his right hand and translator. With Hilletie's aid, Dellius had also translated several religious texts into Mohawk, and by the end of the decade he had baptized at least 131 Indigenous people, most of them Mohawks. Hilletie continued to demonstrate her usefulness in both "religious and diplomatic interpreting" in the interconnected Anglo-Iroquois "politics" of colonial New York. Knowledgeable regarding both European and Native cultures and with "the linguistic abilities to facilitate communication between them," she found her "talents in demand in all arenas of contact."[49] While few of the Iroquois transformed overnight into orthodox Protestant Christians and most continued to retain important Indigenous spiritual components in their religious approach, the "political import" of these baptisms continued to be substantial in strengthening the Anglo-Iroquois alliance and uniting the two groups against the French.[50]

In the summer of 1696, the political influence of Schuyler and Dellius, along with their Anglophile Iroquois cohorts like Lawrence and Hilletie, continued to be strong with the Iroquois due to the well-earned trust of these cross-cultural emissaries. Many of the anti-French Haudenosaunee who embraced Christianity looked upon their baptism by Dellius as a symbolic "conversion" in which they were entering into league with the English nation in the traditional Iroquois manner that placed a premium on reciprocity and mutuality.[51] In Dellius's instruction, they discovered "a spiritual counterweight to the rise of French power and the decline of their own fortunes." Protestant Christianity also offered them "a profound ideal that they hoped to internalize and use to restructure their community relations."[52] Many baptized Mohawks like Lawrence and his wife Maria, thus regarded Christianity as a restorative mechanism not merely for themselves but the entire Five Nations. They believed that Protestant ministers, strongly built forts, and trustworthy traders brought "prosperity, protection, power, and privilege to all."[53]

However, by the fall of 1696, with the recent devastating French attacks and continued reduction in the Five Nations' warrior population, the drying up of the fur trade, and the inability of New York and the other English colonies to coordinate among themselves or deliver on the distant Crown's promises, the influence of Schuyler, Dellius, their fellow Albanians, and the Anglophile Christian Iroquois faction began to wane. Their diminished influence was an important reason why a group of Oneidas and other League Iroquois were willing to defy English demands and send out peace feelers to the French and their Indigenous enemies that they hoped would lead to official treaties.[54]

By this time, the thirty-three-year-old Lawrence had become as much a proponent of peace as a leader of raiding parties into Canada. He now spent more of his time hunting, participating in the "Creator's game" of lacrosse, praying for the resurgence of his people, and raising his two sons, Adam and Henry, with his young wife Maria than carrying the tomahawk against the French.[55] Like most Protestant Mohawks, he and Maria combined traditional Christian practices with Haudenosaunee sacred practices, seeking to restore their lives by performing aspects of Christianity while still embracing the traditional shamans, dreams, and ceremonies of the Iroquois.[56]

What the Mohawk war captain wanted most of all was for the Five Nations to have true peace and undergo a renaissance. Having lost his two friends and fellow war leaders Onnonouagaren and Garistatsi and dozens of his fellow Mohawks to war and disease, he felt the balance and harmony of Haudenosaunee society coming apart and could not help but blame his English allies for much of the Five Nations' misery.[57] The adoption of war captives at this time could not keep pace with the mortality rate among the League Nations, which continued to lead to increased friction between the Christian and traditional Iroquois, as well as mass northward Iroquois defections to French Canada.[58] The families of the war victims and their communities remained out of balance because there were insufficient headmen to perform requickening ceremonies and too few warriors to secure captives. The result was widespread resentment among the Iroquois over "their inability to condole their dead," which, in turn, threatened their diplomatic relations with their English allies.[59]

Throughout the fall of 1696, with intelligence continuing to indicate Frontenac was planning an all-out attack on Albany, New York remained in a state of high alert. The threat became so serious that on November 10, Benjamin Fletcher set sail up the Hudson to spend the winter in Albany directing military operations. Like Schuyler, he was deeply troubled by the dramatic reduction in the region's warrior population. If the Iroquois Confederacy suffered defeat, it continued to be widely believed, all of New York Province, the mid-Atlantic colonies, and Virginia would fall in rapid succession, like dominoes, until Frontenac controlled all English America.[60]

Before setting out for Albany, Fletcher met with several League headmen, who had traveled down the Hudson from the Mohawk River Valley to meet with him. Not only did he hold a formal council and reaffirm England's commitment under the Covenant Chain, he squired them around town in his six-horse coach, fired off cannons to impress them, and lavishly feted them at his dinner table in a manner that would have impressed even the notoriously extravagant and foppish Count Frontenac. Schuyler and Hilletie had given the governor solid instruction on proper etiquette when it came to Haudenosaunee diplomacy, which was built upon reciprocity, mutual respect, and gift exchange. Despite his many flaws and that he could never look upon Native Americans as equals, Fletcher genuinely respected the Iroquois as bold fighters and sagacious statesmen and truly seemed to enjoy his interactions with them as the generous "Corlaer." As he wrote to his bewigged masters in London in the fall of 1696:

> I have been at great pains to gain the hearts of the Heathen, and have . . . taken their Chief Sachems to my table. Some of the principal leading men of the Five Nations came down the river to pay me a visit, whom I treated with all manner of kindness and courtesy. I ordered them on board the greatest ships we have and the guns to be fired, the King's birthday happening at that time. I ordered them to be by when all the guns were fired, I caused some of them to be loaded with ball, to show them how far they could carry upon the river, I caused Granada shells to be fired before them and let them see the armory. I ordered six horses to be put into my coach and my coachmen to drive them round the City and into the Country to take the air, by which they were extremely obliged, and dismissed them with considerable presents, at which they did express great satisfaction.[61]

During his northward journey to Albany in mid-November to reassure the Iroquois, the governor was forced aground twice by contrary winds, and winter ice eventually locked in his sloop more than thirty miles south of Albany. After abandoning the vessel and tromping to shore across the ice, he and his entourage trudged five miles east to Patcoke (Claverack) and were soon thereafter met by Schuyler, who happened to be leading a scouting patrol in the area. Rescued by the major, they hiked to Albany on snowshoes and sleds, crossing from Greenbush on the thickening ice and reaching the fur-trading outpost on November 21.[62]

Although no enemy appeared that winter, New York's royal governor remained at Albany until late March 1697, when it was clear the alarm had passed. During his stay, he worked closely with Schuyler to oversee repairs to the fort, train the troops, and reaffirm the commitment to their Indigenous allies. Following Schuyler and Hilletie's advice, he sent wampum belts and messages of encouragement to the Iroquois and Mahicans in the more distant villages "to let them know that he was there to protect them."[63] But the Five Nations continued to be dispirited from their recent losses. Because of Frontenac's destruction of their villages and his continuing threats, at least thirty war-ravaged Oneidas migrated to Canada during the winter to take refuge with their kin; and other Iroquois would trickle into Kahnawake and other settlements outside Montreal throughout the spring and summer.[64]

By this time, the settlers of Albany and Schenectady, too, had reached the end of their tether after eight years on the front lines of King William's War. With the recent decline of the fur trade, the constant threat of French and Indian attacks, and the returning League war parties turning the countryside into a barren wasteland, many of the European inhabitants of the Hudson and Mohawk River Valleys had fled.[65] Feeling as unprotected and betrayed by their English government as the Iroquois, the region's residents were now open to making peace provided "the French and their allies would spare New York" and allow them to continue trading, thereby relieving them from "both loss of life and the cost of defensive measures."[66]

In the end, Frontenac was unable to carry out his threat of an all-out winter invasion due to his own weaknesses. Unlike in 1690 and 1693, New France in the winter of 1696–1697 experienced severe famine and war fatigue. But Fletcher's well-publicized presence in Albany at this time also played a role in the pugnacious French leader's decision not to attack.[67]

When Fletcher returned to New York City in late March 1697, the Albany frontier was stabilized through his and Schuyler's efforts, with Fort Frederick refurbished and the Five Nations secure in their rebuilt stockades. The Iroquois greatly appreciated that the Great Swift Arrow had spent the entire winter in their country as their supporter and protector. That was something no Brother Corlaer had ever done before.[68]

However, by this stage of the war it was too late for the English to maintain the hearts and minds of the Five Nations. For Lawrence and his fellow Iroquois had come to the realization that the military aid provided by the English would never be enough to free their people from French domination, to help them gain control of the Great Lakes hunting territories, or to allow them to seize hundreds of Indigenous captives to replenish their ranks and renew their people. English neglect and impotence had reached the point where the only course of action was to cease, or at least restrain, all hostilities between the Five Nations and the Canadian tribes and to maintain a diplomatic balance between the English and French that did not adversely impact ties to either European power. Only then, Lawrence and his fellow Iroquois knew, could they ensure the survival of their Haudenosaunee people.[69]

17
THE TREATY OF RYSWICK

In mid-December 1697, Peter Schuyler, recently promoted to colonel, learned of the October 30 signing of the Treaty of Ryswick, formally ending the grueling nine-year contest between France and the Grand Alliance of England, Spain, Austria, and the Dutch Republic. With the exciting news that the war was over, drums resounded in Albany and New York City, the bell of Father Dellius's Dutch Reformed Church in Albany rang out, and cannons exploded from Fort Frederick in Albany and Fort William in New York City to exclamations of "God save the king!" Two months later, on February 26, Governor Fletcher had his majesty's printer, William Bradford, post the Crown's formal peace proclamation at his shop, the Sign of the Bible, and a day of thanksgiving was celebrated in the City and throughout the province.[1]

Who won the protracted and ferocious imperial conflict that had caused so much death and suffering on both sides? The consensus among historians is that King William's War ended in either an inconclusive stalemate or with a slight edge to the French. Thus, after nine years of savage warfare, the provincial European and Native field armies of Louis XIV and those of the League of Augsburg headed by King William III had essentially fought each other to a bloody, exhausting, money-draining draw. While England had thwarted France's ambitions in the New World, she had accomplished little else. The English had compelled the French to recognize the Dutch William of Orange as the legitimate ruler of England and to make commercial concessions to the Netherlands, and they had gained prestige in some European courts, but William had to restore all territories taken from France during the conflict and was saddled with heavy taxation and war debt. Even worse, in leaving her colonists to defend the northern borderlands of English America all by themselves, the Mother Country had allowed her "subjects" to grow more independent from the Crown, with both New York and the New England colonies recognizing that in the future they could count on little help from London in military campaigns against French Canada. The allegiance of royal colonies like New York and Virginia had always been contingent upon the protection provided by the king—yet William III had sent over a measly four independent companies total during the entire violent war waged in his name.[2]

In the end, there was no clear-cut winner between the two imperial superpowers and the Treaty of Ryswick, far from settling the tangled European issues of the Glorious Revolution that had provoked the conflict, only perpetuated the frustrating stalemate. It settled none of the major causes of war in Europe, the North American colonies, the Caribbean, or the East Indies. In requiring both of "His Most Christian Majesties" to restore "all countries, islands, and fortresses" possessed before the beginning of the war, the treaty left the situations in London, Paris, New York, Canada, and the wild North American frontier precisely where they had been in 1689 before the first shots had been fired.[3]

With respect to the Five Nations, although Frontenac and his Gallic legions had not succeeded in breaking the Covenant Chain between the English and Iroquois, the treaty precluded direct English military aid to the Confederation during future wars. The French had also made it clear that the Francophile Iroquois were an equal counterweight to the neutralists and Anglophiles, that the Great Lakes and Laurentian Iroquois tribes were under French control, and that the English claim to sovereignty over the entire Five Nations was a fanciful dream. Furthermore, while the French failed to drive the English from New York or the Five Nations from Iroquoia, by the time all the treaty's fine-print details were worked out they had adroitly managed to make slight territorial gains in Hudson Bay, successfully stymied English expansion into the French colony of Acadia (modern-day eastern Maine, New Brunswick, Nova Scotia, and Prince Edward Island), and won back Port Royal, the capital of French Acadia.[4]

Despite the signing of the treaty, tensions between English and French colonists and between their Indigenous allies remained high. Because of the lingering hostilities, Indian diplomacy continued to remain of vital importance to Schuyler and Hilletie, New York's provincial leadership, the Crown, and Parliament.[5] While the agreement hashed out in Europe did bring peace for the settlers of New York, the other English colonies, and New France, it had no bearing on the Iroquois in relation to their western Native enemies. The Albany frontier and Iroquoia remained a contested borderland for the Five Nations, Great Lakes tribes, Laurentian Iroquois, and the other Indigenous Peoples of the continental interior and Canada.[6]

Unfortunately for the Iroquois, they would continue to suffer as unwilling pawns in the chess match of international politics between the two European superpowers.[7] Both the English and French continued to act as if they ruled over the Five Nations when the Haudenosaunee had never surrendered their land or sovereignty to anyone.[8] Because both New York and New France claimed the Five Nations as "loyal subjects of the Crown," they insisted that the Natives were not covered under the European pact and had no right to negotiate as independent agents.[9] Caught between the imperial titans and weakened by a decade of warfare, the Iroquois were caught in a political stalemate by the conflicting agendas of demoralized Anglophiles like Lawrence who were beginning to question the benefits of the Covenant Chain, resurgent Francophiles who sought peace with Frontenac at virtually any price, and desperate neutralists like Teganissorens who believed that the only viable path forward to ensure Iroquois security and prosperity was to refrain from participation in European conflicts.[10] Meanwhile, while the treaty brought peaceful relations between the League and the French and Laurentian Iroquois, the Haudenosaunee continued to be fair game for their western Great Lakes and Canadian Algonquin foes, who continued to bushwack their hunting and trading parties throughout the contested borderlands.[11]

Historians also agree that while King William's War in North America may have been indecisive, the human costs on both sides of the conflict were devastating. As expected, the Five Iroquois Nations fared the worst, losing well over a thousand men, women, and children from a combination of war, captivity, disease, and famine. Historian Daniel Richter conservatively puts the number of Iroquois losses during King William's War at around 2,000 people from an estimated prewar 1689 population of approximately 8,600 tribal members.[12] Meanwhile, historian Howard Peckham estimates that the Five Nations "may have mourned as many as thirteen hundred dead from battle and disease."[13] Not only Lawrence and his Mohawks, but the Senecas, Onondagas, and Oneidas all saw their towns and crops destroyed by invading armies and their populations ravaged by combat, starvation, and disease.

According to contemporaneous English estimates, the number of Five Nations warriors, including assimilated Mahicans and other "River Indians," fell from 2,660 warriors in 1689 to 1,280 in 1698, a drop of 1,380 fighters.[14] However, some scholars believe these estimated war casualties too high and that the League Iroquois lost no more than half that number in the armed conflict and never decreased to less than 1,800 fighting men.[15] According to Richter, "by 1700 at least 500 of the approximately 2,150 warriors the Five Nations fielded in 1689 had perished, been captured, or moved to Canadian villages."[16]

For the Five Nations, the loss in numbers in King William's War from combined battle deaths and out-migration to French Canada had indeed been steep, but with the large influx of mourning-war adoptees, in-migration to Iroquoia from Canada, and favorable Five Nations birthrates, the long-term damage to Iroquois communities was not as bad as Schuyler and other English officials believed at the time. The Iroquois were able to replenish many of their wartime losses through the adoption of captured prisoners. This ability of the League Iroquois to rebound quickly is demonstrated by the fact that the male population engaged in an extended winter 1697–1698 hunting season.[17] However, even if many of the losses were made up through adoption, the "constant activity of their war parties and those of the enemy, the desertions to Canada, the smallpox epidemic in 1690, and the destruction of tribal food supplies" took a heavy toll and "would not soon be forgotten."[18]

For the European populations, King William's War left a total of 650 dead settlers and more than 1,000 troops killed from the English-American colonies, with most of the casualties coming from Sir William Phips's ill-fated 1690 attack on Quebec. The French, too, suffered substantial losses from war and disease, with more than 2,000 settler men, women, and children and more than 500 French soldiers and Canadian militia killed in the various battles and frontier raids and dying from accidents, medical afflictions, and famine. Over 600 French-allied Canadian Algonquin and Laurentian Iroquois were killed in frontier skirmishes, died from smallpox and other diseases, or were taken into captivity by the English and Anglophile Iroquois.[19]

The Anglo-Dutch settlers of Schuyler and Hilletie's Albany-Schenectady region sustained particularly heavy losses. While the city and county of Albany suffered eighty-four dead and sixteen captured to go along with thirty-eight natural deaths, what was even more devastating to the region was the four-hundred settler men, women, and children who moved away during the war, resulting in a population decrease of nearly 25 percent in less than a decade. The combination of a reduced fur trade and constant danger of lethal hit-and-run attacks by French and Indian forces contributed significantly to the out-migration of the settler population, which became increasingly worn down and despondent as the war progressed. However, traders and farmers gradually returned to the area, with Schuyler playing a major role in recruitment efforts in the half-decade following the signing of the Treaty of Ryswick.[20]

With open warfare between England and France over in name only and the Great Lakes tribes continuing to attack the Iroquois with arms supplied by the French, it was essential that the English royal troops and provincial militia in New York remain on high alert and close to full strength to protect the frontier. The problem was that Ingoldsby's English army in New York was in a deplorable condition by war's end and merely feeding and clothing the soldiers at Fort Frederick and the other outposts remained a challenge. Soon after Ryswick, Parliament expressed its aversion to standing armies by scaling back England's forces to seven thousand troops and then withholding their salaries. As a consequence, soldier pay arrearages amounted to more than £2,000,000 sterling ($700,000,000 today). In New York, the royal troops faced an even more precarious situation since the paymaster-general had forgotten to include them in his annual estimates to Parliament, ensuring that the troops would continue to suffer and desert in large numbers.[21]

In late January 1698, Fletcher and Schuyler sent a New York diplomatic mission headed by Schuyler's younger cousin Abraham Schuyler and Father Dellius of Albany to communicate news of the Treaty of Ryswick to Louis-Hector de Callière, the governor of Montreal. The two envoys brought with them several French prisoners to exchange for League Iroquois captives, whose Native families wanted them returned to their villages in the Mohawk River Valley. But Fletcher failed to send an official sealed letter or copy of the treaty with the peace envoys. Consequently, neither Callière nor Frontenac considered themselves obligated to cease hostilities against either the English colonies or the Iroquois. Fletcher's diplomatic gaffe and Frontenac's inherent bellicosity and hatred of England continued to play a key role in perpetuating fighting between the Five Nations and the Great Lakes tribes. However, Lawrence and League sachems and war captains of hereditary and meritocratic status continued to work toward securing peace with their Laurentian Iroquois kin—as well as with other tribes to the extent practicable—to limit the bloodshed of their people.[22]

With the war between England and France at an end, Lawrence had to be asking himself what exactly he had been fighting for the past decade. From the beginning, his goal and that of his League Iroquois brothers and sisters had been to liberate themselves from the control of the treacherous Yonondio and the French, to gain control of the Great Lakes hunting territories, to repopulate their hard-hit communities with western Indian captives, and to force a long-term mutual nonaggression pact with their Laurentian Iroquois brethren in Canada and encourage their return to the Mohawk River Valley. Because none of those dreams had been realized, he carried bitter feelings toward the English Crown, who had let the Five Nations down time and again despite the strenuous efforts of Brother Quider, the Great Swift Arrow, and Hilletie van Olinda.

But what he didn't know, in the spring of 1698, was that the situation for him and his people was about to become much worse, even though a formal peace treaty had been signed. Soon, there would be a new Brother

Corlaer to contend with in diplomatic councils, a man who was far from sympathetic and had no interest in learning or understanding Iroquois ways. Already, the Crown's new man handpicked by the Great Father across the ocean was on his way to replace the Great Swift Arrow. A pompous Irish-born aristocrat from London, he would soon upset the balance and harmony of their Indigenous world just as ruinously as Jacob Leisler.

His name was Richard Coote, better known as Lord Bellomont.

Looking southward in the direction of Sandy Hook, New York's Crown-appointed governor's council member Colonel Peter Schuyler saw the square-rigged vessel coming up the Upper Bay beyond the palisaded walls of Fort William and battery of cannons overlooking New York Harbor. On this pleasant afternoon of April 2, 1698, he stood with his second wife, Maria van Rensselaer Schuyler, his family, and a coterie of friends and neighbors at the Great Dock along the East River. The new incoming Whig governor, Lord Bellomont, would be arriving in the next few minutes. He was to be welcomed by Schuyler's friend Benjamin Fletcher, the outgoing Tory governor, who had been formally recalled and would today hand over the keys to the governor's mansion.[23]

To provide pomp and circumstance, the lame-duck Fletcher stood with his wife and daughters alongside the uniformed troops from the fort's garrison. Along with the Schuyler, Philipse, and van Cortlandt families, much of New York's blue-blooded elite had turned out in their Sunday finest to welcome the new governor and witness the passing of the torch.[24]

From his brother-in-law Robert Livingston, Schuyler knew all about Bellomont, the principal sponsor of Captain Kidd's Indian Ocean expedition. The prominent New York merchant ship captain and privateer was still away at sea, but he had been the talk of the town back in 1696 with his commissions to fight the French and hunt down pirates stamped by William III himself, who referred to him as the "trusty and well-beloved Captain Kidd."[25] Like Fletcher, Richard Coote had supported William and Mary early in the Glorious Revolution, having commanded a regiment of

English troops in 1687 and 1688 as captain of horse in the Dutch army, which led to an English peerage in 1689 as the First Earl of Bellomont. His services rendered to the Crown, coupled with his marriage in 1680 to the English heiress Catharine Nanfan, paved the way for his position as a lord justice of Ireland and House of Commons member, after he caught the attention of the powerful Duke of Shrewsbury and other members of the Whig Junto.[26]

Though the owner of a Dover Street mansion near Westminster Abbey, a noble peerage, and extensive land holdings in Ireland, Bellomont had spent most of his adult life desperately short of cash and remained in scandalously heavy debt for a member of Parliament.[27] Due to his financial straits, in the summer of 1695 when Livingston and Kidd visited London, he had been forced to consider the time-honored escape-route from penury for English aristocrats: emigration to America as a colonial official. Shrewsbury had recommended him to the king for the position of governor of the Province of Massachusetts Bay. The scheme worked, and not only was Bellomont confirmed to the post on June 14, 1695, he was soon able to employ his Machiavellian political skills and replace Fletcher in New York as well.[28]

Soon Lord and Lady Bellomont and the lieutenant governor, Captain John Nanfan, a cousin of Bellomont's wife, disembarked from their ship. The governor and his entourage were greeted with military salutes from four of the fort's cannons.[29] Stepping up onto the pier of the Great Dock, they were met by Governor Fletcher as well as Mayor William Merritt and Attorney-General James Graham. The sixty-two-year-old earl and his young wife half his age had been expected two months earlier, but squally weather during their Atlantic crossing had forced them to put in at Barbados for several weeks, delaying their arrival to New York.[30]

On the day Bellomont finally set foot on Manhattan Island, New York Province was, thanks to Benjamin Fletcher, one of the wealthiest colonies in the Atlantic world from a combination of legal trade and illicit smuggling and piracy. In the late 17th century, these were the twin engines that fueled colonial prosperity in a New World without any government or private banking system and with limited access to gold and silver specie under England's stringent Navigation Acts.[31] Under Fletcher's liberal policies, transoceanic and coastal trade had been booming for the past several years from the forty licensed big ships, sixty-two sloops, and sixty-two riverboats owned by Colonel Peter Schuyler, the merchants Frederick Philipse, Robert Livingston, and Stephen DeLancey, and many others. The governor had made the colony secure and profitable through strong shipping and legal trade—but he had also done so by turning a blind eye to what was considered illegal smuggling and sea robbery by the English Crown but not by Schuyler and most colonial Americans.[32] Fletcher's policy of laissez-faire salutary neglect that combined licit and illicit trade and put the commercial interests of New York ahead of those of the Mother Country had bolstered the provincial economy and offset the financial drain of King William's War and the stifling Navigation Acts.[33] Though the province was still recovering from the war, the "treasury was burgeoning" in spite of the strains imposed by maintaining "garrisons along the frontier."[34]

Bellomont now took his place behind the wooden speaking podium to introduce himself to his colonial "subjects" and to read aloud the official policy goals of his incoming administration. With seagulls wheeling overhead, Schuyler studied him against a backdrop of handsome glazed yellow and redbrick buildings and stately Trinity Church with its brown stone façade, towering steeple, and large bronze bell. Tall and portly, Bellomont bore a sharp nose, deeply set eyes, and a determined chin beneath his gray powdered periwig.[35]

As his "first official act," he said, it was important for the citizens of New York Province to embrace "the laws of God and the wholesome laws of England." He called upon the Leislerians and anti-Leislerians to put aside their "heats, animosities, and dissensions" and implored the citizenry to join him in promoting "His Majesty's government over us." He then laid out a laundry list of injunctions. "I do hereby strictly prohibit all inhabitants and sojourners within this province from cursing, swearing, immoderate drinking, Sabbath breaking, and all sorts of lewdness and profane behavior in word or action." He commanded all mayors, aldermen, justices of the peace, sheriffs, constables, and other officers within the province to provide "for the suppression of vice and encouragement of religion and virtue" and made it clear that they would "answer the contrary at their peril."[36]

For Schuyler and most of the audience, it was an inauspicious beginning. Here they had come to the Great Dock to welcome their new royal governor, but instead of greeting them as a benevolent leader, Bellomont was lecturing them like a stern schoolmaster. Councilman Schuyler would soon learn just how much the English aristocrat Bellomont looked down his nose upon the American colonists he had been sent overseas to govern, whom he would refer to in his official correspondence as a "rabble," "country people," and "wicked people."[37]

He closed out his oration by reminding his audience how fortunate they were to be governed and protected by the English Crown. The people of New York, he said, were "under the best constitution of laws" and were "fortunate indeed to be in fellowship with the best and bravest people in the world, the people of England." It was for this reason that they "must be obedient to English laws." With the parting flourish of a showman, he then declared, "I am your Lord Bellomont" and "I sayeth to thee God save the King!"[38]

"God save the King!" echoed Peter Schuyler and the crowd. Though they were nothing but an "American rabble" to Bellomont, all but the most stubborn Dutch Leislerians among them were fiercely devoted to Mother England—except when it came to her money-sucking trade laws.

Schuyler understood Bellomont loud and clear. New York Province may have long condoned morally questionable behavior and looked the other way when it came to smuggling and piracy, the earl was telling the crowd, but there was a new sheriff in the colony.[39] Big changes were coming soon for all New Yorkers, Schuyler realized, for the new governor clearly had the firm backing and full weight of the English Crown behind him.

Over the next week, Schuyler and his brothers Brandt and Philip, Frederick Philipse, and the other council members welcomed Bellomont into their fine New York homes overlooking the East River, Upper New York Bay, and the mighty Hudson. At this early stage, they were on good terms with him, as was the outgoing Fletcher, but soon the former governor and his replacement were no longer speaking, the council turned its back on Bellomont, and it met openly with Fletcher to spite him.[40]

However, the politically moderate Whig Schuyler did his best to remain above the fray and not antagonize Bellomont, knowing that colonial governors had a high turnover rate and it was best not to lean too heavily toward either the Whigs or Tories, Leislerians or anti-Leislerians. Until he had more information, he decided that the most prudent course of action would be to stake out a middle position. Though he had been close to Fletcher during his administration, he recognized that he would have to make himself useful to Bellomont if he wanted to protect his interests. Fortunately, he was already in a strong position due to his expertise in Indian affairs and significant political influence in both Albany and New York City.

However, Schuyler soon discovered that Bellomont was a "proud and overbearing" man who was going to cause him and his family endless grief.[41] Within a week of his arrival to New York, the earl became infuriated when he learned that his predecessor Fletcher had managed to acquire a certificate of his good government, signed by members of the council and other prominent inhabitants of the City, thanking him for the "increase of trade" and "growth and prosperity of the city and province." They credited the outgoing governor for his "prudent management and faithful discharge of duty" that had led to New York's "flourishing state" and his policies that had resulted in "the regular distribution of justice" and "just and native freedom." Their fervent hope was that their beloved "Colonel Fletcher" would enjoy the favor of the king and "that God will reward his piety and justice."[42]

Though Schuyler tried to remain neutral in the dispute, he knew that Bellomont had orchestrated Fletcher's recall and that the festering animosity between the two men did not bode well for the province. But before the political tensions escalated to the level of the 1689–1691 Leislerian turmoil, the militia colonel from Albany and New York's top Indian affairs expert was dispatched on an important mission to French Canada to meet with Count Frontenac.

On May 8, 1698, Colonel Peter Schuyler set out from Albany for Montreal with Father Godfredius Dellius, a small contingent of Mohawk scouts that likely included Lawrence, and twenty French and Indian prisoners recently ransomed from captivity. Following the same route he and Lawrence had taken in their bold thrust into New France seven years earlier, the principal objective of the eight-hundred-mile round-trip expedition was to deliver copies of the Treaty of Ryswick in French and Latin, along with an official letter from Bellomont announcing the cessation of hostilities under the treaty. Schuyler and Dellius were also tasked with arranging for prisoner exchanges, as the League Iroquois were anxious for the return of their family members taken by the French and their Indigenous allies during the last decade of imperial and intertribal warfare.[43]

From Albany, they marched northward until they reached the Great Carrying Place on the Hudson River, just north of where Lieutenant Manthet and his French war party had narrowly escaped from Schuyler and Lawrence following his February 1693 rampage through Mohawk country. Located near present-day Fort Edward, New York, the churning rapids and cascading waterfalls in the area made the river unnavigable. Lawrence and his Mohawks, other northeastern tribes, and fur trappers had long carried their canoes and supplies overland at the Great Carrying Place to continue their northward journey to Lake Champlain and French Canada.[44] For two generations, the Schuyler clan, too, had been crossing the Hudson at the well-known spot during military and diplomatic excursions, and the portage would continue to be used during the next three French and Indian Wars, the American Revolution, and the War of 1812.

After crossing the Hudson at the Great Carrying Place, Schuyler's party made for the headwaters of Lake Champlain at South Bay. Here they had made arrangements with League scouts for a small fleet of birchbark canoes, which they loaded up and paddled northward to Crown Point, arriving on May 16. This was where General Winthrop had turned back to Albany in 1690 after having sent Schuyler's brother Johannes and Lawrence northward for their surprise raid at Fort La Prairie. On the lake, they "met a canoe, with French Indians, loaded with beavers, on their way to trade at Albany" and collected information on the situation up north in Canada.[45]

Schuyler was pleased to see the Laurentians, whom he encouraged for both "strategic and economic" reasons to proceed southward to trade in peace and visit their kin. While King William's War had drastically curtailed Albany's supply of high-quality beaver pelts, the last decade of westward expansion had had the opposite effect of glutting the New France market with furs from the Great Lakes tribes, Canadian Algonquians, and Laurentian Iroquois. Schuyler recognized that the two Native fur traders, whether they were acting on their own behalf or as "porters" for French commercial traders in Montreal, represented "a promising means of gaining access to this market."[46] He decided that when he reached Montreal, he would put the word out at the Jesuit mission villages on the St. Lawrence that Albany was open for business for the "French Indians," whom he believed would help resuscitate the town's peltry market.[47]

The next day, they encountered two French Canadian braves donning full war regalia, including fresh war paint on one of the men, and asked where they were heading. The warriors responded that they had been sent by Louis-Hector de Callière, the governor of Montreal, to bring the two Laurentian fur traders heading for Albany back to Canada. However, with a frisson of danger in the air and neither side trusting the other, Schuyler learned from one of his ransomed Native female captives that the Canadian warriors were on their way to Albany to take prisoners and gather intelligence. Not wanting enemy spies to be prowling around his backyard, Schuyler decided to take the two braves into custody and have them travel northward with his group.[48] He and his scouts disarmed and stuffed them in their canoes to, as Schuyler wrote in his journal, "prevent the inconveniences that might happen from their going toward Albany."[49]

From Crown Point, he and his party crossed the full length of Lake Champlain, passing abandoned Fort La Motte, before paddling down the Chambly River to a point just south of Fort Chambly. Tucking their canoes in the brush alongside the river, they struck northwest on foot to Montreal, reaching the wooden gates of the French bastion on May 19 after a twelve-day journey. Once again, the South Bay and Wood Creek route had allowed them to travel on a nearly continuous waterway for more than 150 miles of their journey.[50]

At Montreal, he and Dellius met with Callière, informed him of the signing of the peace treaty, and delivered Bellomont's cover letter addressed to the governor and the formal treaty documents. They also handed over for ransom the twenty French and Indian prisoners in their care and told him that they hoped to commence a formal prisoner exchange. During their meetings on May 19 and 20, Callière informed them that Five Nations' emissaries were expected very soon to conclude a separate peace and that they would exchange prisoners at that time. Schuyler replied that such a treaty was unnecessary since the Iroquois were the lawful subjects of King William III of England, who had claimed suzerainty over the Five Nations since 1664, and as such were included under the Treaty of Ryswick.[51] Callière parried by maintaining that the Iroquois were, in fact, the subjects of France. French Jesuit missionaries, he pointed out, had lived and worked among the Five Nations for decades before the English had seized New York from the Dutch, and furthermore they habitually addressed the governor of Canada as "Father."[52]

On the morning of May 20, Schuyler and Dellius were visited by several Laurentian Iroquois men and women, whom they received "very civilly, and made them some small presents."[53] The informants, who hailed from Kahnawake outside Montreal, were the family kin and friends of Lawrence, his wife Maria, and other Mohawks who had previously lived at the mission with the late Chief Togouiroui, the Great Mohawk, and other Jesuit-influenced Iroquois, but who had moved south to the Mohawk River Valley at the beginning of King William's War. Back in March 1691, Lawrence and Onnonouagaren had tried to forge a peace agreement with their Kahnawake kin to preserve Iroquois lives but had been stymied by Frontenac, Sloughter, and the other Four Nations. Father Dellius, who had with Hilletie's help personally baptized Lawrence and Maria's adopted son and reaffirmed the married couple's Christian vows, was now working secretly with these very same Laurentians to whom Lawrence and Onnonouagaren had extended diplomatic outreach years earlier.

When Schuyler and Dellius met with the Laurentian informants, the messengers told them that six Onondagas were being detained as war captives in the fort's rancid prison inside the gates of Montreal. Schuyler made arrangements to visit the prisoners, whom he and Dellius found badly wounded from a recent bloody battle with a large war party of Canadian

Algonquians, in which twenty-four League braves had been killed and six wounded. Giving them food and water, the two men were outraged by the warriors' harsh treatment under French imprisonment.[54]

Schuyler demanded the immediate release of the Onondagas on moral grounds and their ostensible status as English subjects, but Callière refused. The governor maintained that he could not liberate them from prison without an express order from his superior Frontenac. Schuyler then pressed him about the two Albany-bound Canadian Indians "arrayed as warriors" he had taken captive en route to Montreal, but the French official "was unwilling to admit that they had been sent out to take prisoners."[55]

With the two sides unable to reach an agreement regarding prisoner exchange, Schuyler and his party continued to Quebec to meet with Frontenac himself. On May 25, they reached the clamorous and thriving capital of New France, perched high on the cliffs overlooking the St. Lawrence River, where Sir William Phips had been humiliatingly turned back in 1690. The French royal governor and his entourage, bedecked in sartorial splendor in their freshly powdered periwigs, gold and silver lace, and plumed hats, received them with the usual over-the-top Gallic formality as Schuyler handed over Bellomont's introductory letter and the signed treaty in French and Latin.[56] "I transmit this letter by Colonel Schuyler, member of His Majesty's Council in this Province, and Mr. Dellius," wrote New York's new colonial governor, "both gentlemen of character and merit, in order to evince to you the esteem I entertain for a person of your rank."[57] After their long journey, Schuyler and Dellius conversed only briefly that day with Frontenac, but the next morning they conducted detailed discussions not only with him but the Jesuit superior and his clergy, who came to pay their respects to the high-level functionaries.[58]

The negotiations with Frontenac, conducted over a full week, were polite but contentious. Schuyler stated that he and Dellius had come to New France in good faith with all French and Indian prisoners held by the English in New York and that Bellomont promised to order the Iroquois to deliver to him all those in their possession, who would be sent to Canada. In return, Schuyler requested the release of all English prisoners still held by Frontenac and the French-allied tribes and the termination of all hostile attacks upon the English and the Iroquois.[59]

The French governor graciously but forcefully refused to recognize English imperial claims in North America, presenting many of the same objections as his subordinate Callière. Though he agreed to return any English soldiers or subjects still held under confinement in Canada, he refused to release any League captives until the Five Nations sued for peace. The Iroquois were French subjects, he said, by right of discovery and occupancy of their country by forts and missions. Schuyler civilly disagreed. He contended that, as a free and independent people, the Iroquois had placed themselves and their country under English protection, and had always been recognized as firm English allies.[60]

He and Dellius further argued that the Iroquois tribal leaders had never recognized France as the master of their people and, therefore, the claim that they were subjects of the French Crown carried no weight under the Treaty of Ryswick.[61] The Jesuit missions, they pointed out, "had been tolerated by the English merely through indulgence." The English, on the other hand, had acquired their rights by conquest from the Dutch, and "it cannot be disputed but the Dutch had the Five Nations under their dependence."[62]

In the end, Schuyler and Dellius failed to convince Frontenac of Iroquois sovereignty under the English Empire and the French count firmly but courteously refused to entertain Bellomont's proposed prisoner exchange program. He instead concluded that he and his English counterpart would never agree on the issue and that it would have to be settled by their respective Crowns.[63] Meanwhile, he had precise orders from his king, he said, and if the Iroquois "did not come to him to make peace, he knew the way to their country, and would go and force them to do so."[64]

During the negotiations, the English prisoners held by the French at Quebec, some of whom had been taken captive nearly a decade earlier at Schenectady, were brought before Schuyler and his party to be returned to their families. However, all but two or three refused to return to New York or the New England colonies. Having been seized from their homes as children, they had been well treated in Canada since their abduction, had moved on from their previous lives, and preferred to remain in New

France. Thoroughly indoctrinated in Roman Catholicism, those that had been captured at a young age had been raised by nuns, while the older children had been adopted into Canadian families, with the result that both groups had formed new associations and refused to return to the English colonies. In response, Father Dellius requested that children under fourteen be forced to return whether they wished to or not, on the grounds that they were too young to know what was best when it came to matters of religion, but this, too, became a point of contention. In the end, Frontenac reluctantly agreed that all the children under twelve would be rounded up and sent to Albany at the first opportunity.[65]

On May 31, after arguing back and forth for a week, Schuyler and his contingent started off on their long return journey home, accompanied by several English captives. At Three Rivers halfway between Quebec and Montreal, he and Dellius gathered additional English prisoners to take home with them, and upon their return to Montreal, their previous diplomatic outreach to the Laurentians paid off handsomely. Although they were unable to convince Callière to release the six captive Onondaga warriors, they managed to recruit forty Iroquois from the Montreal region, who agreed to abandon Canada, head south with them, and return to their ancestral homeland in the Mohawk River Valley. The Laurentians carried with them at least five hundred beaver pelts to ease their return and establish a trading nexus between Albany and Montreal through new commercial and kinship ties.[66]

Schuyler and Dellius not only wanted to rebuild the League communities decimated by war, but to provide an open invitation to the transplants living in the Kahnawake and La Montagne missions to trade directly at Albany. In subsequent years, Schuyler and Albany's leaders renewed the invitation and countless Canadian Indians accepted, establishing a new important trading link that would thrive for much of the next century.[67]

The colonel and his exhausted party arrived in Albany on June 22, with twenty-five liberated English prisoners, forty Laurentian Iroquois with kinship ties to the region, and five hundred beaver skins.[68] But no sooner had Schuyler and Dellius reached home than Hilletie van Olinda notified them that their Leislerian enemies had been busy plotting against them while they were gone.

18
THE WRATH OF LORD BELLOMONT

By mid-June, a mere two months after taking office, Richard Coote was as despised from Manhattan to Albany as the tyrannical Leisler before him. Although he at first tried to straddle the fence between the Leislerians and anti-Leislerians, the Earl of Bellomont quickly put aside any semblance of bipartisanship by removing lawyer William Nicoll, customs collector Chidley Brooke, and merchant William Pinhorne from his governor's council, despite the fact they had all been handpicked by the Crown. By September 28, he would suspend the remaining councilors except the political moderates Schuyler, Stephanus van Cortland, and William Smith, as well as Frederick Philipse, who at age seventy-three was forced into retirement. As their replacements, he appointed several rabid Leislerians and a pair of moderates.[1]

In retribution for the council's signed certificate of Fletcher's good government, Bellomont slapped his predecessor with a £10,000 ($3,5000,000 today) bond before the ex-governor departed for England to answer the charges against him. He then deluged the Board of Trade in London with endless accusations against Fletcher. While some were true, or at least partly true, many were slanderous falsehoods. He also pointed a finger at New York's Assembly, which remained an obstacle to his ambitious agenda.[2] On June 14, he disbanded the Assembly in a fit of rage as Leisler had done before him, claiming that his American representatives were "altogether obstructing the king's service."[3]

Over the next two months, Bellomont dug deep into New York's public records to uncover damaging material on Fletcher and he continued to make enemies in Manhattan, Albany, and throughout the province. While his initial investigations focused on his predecessor's cozy relationship with the Red Sea pirates—the same bandits Bellomont had coerced Captain Kidd into hunting down in the Indian Ocean—the earl's inquiries soon uncovered Fletcher's extravagant land grants to his political favorites. Seven of the nineteen New York manors that existed by the 18th century, including 57,000-acre Philipsburg Manor awarded to Frederick Philipse in 1693, were granted by Fletcher between 1692 and 1697. However, Bellomont's actions proved to be highly selective and politically motivated, as he singled out only the deeds of Schuyler, Philipse, and other members of the anti-Leislerian faction who had supported Fletcher, while ignoring large holdings acquired by Leislerians. Eventually, Bellomont would expand his policing efforts to include all large grants in New York, making him unpopular with virtually every prominent landholder.[4]

While Bellomont focused on exposing the past activities of Fletcher and the anti-Leislerians, he continued to work strenuously to combat illegal smuggling and piracy. In June, he ordered customs agents to raid the home of Dutchman Ounziel van Sweeten in search of East India goods. However, an angry mob of New York merchants, led by Philipse and his English son-in-law Philip French, rushed to the aid of van Sweeten. The "rabble of colonials" not only freed van Sweeten but turned the tables on the Crown officials by locking them up in the house. After the Philipse family thwarted the arrest of van Sweeten, the governor was forced to call upon armed soldiers from Fort William to disperse the crowd and rescue the officers, whom Bellomont claimed "were in danger of being murdered."[5]

By July, many citizens were complaining that his stringent anti-piracy measures had already "prevented £100,000 from being brought into the city since his arrival," thus severely depleting the coffers of the provincial treasury and limiting the money available on the streets.[6] Though Bellomont retained the support of the Leislerian faction, he remained unaware of how precarious the colony's economy was without the massive influx of specie and trade goods from smuggling and piracy.[7] In his efforts to clean up the City and province, he also alienated many of the Dutch, French, Walloon, German, and Jewish citizens with his heavy-handed anglicization efforts, which far exceeded those of his predecessor. In his mind, victory in the struggle over Crown authority required not only recruiting more Britons and strengthening English institutions but weakening the hold of Dutch culture on the province's longtime residents. This he accomplished by filling prominent political and commercial positions with Englishmen and by enhancing the already central position of the Church of England.[8]

Like many New Yorkers, Peter Schuyler and his brothers Brandt and Philip quickly came to despise Bellomont, who within six months of taking office had become the torchbearer of the Leislerians.[9] The changeover was symbolized on October 20, 1698, when a large crowd accompanied the governor to the former gallows where the bodies of Jacob Leisler and Jacob Milborne were interred. To the sound of beating drums and blaring trumpets, the Leislerians dug up the bodies of the two insurrectionists who had been hanged and beheaded seven years earlier, sewed their decapitated heads back on, and paraded the decomposed corpses through the streets. The bodies of the Protestant martyrs were taken to the Dutch Reformed Church to lay in state for several days before being reinterred in consecrated ground, which the anti-Leislerians called "a pompous burial." Over a thousand people attended the grim ceremony to witness Bellomont's public vindication of their slain leader and his son-in-law.[10]

The whole scene struck such a terror into the anti-Leislerian inhabitants and itinerant seamen that most remained in their homes or aboard their ships during the burial for their own safety. Though the act solidified Bellomont's support with the Leislerians, it "reopened seven-year-old wounds and once again split the city like a cleaver."[11]

By December, many lukewarm Leislerians and political moderates had joined in the formal petition for the governor's recall, and former council members Chidley Brooke and Nicholas Bayard had joined Fletcher in London to lodge complaints against Bellomont. Reports were soon being transmitted from across the Atlantic that he was running the colony into the ground financially, packing key government posts with Leislerians, and casting aside the Anglican Church in favor of Dutch Calvinism.[12]

But the colony's staunch anti-Leislerians like Nicholas Bayard and political moderates like Schuyler were not the only ones to take a dislike to Bellomont and who wanted to send him packing. Soon after taking office, he managed to alienate New York Province's most important military ally in combating the ever-encroaching French.

When the new "Brother Corlaer" arrived in Albany on July 20, 1698, to renew the Covenant Chain, Lawrence and his fellow Iroquois were taken aback by Bellomont's bombastic demeanor and physical infirmity compared to his predecessor Cayenquiragoe, the Great Swift Arrow. While the humble-born soldier Fletcher had always observed formal etiquette and protocol in Indian diplomacy, possessed a strong military bearing that the Natives admired, and genuinely respected the Iroquois as human beings, the aristocrat Lord Bellomont made a miserable first impression. He limped and groaned from his gout, sniffled and sneezed from a nasty cold, and complained endlessly about his long voyage and ill health. All this was bad enough, but what was most off-putting to the Iroquois was his arrogant demeanor and lack of hospitality.[13]

During the multiday conference, Colonel Peter Schuyler served in his customary role as Indian Affairs commissioner and Hilletie van Olinda as Crown interpreter. After delivering nine beaver skins to open the treaty negotiation, the Onondaga Anglophile Sadekanaktie, speaking on behalf of all Five Nations, congratulated New York's new royal governor for his "safe arrival over the Great Sea"; invoked a "tree of welfare and peace" between the Iroquois and English; reminded Bellomont of the Iroquois's "great losses" sustained during King William's War; and informed him that, since receiving notification of the 1697 Treaty of Ryswick, his people had suffered ninety-four warriors killed in skirmishes with the French-allied Great Lakes tribes.[14] The Onondaga headman lavished particular praise upon "Brother Quider," whom he said never failed to come to the assistance of the Iroquois "in time of need."[15] For more than a decade, pronounced Sadekanaktie, Schuyler had been their strongest advocate and link in the Covenant Chain.[16]

Sadekanaktie also had many grievances. He demanded that the English live up to their obligations as alliance partners "to see justice done" for the attacks upon them by their Native enemies to the north and west. He also complained about the high prices of trade goods and blacksmithing repairs in Albany and the English inability to supply timely military aid. The Mohawk headman Sanonguirese and another Haudenosaunee speaker also raised several concerns. One of the most pressing was the need to recover the twenty-five men, forty-two women, and three children belonging to the Oneida, Onondaga, Cayuga, and Seneca Nations still detained as prisoners by Frontenac in Canada. Because of the importance of recovering the prisoners to restock their war-ravaged population, the headmen informed Bellomont that they had already extended an olive branch to their kindred "praying Indians of Canada" and reached out to Frontenac to recover the prisoners.[17]

The sickly royal governor was in no mood to be lectured by a pack of wild "savages" and scolded the League spokesmen several times like errant children. Not only did he blame their losses since the end of the war on their "own neglect," he insisted that all negotiations with the French for the release of captives must be left in English hands.[18] You should "not upon any account whatsoever" hold council or negotiate "with the French of Canada," he warned the Iroquois headmen through Hilletie, for "you will then break the Covenant Chain, and the promise you have made of continuing firm under the obedience and protection of the king, my great master."[19]

Though the two sides remained apart on several issues, Schuyler managed to act in his usual conciliatory fashion and bring the two sides closer together, with Hilletie's help, by the end of the meeting. Through the soft-touch diplomacy of Schuyler and Hilletie, Bellomont managed to garner continued Anglophile support and to obtain a pledge that the Iroquois would not pursue a separate peace with the French without consulting their English allies.[20]

During the first two days of negotiations, the cranky earl found the Iroquois "sullen and cold in their carriage." But by the end of the proceedings, he claimed to have "quite retrieved their affections to the king's government" and believed that "they were never known to part with any governor in so good humor as they did with me."[21] So pleased was he with his performance that he ordered the publication of the negotiations by William Bradford, New York's official printer to the Crown.[22]

However, Bellomont badly misinterpreted what had transpired due to his failure to grasp the highly personal and reciprocal nature of Iroquois diplomacy, for which he had been given a crash-course by Schuyler and Hilletie but proved a poor pupil. Like their Brother Quider, the Indigenous leaders immediately distrusted and disdained his lordship because he came across as a pompous ass who had no respect nor interest in the Iroquois or their fate. In the eyes of Lawrence, Sadekanaktie, Sanonguirese, and their fellow headmen and war captains, the difference between him and his predecessor couldn't have been starker. While the Great Swift Arrow had rushed upriver from New York City to help the Iroquois during moments of crisis, supped with them at his dining table, squired them around in his six-horse carriage, and treated them to a display of his majesty's naval firepower in New York Harbor on King William III's birthday, the new governor treated his Indian allies like serfs.[23] "[I]n the midst of a fit of the gout . . . and a cold taken upon Hudson's River," wrote Bellomont, "I had like to have died when I came to Albany . . . and was strangely surprised and discouraged at the behavior of *those people* the first two or three days conference (italics added)."[24]

The prodigious gift of muskets, lead, powder, shirts, kettles, knives, hats, rum, tobacco, flints, and loaves of bread was appreciated, but in the eyes of *those people*, Bellomont was just another tone-deaf Crown official in the Leisler mold, who preferred to lecture them instead of listening to their concerns.[25]

The most far-reaching outcome of the meeting was Bellomont's undermining of the authority of Schuyler and Hilletie and the severing of the all-important ties between Albany's most experienced Indian agents and the League Iroquois. The cause of the governor's displeasure was a pair of questionable, Fletcher-approved land deeds in the Hudson and Mohawk River Valleys.

In early June, Bellomont had been visited in New York City by the Protestant Mohawks Hendrick and Joseph, both friends of Lawrence, about the deeds as well as alleged mismanagement by Father Dellius, Schuyler, Hilletie, and other Fletcher appointees. The first deed had originated in a 1695 sale by six Mohawks of a large tract of land at Schoharie to Schuyler's younger brother Arent, who had acted on behalf of Nicholas Bayard. The second had involved a July 1697 title to a fifty-mile-long and four-mile-wide land tract in the Mohawk River Valley and another enormous parcel surrounding Schaghticoke on the upper Hudson to Dellius and several public officials, including Peter Schuyler. With Hilletie acting as interpreter, Dellius somehow persuaded eight Protestant Mohawks to sign the confirmatory deed on the parcel, which was valued at £25,000 ($8,750,000 today).[26]

Though the Dellius land deal had been put forward to the Protestant Mohawks years earlier as a wartime measure to place the deed holders in the position of "guardians or trustees," the deponents Hendrick and Joseph claimed they had been duped by the reverend into signing away much of their land instead of ensuring its security against French seizure. They demanded that the governor vacate and destroy the agreements. Based on Hendrick and Joseph's complaint and the testimony of two Leislerian Albany officials, Bellomont requested official power to "vacate" Fletcher's grants prior to his July meeting with League delegates in Albany.[27]

Confronted with what he believed was overwhelming evidence of malfeasance by Fletcher and his appointees, Bellomont had arrived at the Albany council on July 20 with his mind already made up and hoping to gather explicit evidence of illegal activity. Due to his heavy bias against Fletcher and the anti-Leislerians, he mistook the Indians initial sullenness toward him as confirmation that Dellius, Schuyler, and Hilletie had abused their governmental positions. He saw their behavior as proof of Hendrick and Joseph's complaint that the commissioners had defrauded the Indians to further their positions and line their own pockets—without any intention of protecting Iroquois interests. But the motivations of the principal parties were not as black-and-white as the governor wanted to believe.[28]

During the council and shortly afterward, Bellomont conducted a hasty investigation to confirm the charges, further smear Fletcher, and justify stripping Albany's anti-Leislerians of power. Under questioning by the governor, Dellius argued for his innocence and maintained that his primary aim had been to secure the Mohawk land rights to protect against seizure by the French and their Indian allies.[29] Though the evidence supported Dellius's claim, he and his fellow New Yorkers also clearly "sought to prosper in the long run from their enormous grant."[30] In his defense, Dellius argued that the deed was supposed to have included parcels of land reserved for the Mohawks, but Fletcher's attorney general had refused to include them because the Crown could not approve the granting of a conditional patent to the Mohawks, since, according to English law, "uncivilized" Natives could not possess legal title to their lands. But Bellomont refused to accept Dellius's more nuanced explanation of the sequence of events that had led to the controversial land deed.[31]

Recognizing that he had made a mistake and to remove himself from the controversy, Peter Schuyler swiftly resigned his share with a "frank and genteel" renunciation along with two of his fellow Albany Indian commissioners. In the end, most of the blame fell on Dellius, who had been the leading figure in two of the three Mohawk land deals under Bellomont's review.[32] Even though he survived the debacle relatively unscathed, Schuyler would be at odds with Bellomont for as long as the earl retained the governor's chair. Neither trusting nor liking the militia colonel and former mayor of Albany, Bellomont retained Schuyler solely because he was "the most popular man" in New York Province with the Five Nations and he could not do without him.[33] At the same time, the governor had the treacherous Robert Livingston "keep a watchful eye on his brother-in-law."[34]

In parting from Albany, Bellomont promised the Iroquois that he would do all in his power to have the grants revoked and urged them to apply to the still-trusted Schuyler if they encountered further difficulties. By the spring of 1699, the gouty earl had pushed through the New York Assembly a bill that revoked the Mohawk River Valley grant along with several others. At the same time, he removed Dellius from his Albany pulpit. Intent on revenge, the Leislerians in the lower House insisted upon a provision that officially suspended the dominie from his ministerial duties. With his career in ruins, Dellius collected testimonials protesting his innocence and proclaiming his good character from influential church leaders, merchants, and officials throughout the province and sailed for the Netherlands.[35] Upon his arrival in Amsterdam, Dellius made life difficult for Bellomont back in America by making "sure that both the classis of Amsterdam and the bishop of London were acquainted with his side of the controversy."[36]

Hilletie van Olinda, who had faithfully supported Dellius for a decade, was another casualty of Bellomont's anti-Leislerian purge. Having served as interpreter in the two Dellius land transactions and having been accused by Bellomont's military engineer, Wolfgang Romer, of being the major reason Indian diplomacy was "managed, with extraordinary division and jealousy," she was dismissed by the governor from her position as Crown interpreter. In the process, she lost her £20 ($7,000 today) yearly stipend needed to help support her family. In undermining Hilletie, Romer was driven by both chauvinism and his Leislerian agenda, writing to Bellomont that although "a *woman* may answer you as an interpreter, it will be, my Lord, only for the purpose of deceiving you, and keeping you in ignorance of important affairs (italics added)."[37]

Referring to Hilletie as "the Mohawk interpretress," Bellomont grilled her about the Mohawk land deal, both in the presence of Dellius and on her own so that the reverend could not "overawe" her. Under oath, she swore that "the Indians had signed the deed as a deed of trust only" and that the land would only "go to Dellius and his partners" if the Mohawks no longer lived in the region.[38] Bellomont appeared satisfied with her deposition, claiming that she was very "frank" under oath and had given valuable evidence against the man who had "converted" her to Protestantism, thus exposing Dellius's "sinister practices."[39] Unfortunately for the Mohawk translator, her forthcoming testimony meant little to Bellomont. Not only did he remove her from her Crown position, he tried to banish her from Albany altogether and replaced her with the elderly Dutch trader Arnout Viele, a Leislerian who had lost his position as Crown interpreter in 1691.[40]

The drastic changes instituted by Bellomont were not only hard on Hilletie, Schuyler, and many others in Albany and Iroquoia who had worked vigorously on behalf of the English and Five Nations—they threatened to undermine New York-Iroquois relations altogether. Although many Iroquois were angry at Father Dellius for what they viewed as a grubby land scam, and at least some held Schuyler, Hilletie, and other Albany officials accountable for poor decision-making, Lawrence and other teetering Anglophiles believed it was far worse that Dellius and Hilletie had been stripped of authority and that Schuyler's role was significantly reduced.[41]

19
THE END OF AN ERA

By the fall of 1698, communications between the Five Nations and English of New York continued, but Lawrence, his fellow Mohawks, and many other Iroquois remained angry with the royal governor for removing Hilletie and demoting Schuyler, whom they now referred to as "the Colonel" in addition to "Brother Quider." Although Hilletie still remained an invaluable liaison in Indian affairs due to her mastery of Dutch, Mohawk, and rudimentary English, she no longer traveled to the Five Nations villages or attended the Albany treaty councils as the Crown's official interpreter. With the reduced influence of Schuyler and Hilletie in Indian affairs and the lingering odor of the Dellius land deal, the Anglophile Iroquois receded into the background as winter progressed, while the power of the neutralist and Francophile factions correspondingly grew.[1]

While the Francophiles sought a separate peace with New France, the neutralist leaders continued to search for a middle ground between Bellomont's and Frontenac's diametrically opposed interpretations of the status of the Five Nations under the Treaty of Ryswick. Despite the termination of hostilities, Lawrence and the Iroquois continued to grapple with the need to find a balance between the still-competing English and French. Meanwhile, Frontenac and Callière continued to supply arms to their Native allies of the Great Lakes region and to press for the western Iroquois to move north into the St. Lawrence Valley. The Five Nations' longtime diplomatic ties with New York served as a counterweight to the aggressive aspirations of New France, but the combination of the relentless diplomatic pressure by Canadian officials and their Indigenous allies and the inadequate supply of weapons, powder, and supplies from the English Crown threatened to undermine the Confederacy.[2]

As Bellomont and Frontenac pressed forward with ambitious fort-building projects designed to secure a foothold in Iroquois territory, the Five Nations headmen like Teganissorens, Sadekanaktie, Sanonguirese, and Rode, and war captains like Lawrence, continued to search for a way to maintain both alliances, while not selling out their interests or losing control of their territory. With few viable options open to them, Lawrence and others seeking a peaceful resolution focused on the traditional role of Iroquois leaders as diplomatic peacemakers and mediators between competing or warring interests. Their goal was to reduce Iroquois deaths, preserve League villages, ensure access to the rich western hunting grounds, and reestablish a strong fur trade.[3]

The problem was that Bellomont was no man of peace. He continued to argue strenuously that the Iroquois were "English subjects" under the Covenant Chain and that a diplomatic treaty between the Iroquois and the French could only be consummated by the Crown. As the western Iroquois continued to send out peace feelers to New France, Bellomont persisted in demanding that the English alone handle negotiations with Frontenac over peace and prisoner exchanges. Meanwhile, neutralists like Teganissorens and neutral-leaning Anglophiles like Lawrence, unwilling to make peace with the French at the cost of severing their Covenant Chain link with the English, refused the demands of the French.[4]

The result was a political stalemate. While Iroquois leaders struggled to escape the diplomatic bind, the Wendats, Odawas, Miamis, and Illinois Confederation continued to wage bloody war against their traditional Iroquois enemies. Between 1697 and 1699, the western offensives by the Indigenous allies of New France against the Five Nations killed enormous numbers of Onondaga, Seneca, and other Iroquois warriors with powder and weapons provided by the French. With the increasing casualties of the deadly western Indian war, the neutralists' tenuous position became difficult to sustain.[5]

But then after a short illness, Count Frontenac, that wily old French courtier who had been a thorn in the side of Schuyler and the English for a generation, departed the mortal world.[6] The passing of the larger-than-life statesman in late November 1698 resulted in a major shift in France's policy regarding her tempestuous and financially costly relationship with the Iroquois.[7] The last decade of fighting on the New York-Canadian frontier had demonstrated that trying to bring the Iroquois under imperial control threatened perpetual "hostilities, misunderstanding, and division." The French believed that England would never stop unleashing the Iroquois upon Canada and that the Indians inflicted far more death, injury, and terror "than the English."[8] By early 1699, the Roi du Soleil supported a peace that recognized the Five Nations' neutral and independent status and the Confederation's right to trade with both England and France without restrictions.[9]

The dramatic change in diplomacy coincided with Bellomont's vacating of Fletcher's controversial land grants through an act of the New York Assembly. Although the May 26, 1699, act vested title to the lands with the English Crown instead of returning them to the Five Nations as Bellomont had promised, he assured the Mohawks that they possessed their lands as fully as if the contested deed had never been written. But he was bamboozling them. With the future disposition of the lands under his control as the Crown's man in New York, he was anxious to construct forts and trading posts in the Onondaga region to the west, believing this was his best means of retaining long-term Iroquois fealty to the English.[10]

Reinstated Indian agent Robert Livingston, always on the lookout for ways to line his own pockets, had recommended building a fort and stationing a garrison in the contested region of Detroit. He believed it would demonstrate English power and influence in the upper Great Lakes country and promote peace between the Five Nations and western Pays d'en haut tribes. This would, in turn, allow Mother England to stake "a claim to the region's promising peltry trade," from which Livingston would make a fortune.[11]

A mere three months after the passing of the act vacating the Dellius grant and other questionable deeds, Bellomont proposed to the Board of Trade in London that the sacred Iroquois lands be distributed among the Crown's officers and soldiers at Albany. He believed this would help prevent troop desertion and allow English expansion into the North American interior. "With peaceful thoughts prevailing nowhere," observes historian Daniel Richter, "the Iroquois were caught between the rock of Redcoats stationed in their villages and the hard place of surrender to their French and western Indian enemies."[12]

For the Five Nations, their new "Brother Corlaer," Lord Bellomont, had stabbed them in the back.

Although the Treaty of Ryswick in late 1697 had ostensibly ended King William's War between England and France, two years later the imperial superpowers continued to actively spy upon one another and grapple behind the scenes for control of northeastern North America, knowing that formal hostilities between the two countries would likely soon recommence. To investigate the growing rumors of a planned pan-Indian assault upon New York and the New England colonies, Bellomont recalled Schuyler from the political wilderness and dispatched him in March 1700 to travel to Onondaga with Livingston and Albany trader Hendrick Hansen for some answers. The interpreter Hansen was one of the replacements for Hilletie following her dismissal from her position as Crown interpreter by the spiteful royal governor, who continued to believe there was an active conspiracy against the English by the French and western League Iroquois.[13]

On April 9, Schuyler and his party set out for the seat of the Iroquois Confederacy to meet with the "Keepers of the Central Fire." They traveled the first day on foot, hiking the twenty miles to Schenectady. There they outfitted two canoes with supplies and the next morning started paddling upstream on the Mohawk River toward their destination.[14] Neither Schuyler nor Livingston had ever used the river-borne conveyances to journey to Onondaga country before, but they decided to on this occasion so "that we might be satisfied how canoes can go thither."[15]

Although Schuyler and Livingston seem to have gotten along reasonably well, had both made their fortunes in the fur trade and oceangoing commerce, shared many of the same friends, and were closely aligned in their views when it came to Indian Affairs, the two brothers-in-law—one a Dutch-American born on the wild Indian frontier, the other a Scottish emigrant of noble blood—could not have been more different. While Schuyler was the man of action whose word carried the weight of gospel in the borderlands and who was both beloved and venerated by the Five Nations and those with whom he lived, worked, and fought, Livingston was the entrepreneurial man of vision. However, he was not very likable, looked down upon Native Americans, was known for his greedy nature, and was considered untrustworthy and unscrupulous by many of his peers.[16] As historian Allen Trelease has written:

> The lives of Livingston and Schuyler, whose personalities in some respects were complimentary, ran parallel until their deaths in the 1720's. Both men . . . enjoyed considerable political power at various times. Livingston was the more clever and acquisitive of the two and by material standards was more successful. Schuyler, on the other hand, was more popular. His physical courage and personal integrity contrasted markedly with the shrewdness of his brother-in-law, which savored more of the court and the countinghouse. Schuyler managed to stay in the good graces of every successive governor—a feat requiring supreme tact as well as agility—whereas Livingston's initial good impression often soured on longer acquaintance.[17]

Paddling their lead canoe upriver against the stiff current with a second birchbark canoe tied to first to carry supplies, Schuyler, Livingston, and Hansen followed alongside the Old Mohawk Turnpike. This was the same trail that Schuyler, Hilletie, and Dirck Wessels had taken in January 1694 during their aborted journey to Oneida, plodding through the deep winter snow on horseback and with snowshoes. The heavily used trail spanning the entire east-west length of the Mohawk River Valley had been used by Haudenosaunee hunting, trading, and war-making parties for centuries and Schuyler and his group saw Indigenous traffic moving up and down the busy thoroughfare. As much frontier explorers as Indian Affairs commissioners,

Schuyler and Livingston recorded their observations of the riverside settlements and the estimated distances to key landmarks all along their route from Albany to Onondaga.[18]

From Schenectady by water, their first stop was the relocated Mohawk "Lower Castle" of Tiononderoge, where Lawrence and his wife Maria lived with their three Mohawk children. Still the home of many Protestant Mohawks baptized by Father Dellius and Hilletie, the village was gaining in strength and burgeoning with people, with Lawrence's Wolf Clan "still a substantial force" among the villagers despite the negative fallout from Dellius's ill-advised land scheme. During their overnight stay in Tiononderoge, Schuyler and his party ate dinner and held a council with Lawrence and other Mohawk leaders, sounding them out regarding the political situation in Onondaga country and inviting them to the planned conference in Albany scheduled for August.[19]

From Tiononderoge, they paddled upriver to the "Upper Castle" of Canajoharie and "from thence till ye place where ye great Castle stood called Tionnontoguen burnt by ye French" in 1693, located twelve miles farther up the Mohawk River Valley.[20] The scorched remainder of the once powerful Mohawk fortress overlooking the meandering river stood like a raven-pecked carcass, reminding Schuyler of just how brutal the "Nine Years' War," as many were now calling it, had been to his Iroquois brethren as well as his fellow settlers along the Albany frontier.

From the old burnt-down "castle" at Tionnontoguen, Schuyler and his party navigated their way westward up the Mohawk River, passing the Little Carrying Place at modern-day Little Falls, where they were forced to disembark from the river's whitewater rapids to portage their two canoes loaded with their weapons, supplies, and gifts for the Iroquois. Days later, after traveling nearly ninety miles upriver from the burnt-down settlement at Tionnontoguen, they reached the Great Carrying Place of the Oneidas, where they once again disembarked to go around the cascading waterfalls due to the difficulty of navigation. The portage was a narrow trail across a low ridge between the Mohawk River and Wood Creek, located near present-day Rome, New York. The calcareous limestone and dolostone ridge lay between two major watersheds—the Mohawk River flowing eastward to the Hudson River and the Atlantic, and Wood Creek flowing westward to the Great Lakes by way of Oneida Lake and the Oswego River. Because of the spring thaw, both natural watersheds were full and the river was running high, making the distance for them to carry their canoes and supplies around a mile.[21]

Continuing west, Schuyler and his party soon learned just how far the support for the English had fallen among the western League Iroquois Nations. At an Onondaga fishing camp on the south shore of Oneida Lake, they stopped to talk to the Mohawk Bear Clan headman Sanonguirese and the old Anglophile sachem Onnucheranorum, who informed them that many of their people now distrusted the English. The French officers and Jesuit leaders were circulating rumors of English treachery, impotence in Indian Affairs, and diminished prestige on the world stage. Although both Anglophile leaders claimed not to believe "the French lies," they proceeded to recount in excruciating detail the various rumors of English plots to destroy the Five Nations through poisoning and other macabre schemes.[22] After traveling more than two hundred miles by water to parley with Iroquois sachems and invite them to the planned meeting with the governor, the Albany emissaries were flabbergasted.[23]

The headmen also repeated a story that the French intended to build forts in Iroquois territory and that England was too weak to stop them. Even more alarming, rumors were floating around that the English intended to disarm the Five Nations and destroy them altogether. The headmen claimed not to believe these unsubstantiated reports either—and yet they wondered why their gifts of weapons, powder, and food stores were always late and short of what was needed to secure themselves against their mutual enemies.[24] The French governor Callière, Frontenac's successor, often upbraided them and their people, they said, by scoffing, "Why, if your [English] Governor loved you so well as I do my Children the Indians, he would clothe you as I do."[25]

The prejudicial rumors were denied by Schuyler, Livingston, and Hansen, but it was clear that the Iroquois pro-French faction had grown in strength over the past year. To demonstrate their good will, the envoys reminded the headmen that they were cordially invited to Albany in August to meet with Bellomont, where they would be able to settle all matters to their satisfaction in the usual manner under the Covenant Chain.[26] But it was clear to Schuyler that neither Sanonguirese nor Onnucheranorum thought much of the new "Corlaer," whom they and their fellow League leaders continued to resent for continuing to restrict their freedom to travel to New France for trade and to conclude a peace agreement on their own with Callière and the Great Lakes tribes of the Pays d'en haut.[27]

As the New York envoys proceeded westward toward Onondaga, they found the political situation even more unsettling. Though the Iroquois elders and some of the younger men typically dispersed across the freshwater streams and lakes around the Great Carrying Place, Oneida Lake, and Onondaga Lake in the spring, it soon became clear to Schuyler that many of the headmen had not gone to their fishing camps so much for subsistence as to escape from the ongoing political turmoil and factionalism that was tearing apart the Five Nations in the aftermath of King William's War.[28]

At one fishing spot, Schuyler's party encountered Sadekanaktie and several followers. The Anglophile leader reported similar negative rumors, including one from an interpreter at Fort Frontenac that Bellomont himself was plotting to destroy the Five Nations. Though Schuyler and his cohorts refuted the baseless French propaganda, it was clear that damage had been done and that support for the English under the Covenant Chain was dwindling among the western League Iroquois. But Schuyler and his party were even more shocked when they learned from Sadekanaktie that he and his fellow Anglophiles were no longer welcome in their own village at Onondaga.[29]

When the New Yorkers asked the headmen to join them as they traveled from the fishing village to Onondaga, only one person accompanied them, and when they reached their destination, they were stunned to find a gathering of only eight sachems. Both the Anglophile Sadekanaktie and the neutralist Teganissorens were conspicuous by their absence. The Onondagas' orator was the Francophile Aradgi, whom Schuyler had learned was a favorite of Callière and his French officials.[30]

At this point, Schuyler's biggest fear was that the pro-French Iroquois faction would lead a delegation to Montreal that would completely capitulate to the French government, the western Great Lakes tribes, and the Laurentian Iroquois. In his view, this would pose a serious threat to England's current and future interests in North America. He could only hope that the traditional Iroquois neutralist principle of balance would serve as a counterweight to the Francophile faction that had taken over Five Nations politics.[31]

Realizing that he had to reframe the English narrative, Schuyler pushed back with his usual combination of polite diplomacy, reciprocal generosity, and patriarchal firmness. During the proceedings, he declared that he had discovered the most potent tool the Francophiles were using to purge their political opponents. "The French tell you that the English will poison you," he told Aradgi and the others, "but we have great cause to suspect the French have a hand in seducing you to poison one another; for we observe those Indians that have done signal services for your Nation against the French and are true to the English interest, their whole families are poisoned, and dwindle away to nothing."[32] He was not joking: many people believed that toxins, or witchery, were taking the lives of prominent Anglophile families and the Iroquois were terrified of the unexplained illnesses gripping their fragile communities. The actual cause did not matter, as Aradgi's opponents at Onondaga were intimidated by him and the Francophile faction, who seemed to wield supernatural powers.[33]

It was clear to Schuyler that the Five Nations were in a state of profound demoralization and uncertainty regarding their future and that they were continuing to lose considerable numbers of their people to New France. The factionalism and out-migration were driven by heavy recruitment efforts by French political brokers and the Laurentian Iroquois; the superior weaponry, clothing, gifts, and soldierly protection provided by the French; the shrinking influence of Albany in the wake of the disastrous Dellius affair; Bellomont's heavy-handed and tone-deaf approach to Indian Affairs; the continued neglect and ineffectiveness of the English Crown; and the persistent thrashing by the western Great Lakes tribes. As Schuyler had suspected, the Five Nations were not involved in a nefarious plot to join forces with the eastern Algonquin tribes and destroy the English, as the paranoid Bellomont had suspected, but they *had* fallen victim to the bizarre French-inspired rumors that the English were planning to annihilate them. The English were simply being outmaneuvered by New France, which he and Livingston found humiliating. The League Iroquois were now more divided than ever before between those who sided with the French like Aradgi, those who opted for the middle course of neutrality like Teganissorens, and those who believed that remaining committed to the English under the Covenant Chain was the best path for the Haudenosaunee like Sadekanaktie.[34]

To undercut Aradgi's rising authority and prevent the Iroquois from French domination, Schuyler chastised him and the other Onondaga headmen for their willingness to cut a deal with the devil. He then invited them to meet with the new "Corlaer" Bellomont at Albany in three and a half months' time to rectify the dire situation. However, the clever Aradgi politely declined the offer. Because the pendulum had swung back to the League's Francophiles and to France's Native allies in the two and a half years since the end of the war, the French and their Indigenous supporters now wielded significantly more power than the English, the Mohawks, and the Anglophile factions of the other Four Nations.[35]

When Schuyler and his party left Onondaga for the return journey to Albany, they realized that Mother England had lost the diplomatic battle for the hearts and minds of the Iroquois. Paddling downriver on their return journey, they made good time and reached Albany on May 2, having been in the backcountry for a full three weeks. After completing a round trip of 540 miles by land and water through territory only rarely traversed before by White Europeans, Livingston, Schuyler, and Hansen were not only exhausted but remained alarmed by what they had witnessed in Indian country.[36]

They immediately prepared their individual and joint reports for Bellomont to stem the pro-French tide and aggressive political maneuvering taking place in the distant western borderlands. With so many League Iroquois fleeing to the St. Lawrence River Valley and Montreal region over the past decade, they believed quick and decisive action was necessary to prevent the continued mass exodus to Canada.[37] To frustrate the French, they endorsed Bellomont's plan to build an English fort and send missionaries among the Iroquois and they proposed that the Five Nations be resettled, with the Mohawks and Oneidas moving closer to Albany. With a fort built to protect them and ministers sent to instruct them, they would be less inclined to trade with the French or support them in the next imperial war. They proposed that the English fort for the region be placed between Lake Ontario and Lake Oneida.[38] Because this was the main route between Canada and the western Iroquois, this would secure "all the 5 Nations from the French at once."[39]

No sooner had Schuyler and the commissioners filed their reports than Sadekanaktie arrived from Onondaga with twenty-five bedraggled supporters, who, under heavy pressure from Aradgi and his acolytes, had been "forced to fly" from Onondaga.[40] Schuyler not only took in the excommunicated villagers, but gave them food and allowed them to live on his property at Schuyler Flatts outside Albany for several months. The widely respected Sadekanaktie and his family had been forced to leave behind the headman's son, who was dying of an alleged combination of poisoning and witchcraft and was too sick to be moved.[41]

Upon receiving the reports from Schuyler, Livingston, and Hansen, Bellomont promptly forwarded them to England. Not only did he take all the credit for their suggestions with the Crown, he claimed them as his own personal policy initiative. But before any of the plans could be implemented, he passed over to the other side just like Frontenac. After suffering a severe attack of gout, Bellomont died in New York City in March 1701 at age sixty-five.[42]

The man who drove him into his grave was none other than Peter Schuyler's friend and Bellomont's business partner, Captain William Kidd, who had returned home to America from the Indian Ocean with a shipload of treasure in June 1699 and was now imprisoned in London for piracy. Despite the countless challenges he had faced during his perilous voyage and the mutiny of ninety-seven of his seamen because he refused to go all-in on piracy, Kidd miraculously made it back to the colonies from Madagascar with around £40,000 ($14,000,000 today) of plunder in his hold and French passports that proved he had taken two ships, the *Rouparelle* and *Quedagh Merchant*, legally in accordance with his commissions. However, the treasure-rich *Quedagh* was connected to the Great Mughal of India, King Aurangzeb I, and the East India Company had brokered the shipping, which caused a political uproar in India and threats from the Great Mughal to terminate all trade with England. When the "trusty and well-beloved Captain Kidd" of King William III and his small band of loyalists reached Antigua on April 2, 1699, they were stunned to learn that the Crown, at the urging of the East India Company, had declared them pirates in late November 1698 and had ordered an all-out manhunt to capture and bring them to justice. With the brutal English pirate Henry Every and other notorious Red Sea outlaws still at large, Bellomont's law-abiding protégé Captain Kidd had become Public Enemy No. 1 because he took the wrong ship at the wrong time.[43]

Kidd decided to present his case for his innocence and obtain a pardon from his sponsor Bellomont. After burying a portion of his legally obtained treasure on Gardiners Island in Long Island Sound and distributing goods to several trusted community leaders as a precautionary measure, Kidd sailed into Boston on July 3, 1699, to meet with Bellomont, who had recently left New York to administer his office as governor of Massachusetts and had promised him a full pardon. But with Kidd now a wanted criminal and Henry Every still at large, Bellomont, Livingston, and the other backers, members of the once powerful Whig Junto that had fallen from power to the Tories, wanted nothing to do with the scandal. Having merely lured his business partner into Boston by dangling the possibility of clemency before him, Bellomont arrested him and his seamen shortly after their arrival in port. Meanwhile, Livingston distanced himself from Kidd and pleaded with Bellomont not to throw him in prison with the man they had both strong-armed into commanding the risky expedition in the first place.[44]

After being stripped of his lawfully seized plunder and enduring six months of incarceration in Boston, Kidd was shipped to England to stand trial. Abandoned by Bellomont, Livingston, and his other wealthy Whig sponsors, he was found guilty and hung in public shame on May 23, 1701, where he proclaimed his innocence and castigated Bellomont and Livingston for their treacherous betrayal before a drunken, jeering mob of Londoners.[45] Days later, the New York war hero's corpse was coated with tar and hoisted in a gibbeted iron cage downriver at Tilbury Point near the mouth of the Thames, where it would remain for the next twenty years to serve as the English State's grisly warning to other would-be pirates of the fate that awaited them if they dared threaten England's valuable trade relations with India by pursuing the short but merry life of a pillaging freebooter.[46]

From March 10, 1700, the day he shipped Kidd to London in chains, until his death on March 5, 1701, Bellomont was under siege from his American critics due to his connection to Captain Kidd. While waiting anxiously for Kidd to swing from the gallows, he continued to grapple with colonial administrators and citizens alike, first in Boston and then upon his return to New York, "as one accusation after another was leveled at him." Implicated in the Madagascar pirate trade as the chief backer of Kidd's venture and due to his close association with the now-tainted Whig Junto, he was under severe strain and his health deteriorated.[47]

With his gout flaring up and barely able to clutch a pen, he wrote letter after letter to the Junto and London officials sanctimoniously defending his actions as governor. He maintained that he had never financed any illegal privateering voyages, had never been in league with the "pirate" Kidd, and had never taken payoffs like Fletcher. Much of this was true, but his voluminous correspondence showed that he was still obsessed with finding a way to profit from the hare-brained scheme that he and Livingston had concocted and forced upon a reluctant Captain Kidd.[48]

While Peter Schuyler, Hilletie van Olinda, and most of their fellow New Yorkers celebrated Bellomont's death, or at least did not shed a tear, the Leislerians did their best to ensure that he received posthumous sainthood despite his dictatorial tenure. The governor's New York funeral featured a full military parade by a King's and Queen's County infantry regiment and two troops of cavalry. Following the lavish procession, Bellomont's remains "were interred with becoming honors" in the Fort William chapel. The expensive burial organized by the Leislerians had to be paid at government expense because his lordship was dead broke.[49]

In the final gout-ridden year of his life, Bellomont was an angry and disillusioned man. His Iroquois policy and naval stores scheme to use Native lands to manufacture tar, pitch, turpentine, and masts for English naval and merchant vessels both proved abject failures; and his anti-piracy campaign, while more successful, came to imperil him due to his close connection to Captain Kidd and the Junto.[50] Taking advantage of his unpopularity and the decline of the Whigs, Fletcher's sponsor William Blathwayt and the Tories, the Bishop of London, and the Classis of Amsterdam, the governing body that oversaw the Dutch Reformed Church in New York, all worked to remove him from power and confiscate his estates seized from Catholics in Ireland.[51]

Upon his death, he left Lady Bellomont in heavy personal and public debt. He and his much younger wife had racked up bills like drunken sailors in America and still owed £10,000 ($3,500,000 today) in salary to the English soldiers protecting the frontier and for building the fort at Onondaga. With a mountain of outstanding debt, the New York authorities forced "Countess Cate" to sign an agreement guaranteeing to pay and not to flee.[52] However, she instead escaped justice by cajoling one Captain Caldwell into sneaking her out of New York and carrying her across the Atlantic to her wealthy family living in London, which infuriated Schuyler and New York's leadership responsible for guarding the underfunded frontier.[53] Remaining one step ahead of the law, she eventually returned to Bellomont's family seat in Sligo, Ireland, without ever paying a single penny on her late husband's outstanding debts to the settlers and troops of New York.[54]

For Lawrence and the Iroquois, the 18th century brought an end to a decade of warfare, disease, and misery and gave rise to a newfound sense of hope with a fresh "Tree of Peace." By this time, the eclipse of the Anglophile and rise of the Francophile factions paved the way for the neutralist principle of balance of Teganissorens to return and once again prevail in negotiations with the western Indigenous tribes and the French. By the first months of 1701, Sadekanaktie and Teganissorens had reestablished themselves as the true leaders of their people and forged an agreement that benefitted all the Iroquois. By working collaboratively with the Anglophiles, Francophiles, and neutralists to reunite the factionally divided Confederacy, they were able to reestablish Iroquois independence. Through their tireless efforts and those of others, in July and August 1701, League Iroquois delegations negotiated simultaneous treaties with New France and English New York that would have long-lasting positive consequences for the Haudenosaunee through a policy of neutrality toward the two competing European empires.[55]

Under the terms of what became known as the "Grand Settlement of 1701," the parallel treaties conducted in Montreal and Albany allowed the Five Nations freedom of movement in Iroquoia, provided neutrality in future conflicts between England and France, and secured improved trading status with both European powers. At Montreal, Louis-Hector de Callière, the governor-general of New France and Frontenac's successor, ratified agreements with representatives of more than thirty French-allied Canadian tribes, including the Odawas, Wendats, Miamis, Sauks, and Ojibwas, together with some two hundred League Iroquois. The French concessions were a huge coup for Lawrence and the Five Nations, for not only would Indigenous lives be spared in conflicts between England and France through neutrality, they gained valuable trading rights in contested territory claimed by the King of England.[56]

The diplomatic council with English New York was held between July 10 and 21, 1701, at Albany's City Hall. The negotiations were conducted between thirty-two headmen from all Five Nations, the town's Indian Affairs officials, and Lieutenant-Governor Nanfan, who had taken the governor's office following Bellomont's death in March. Colonel Peter Schuyler and Hilletie van Olinda, the latter reinstated as one of three Crown interpreters at her former salary, were both in attendance to represent the Albany Indian commission.[57]

At this stage of their lives, Schuyler was forty-three and Hilletie fifty-four. Still living most of the time in Albany, Schuyler continued to serve as a New York governor's council member, commander of the Albany militia, and the lead commissioner for Indian Affairs. Since the death of his first wife, Angelica van Schaick Schuyler, in 1689, his third child from his first marriage, daughter Anna, had passed away; while his eldest daughter, Margarita, had married his brother-in-law Robert Livingston's nephew, Robert Livingston the Younger, and the couple had produced a daughter, Angelica, making Schuyler now a grandfather. Between 1692 and 1698, he and his second wife, Maria van Rensselaer Schuyler of the powerful Dutch van Rensselaer family, had been blessed with the birth of three healthy sons and two daughters—Maria, Gertruj, Philip, and the twins Peter and Jeremiah—making for a very loving and rambunctious household for the married frontier couple.[58] An elderly woman at this point of her career as a translator and cross-cultural liaison, Hilletie continued to live with her Dutch tailor husband, Peter Danielse van Olinda, in their Amsterdam-style home a stone's throw from the rebuilt fort overlooking the Mohawk River in Schenectady. Two of their three sons—Daniel and Jacob—were now fully grown and married with children of their own, but their youngest son, the nonspeaking Matthew, remained unmarried.[59]

During the council, Schuyler and Nanfan renewed the Covenant Chain, and doled out a significant gift from the Crown, valued at £800 ($280,000 today).[60] The Mohawk headman Onnucheranorum and Onondaga leader Sadekanaktie, speaking at the conference for all Five Nations, pursued the neutralist agenda of peace with New France without alienating the English.[61] To protect against invasion by the French and their Indian allies, the headmen came up with a novel approach to counterbalance French Canada and ensure favorable fur prices. They offered to give William III all the Five Nations' western beaver-hunting grounds they had won "with the sword eighty years ago" in return for the permanent protection of the English Crown.[62] The "Deed from the Five Nations to the King of their Beaver Hunting Ground," drawn up by Robert Livingston, was signed on July 19, 1701, by twenty sachems from all Five Nations. The vast tract of land deeded to the king stretched westward from present-day Erie,

Pennsylvania, to what is today Chicago, Illinois, and northward to upper Michigan.[63]

For Lawrence and the Iroquois, the purpose of the deed was not to legally transfer ownership of their land to the Crown, but to gain English military protection from encroachments on their western hunting grounds and to obtain a clear definition of England and France's territorial boundaries in North America.[64] In return for the territory between the Hudson and Detroit previously conquered by the Five Nations, England was obligated to serve as their "protector and defender," thereby ensuring that the Iroquois would continue to have unimpeded access to their vital hunting and fur-trading grounds within the donated lands. Thus, far from an outright surrender of their territory, the deed committed their English allies to protecting the Haudenosaunee and their way of life for the foreseeable future.[65]

Many of the Iroquois diplomats who helped seal the peace and their descendants credited Peter Schuyler for standing by them during King William's War and its aftermath that led to the signing of the Grand Settlement of 1701. Though he repeatedly led and fought bravely alongside his Native allies and honored their customs, his battlefield exploits and respect for Indigenous rituals were not the only things that endeared him to the Iroquois and Mahicans. They remembered how he had intervened on their behalf, how he had personally vouched for those falsely accused of crimes, and how on several critical occasions, he had traveled to Mohawk, Oneida, and Onondaga country to provide food, supplies, and weapons and to hold council in a mutually beneficial manner.[66] Guided "by the principles of kindness and justice" toward Indigenous Peoples from the examples set by his Dutch father and grandfather, he always advocated for New York's royal governors to give generous gifts to his Iroquois brethren and instructed them to respect and honor Native protocols when it came to reciprocity.[67]

In the aftermath of the 1701 treaty negotiations, Schuyler, Lawrence, and Hilletie all recognized that the Albany conference was a transformative moment in Anglo-Iroquois relations. The long and trusted partnership between Albany's colonial officials and the Anglophile Iroquois—represented by Schuyler as Indian Affairs commissioner, Hilletie as interpreter, and Lawrence as war leader and peacemaker—had been seriously tested during the past decade, but the reciprocal alliance still remained strong.[68] While the bond between New York and the Keepers of the Longhouse's Eastern Door and the other Four Nations was no longer as militarily strong as it once was following the Grand Settlement, both New York and the Iroquois could claim victory. Lawrence and his fellow Iroquois were able to distance themselves from the existential threat of imperial France to the north and to promise only neutrality going forward in future Anglo-French conflicts, while the English ensured an even closer partnership with the Five Nations in the vast interior frontier.[69]

The neutralist strategy had not only created a stable balance of power in Iroquoia, sealed the bonds of kinship between the Iroquois of New France and New York, and more sharply delineated European colonial boundaries, the Grand Settlement affirmed the efforts of Schuyler, Hilletie, and Lawrence to strengthen the Covenant Chain. The Five Nations now possessed a counterweight to French influence in Iroquoia, while gaining an even closer tie to New York.[70]

Though the League Iroquois would continue to rely upon Brother Quider, Hilletie, and other Albanians as brokers between their communities and the outside world, with the treaties at Montreal and Albany they now possessed greater independence than at any time since the 1664 English conquest. What made the situation different was that they for the first time stood resolutely on their own two feet without binding obligations to either imperial power.[71] Furthermore, while their arms were now linked with both the English and the French through neutrality, they were still a formidable military and economic power in North America and would remain so through the American Revolution.[72]

AFTERWORD

The Legacy of King William's War and Peter Schuyler, Lawrence, and Hilletie van Olinda

Although Peter Schuyler, Lawrence the Mohawk, Hilletie van Olinda, and the other historical figures of this book did not know it at the time, they played a huge role in forging the distinctive character of both New York Province and northeastern North America in the colonial era that still resonates today. The Albany frontiersman and scion of one of America's most influential families and his Iroquois brethren with whom he lived and fought alongside set the tone for Anglo-Iroquois relations through the American Revolution. Decades ahead of his time in his respect for Native diplomacy and sovereignty, Schuyler not only helped forge and sustain the fragile Covenant Chain alliance between Anglo-Dutch colonists and the Haudenosaunee during a decade of brutal warfare, he played a major role in checking French ambitions in North America and in shaping the political and military landscape of the American frontier for the next hundred years.

The first clash between England and France for control of North America during King William's War set the stage for the strategies and tactics of frontier warfare between the two European empires through the fourth and final French and Indian War, fought between 1754 and 1763. King William's War, thus, set a precedent for future colonial conflicts, providing a roadmap for how European wars would play out on American soil as both sides sought to expand their territories and enrich their respective Crowns. This warfare marked a continuation of Euro-Indigenous alliances and an increase in military fortifications along the frontier, as communities prepared for further conflicts with rival European powers and Native Americans.

In the end, it was the Iroquois who won in the epic struggle of King William's War and the subsequent Grand Settlement of 1701. Despite the high cost in Native lives, they were able to gain both long-term security and independence from the English by making a separate peace with the French. Through a combination of diplomatic skill and patience despite their divided Anglophile, neutralist, and Francophile factions, they were in the unique position following the 1701 treaty to dictate terms to England and France in future conflicts and would be courted by both powers in the next three French and Indian Wars, the American Revolution, and the War of 1812.

By preserving their valuable alliance under the Covenant Chain and close ties to the English through military protection and regular supplies of trade goods, weapons, and food, while simultaneously remaining neutral toward New France, the Iroquois were able to preserve much of their territory until the end of the American Revolution. Today, the Haudenosaunee Confederacy or Six Nations of the Iroquois are one of the top ten largest Indigenous tribes or confederations in North America and the Oneida Nation alone is among the top five in wealth. Unlike the Mohawks, Onondagas, Cayugas, and Senecas, the Oneidas and the Tuscaroras who joined the Confederacy in 1722 fought on the side of the American colonists in the Revolutionary War, breaking from the League to support the American cause of liberty and becoming one of the first and most important allies of the fledgling nation. Unfortunately, the Six Iroquois Nations were forced to pick a side during the Revolution just as they were in King William's War, and for the Mohawks, Onondagas, Cayugas, and Senecas, their alliance with Great Britain cost them dearly. Regrettably, even though the Oneidas sided with the eventual victors, they saw few tangible long-term benefits to supporting "the Cause," as their homes, fortunes, and way of life were destroyed by the fighting and they did not receive any restitution from their former allies, the U.S. Government, until 1794, eleven years after the signing of the Treaty of Paris.

Three generations before the American Revolution and the infant republic's alliance with France to defeat Great Britain, King William's War and the Grand Settlement of 1701 were the catalysts for a huge paradigm shift in the struggle for North America between the English and French. Collectively, the two landmark events demonstrated that the best imperial France could ever hope for in its struggle with England over the continent was either a draw or pyrrhic victory because the English colonies would only grow stronger in the future, with a total population that would dwarf New France, and they would learn to work together more closely, which would be the death knell for French Canada. In Albany, Boston, New York City, and elsewhere, the idea was planted that the only way to achieve permanent peace, security, and prosperity was for the independent colonies to work collaboratively and to push the French off the North American continent. Though the intercolonial cooperation between New York and the New England colonies, Pennsylvania, and Virginia in the 1690s experienced more failure than success, significant progress was made from the multi-colony war planning conferences held by Leisler, Fletcher, and others as well as by the extensive letter correspondence, resource sharing, and joint intelligence-gathering initiatives. Peter Schuyler and Hilletie van Olinda's New York and the other English colonies understood, for the first time, that military defense and offensive land-sea operations against French Canada were the concern and responsibility of English America as a whole and not thirteen bickering individual colonies, and that success could only be accomplished through collaborative support and joint military action.

Across the decade of war, espionage, and political intrigue covered in this book—from the 1689 Leisler's Rebellion, 1690 Schenectady Massacre, and 1691 Battles of La Prairie to the climactic Grand Settlement of 1701—the intertwined stories of Peter Schuyler, Lawrence, and Hilletie van Olinda reveal the human cost and political complexity behind one of early America's most consequential alliances and one of our country's most significant military conflicts. Through a unique combination of ethnic, religious, economic, and regional subcultures that somehow fused together to create something new, different, and uniquely "American," Schuyler and the other historical figures presented in this narrative of the first French and Indian War have left an indelible mark. Below is what ultimately happened to Schuyler, Lawrence, and Hilletie, three largely unknown but important early Americans who played a vital role in our national heritage.

Peter Schuyler

Colonel Peter Schuyler remained a prominent New York official and leading citizen until his death in 1724 at age sixty-six. The American-born backwoodsman and longtime mayor of Albany would remain on the New York governor's council from 1692 until 1720, serving under seven different administrations; and he would hold office as acting governor twice himself, in 1709 and again in 1719–1720. Throughout his life, he remained fiercely devoted to his fledgling colony of New York, his hometown of Dutch Albany, and his Iroquois brethren.[1]

In the summer of 1709, during the War of Spanish Succession, or Queen Anne's War, he served as second-in-command of a force of 1,500 combined English troops and Five Nations warriors for yet another land-sea attack upon Montreal and Quebec. However, the joint operation against New France in the second French and Indian War proved to be a reenactment of the failed 1691 attack by Winthrop and Phips. This time, the Royal Navy fleet that was supposed to transport the English soldiers north to Quebec was diverted to fight on the Iberian Peninsula and never arrived in Boston.[2]

In the aftermath of the failed military expedition, Schuyler and his New York officials had once again to bear severe criticism from their Iroquois allies. However, the colonel remained convinced that the attack plan was sound and hoped to carry out the mission the following year.[3] To regain credibility among the Five Nations and obtain Crown backing, he organized a Native American delegation to make a transatlantic journey to London, where he would present them as Indigenous sovereigns and persuade Queen Anne to financially and militarily support a renewed invasion. In addition to Schuyler and his cousin Abraham who served as interpreter, the delegation consisted of three Anglophile Christian Mohawks and one Mahican, all with close ties to Brother Quider and the Albany community. Two of the Indian leaders, Tejonihokarawa (baptized Hendrick) and Etowaucum (baptized Nicholas), had fought alongside Schuyler and Lawrence in the joint English-Iroquois raids upon French Canada in the 1690s.[4]

The 1710 journey to London turned out to be far more than a diplomatic success—it was a cross-cultural sensation. For two weeks, the Mohawk Hendrick and his three Indigenous companions were the toast of London society as men, women, and children of all social classes flocked to see the celebrated "Four Indian Kings of Iroquoia" in the flesh. They were feted, banqueted, and greeted as celebrities wherever they ventured, inspiring a romantic view of Native Americans among their British hosts, just as Pocahantas had at the court of James I nearly a century earlier. When a poor, pregnant London woman attempted to reach out and kiss one of the delegates' hands, his "Indian Majesty" not only permitted the kiss but generously gave her a half guinea so she could buy herself some blankets.[5]

Schuyler and his entourage's much-anticipated audience with Queen Anne was held at the Court of St. James on April 19, 1710. Following the historic meeting, the "Four Indian Kings" were eulogized in a torrent of broadsides, poems, ballads, and music. The queen even arranged for John Verelst, a famous Dutch portrait artist residing in London, to paint state portraits of each of the Indian diplomats to record this never-before-seen cultural extravaganza between the Haudenosaunee and British Crown. The four earliest surviving painted portraits in Europe of the Indigenous Peoples of North America, the paintings were hung in a small room in Kensington Palace next door to a larger chamber showcasing portraits of fourteen British admirals. So popular were the "Four Indian Kings" that a London printmaker created mezzotints that would flood both London and colonial American cities the following year.[6]

Schuyler, too, was treated like a king. For his service on behalf of England, Queen Anne offered to confer upon him the order of knighthood as she had Isaac Newton five years earlier; however, the colonial American man of action, raised in the wilds of Iroquoia and the Albany frontier, cared little about royal titles and politely declined the honor. However, he did accept from her majesty "his portrait painted by her order, a gold snuff box, and some pieces of silverplate; and for his wife, a diamond brooch and earrings."[7]

Schuyler and the Indian delegation's lobbying efforts resulted in not only Crown backing for an assault on the French outpost of Port Royal in Acadia, but a full-scale invasion of Canada, a commitment to build forts and chapels in Mohawk and Onondaga country, and a promise to staff them with Protestant missionaries over the next two years. Unfortunately, despite the public relations coup in London, the English invasion conducted during July and August 1711 proved an unmitigated disaster. In the end, all the hard work and good will built up by Schuyler and his "Indian Kings" went for naught and he never again led a military expedition into French Canada.[8]

Following his death in February 1724, Colonel Peter Schuyler was buried in a vault beneath the Dutch Reformed Church in Albany. Without question, his greatest legacy is his respectful and skillful management of Native American affairs for almost forty years. For this, he received high praise from the Five Nations not only in his own lifetime but all the way up to the American Revolution.[9] Throughout his life, he continued to invite "sachems to his table," treating them as equals and making them "welcome guests" at his Albany home.[10] When Sadekanaktie and twenty-five Iroquois had been forced to flee their country, he had allowed them to seek refuge for months on his Albany farm.[11] Perhaps most important, throughout his life, he appreciated how crucial Iroquois condolence ceremonies for fallen warriors and family members were for maintaining balance and harmony in Haudenosaunee society.[12]

The unity between New York and the Five Nations under the Covenant Chain was sometimes fragile and seriously tested, but the chain remained unbroken throughout his nearly forty years as a government liaison to the Iroquois. Anne Grant, an Englishwoman who lived in Albany in the 18th century and had a close relationship with Schuyler's descendants, judged him favorably for many of the same virtues as the Iroquois and Mahicans: "The powerful influence that his knowledge of nature and of character, his sound judgment and unstained integrity had obtained over both parties, made him the bond by which the aborigines were united with the colonists."[13] "We remember how it was in former times when we were a strong and powerful People," wrote Lawrence's good friend Hendrick thirty years after Brother Quider's death. "Colonel Schuyler used frequently to come among us, and by this means we were kept together."[14] A "fire of prudence and friendship" had been kindled "at the habitation of Quider," pronounced another venerable Mohawk leader many years after the great battles of the 1690s. "This fire never burnt clear and was almost extinguished."[15] The key word is *almost*, thanks to the tireless efforts of Schuyler.

To the Iroquois, he would always be "Brother Quider," the one Euro-American who could always be counted on to stand by the Five Nations in times of war and peace.

Lawrence the Mohawk

Following the Grand Settlement of 1701, Lawrence was in his late thirties and had put aside the trade musket, war club, and scalping knife in favor of spending more time hunting, engaging in the "Creator's game" of lacrosse, and being with his family. Though he continued to serve as a war captain and peace negotiator, he no longer appears to have led large-scale military expeditions deep into Canadian territory. If he did serve as a war leader during the failed 1709 and 1711 campaigns, in which "virtually every Mohawk fighter" participated, he likely once again came away disappointed with his English allies for failing to successfully carry out the joint land-sea invasion of New France.[16]

Like many Iroquois who survived the bloody imperial and intertribal conflicts of the 1690s, he focused on regrouping, rebuilding, and restoring "a measure of the way of life so long disrupted by warfare."[17] He continued to call Tiononderoge home with his wife Maria and their three sons, Adam (Sagonorasse), Henry, and Hendrick. Named after his friend and fellow Wolf Clan member Hendrick Tejonihokarawa, Lawrence's third son was christened in the First Reformed Dutch Church in Schenectady on April 15, 1704.[18]

It is not known what year either Lawrence or his wife Maria passed away. Their friend Hendrick, one of the "Four Kings" who had visited the Queen in London, would live until 1735 to the age of seventy-five, so perhaps Lawrence was lucky enough to live to a ripe old age as well. Because of his military success, long-term close relationship to Peter Schuyler and the Albany elite, and influential Mohawk hereditary status, he remained in high esteem throughout his life among both the Five Nations and the survivors of the 1690 Schenectady attack, whose descendants to this day continue to celebrate him for coming to their ancestors' aid. In his later years, he likely also kept in contact with the Kahnawake Iroquois living outside Montreal, with whom he also had family ties.

For his many sacrifices on behalf of his Iroquois people and the Anglo-Dutch colonists of New York, it is only fitting that the prominent Mohawk war captain and peace negotiator is memorialized to this day in an iconic statue in Schenectady. Erected at the intersection of North Ferry, Green, and Front Streets in the Stockade Historic District, the "Lawrence the Indian" statue went up in 1887 and has been a popular attraction for nearly 140 years. Bolted onto a painted cast-iron base, the zinc sculpture stands six-foot-three-inches tall, including the three upright eagle feathers in Lawrence's hair. Standing in an alert "semi-action" pose, he stares to his left, standing with his left knee bent on a rock outcropping and clutching a bow in his left hand and an arrow in his right. He wears a breechclout and fringed buckskin leggings, while suspended from his neck is a bear claw necklace and medallion and wrapped around his waist and shoulder is a belt to hold his scalping knife and war club.[19]

Though it is doubtful that the actual Mohawk war captain closely resembled the much-visited statue that bears his name and although his Native name regrettably remains unknown to this day, the heroic Lawrence remains a source of great pride to the Haudenosaunee and people of Schenectady. The multi-pieced casting assemblage of "Lawrence the Indian" is, in fact, a widely reproduced sculpture produced by J. L. Mott Iron Works on the Harlem River in the Bronx and listed in the Mott Statuary catalog as "No. 53 Indian Chief." Originally selling for $500, there are today more than twenty-five No. 53 Indian Chiefs in existence, including Tecumseh in Ohio and Hiawatha in Maryland.[20]

Despite its lack of uniqueness, the sculpture, refurbished in 2012, continues to be a venerated cultural attraction. Today, the people of Schenectady consider Lawrence not only a source of profound historical inspiration but their personal protector watching over their city, just like the original warrior and peacemaker who defended the Hudson and Mohawk River Valleys in the late 17th century.

Hilletie van Olinda

Following her brief hiatus as a government interpreter by order of Bellomont, Hilletie van Olinda returned to the post from 1701 until her death in 1707. Although her association with Father Dellius and role in his sketchy land deal caused her a temporary fall from favor during Bellomont's administration, she quickly reestablished herself as a well-respected member of the Albany-Schenectady community and a valuable resource to both the Iroquois and Anglo-Dutch settlers due to her linguistic skills.

Judging by how many petitions she had to file to collect her salary throughout her working career and how excruciatingly long it took to receive payment, it is clear that "New York government interpretess" was a thankless job. All the same, she served more than twenty-two years as a paid religious document translator, provincial council interpreter, and Mohawk language instructor to incoming Protestant ministers. In 1702, she taught Albany's new dominie of the Dutch Reformed Church, Johannes Lydius, the Mohawk language so that he could better serve the Five Nations in the work of the gospel. Due to her capable instruction, within two years Father Lydius became highly regarded by the Mohawks for his ability to communicate in his Protestant Christian mission work.[21]

In 1704, three Christian Mohawk headmen conveyed a small tract of land near Albany in her name for her religious and linguistic contributions over the decades, "affirming her continued importance to her mother's kin."

In the deed, she is referred to as "Hilletie van Olinda one of the Natives," underscoring her Mohawk roots.[22] Thus, while the ill-advised Dellius land deal did briefly tarnish her career, she was able to prove her worth as a cross-cultural communicator and translator, thereby regaining her stature among her Mohawk people who had raised her until she was a young woman.

Throughout her life, the biracial Hilletie straddled two worlds, the Native American world of her Mohawk Wolf Clan mother, Ots-Toch, and the European world of her Dutch father and husband. Time and again, she was compelled to draw upon her experiences in these very different and conflicting worlds in deciphering and translating the delicate diplomatic negotiations between the northeastern tribes and Euro-American public officials.

She was a strong-willed, intelligent, confident, energetic, and independent woman in a male-dominated world and, as one historian has written, she was "clearly a person to be reckoned with."[23] Though women maintained a strong position in both matriarchal Iroquois and Dutch society compared to English and other less tolerant European cultures, many Native headmen and Euro-American leaders still considered diplomacy to be the exclusive province of men. But through her skill, persistence, and strength of character, Hilletie was able to win over the Iroquois headmen and play a prominent role in the day-to-day workings of intercultural relations between the Five Nations and colonists of New York. Even more importantly, she served both communities through extremely challenging times characterized by outbreaks of highly contagious diseases, virtually constant warfare, and many broken or unfulfilled promises by the English Crown.[24]

Not only was she invaluable in treaty negotiations and the conversion of the Iroquois to Protestant Christianity, she was among the first who understood Mohawk spiritual concepts and practices as well as the protocols of the Dutch Reformed Church. In the decade she worked on behalf of Father Dellius, she translated several religious texts into Mohawk, and by the end of the century she had helped him baptize at least 131 Native Americans, most of them Mohawk residents of Tiononderoge. Due to her unique and detailed understanding of the languages and spiritual traditions on both sides, she was able to explain religious concepts where others struggled merely to translate the words. In doing so, she helped Lawrence, his wife Maria, and many other Protestant Iroquois combine their Indigenous spirituality with Christianity to suit their individual needs, while at the same time strengthening the bonds of the Covenant Chain and laying the groundwork for the Mohawks to remain loyal allies of the English through the American Revolution.[25]

Hilletie van Olinda died in Albany on February 10, 1707, at the age of sixty-one. She left behind her husband, Peter, who would outlive her by nine years, and her three grown sons—Daniel, Jacob, and Matthew.[26] By the time of her passing, New York was no longer defined by Lenape, Mahican, or Mohawk history, Dutch versus English, Calvinist as opposed to Anglican, or wealthy versus poor. While each of these ethnic, religious, and socioeconomic strands remained important, pluralism, trading partnerships, collaboration, and cross-cultural coalitions were the new order of the day. By this time, social, political, and economic connections and alliances were forged in the City and Province of New York that cut across ethnicity, race, religion, and political affiliation, and in the process, formed a distinctive "American" character.[27]

The collision of cultures, religions, and classes did not result in a "melting pot." Rather, Peter Schuyler, Lawrence the Mohawk, Hilletie van Olinda, and their contemporaries blazed a new trail. Through their tireless efforts, they served as the building blocks for not merely the New York we know today but a new, wondrous, multiethnic, and democratic United States of America—the first nation in world history founded expressly on the principle of freedom and the first to lead a successful mass rebellion against imperialism and colonialism.

ACKNOWLEDGMENTS

The foundation for the research presented in this book came from writing a biography of my ninth-great-grandfather, the legendary New York privateer Captain William Kidd, entitled *Captain Kidd: A True Story of Treasure and Betrayal* (2025). Both *Empire and Frontier* and *Captain Kidd* attempt to bring to life colonial New York, King William's War, and Leisler's Rebellion from 1689 to 1701, but from far different vantage points. While *Empire and Frontier* explores the First French and Indian War on the Albany frontier and the Covenant Chain alliance between the English and the Haudenosaunee, as seen through the eyes of Colonel Peter Schuyler, Lawrence the Mohawk, and Hilletie van Olinda, *Captain Kidd* recreates Kidd's life in New York and Boston with his wife, Sarah, his privateering voyages, and his political struggles with the British Crown in London. The two books can, thus, be considered companion volumes since they both feature King William's War and many of the same historical figures; yet, they have a significantly different narrative emphasis as well as distinctive primary characters as England and France battle for possession of North America during the global conflict.

In writing *Empire and Frontier*, I have enjoyed the support and encouragement of several people and scholarly institutions. First and foremost, I would like to thank my wife, Christine, and my daughter, Cassidy, for their outstanding contributions to the final manuscript. In preparing and formatting the endnotes, bibliography, and draft index for publication and in acquiring and preparing the historical photographs and images presented in this book, they have made *Empire and Frontier* significantly better. I am a very fortunate man and author to have two such dedicated and talented individuals packing a punch on my publishing team.

At Pegasus Books, I would like to thank Claiborne Hancock, Jessica Case, and Nicole Maher for their tremendous efforts in editing, publishing, and promoting *Empire and Frontier.* Freelance copyeditor Drew Wheeler, a consummate professional, significantly improved the quality of the final book through his judicious editorial work, proofreading, and fact-checking. At Maria Fernandez LLC, designer and producer for Pegasus Books, I would like to thank Maria Fernandez and her outstanding team for their extensive editorial and production support for *Empire and Frontier.* A special thank you also goes to cover designer Kate Gendruschke at Faceout Studio for the impressive jacket design and to the stellar historian and cartographer Gene Thorp at Cartographic Concepts Inc. for creating the outstanding large, two-page map of Colonial New York, Iroquoia, and New France during King William's War (1689-1701).

There were several important libraries, archives, and organizations upon which I relied in the acquisition of the extensive primary source materials for *Empire and Frontier* and which deserve a special shout out. These first-rate institutions and organizations include the National Archives of the United Kingdom, Public Records Office, at Kew outside London; the New York State archives and New York Historical Society; the Gilder Lehrman Institute of American History; the Massachusetts Historical Society; the Huntington Library in San Marino, California; the Schenectady County Historical Society, who provided the image of Hilletie van Olinda and several important references for this book; and Adam Matthew Digital Limited.

While contemporaneous primary sources form the backbone of this book, I would like to thank several trailblazing historians whose research proved indispensable in chronicling and interpreting King William's War, New York's colonial history, and the Five Nations of the Iroquois, as well as for making my job much easier in locating the most critical primary references. The major academic researchers and authors whose work was most critical in shaping *Empire and Frontier*—acknowledging that they have not endorsed the book, that I have not met them in person, and that all interpretations and opinions of their work are my own—include the following: Dr. Daniel Richter, author of the seminal *The Ordeal of the Longhouse* and other important scholarly works on the Iroquois; Dr. Lawrence Leder, editor and author of many detailed and comprehensive works on New York colonial history, Indian Affairs, and Leisler's Rebellion; George Schuyler, author of *Colonial New York: Philip Schuyler and His Family*, published in 1885 and the only detailed biography of Colonel Peter Schuyler until *Empire and Frontier*; Dr. Alan Taylor, author of *American Colonies: The Settling of North America*; Dr. Jon Parmenter, author of *The Edge of the Woods* and other important academic articles on the Five Nations; Michael Laramie, author of *King William's War: The First Contest for North America*; Barbara Sivertsen, author of *Turtles, Wolves, and Bears: A Mohawk Family History*; and Allen Trelease, author of *Indian Affairs in Colonial New York*. Other academic scholars and writers whose books and articles proved indispensable in helping me put together the story of Colonel Peter Schuyler, Lawrence, and Hilletie van Olinda and who deserve special thanks are Ned Blackhawk, Patricia Bonomi, James Bradley, J.A. Brandão, Thomas Burke, W.J. Eccles, Gretchen Lynn Green, Nancy Hagedorn, William Hart, Eric Hinderaker, Michael Kammen, Francis Parkman, John Pell, Robert Ritchie, Timothy Shannon, Susan Staffa, Owen Stanwood, and William Starna.

In closing, I would also like to thank my brilliant literary agent, Max Sinsheimer, who negotiated the contract with Pegasus and provided invaluable editorial guidance, as well as my growing legion of book fans and supporters who have helped promote *Empire and Frontier*, *Captain Kidd*, and my other books over the years. Once again, you know who you are and I offer you a hearty Mile High Salute!

BIBLIOGRAPHY

ARCHIVAL MANUSCRIPTS

United Kingdom
Board of Trade and Plantations (BOT)
Calendar of State Papers, Colonial Series (CSPC)
Journals of the House of Commons (Commons *Journals*)
Public Record Office, London (PRO)
Admiralty Records (ADM)
Colonial Office Records (CO)
High Court of Admiralty Records (HCA)

United States
Calendar of Historical Manuscripts (Cal. Hist. MSS)
Documents Relative to the Colonial History of the State of New York (NYCD)
Huntington Library, San Marino, Calif. (HL)
Massachusetts Historical Society Collections (MHS *Collections*)
Documentary History of the State of New York (DHNY)
Minutes of the Common Council of the City of New York 1675–1776 (NYM)
New York Calendar of Council Minutes 1668–1783 (NYCCM)
New-York Historical Society *Collections*, New York (NYHS *Collections*)

Newspapers
The Flying Post, London, 1698–1701, British Library.
The Post Boy, London, 1698–1701, British Library.
The Post Master, London, 1698–1701, British Library.

PRIMARY SOURCES (PRINTED AND DIGITAL)

Anonymous (likely John Tuder). *Account of What Happened at New York*, June 5–8, 1690, in Leder, Lawrence H., ed., "'. . . Like Madmen Through the Streets': The New York City Riot of 1690." *The New-York Historical Society Quarterly* 39, no. 4 (Oct. 1955): 405–415.

Bellomont, Richard Earl (Richard Coote). Proclamation of His Excellency Richard Earl of Bellomont, New York, April 2, 1698. William Bradford, 1698.

Boyer, Paul and Stephen Nissenbaum (eds). *The Salem Witchcraft Papers: Verbatim Transcripts of the Legal Documents of the Salem Witchcraft Outbreak of 1692; Compiled and Transcribed in 1938 by the Works Progress Administration, under the Supervision of Archie N. Frost; Edited and with an Introd. and Index by Paul Boyer and Stephen Nissenbaum.* Da Capo Press, 1977.

Boyles, David A. Personal Communications with Dr. David A. Boyles, Jack R. Gaines Emeritus Professor of Chemistry of the Department of Chemistry and Applied Biological Sciences of the South Dakota School of Mines and Technology, June 2020–September 2024.

Bullivant, Dr. Benjamin and Wayne Andrews, eds. "A Glance at New York in 1697: The Travel Diary of Dr. Benjamin Bullivant." *New York Historical Society Quarterly* 60 (1956): 55–73.

Earle, Alice Morse. *Colonial Days in Old New York: Before, During and After the American Revolution.* HVA Press, 2018.

Grant, Anne MacVicar. *Memoirs of an American Lady.* 2 vols. George Dearborn, 1808.

Holland Society of New York. *Records of the Reformed Dutch Church of Albany, New York, Part 1, 1683–1700.* Holland Society of New York, 1904.

Hutchinson, Thomas, ed. *The History of Massachusetts, from the First Settlement Thereof in 1628, Until the Year 1750, Vol. I.* Thomas and Andrews, 1795.

James, B. Burleigh and J. Franklin Jameson, eds. *Journal of Jasper Danckaerts, 1679–1680.* C. Scribner's Sons, 1913.

Journals of the House of Commons, 1547–1714. 17 vols. His Majesty's Stationery Office, 1742.

Journal of the Votes and Proceedings of the General Assembly of the Colony of New York. Vol. 1, 1691–1743. Hugh Gaine, 1764.

Lahontan, Louis Armand de Lom d'Arce, Baron de. *New Voyages to North-America.* Riviere & Son, 1703.

Leder, Lawrence H., ed. *The Livingston Indian Records, 1666–1723.* Pennsylvania Historical Association, 1956.

Lincoln, Charles Z., ed. *State of New York Messages from the Governors: Comprising Executive Communications to the Legislature and Other Papers Relating to Legislation from the Organization of the First Colonial Assembly in 1683 to and Including the Year 1906,* with notes, v. 1. J.B. Lyon Co., 1909.

Lorrain, Paul. *The Ordinary of Newgate, His Account of the Behaviour, Confessions and Dying-words of Captain W. Kidd, and Other Pirates, that Were Executed at the Execution Dock in Wapping, Friday, May 23, 1701.* Printed for E. Mallet at the Hat and Hawk in Bride-lane, 1701.

Mather, Cotton. *Pietas in Patriam: The Life of His Excellency Sir William Phips.* Sam, Bridge in Austin-Friars, 1697.

Miller, John. *A Description of the Province and City of New York; With Plans of the City and Several Forts as They Existed in the Year 1695, Or New York Considered and Improved, With Introduction and Notes by Victor Hugo Paltsits.* Burrows Brothers, 1903.

Newton, Thomas. Letter to Lieutenant Governor Francis Nicholson, April 8, 1691, quoted in Lawrence Leder, "Captain Kidd and the Leisler Rebellion." *The New-York Historical Society Quarterly* 38 (1954): 48–53.

Propositions Made by the Five Nations of Indians, viz. the Mohaques, Oneydes, Onnondages, Cayouges & Sinnekes, to His Excellency Richard, Earl of Bellomont, Capt. general and Governour in Chief of His Majesties Province of New York, &c. in Albany, the 20th of July, Anno Dom. 1698. William Bradford, 1698.

Savage, Thomas, 1640–1705. *An Account of the Late Action of the New-Englanders Under the Command of Sir William Phips Against the French at Canada.* Printed for Thomas Jones . . ., 1691.

Sewall, Samuel. *The Diary of Samuel Sewall, 1674–1729*, vols. 1 and 2. Massachusetts Historical Society, 1878–1882.

The Trial of Captain William Kidd, at the Old-Bailey, for Murder and Piracy upon the High Seas; and of Nicholas Churchill, James Howe, Robert Lamley, William Jenkins, Gabriel Loff, Hugh Parrot, Richard Barleycorne, Abel Owens, and Darby Mullins, for Piracy, in Howell, T.B., ed., *A Complete Collection of State Trials and Proceedings for High Treason and Other Crimes and Misdemeanors, from the Earliest Period to the Present Time* . . ., v. 14. T.C. Hansard, 1812, 123–234.

Van Cortlandt, Stephanus, and Nicholas Bayard. *A journal kept by Coll. Stephen Courtlandt, & Coll. Nich. Bayard, of Their Majesties Council for the Province of New-York, being appointed by the Council to attend His Excellency Benjamin Fletcher . . . to Albany in treating with the Indians of the Five Nations, and river Indians of that province, in the months of June and July, 1693: Together with the propositions and conferences of the said Indians with His Excellency. And His Excellency's answers, &c.* William Bradford, 1693.

DOCUMENT COLLECTIONS (PRINTED AND DIGITAL)

Fernow, Berthold, ed. *Calendar of Wills on File and Recorded in the Offices of the Clerk of the Court of Appeals, of the County Clerk at Albany, and of the Secretary of State: 1626–1836.* The Knickerbocker, 1896.

Hamlin, Paul M. and Charles E. Baker, eds. *Supreme Court of Judicature of the Province of New York, 1691–1704.* Volume I, *Introduction;* Volume II, *The Minutes, Annotated;* Volume III, *Biographical Dictionary, Glossary, Sources, Indexes*, The New-York Historical Society Collections [1945–1947]. New-York Historical Society, 1952–1959.

Hastings, Hugh, ed. *Ecclesiastical Records, State of New York*, v. 2. James B. Lyon, State Printer, 1901.

Index of Conveyances Recorded in the Office of Register of the City and County of New York, Provo, Utah, Grantees, v. L.

James, G.P.R., ed., and James Vernon. *Letters Illustrative of the Reign of William III, from 1696 to 1708: Addressed to the Duke of Shrewsbury.* Henry Colburn, 1841.

Leder, Lawrence H. "Records of the Trials of Jacob Leisler and His Associates." *The New-York Historical Society Quarterly* 36, no. 4 (Oct. 1952): 431–457.

———, ed. "Rolls of the Trial of Leisler et al. for Treason," in "Records of the Trials of Jacob Leisler and His Associates." *The New-York Historical Society Quarterly* 36, no. 4 (Oct. 1952).

Minutes of the Common Council of the City of New York 1675–1776, v. I and II. Dodd, Mead and Company, 1905.

New York Calendar of Council Minutes 1668–1783, History 6. *New York State Library Bulletin* 58. University of the State of New York, 1902.

New York (Colony). Governor (1698–1701: Bellomont). *By His Excellency Richard Earle of Bellomont, captain general and governour in chief of His Majesties province of New York, &c. A proclamation: Whereas it is of absolute necessity for the good and prosperity of this province . . . Given at New York the second day of April, 1698.* Printed by William Bradford, Printer to the King's Most Excellent Majesty in the City of New York, 1698.

New York Title and Guarantee Company. *New York Land-Holding Sea Rover.* Lotus Press, 1901, 1–5.

O'Callaghan, E. B., ed. *Calendar of Historical Manuscripts in the Office of the Secretary of State, Albany, New York. Part II, English Manuscripts, 1664–1776.* Weed, Parsons & Company, 1866.

———. *Journal of the Legislative Council of the Colony of New York.* Weed, Parsons & Company, 1861.

———. *Documentary History of the State of New York.* 4 vols. Weed, Parsons, & Company, 1849–1851.

——— and Berthold Fernow, eds. *Documents Relative to the Colonial History of the State of New York.* 15 vols. Weed, Parsons & Company, 1856–1887.

Report on the Manuscripts of His Grace the Duke of Portland, Preserved at Welbeck Abbey, vols. 8 and 9. Historical Manuscripts Commission, 1907 and 1923.

Report on the Manuscripts of the Duke of Buccleuch and Queensberry, Preserved at Drumlanrig Castle. v. II, part 2, Historical Manuscripts Commission, 1908.

Sainsbury, Noel, et al., eds. *Calendar of State Papers, Colonial Series, America and West Indies, 1574–1738.* 42 vols. Her Majesty's Stationery Office, 1860–1969.

Stokes, Isaac Newton Phelps. *Iconography of Manhattan*, v. 1–6, Robert H. Dodd, 1915–1928.

Valentine, David T., ed. *Manual of the Corporation of the City of New York for 1858.* C.W. Baker, 1858.

The Winthrop Papers. Collections of the Massachusetts Historical Society, 5th series, v. 8. University Press, John Wilson and Son, 1882.

PRINTED SECONDARY SOURCES

Archdeacon, Thomas J. *New York City, 1664–1710: Conquest and Change.* Cornell University Press, 1976.

Baer, Joel H. *Pirates of the British Isles.* Tempus, 2005.

Baker, Emerson and John Reid. *The New England Knight: Sir William Phips, 1651–1695.* University of Toronto Press, 1998.

Balmer, Randall Herbert. *A Perfect Babel of Confusion: Dutch Religion and English Culture in the Middle Colonies.* Oxford University Press, 2002.

———. "Traitors and Papists: The Religious Dimensions of Leisler's Rebellion." *New York History* 70, no. 4 (1989): 341–372.

Barnes, Viola F. "The Rise of William Phips." *The New England Quarterly* 1, no. 3 (1928): 271–94.

Barth, Jonathan. *The Currency of Empire: Money and Power in Seventeenth-Century English America.* Cornell University Press, 2021.

Berlin, Ira, and Leslie M. Harris, eds. *Slavery in New York.* The New Press in conjunction with The New-York Historical Society, 2005.

Bialuschewski, Arne, "Pirates, Markets and Imperial Authority: Economic Aspects of Maritime Depredations in the Atlantic World, 1716–1726." *Global Crime* 9 (2008): 52–65.

Bielinski, Stefan. "How a City Worked: Occupations in Colonial Albany." *A Beautiful and Fruitful Place, Selected Rensselaerswijck Seminar Papers, Volume 1* (1991): 199–236.

Biggar, H. P. "Frontenac's Projected Attempt on New York in 1689." *The Quarterly Journal of the New York State Historical Association* 5, no. 2 (1924): 139–147.

Blackhawk, Ned. *The Rediscovery of America: Native Peoples and the Unmaking of U.S. History.* Yale University Press, 2023.

Boatfield, Helen C., "Fletcher, Benjamin." *Dictionary of American Biography*, v. 21, Dumas Malone, Harris Elwood Starr, eds. C. Scribner's Sons (1944): 315–316.

Bonomi, Patricia. *A Factious People: Politics and Society in Colonial New York.* Cornell University Press, 2015.

Bradley, James W. "Before Albany: An Archaeology of Native-Dutch Relations in the Capital Region 1600–1664." *New York State Museum Bulletin*, 509 (2006).

Brandão, J. A., and William A. Starna. "The Treaties of 1701: A Triumph of Iroquois Diplomacy." *Ethnohistory* 43, no. 2 (1996): 209–244.

Buffinton, Arthur H. "The Policy of Albany and English Westward Expansion." *The Mississippi Valley Historical Review* 8, no. 4 (1922): 327–366.

Burgess, Douglas R. *The Pirates' Pact: The Secret Alliances Between History's Most Notorious Buccaneers and Colonial America.* International Marine/Ragged Mountain Press, 2008.

———. *The Politics of Piracy: Crime and Civil Disobedience in Colonial America.* University Press of New England, 2014.

Burke, Thomas E. "Leisler's Rebellion at Schenectady, New York, 1689–1710." *New York History* 70, no. 4 (1989): 405–430.

———. *Mohawk Frontier: The Dutch Community of Schenectady, New York, 1661–1710.* State University of New York Press, 2009.

Burrows, Edwin, and Mike Wallace. *Gotham: A History of New York City to 1898.* Oxford University Press, 2000.

Chet, Guy. *The Colonists' American Revolution: Preserving English Liberty 1607–1783.* John Wiley and Sons, Inc., 2020.

Clark, George, "The Character of the Nine Years War, 1688–97." *The Cambridge Historical Journal* 11, no. 2 (1954): 168–182.

Colden, Cadwallader. *The History of the Five Indian Nations Depending on the Province of New-York in America: A Critical Edition*. Cornell University Press, 2016.

Crouse, Nellis M. *The French Struggle for the West Indies*. Columbia University Press, 1943.

Davis, Alice. "The Administration of Benjamin Fletcher in New York." *The Quarterly Journal of the New York State Historical Association* 2, no. 4 (1921) 213–250.

De Peyster, Frederic. *The Life and Administration of Richard, Earl of Bellomont, Governor of the Provinces of New York, Massachusetts, and New Hampshire from 1697–1701*. New York Historical Society, 1879.

Eccles, W. J. *Frontenac: The Courtier Governor*. University of Nebraska Press, 2003.

Finnegan, Oliver John. "Pirates in the Age of Projects, 1688–1707." PhD diss., University of Cambridge Pembroke College, 2018.

Foote, Thelma Wills. *Black and White Manhattan: The History of Racial Formation in Colonial New York City*. Oxford University Press, 2004.

Geanacopoulos, Daphne Palmer. "Eighteenth Century Piracy through a Wider Lens: Recasting the Image of Pirates to include their Wives, Families and Communities." PhD diss., Georgetown University, 2014.

———. *The Pirate Next Door: The Untold Story of Eighteenth Century Pirates' Wives, Families and Communities*. Carolina Academic Press, 2017.

———. *The Pirate's Wife: The Remarkable True Story of Sarah Kidd*. Hanover Square Press, 2022.

Gélinas, Cyrille. *The Role of Fort Chambly in the Development of New France, 1665–1760*. National Historic Parks and Sites Branch, Parks Canada, Environment Canada, 1983.

Goodfriend, Joyce D. *Before the Melting Pot: Society and Culture in Colonial New York City, 1664–1730*. Princeton University Press, 1994.

———. *Who Should Rule at Home?: Confronting the Elite in British New York City*. Cornell University Press, 2017.

Gray, Linda Breuer. "Narratives and Identities in the Saint Lawrence Valley, 1667–1720." PhD diss., McGill University, May 1999.

Green, Gretchen Lynn. "A New People in an Age of War: The Kahnawake Iroquois, 1667–1760." PhD diss., College of William & Mary, 1991.

Greene, Nelson. *The History of the Mohawk Valley, Gateway to the West 1614–1925*. S.J. Clarke Publishing Company, 1925.

———. *The Old Mohawk Turnpike Book*. Nelson Greene, 1924.

Haan, Richard L. "Covenant and Consensus: Iroquois and English, 1676–1760." *Beyond the Covenant Chain: The Iroquois and Their Neighbors in Indian North America, 1600–1800*, eds. James H. Merrell, et al. Penn State University Press, 2003.

Haefeli, Evan. "Dutch New York and the Salem Witch Trials: Some New Evidence." *Proceedings of the American Antiquarian Society* 110, no. 2 (Oct. 2000): 277–308.

Hagedorn, Nancy L. "Brokers of Understanding: Interpreters as Agents of Cultural Exchange in Colonial New York." *New York History* 76, no. 4 (1995): 379–408.

———. "A Friend to Go Between Them: Interpreters among the Iroquois, 1664–1775." PhD diss., College of William and Mary, 1995.

Hall, Michael G., Lawrence H. Leder, Michael Kammen, eds. *The Glorious Revolution in America: Documents on the Colonial Crisis of 1689*. Omohundro Institute of Early American History and Culture and University of North Carolina Press, 2012.

Handley, Stuart. "Coote, Richard, 1st Earl of Bellomont [I] (c. 1655–1701)." in *The History of Parliament: The House of Commons 1690–1715*, eds. David Hayton, Eveline Cruickshanks, and Stuart Handley. Cambridge University Press, 2002.

Hanham, Andrew A. "Blathwayt, William (1649–1717), of Little Wallingford House, Great Street, Westminster and Dyrham Park, Glos." *The History of Parliament: The House of Commons 1690–1715*, eds. David Hayton, Eveline Cruickshanks, and Stuart Handley. Cambridge University Press, 2002.

Hanna, Mark G. *Pirate Nests and the Rise of the British Empire, 1570–1740*. University of North Carolina Press, 2015.

———. "Well-Behaved Pirates Seldom Make History: A Reevaluation of English Piracy in the Golden Age." *Governing the Sea in the Early Modern Era: Essays in Honor of Robert C. Ritchie*, eds. Peter C. Mancall and Carole Shammas. USC-Huntington Library Press (2015): 129–168.

Hart, William. *"For the Good of Their Souls": Performing Christianity in Eighteenth-Century Mohawk Country*. University of Massachusetts Press, 2020.

Hawkins, Cole. "Across the Great Water: Indigenous Tobacco and Haudenosaunee Diplomacy in Early Modern England, 1550–1750." MA thesis, University of Alberta, 2020.

Head, David, ed. *The Golden Age of Piracy: The Rise, Fall, and Enduring Popularity of Pirates*. University of Georgia Press, 2018.

Hinderaker, Eric. *The Two Hendricks: Unraveling a Mohawk Mystery*. Harvard University Press, 2010.

Hinrichs, Dunbar Maury. *The Fateful Voyage of Captain Kidd*. Bookman Associates Inc., 1955.

Howe, Adrian. "The Bayard Treason Trial: Dramatizing Anglo-Dutch Politics in Early Eighteenth-Century New York City." *The William and Mary Quarterly* 47, no. 1 (1990): 57.

Jennings, Francis. *The Ambiguous Iroquois Empire: The Covenant Chain Confederation of Indian Tribes with English Colonies*. W.W. Norton & Company, 1984.

———, ed. *The History and Culture of Iroquois Diplomacy: An Interdisciplinary Guide to the Treaties of the Six Nations and Their League*. Syracuse University Press, 1995.

Kammen, Michael. *Colonial New York: A History*. Scribner, 1975.

Keener, Craig S. "An Ethnohistorical Analysis of Iroquois Assault Tactics Used against Fortified Settlements of the Northeast in the Seventeenth Century." *Ethnohistory* 46, no. 4 (1999): 777–807.

Kierner, Cynthia A. *Traders and Gentlefolk: The Livingstons of New York, 1675–1790*. Cornell University Press, 2010.

Laramie, Michael G. *King William's War: The First Contest for North America, 1689–1697*. Westholme Publishing, 2017.

Lavin, Lucianne, ed. *Dutch and Indigenous Communities in Seventeenth-Century Northeastern North America: What Archaeology, History, and Indigenous Oral Traditions Teach Us about Their Intercultural Relationships*. SUNY Press, 2021.

Leamon, James S. "Governor Fletcher's Recall." *William and Mary Quarterly* 20, no. 4 (1963): 527–542.

Leder, Lawrence H. "Captain Kidd and the Leisler Rebellion." *The New-York Historical Society Quarterly* 38 (1954): 48–53.

———. "'. . . Like Madmen Through the Streets': The New York City Riot of 1690." *The New-York Historical Society Quarterly* 39, no. 4 (Oct. 1955): 405–415.

———. "The Politics of Upheaval in New York, 1689–1709." *The New-York Historical Society Quarterly* 44, no. 4 (Oct. 1960): 413–427.

———. *Robert Livingston, 1654–1728, and the Politics of Colonial New York.* University of North Carolina Press, 1961.

———, and Vincent P. Carosso. "Robert Livingston (1654–1728): Businessman of Colonial New York." *The Business History Review* 30, no. 1 (1956): 18–45.

Leonard, John William. *History of the City of New York 1609–1909: From the Earliest Discoveries to the Hudson-Fulton Celebration, Together with Brief Biographies of Men . . . Interests of the City.* Forgotten Books, 2017.

Le Sueur, William D. *Count Frontenac.* Morang & Co., Limited, 1909.

Lincoln, Margarette. *British Pirates and Society, 1680–1730.* Routledge, 2014.

Lovejoy, David S. *The Glorious Revolution in America.* University Press of New England, 1987.

Lozier, Jean-François. "In Each Other's Arms: France and the St. Lawrence Mission Villages in War and Peace, 1630–1730." PhD diss., University of Toronto, 2012.

Marquis, Samuel. *Captain Kidd: A True Story of Treasure and Betrayal.* Diversion Books, 2025.

Marsh, James H. "Birchbark Canoe." *The Canadian Encyclopedia. Historica Canada.* Article published May 29, 2006; last edited January 18, 2021.

Mason, Bernard. "Aspects of the New York Revolt of 1689." *New York History* 30, no. 2 (1949): 165–180.

Matson, Cathy D. *Merchants and Empire: Trading in Colonial New York.* Johns Hopkins University Press, 1998.

McCormick, Charles H. "Governor Sloughter's Delay and Leisler's Rebellion, 1689–1691." *The New-York Historical Society Quarterly* 62, no. 3 (July 1978): 238–252.

McCully, Bruce T. "Catastrophe in the Wilderness: New Light on the Canada Expedition of 1709." *William and Mary Quarterly*, 3rd ser., 11, no. 3 (July 1954): 441–456.

Merwick, Donna. "Being Dutch: An Interpretation of Why Jacob Leisler Died." *New York History* 70, no. 4 (1989): 373–404.

———. *Possessing Albany, 1630–1710: The Dutch and English Experiences.* Cambridge University Press, 2002.

Midtrøød, Tom Arne. "The Flemish Bastard and the Former Indians: Métis and Identity in Seventeenth-Century New York." *American Indian Quarterly* 34, no. 1 (Winter 2010): 83–108.

Muller, Kevin R. "From Palace to Longhouse: Portraits of the Four Indian Kings in a Transatlantic Context." *American Art* 22, no. 3 (2008): 26–49.

Munsell, Joel. *Collections On the History of Albany: From Its Discovery to the Present Time.* J. Munsell, 1865.

Murrin, John M. "English Rights as Ethnic Aggression: The English Conquest, the Charter of Liberties of 1683, and Leisler's Rebellion in New York." *Authority and Resistance in Early New York*, eds. William Pencak and Conrad E. Wright. The New-York Historical Society, 1988.

———. "The Menacing Shadow of Louis XIV and the Rage of Jacob Leisler: The Constitutional Ordeal of Seventeenth-Century New York." in *New York and the Bicentennial: Contributions to the American Constitutional Experience*, Stephen L. Schechter and Richard B. Bernstein, eds. New York State Commission on the Bicentennial of the United States Constitution, 1990.

Norton, Mary Beth. *In the Devil's Snare: The Salem Witchcraft Crisis of 1692*. Vintage Books, 2003.

Otterbein, Keith F. "Why the Iroquois Won: An Analysis of Iroquois Military Tactics." *Ethnohistory* XI (1964): 56–63.

Palfrey, J. Gorham. *History of New England*. Little, Brown and Co., 1890.

Parker, Amasa, ed. *Landmarks of Albany County, New York*. D. Mason & Co., 1897.

Parkman, Francis. *Count Frontenac and New France under Louis XIV, Volume One*. Little, Brown, and Company, 1897.

———. "Sir William Phips's Attack on Quebec." *The Atlantic Monthly* 38 (Dec. 1876): 719–732.

Parmenter, Jon. *The Edge of the Woods: Iroquoia, 1534–1701*. Michigan University Press, 2010.

———. "After the Mourning Wars: The Iroquois as Allies in Colonial North American Campaigns, 1676–1760." *The William and Mary Quarterly* 64, no. 1 (2007): 39–76.

Paterek, Josephine. *Encyclopedia of American Indian Costume*. W.W. Norton & Company, 1996.

Pearson, Jonathan, and J. W. MacMurray, eds. *A History of the Schenectady Patent in the Dutch and English Times*. Joel Mansell's Sons, 1883.

Peckham, Howard H. *Colonial Wars, 1689–1762*. The University of Chicago Press, 1965.

Pencak, William and Conrad Wright, eds. *Authority and Resistance in Early New York*. New-York Historical Society, 1988.

Rainbolt, John C. "The Creation of a Governor and Captain General for the Northern Colonies: The Process of Colonial Policy Formation at the End of the Seventeenth Century." *The New-York Historical Society Quarterly* 57, no. 2 (April 1973): 101–120.

———. "A 'great and usefull designe:' Bellomont's Proposal for New York, 1698–1701." *The New-York Historical Society Quarterly, 1917–1980* 53, no. 4 (Oct. 1969): 333–351.

Ranlet, Philip. "A Safe Haven for Witches? Colonial New York's Politics and Relations with New England in the 1690s." *New York History* 90, no. 1/2 (2009): 37–57.

Reich, Jerome R. *Leisler's Rebellion: A Study in Democracy in New York, 1664–1720*. University of Chicago Press, 1953.

Reynolds, Cuyler. *Albany Chronicles: A History of the City Arranged Chronologically from the Earliest Settlement to the Present Time*. J.B. Lyon Company, 1906.

Reynolds, Neil B. "Lawrence the Maquase." *Bulletin of the Schenectady County Historical Society* 6, no. 1 (Sept. 1962).

Richter, Daniel K. "Cultural Brokers and Intercultural Politics: New York-Iroquois Relations, 1664–1701." *The Journal of American History* 75, no. 1 (1988): 40–67.

———. *The Ordeal of the Longhouse: The Peoples of the Iroquois League in the Era of European Colonization*. University of North Carolina Press, 1992.

———. *Trade, Land, Power: The Struggle for Eastern North America*. University of Pennsylvania Press, 2013.

———. "War and Culture: The Iroquois Experience." *The William and Mary Quarterly* 40, no. 4 (1983): 528–559.

Ritchie, Robert C. *Captain Kidd and the War against the Pirates*. Harvard University Press, 1986.

———. *The Duke's Province: A Study of New York Politics and Society, 1664–1691*. University of North Carolina Press, 1977.

Rowlands, Edward. "Coote, Richard, 2nd Baron Coote of Coloony [I] (c. 1655–1701)." *The History of Parliament: The House of Commons 1660–1690*, B. D. Henning, ed. Boydell and Brewer, 1983.

Runcie, John D. "The Problem of Anglo-American Politics in Bellomont's New York." *William and Mary Quarterly* 26, no. 2 (1969): 191–217.

Schuyler, George W. *Colonial New York: Philip Schuyler and His Family*, v. 2. Charles Scribner & Sons, 1885.

Shannon, Timothy J. *Iroquois Diplomacy on the Early American Frontier*. Penguin Books, 2009.

Silverman, David J. *Thundersticks: Firearms and the Violent Transformation of Native America*. Belknap Press, 2016.

Sivertsen, Barbara J. *Turtles, Wolves, and Bears: A Mohawk Family History*. Heritage Books, 2006.

Smith, Jr., William and Michael Kammen. *The History of the Province of New-York, Volume 1: From the First Discovery to the Year 1732*. Harvard University Press, 2013.

Snow, Dean, Charles Gehring, and William Starna, eds. *In Mohawk Country: Early Narratives of a Native People*. Syracuse University Press, 1996.

Snyderman, George S. "Behind the Tree of Peace: A Sociological Analysis of Iroquois Warfare." MA thesis, University of Pennsylvania, 1948.

Stackpole, Everett S. *History of New Hampshire*. The American Historical Society, undated.

Staffa, Susan J. *Schenectady Genesis: How a Dutch Colonial Village Became an American City, Circa. 1661-1800, Volume I: The Colonial Crucible, Ca. 1661-1774*. The Colonial Schenectady Project, 2023.

Staggs, Stephen T. *Calvinists and Indians in the Northeastern Woodlands*. Amsterdam University Press, 2023.

———. "Declarations of Interdependence: The Nature of Dutch-Native Relations in New Netherland, 1624–1664." *Dutch and Indigenous Communities in Seventeenth-Century Northeastern North America: What Archaeology, History, and Indigenous Oral Traditions Teach Us about Their Intercultural Relationships*, Lucianne Lavin, ed. 43–78. SUNY Press, 2021.

Stahlhut, Andrew Thomas, "Creating Borderlands Authorities: The Albany Commissioners for Indian Affairs and the Iroquois Nations, 1691–1755." PhD diss., Lehigh University, 2016.

Stanwood, Owen. "Catholics, Protestants, and the Clash of Civilizations in Early America," in *The First Prejudice: Religious Tolerance and Intolerance in Early America*, Chris Beneke and Christopher Grenda, eds. 218–240. University of Pennsylvania Press, 2011.

———. *The Empire Reformed: English America in the Age of the Glorious Revolution*. University of Pennsylvania Press, 2011.

———. "The Protestant Moment: Antipopery, the Revolution of 1688–1689, and the Making of an Anglo-American Empire." *Journal of British Studies* 46, no. 3 (2007): 481–508.

Sullivan, James, prep. *The Papers of Sir William Johnson*. v. 9. SUNY, 1922.

Sylvester, Nathaniel Bartlett. *History of Saratoga County, New York*. Everts & Ensign, 1878.

Taylor, Alan. *American Colonies: The Settling of North America*. Penguin Books, 2002.

———. *American Revolutions: A Continental History, 1750–1804*. W.W. Norton & Company, 2016.

Trelease, Allen W. *Indian Affairs in Colonial New York: The Seventeenth Century*. University of Nebraska Press, 1997.

Van Rensselaer, Mariana Griswold. *History of the City of New York in the Seventeenth Century: Volume II: New York Under the Stuarts*. Cosimo Classics, 2013.

Voorhees, David William. "The 'fervent Zeale' of Jacob Leisler." *William and Mary Quarterly* 51, no. 3 (1994): 447–472.

Waterman, Kees-Jan. "'We Must Stick to Brother Quider': Reverberations of Leisler's Rebellion and Its Aftermath among the League Iroquois, 1688–1693." *De Halve Maen, Magazine of the Dutch Colonial Period in America* 67, no. 1 (Spring 1994): 21–27.

Wilson, David. "Piracy, Patronage & Political Economy: Captain Kidd and the East India Trade." *International Journal of Maritime History* 27, no. 1 (2015): 26–40.

Winsor, Justin, ed. *The Memorial History of Boston: Including Suffolk County, Massachusetts, 1630–1880, vol. II*. Ticknor and Company, 1881.

Winston, Alexander. *No Man Knows My Grave: Sir Henry Morgan, Captain William Kidd, Captain Woodes Rogers in the Great Age of Privateers and Pirates, 1665–1715*. Houghton Mifflin, 1969.

Wood, Barry. *Invented History, Fabricated Power: Narratives Shaping Civilizations*. Anthem Press, 2020.

Woodard, Colin. *American Nations: A History of the Eleven Rival Regional Cultures of North America*. Penguin Books, 2012.

Worcester, Donald E., and Thomas F. Schilz. "The Spread of Firearms among the Indians on the Anglo-French Frontiers." *American Indian Quarterly* 8, no. 2 (1984): 103–115.

Zacks, Richard. *The Pirate Hunter: The True Story of Captain Kidd*. Hyperion, 2002.

Zahedieh, Nuala. *The Capital and the Colonies: London and the Atlantic Economy, 1660–1700*. Cambridge University Press, 2012.

Zimmerman, Jean. *The Women of the House: How a Colonial She-Merchant Built a Mansion, a Fortune, and a Dynasty*. Harcourt Books, 2007.

DIGITAL SECONDARY SOURCES

Béchard, Henri. "Togouiroui, Joseph, Great Mohawk." *Dictionary of Canadian Biography*, v. 1, University of Toronto/Université Laval, 2003. http://www.biographi.ca/en/bio/togouiroui_1E.html.

Blain, Jean. "Ailleboust de Manthet (Menthet), Nicolas D'." *Dictionary of Canadian Biography*, v. 2, University of Toronto/Université Laval, 2003. https://www.biographi.ca/en/bio/ailleboust_de_manthet_nicolas_d_2E.html.

———. "Le Moyne de Sainte-Hélène, Jacques'." *Dictionary of Canadian Biography*, v. 1, University of Toronto/Université Laval, 2003. http://www.biographi.ca/en/bio/le_moyne_de_sainte_helene_jacques_1E.html.

Dr. David Boyles Family Tree, Ancestry.com. https://www.ancestry.com/family-tree/person/tree/72250632/person/34520905601/facts. https://www.ancestry.com/family-tree/person/tree/72250632/person/34482811293.

Burleigh, H. C. "Ourehouare (Orehaoue, Horehouasse)." *Dictionary of Canadian Biography*, v. 1, University of Toronto/Université Laval, 2003. https://www.biographi.ca/en/bio/ourehouare_1E.html.

Clothing-Haudenosaunee Confederacy. https://www.haudenosauneeconfederacy.com/historical-life-as-a-haudenosaunee/clothing/.

Dunn, Richard S. "The Glorious Revolution and America." *The Oxford History of the British Empire: Volume I: The Origins of Empire: British Overseas Enterprise to the Close of the Seventeenth Century*, Nicholas Canny and Wm Roger Louis, eds. Oxford University Press, 1998. Online edition, Oxford Academic, Oct. 3, 2011. https://doi.org/10.1093/acprof:oso/9780198205623.003.0020.

Eccles, W. J. "Buade, Louis De, Comte de Frontenac at de Palluau." *Dictionary of Canadian Biography*, v. 1, University of Toronto/Université Laval, 2003. http://www.biographi.ca/en/bio/buade_de_frontenac_et_de_palluau_louis_de_1E.

———. "Clément Du Vuault (Vault) De Valrennes, Phillippe." *Dictionary of Canadian Biography*, v. 2, University of Toronto/Université Laval, 2003. https://www.biographi.ca/en/bio/clement_du_vuault_de_valrennes_philippe_2E.html.

Farrell, Michael P. "A Little Work for Lawrence." *Albany Times Union*, May 3, 2012. https://www.timesunion.com/news/slideshow/a-little-work-for-lawrence-42476.php.

Giacalone, David. "Looking for Lawrence." *Suns Along the Mohawk* (blog), Oct. 11, 2009. https://giacalonephotos.com/2009/10/11/looking-for-lawrence/.

Gilmore, Frank F. "Lawrence the Indian Proves to Be Example of Ship Carver's Art." *Daily Gazette*, June 3, 2012. https://www.dailygazette.com/opinion/op-ed-column-lawrence-the-indian-proves-to-be-example-of-ship-carver-s-art/article_d7cd1502-f446-5a7b-a1a6-a79becfc8635.html.

The Gleason Book Company, Schenectady, NY. *Street View of Lawrence the Indian Statue, Stockade, Schenectady, NY.* 1908. Schenectady County Historical Society, *Schenectady County Historical Society Digital Collections*. https://cdm16694.contentdm.oclc.org/digital/collection/p16694coll45/id/145.

Grems-Doolittle Library (blog). "A Stockade Icon: Lawrence the Indian." *Grems-Doolittle Library Collections Blog*, September 12, 2013. https://gremsdoolittlelibrary.blogspot.com/2013/09/a-stockade-icon-lawrence-indian.html.

Hardy, James. *Leisler's Rebellion: A Scandalous Minister in a Divided Community 1689–1691.* https://historycooperative.org/leislers-rebellion/.

Historical Society of the New York Courts. *The Jacob Leisler Treason Trial, 1691.* https://history.nycourts.gov/case/jacob-leisler-treason-trial.

Inglish, Patty. "Traditional Mohawk Nation: Daily and Ceremonial Clothing." *HubPages*, https://discover.hubpages.com/style/Traditional-Mohawk-Nation-Daily-and-Ceremonial-Clothing.

Konstam, Angus. *The Sacrifice of Captain Kidd.* https://www.historyextra.com/period/stuart/the-sacrifice-of-captain-kidd/.

Law Library-American Law and Legal Information. *Notable Trials and Court Cases, 1637 to 1832, Jacob Leisler Trial, 1691.* https://law.jrank.org/pages/2336/Jacob-Leisler-Trial-1691.html.

Lienhard, John H. *The Indian Canoe.* https://www.uh.edu/engines/epi1620.htm.

Morgan, Kenneth. "British American Port Cities," Oxford Bibliographies. https://www.oxfordbibliographies.com/view/document/obo-9780199730414/obo-9780199730414-0094.xml.

National Park Service. *A Timeline History of the Oneida Carry, Fort Stanwix National Monument.* https://www.nps.gov/articles/000/a-timeline-history-of-the-oneida-carry.htm.

Nye, Eric. "Pounds Sterling to Dollars: Historical Conversion of Currency." https://www.uwyo.edu/numimage/currency.htm.

Pell, John H. G. "Schuyler, Johannes." *Dictionary of Canadian Biography*, v. 3, University of Toronto/Université Laval, 2003. http://www.biographi.ca/en/bio/schuyler_johannes_3E.html.

———. "Schuyler, Peter (1657–1723/24)." *Dictionary of Canadian Biography*, v. 2, University of Toronto/Université Laval, 2003. https://www.biographi.ca/en/bio/schuyler_peter_1657_1723_24_2E.html.

Silverman, David J. "Guns, Empires and Indians." *Aeon*, April 11, 2018. https://aeon.co/essays/how-did-the-introduction-of-guns-change-native-america.

ENDNOTE ABBREVIATIONS

The names of authors and book and journal article titles have been abbreviated in the endnotes with only last name given for authors and editors and book/journal titles shortened for the sake of brevity. The reader is referred to the comprehensive bibliography for complete and pertinent historical reference information.

ADM: Admiralty Records, Public Record Office, London.

BOT: Board of Trade and Plantations (beginning May 15, 1696) and Lords of Trade and Plantations (before May 15, 1696).

Cal. Hist. MSS: *Calendar of Historical Manuscripts in the Office of the Secretary of State, Albany, New York. Parts I and II, English Manuscripts, 1664–1776.* Weed, Parsons, 1866.

CO: Colonial Office Papers, Public Record Office, London.

Commons *Journals*: *Journals of the House of Commons*, 1547–1714. 17 vols. London, 1742.

CSPC: *Calendar of State Papers, Colonial Series, America and West Indies*, 1574–1738, Noel Sainsbury et al. (eds.). 42 vols. London: Her Majesty's Stationery Office, 1860–1969.

DAB: Dictionary of American Biography.

DHNY: *Documentary History of the State of New York*, ed. E. B. O'Callaghan. 4 vols. Weed, Parsons, 1849–1851.

ERNY: Ecclesiastical Records, State of New York, ed. Hugh Hastings, v. 2.; James B. Lyon, State Printer, 1901.

HCA: High Court of Admiralty Records, Public Record Office, London.

HL: Huntington Library, San Marino, Calif.

JLCNY: *Journal of the Legislative Council of the Colony of New-York, Began the 9th Day of April, 1691; Ended the 27 of September, 1743.* Weed, Parsons & Company, 1861.

JR: *The Jesuit Relations and Allied Documents*, ed. Reuben Gold Thwaites. 73 vols. Burrows, 1896–1901.

MHS *Collections*: Massachusetts Historical Society *Collections*, 1793.

NYCCM: *New York Calendar of Council Minutes 1668–1783, History 6*. New York State Library Bulletin 58. University of the State of New York, 1902.

NYCD: *Documents Relative to the Colonial History of the State of New York*, ed. E. B. O'Callaghan and Berthold Fernow. 15 vols. Weed, Parsons, 1856–1887.

NYHS *Collections*: New York Historical Society *Collections*, 1811.

NYM: *Minutes of the Common Council of the City of New York 1675–1776, Vols. I and II.* Dodd, Mead and Company, 1905.

PRO: Public Record Office, London.

***State Trials*:** *A Complete Collection of State Trials and Proceedings for High Treason and Other Crimes and Misdemeanors, from the Earliest Period to the Present Time, Vols. 13 and 14*, T. B. Howell, ed. (T.C. Hansard, 1812 and 1816).

ENDNOTES

Chapter 1: Leisler's Rebellion

1 *Memorial of William van Breen and others of the Occurrences in New York in 1690–1691*, The Hague, Oct. 15, 1691, CSPC (hereafter *van Breen Memorial)*, v. 13, no. 1,840; New York Council to Shrewsbury, June 10, 1689; Abstract of Colonel Bayard's journal; *Bayard's Narrative of Occurrences in New York from April to December 1689*, (hereafter *Bayard's Narrative*), Dec. 13, 1689, NYCD, v. 3, 585–586, 599–604, 636–648; Ritchie, *Duke's*, 198–203; Howe, *Bayard*, 62; Archdeacon, *New York*, 97–118; Hardy, *Leisler's*.

2 Livingston to Andros, Hartford, April 14, 1690; Van Cortlandt to Andros, New York, May 19, 1690, NYCD, v. 3, 708–710, 715–719; Bullivant and Andrews, *Glance*, 61–63; Burrows and Wallace, *Gotham*, 21, 35–37, 63–64, 91–98; Earle, *Colonial*, 70–71, 98–114; Zimmerman, *Women*, 26–29.

3 Council of New York to Shrewsbury, June 10, 1689; Livingston to Andros, Hartford, April 14, 1690; Van Cortlandt to Andros, New York, May 19, 1690, NYCD, v. 3, 585–586, 708–710, 715–719; *Van Breen Memorial*, v. 13, no. 1,840; Hall, Leder, and Kammen, *Glorious*, 99–114; Ritchie, *Duke's*, 198–203; Archdeacon, *New York*, 97–118.

4 Bonomi, *Factious*, 19; Kammen, *Colonial*, 28–30; Taylor, *American Colonies*, 251–252.

5 Bullivant and Andrews, *Glance*, 61–67; Burrows and Wallace, *Gotham*, 21, 35–37, 63–64, 91–98; Earle, *Colonial*, 70–71, 98–114; Zimmerman, *Women*, 26–29; Hall, Leder, and Kammen, *Glorious*, 99–114; Ritchie, *Duke's*, 198–203; Archdeacon, *New York*, 97–118.

6 Livingston to Andros, Hartford, April 14, 1690; Van Cortlandt to Andros, New York, May 19, 1690, NYCD, v. 3, 708–710, 715–719; Kammen, *Colonial*, 118–127; Ritchie, *Duke's*, 230; Leder, *Livingston*, 57–76.

7 Modest Narrative, NYCD, v. 3, 669.

8 Lovejoy, *Glorious*, 225–234; Burgess, *Pirates'*, 82; Burrows and Wallace, *Gotham*, 95; Taylor, *American Revolutions*, 12.

9 Ibid.

10 Taylor, *American Colonies*, 278; Chet, *Colonists'*, 23.

11 Chet, *Colonists'*, 23; Ritchie, *Duke's*, 198; Taylor, *American Colonies*, 278.

12 Taylor, *American Colonies*, 278.
13 Lovejoy, *Glorious*, 225–234; Taylor, *American Colonies*, 278, 288, *American Revolutions*, 12; Burgess, *Pirates'*, 82.
14 Nicholson and New York Council to BOT, May 15, 1689; Randolph to BOT, May 29, 1689; Address of Militia to William and Mary; New York Council to Shrewsbury, June 10, 1689, NYCD, v. 3, 574–576, 578–586; Stanwood, *Protestant*, 481–508; Foote, *Black*, 100; Bonomi, *Factious*, 75; Goodfriend, *Who*, 24.
15 Dunn, *Glorious*, 445–466; Stanwood, *Protestant*, 481–507; Bonomi, *Factious*, 76.
16 Murrin, *Menacing*, 29–36; Lovejoy, *Glorious*, 235–239, 251–257.
17 *Van Breen Memorial*, v. 13, no. 1,840; New York Council to Shrewsbury, June 10, 1689; Abstract of Colonel Bayard's journal; *Bayard's Narrative*, Dec. 13, 1689, NYCD, v. 3, 585–586, 599–604, 636–648; Ritchie, *Duke's*, 198–203; Howe, *Bayard*, 62; Archdeacon, *New York*, 97–118; Hardy, *Leisler's*.
18 Bayard to Nicholson, Albany, July 23, 1689; Abstract of Colonel Bayard's journal; Phillips and Van Cortlandt to Blathwayt, Aug. 5, 1689; Van Cortlandt to Nicholson, Aug. 5, 1689; *Bayard's Narrative*, Dec. 13, 1689, NYCD, v. 3, 585–586, 599–604, 608, 609–610, 636–648; Lovejoy, *Glorious*, 256–257; Hall, Leder, and Kammen, *Glorious*, 99–114; Archdeacon, *New York*, 107–108; Ritchie, *Duke's*, 200–203.
19 Ibid.
20 Council of New York to Shrewsbury, June 10, 1689, NYCD, v. 3, 585–586.
21 Bayard to Nicholson, Albany, July 23, 1689; Abstract of Colonel Bayard's journal; Phillips and Van Cortlandt to Blathwayt, Aug. 5, 1689; Van Cortlandt to Nicholson, Aug. 5, 1689; *Bayard's Narrative*, Dec. 13, 1689, NYCD, v. 3, 585–586, 599–604, 608, 609–610, 636–648.
22 Bayard to Nicholson, Albany, July 23, 1689; Abstract of Colonel Bayard's journal; Phillips and Van Cortlandt to Blathwayt, Aug. 5, 1689; Van Cortlandt to Nicholson, Aug. 5, 1689; *Bayard's Narrative*, Dec. 13, 1689, NYCD, v. 3, 585–586, 599–604, 608, 609–610, 636–648; Lovejoy, *Glorious*, 256–257; Hall, Leder, and Kammen, *Glorious*, 99–114; Archdeacon, *New York*, 107–108; Ritchie, *Duke's*, 200–203.
23 Ritchie, *Captain*, 43–44; Zahedieh, *Capital*, 114; Stanwood, *Protestant*, 489; Lincoln, *British*, 93–97.
24 Balmer, *Traitors*, 344.
25 Modest Narrative, NYCD, v. 3, 665–684; *Van Breen Memorial*, v. 13, no. 1,840; Balmer, *Traitors*, 343; Hardy, *Leisler's*; Ritchie, *Duke's*, 198–203; Archdeacon, *New York*, 97–118.
26 Hardy, *Leisler's*; Reich, *Leisler's*, 1–180; Murrin, *English*, 56–84; Merwick, *Being*, 373–400; Balmer, *Traitors*, 341–370.
27 Murrin, *English*, 73–77; Stanwood, *Protestant*, 497–498, 503–506; Voorhees, *Zeale*, 447–472.
28 Voorhees, *Zeale*, 452; Foote, *Black*, 102.
29 Voorhees, *Zeale*, 447–472; Ritchie, *Duke's*, 145–146; Archdeacon, *New York*, 110–112; Foote, *Black*, 102–103.
30 Stokes, *Iconography*, v. 4, 178; Voorhees, *Zeale*, 449–451; Archdeacon, *New York*, 97–118; Stanwood, *Protestant*, 497–498, 503–506.

31 *Van Breen Memorial*, v. 13, no. 1,840; *Bayard's Narrative*, Dec. 13, 1689, NYCD, v. 3, 636–648; Stokes, *Iconography*, v. 3, 222, 297; Leder, *Livingston*, 58–59; Howe, *Bayard*, 62; Voorhees, *Zeale*, 449; Balmer, *Traitors*, 351, *Perfect*, 31; Lovejoy, *Glorious*, 104; Mason, *Aspects*, 168; Stanwood, *Protestant*, 503–507; Kierner, *Traders*, 30; Reich, *Leisler's*, 77–99; Merwick, *Being*, 373–404; Archdeacon, *New York*, 97–118.

32 Ibid.

Chapter 2: The Gathering Storm

1 Matson, *Merchants*, 36–37, 49–56; Goodfriend, *Who*, 27, 33–36, *Before*, 40–48, 60–64; Archdeacon, *New York*, 32–96; Bonomi, *Factious*, 24–26.

2 Leisler to Treat, New York, Feb. 14 and 15, 1689; Albany Convention Records, Aug. 1 and Oct. 25, 1689, DHNY, v. 2, 68–69, 80, 104; Leder, *Livingston*, 63; Richter, *Ordeal*, 164; Staffa, *Schenectady*, 59.

3 Miller, *Description*, 29–30, 91, 95, 96; James and Jameson, *Journal*, 216–217; Parker, *Landmarks*, 53; Zimmerman, *Women*, 139–142; Hinderaker, *Hendricks*, 44–45; Bielinski, *How*, 132.

4 Ibid.

5 Albany Convention Records, Nov. 9–16, 1689 and Jan. 11–13, 1690; Sheriff Pretty to Milborne, Albany, Jan. 15, 1690; Leisler to Albany Convention, New York, Dec. 28, 1689; DHNY, v. 2, 59–60, 113–114, 120–132, 144–154; Memorial of Albany to Connecticut, March 12, 1690, NYCD, v. 3, 692–694; Leder, *Livingston*, 62–63; Waterman, *We Must*, 22; Richter, *Ordeal*, 164–165, 171–172.

6 Albany Convention Records, Aug. 5–Nov. 5, 1689, DHNY, v. 2, 82–111; Ritchie, *Duke's*, 206; Kammen, *Colonial*, 124–125; Lovejoy, *Glorious*, 313.

7 *Bayard's Narrative*, December 13, 1689, NYCD, v. 3, 675; Albany Convention Records, Sept. 17–Nov. 9, 1689, DHNY, v. 2, 92–116; Ritchie, *Duke's*, 206–207.

8 Ibid.

9 Bullivant and Andrews, *Glance*, 61–63; Burrows and Wallace, *Gotham*, 21, 35–37, 63–64, 91–98; Earle, *Colonial*, 70–71; Merwick, *Being*, 404; Zimmerman, *Women*, 26–29.

10 Shannon, *Iroquois*, 23–24; Richter, *Ordeal*, 1, 30; Staffa, *Schenectady*, 317; Sivertsen, *Turtles*, 11–12; Jennings, *History*, 7; Hinderaker, *Hendricks*, 16.

11 Schuyler, *Colonial*, v. 1, 306, 321, 365, 383, 405, 479, 497; Taylor, *American Colonies*, 251–253; Foote, *Black*, 25; Burrows and Wallace, *Gotham*, 23–24; Bonomi, *Factious*, 18–26.

12 Parkman, *Count*, 75, 161–162, 187; Kammen, *Colonial*, 124–125; Eccles, *Frontenac*, 227; Waterman, *We Must*, 23.

13 Greene, *History*, 6.

14 Sloughter to Connecticut, New York, July 11, 1691, DHNY, v. 2, 384.

15 Blackhawk, *Rediscovery*, 76–78, 84–104; Richter, *Ordeal*, 17–20; Parmenter, *Edge*, 210–211; Keener, *Ethnohistorical*, 783–784; Hinderaker, *Hendricks*, 19.

16 Schuyler, *Colonial*, v. 1, 302–304; Peckham, *Colonial*, 1689–1762, 17; Reynolds, *Albany*, 43–84; Parmenter, *Edge*, 4, 11, 16; Richter, *Ordeal*, 1–4, 6–8, *War*, 529; Munsell, *Collections*, v. 1, 38–50.

17 Schuyler, *Colonial*, v. 1, 302–304; v. 2, 1; Pell, *Schuyler, Peter*; Trelease, *Indian*, 209–210; Stahlhut, *Creating*, 52–53; Greene, *History*, 277; Hagedorn, *Friend*, 56–57; Peckham, *Colonial*, 17; Reynolds, *Albany*, 43–84; Parmenter, *Edge*, 4, 11, 16; Richter, *Ordeal*, 1–4, 6–8, *War*, 529; Munsell, *Collections*, v. 1, 38–50; Blackhawk, *Rediscovery*, 84–86.

18 DHNY, v. 1, 255, 266, 303, 313, 315, 318; DHNY, v. 2, 80–218; Schuyler, *Colonial*, v. 1, 169, 323–324; Munsell, *Collections*, v. 1, 42, 44, 47, 48; Leder, *Livingston*, 45.

19 Leder, *Livingston Indian*, 176, 186–187, 193, 196, 197; Richter, *Ordeal*, 164, *Trade*, 118.

20 Haan, *Covenant and Consensus*, 43–45; Kammen, *Colonial*, 114; Parmenter, *Edge*, 151–152; Richter, *Ordeal*, 135–137.

21 Richter, *Ordeal*, 137.

22 Taylor, *American Colonies*, 262; Richter, *Ordeal*, 136–137.

23 Taylor, *American Colonies*, 262.

24 Kammen, *Colonial*, 114; Richter, *Ordeal*, 136–137; Leder, *Livingston*, 12.

25 Leder, *Livingston Indian*, 133–189; Bonomi, *Factious*, 65; Stahlhut, *Creating*, 52–54; Richter, *Ordeal*, 164, 172, 249, 346.

26 Livingston to Nicholson, June 7, 1690, NYCD, v. 3, 727, and DHNY, v. 1, 311–312; Albany Convention Records, Nov. 9, 1689, DHNY, v. 2, 113–115; Murrin, *English*, 67; Ritchie, *Duke's*, 146, 207; Archdeacon, *New York*, 112.

27 Albany Convention Records, Nov. 9–11, 1689, DHNY, v. 2, 113–124; *Bayard's Narrative*, Dec. 13, 1689, NYCD, v. 3, 675; Lovejoy, *Glorious*, 313; Leder, *Livingston*, 62–63; Schuyler, *Colonial*, v. 1, 350.

28 *Bayard's Narrative*, Dec. 13, 1689, NYCD, v. 3, 675; Waterman, *We Must*, 22.

29 Albany Convention Records, Nov. 9, 10, and 11, 1689, DHNY, v. 2, 114, 116–117, 123; Lovejoy, *Glorious*, 313; Burke, *Leisler's*, 411.

30 Albany Convention Records, Nov. 10, 1689, DHNY, v. 2, 121.

31 Leder, *Livingston*, 63.

32 Schuyler, *Colonial*, v. 1, 350–352; Albany Convention Records, Nov. 11, 1689, DHNY, v. 2, 123; Lovejoy, *Glorious*, 313; Ritchie, *Duke's*, 207–208.

33 Albany Convention Records, Nov. 9–15, 1689, DHNY, v. 2, 113–131; Lovejoy, *Glorious*, 313–314.

34 *Bayard's Narrative*, Dec. 13, 1689, NYCD, v. 3, 675; Leder, *Livingston*, 63.

35 Albany Convention Records, Nov. 15, 1689, DHNY, v. 2, 130; Merwick, *Possessing*, 245.

36 Albany Convention Records, Nov. 9–16, 1689, DHNY, v. 2, 113–132; Memorial of Albany to Connecticut, March 12, 1690, NYCD, v. 3, 693; Richter, *Trade,* 18; Merwick, *Possessing*, 245.

37 Sivertsen, *Turtles*, 22–26; Hinderaker, *Hendricks*, 40–41; Hart, *For*, 51–54; Parmenter, *Edge*, 211; Blackhawk, *Rediscovery*, 78; Staffa, *Schenectady*, 65.

38 Lamberville to Millet, May 6, 1690; Leisler to Shrewsbury, Oct. 20, 1690, NYCD, v. 3, 715, 753; NYCD, v. 4, 26; Letter from gentleman, DHNY, v. 2, 431; Richter, *Trade*, 118–119, *Ordeal*,165; Midtrøød, *Flemish*, 91; Hinderaker, *Hendricks*, 40–44; Hart, *For*, 51–54; Sivertsen, *Turtles*, 7–9, 20–21, 25–26; Hagedorn, *Friend*, 71–76; Waterman, *We Must*, 22.

39 Albany Convention Records, Nov. 15–16, 1689, DHNY, v. 2, 130–132; Reynolds, *Albany*, 120; Schuyler, *Colonial*, v. 1, 351; Ritchie, *Duke's*, 208; Merwick, *Possessing*, 245.
40 Ibid.
41 Ibid.
42 Paterek, *Encyclopedia*, 55–58; Inglish, *Traditional*; Clothing-Haudenosaunee Confederacy.
43 Ibid.
44 Keener, *Ethnohistorical*, 787; Worcester and Schilz, *Spread*, 107; Silverman, *Thundersticks*, 8–9, *Guns*.
45 Silverman, *Thundersticks*, 28–29, *Guns*; Richter, *War*, 538; Otterbein, *Why*, 58; Worcester and Schilz, *Spread*, 104–108.
46 Silverman, *Thundersticks*, 24–39, *Guns*; Parmenter, *Edge*, 48–49; Laramie, *King*, 6–7.
47 Albany Convention Records, Nov. 15–16, 1689, DHNY, v. 2, 130–132; Richter, *Ordeal*, 178; Sivertsen, *Turtles*, 3–10, 20–26; Staffa, *Schenectady*, 27.
48 Richter, *Ordeal*, 164; Reich, *Leisler's*, 94; Trelease, *Indian*, 115–118; Le Sueur, *Frontenac*, 253. Throughout the late 17th century, the Iroquois referred to the governors of New York as "Brother Corlaer" or simply "Corlaer" based on the Dutch settler and fur trader Arent van Curler (1619–1667), whose name they continued to use as a government title even after his death due to the high esteem in which they had held him during his lifetime.
49 Albany Convention Records, Nov. 15, 1689, DHNY, v. 2, 130–131; Waterman, *We Must*, 22.
50 Albany Convention Records, Nov. 15, 1689, DHNY, v. 2, 130–132; Schuyler, *Colonial*, v. 1, 351; Waterman, *We Must*, 22; Reynolds, *Albany*, 120.
51 Albany Convention Records, Nov. 15, 1689, DHNY, v. 2, 131–132.
52 Albany Convention Records, Nov. 16, 1689, DHNY, v. 2, 132; Burke, *Leisler's*, 411–412.
53 Albany Convention Records, Nov. 9–16, 1689 and Jan. 11–13, 1690; Sheriff Pretty to Milborne, Albany, Jan. 15, 1690; Leisler to Albany Convention, New York, Dec. 28, 1689; DHNY, v. 2, 59–60, 113–114, 120–132, 144–154; Memorial of Albany to Connecticut, March 12, 1690, NYCD, v. 3, 692–694; Leder, *Livingston*, 62–64.
54 Albany Convention Records, Nov. 25, 1689, DHNY, v. 2, 132; Merwick, *Possessing*, 245.
55 Albany Convention Records, Nov. 29, 1689–January 21, 1690, DHNY, v. 2, 132–156; Greene, *History*, v. 1, 197; Schuyler, *Colonial*, v. 1, 352; Parkman, *Count*, 212–213; Leder, *Livingston*, 63–64; Reynolds, *Albany*, 120.
56 Ibid.
57 Ibid.
58 Albany Convention Records, Sept. 4, 1689, DHNY, v. 2, 90.

Chapter 3: The Attack on Schenectady

1 Monseignat, Occurrences, Nov. 1689 to Nov. 1690; Albany Council, Feb. 9, 1690; Leisler to Maryland, New York, March 4, 1690; Livingston to Andros, Hartford, April 14, 1690; Leisler to Andros, New York, May 17, 1690; Van Cortlandt to Andros, DHNY, v. 1, 297–311; Leisler to Bishop of Salisbury, New York, March 31, 1690, NYCD, v. 3, 701–702; Pearson, *History*, 244–251.

2 Ibid; Blain, *Le Moyne*; Parmenter, *Edge*, 210; Laramie, *King*, 119–121.

3 Monseignat, Occurrences, November 1689 to November 1690, DHNY, v. 1, 297–302; Béchard, *Togouiroui*; Parmenter, *Edge*, 137, 146, 173, 197, 210, *After*, 45, 47; Richter, *Ordeal*, 126; Trelease, *Indian*, 14–24; Hart, *For*, 35; Sivertsen, *Turtles*, 84.

4 Monseignat, Occurrences, Nov. 1689 to Nov. 1690, DHNY, v. 1, 299; Le Sueur, *Frontenac*, 246; Parmenter, *After*, 47; Laramie, *King*, 120–121.

5 Sylvester, *History*, 35; Monseignat, Occurrences, Nov. 1689 to Nov. 1690, DHNY, v. 1, 298–300; Pearson, *History*, 244–251; Laramie, *King*, 120; Burke, *Mohawk*, 103–108.

6 Greene, *History*, 197; Sylvester, *History*, 14, 28.

7 Albany Council, Nov. 29, 1689, DHNY, v. 2, 132; Monseignat, Occurrences, Nov. 1689 to Nov. 1690; Albany Council, Feb. 9, 1690; Leisler to Maryland, New York, March 4, 1690; Livingston to Andros, Hartford, April 14, 1690; Leisler to Andros, New York, May 17, 1690; Van Cortlandt to Andros, DHNY, v. 1, 297–311; Robert Livingston, Examination of three French Prisoners, Albany, March 3, 1690, in Leder, *Livingston Indian*, 158–160; Leisler to Bishop of Salisbury, New York, March 31, 1690, NYCD, v. 3, 701–702.

8 Albany Council, Feb. 9, 1690; Jacob Leisler to Maryland; Livingston to Andros, Hartford, April 14, 1690, DHNY, v. 1, 302–303, 306, 307, 309–310; Pearson, *History*, 244–251; Burke, *Mohawk*, 103–108; Laramie, *King*, 121; Staffa, *Schenectady*, 62; Greene, *History*, 380–396.

9 Memoir of Instructions to Frontenac, June 7, 1689; Monseignat, Occurrences, Nov. 1689 to Nov. 1690, DHNY, v. 1, 292–299; Waterman, *We Must*, 22; Trelease, *Indian*, 297–298, 301; Le Sueur, *Frontenac*, 224–247; Biggar, *Frontenac's*, 142–147; Parmenter, *Edge*, 206–207, *After*, 47; Sylvester, *History*, 34–35.

10 Memoir of Instructions to Frontenac, June 7, 1689, DHNY, v. 1, 292–297; Trelease, *Indian*, 297–298; Le Sueur, *Frontenac*, 234; Biggar, *Frontenac's*, 142–147; Parmenter, *After*, 47, *Edge*, 206–207; Eccles, *Frontenac*, 192–194.

11 Memoir of Instructions to Frontenac, June 7, 1689, DHNY, v. 1, 292–297; Bradstreet to Leisler, Boston, May 30, 1690, DHNY, v. 2, 259–260; Greene, *History*, 381; Trelease, *Indian*, 300–301; Le Sueur, *Frontenac*, 234–236.

12 Livingston, Examination of three French Prisoners, Albany, March 3, 1690, in Leder, *Livingston Indian*, 160; Monseignat, Occurrences, Nov. 1689 to Nov. 1690, DHNY, v. 1, 299; Sylvester, *History*, 35–36; Parmenter, *Edge*, 210; Greene, *History*, 380–396; Pearson, *History*, 244–246; Eccles, *Frontenac*, 224; Le Sueur, *Frontenac*, 245–246.

13 Ibid.

14 Livingston, Examination of three French Prisoners, Albany, March 3, 1690, in Leder, *Livingston Indian*, 160; Albany Council, Jan. 20, 1689, DHNY, v. 2, 155; Monseignat, Occurrences, Nov. 1689 to Nov. 1690, DHNY, v. 1, 299–300; Parmenter, *Edge*, 210; Le Sueur, *Frontenac*, 246.

15 Albany Council, Nov. 29, 1689, DHNY, v. 2, 132; Monseignat, Occurrences, Nov. 1689 to Nov. 1690; Albany Council, Feb. 9, 1690; Leisler to Maryland, New York, March 4, 1690; Livingston to Andros, Hartford, April 14, 1690; Leisler to Andros, New York, May 17, 1690; Van Cortlandt to Andros, DHNY, v. 1, 297–311; Livingston, Examination of three French Prisoners, Albany, March 3,

1690, in Leder, *Livingston Indian*, 158–160; Leisler to Bishop of Salisbury, New York, March 31, 1690, NYCD, v. 3, 701–702; Sylvester, *History*, 35–36; Le Sueur, *Frontenac*, 245–248; Parmenter, *Edge*, 210; Greene, *History*, 380–396; Pearson, *History*, 244–257; Burke, *Mohawk*, 103–108; Laramie, *King*, 121–123.

16 Ibid.

17 Ibid.

18 Ibid.

19 Ibid.

20 Albany Council, Feb. 9, 1690; List of Ye People Killed and Destroyed; Leisler to Maryland, New York, March 4, 1690; Livingston to Andros, Hartford, April 14, 1690; Leisler to Andros, New York, May 17, 1690; Van Cortlandt to Andros, DHNY, v. 1, 302–311; Greene, *History*, 333–339, 382–385; Sivertsen, *Turtles,* 7; Burke, *Leisler's*, 408; Staffa, *Schenectady*, 27, 46, 62-65.

21 Albany Council, Nov. 29, 1689, DHNY, v. 2, 132; Monseignat, Occurrences, Nov. 1689 to Nov. 1690; Albany Council, Feb. 9, 1690; Leisler to Maryland, New York, March 4, 1690; Livingston to Andros, Hartford, April 14, 1690; Leisler to Andros, New York, May 17, 1690; Van Cortlandt to Andros, DHNY, v. 1, 297–311; Robert Livingston, Examination of three French Prisoners, Albany, March 3, 1690, in Leder, *Livingston Indian*, 158–160; Leisler to Bishop of Salisbury, New York, March 31, 1690, NYCD, v. 3, 701–702.

22 Schuyler to Bradstreet, Albany, Feb. 15, 1690, in Pearson, *History*, 252–256; Sylvester, *History*, 36.

23 Livingston, Examination of three French Prisoners, Albany, March 3, 1690, in Leder, *Livingston Indian*, 160; Monseignat, Occurrences, Nov. 1689 to Nov. 1690; List of Ye People Killed and Destroyed, DHNY, v. 1, 302–306; Parmenter, *Edge*, 210, 357 (Endnote 76); Pearson, *History*, 247.

24 List of Ye People Killed and Destroyed, DHNY, v. 1, 304–306, and Pearson, *History*, 261–266; Parmenter, *Edge*, 357 (Endnote 76).

25 Parmenter, *Edge*, 357 (Endnote 76); List of Ye People Killed and Destroyed, DHNY, v. 1, 304–306, and Pearson, *History*, 261–266.

26 Schuyler to Bradstreet, Albany, Feb. 15, 1690, in Pearson, *History*, 253.

27 Livingston, Examination of three French Prisoners, Albany, March 3, 1690, in Leder, *Livingston Indian*, 160; Monseignat, Occurrences, Nov. 1689 to Nov. 1690; List of Ye People Killed and Destroyed, DHNY, v. 1, 302–306; Parmenter, *Edge*, 210, 357 (Endnote 76); Pearson, *History*, 247.

28 Sylvester, *History*, 36.

29 Monseignat, Occurrences, Nov. 1689 to Nov. 1690; List of Ye People Killed and Destroyed, DHNY, v. 1, 302–306; Parmenter, *Edge*, 210, 357 (Endnote 76); Staffa, *Schenectady*, 65.

30 Monseignat, Occurrences, Nov. 1689 to Nov. 1690; Albany Council, Feb. 9, 1690; The Way Ye Bloody French and Indians committed this Tragedy, Feb. 10, 1690, DHNY, v. 1, 300–303, 306; Staffa, *Schenectady*, 15 (Endnote 21), 316; Sivertsen, *Turtles*, 3–10.

31 Greene, *History*, 209.

32 Burke, *Leisler's*, 408, 415; Sivertsen, *Turtles*, 3; Greene, *History*, 333–339; Staffa, *Schenectady*, 27, 46, 65, 75, 316.

33 Monseignat, Occurrences, Nov. 1689 to Nov. 1690; Albany Council, Feb. 9, 1690; The Way Ye Bloody French and Indians committed this Tragedy, Feb. 10, 1690, DHNY, v. 1, 300–303, 306; Albany Council, Feb. 11, 1690, in Pearson, *History*, 252; Parmenter, *Edge*, 120, 210; Le Sueur, *Frontenac*, 247–248; Greene, *History*, 330–333, 384–385.
34 Sylvester, *History*, 36.
35 List of Ye Prisoners which ye French and their Indians have taken; Albany Council, Feb. 22, 1690, DHNY, v. 1, 305–306; Albany Council, Feb. 22, 1690, DHNY, v. 2, 163; Robert Livingston, Examination of three French Prisoners, Albany, March 3, 1690, in Leder, *Livingston Indian*, 159–160; Parmenter, *Edge*, 210–211; Laramie, *King*, 122–123.
36 Instructions for Capt. Jonathan Bull, Feb. 10, 1690, DHNY, v. 1, 304.
37 Greene, *History*, 385.
38 Propositions made by Mohawk Sachems and answer to Propositions, Feb. 25 and 26, 1690; DHNY, v. 2, 164–169; Richter, *War*, 548; Sivertsen, *Turtles*, 20–21.
39 Albany Council, Dec. 16, 1689; Feb. 11, 12, and 13, 1690, DHNY, v. 2, 137, 157–159; Albany Council, Feb. 9 and 22, 1690, DHNY, v. 1, 303, 306; Reynolds, *Lawrence*; Parmenter, *Edge*, 211.
40 Albany Council, Feb. 11, 1690, DHNY, v. 2, 157; Albany Council, Feb. 22, 1690, DHNY, v. 1, 306.

Chapter 4: A Most Fragile Unity

1 Albany Council, Feb. 11 and 13, 1690, DHNY, v. 2, 157–158; Parmenter, *Edge*, 210–211, 225; Reynolds, *Lawrence*; Staffa, *Schenectady*, 65.
2 Ibid; Richter, *Ordeal*, 178.
3 Albany Council, Feb. 9 and 22, 1690, DHNY, v. 1, 303, 306; Robert Livingston, Examination of three French Prisoners, Albany, March 3, 1690, in Leder, *Livingston Indian*, 159–160.
4 Albany Council, Feb. 13, 1690, DHNY, v. 2, 158–159; Reynolds, *Lawrence.*
5 Albany Council, Feb. 9 and 22, 1690, DHNY, v. 1, 306; Reynolds, *Lawrence.*
6 Albany Council, Feb. 9 and 22, 1690, DHNY, v. 1, 306.
7 Propositions made by Mohawk Sachems, Feb. 25, 1690, DHNY, v. 2, 164–165.
8 Albany Council, Feb. 9 and 22, 1690, DHNY, v. 1, 303, 306; Robert Livingston, Examination of three French Prisoners, Albany, March 3, 1690, in Leder, *Livingston*, 159–160.
9 Schuyler to Bradstreet, Albany, Feb. 15, 1690, in Pearson, *History*, 255.
10 Leisler to Bishop of Salisbury, New York, March 31, 1690, DHNY, v. 1, 309; Livingston to Andros, Hartford, April 14, 1690, NYCD, v. 3, 708; Parmenter, *Edge*, 210–211.
11 Ibid.
12 Parmenter, *After*, 39; Richter, *War*, 528–535.
13 Albany Council, February 13–March 3, 1690, DHNY, v. 2, 158–178.
14 Richter, *War*, 530–531.
15 Richter, *War*, 535.
16 Livingston to Andros, Hartford, April 14, 1690, NYCD, v. 3, 710; Parmenter, *Edge*, 211.

17 Livingston to Connecticut, Hartford, May 9, 1690, NYCD, v. 3, 728–729.
18 Albany Council, Feb. 11, 12, and 13, 1690, DHNY, v. 2, 137, 157–159; Albany Council, Feb. 9 and 22, 1690, DHNY, v. 1, 303, 306; Parmenter, *Edge*, 211.
19 Champigny to Minister, May 10, 1691, NYCD, v. 9, 499.
20 Albany Convention Records, Nov. 15–16, 1689, Feb. 25, 1690, DHNY, v. 2, 130, 131, 164; Blackhawk, *Rediscovery*, 78–79; Hagedorn, *Friend*, 75; Staggs, *Calvinists*, 203–204; James and Jameson, *Journal*, 201–205; Midtrøød, *Flemish*, 85–96; Hart, *For*, 2, 51–54; Staffa, *Schenectady*, 27, 316.
21 Albany Convention Records, Nov. 15–16, 1689, Feb. 25, 1690, DHNY, v. 2, 130, 131, 164; Midtrøød, *Flemish*, 85–96; Staggs, *Calvinists*, 203–204; Staffa, *Schenectady*, 27; James and Jameson, *Journal*, 201–205; Hart, *For*, 51–54.
22 Albany Convention Records, Nov. 15–16, 1689, Feb. 25, 1690, DHNY, v. 2, 130, 131, 164; James and Jameson, *Journal*, 201–205; Midtrøød, *Flemish*, 85–96; Hart, *For*, 51–54; Hagedorn, *Friend*, 21, 23, 57, 60, 73; Hinderaker, *Hendricks*, 41–44.
23 Livingston to Andros, Hartford, April 14, 1690; Livingston to Nicholson, June 7, 1690, DHNY, v. 1, 309–310, 311–312; Burke, *Leisler's*, 413–414.
24 Livingston to Andros, Hartford, April 14, 1690, DHNY, v. 1, 309–310.
25 Leisler to Maryland, Boston, Bishop of Salisbury, and Governor of Barbados, New York, March 4 and 31 and May 17, 1690, DHNY, v. 1, 307–309, 310–311; Burke, *Leisler's*, 414.
26 Ritchie, *Duke's*, 222; Kammen, *Colonial*, 124–125; Eccles, *Frontenac*, 227; Waterman, *We Must*, 23; Trelease, *Indian*, 302.
27 Commission to Bruyn and others to Superintend Albany, March 4, 1690, NYCD, v. 3, 702–703; Stokes, *Iconography*, v. 4, 359.
28 New York Council to Shrewsbury, June 10, 1689; Abstract of Colonel Bayard's journal; Modest Narrative, NYCD, v. 3, 585–586, 599–604, 665–684; Ritchie, *Duke's*, 203–229.
29 Balmer, *Traitors*, 341–372; Leder, *Livingston*, 61–64.
30 Circular to Governors, New York, April 2, 1690, DHNY, v. 2, 211; Hall, Leder, and Kammen, *Glorious*, 101; Eccles, *Frontenac*, 227–229.
31 New York Council, DHNY, v. 2, 211, 237–240, 242, 254–256; Sewall, *Diary*, v. 1, 317–318; Ritchie, *Duke's*, 222; Reich, *Leisler's*, 94–96; Kammen, *Colonial*, 124–125.
32 New York Council, DHNY, v. 2, 237–240; Van Cortlandt to Andros, NYCD, v. 3, 715–719; Ritchie, *Duke's*, 222; Kammen, *Colonial*, 124–125.
33 Leisler to Shrewsbury, New York, June 23, 1690, NYCD, v. 3, 731–733; Stokes, *Iconography*, v. 4, 359; New York Council; Leisler to Treat, New York, May 29, 1690; Bradstreet to Leisler, Boston, May 30, 1690, DHNY, v. 2, 237–240, 242, 254–256, 259–260; Hall, Leder, and Kammen, *Glorious*, 101; Trelease, *Indian*, 302–303.
34 Hall, Leder, and Kammen, *Glorious*, 101; Trelease, *Indian*, 302–303; Parkman, *Count*, 234; Parmenter, *Edge*, 212, 213.
35 Allyn to Leisler, Hartford, May 25, 1690, DHNY, v. 2, 252–253.
36 Livingston to Connecticut, May 13, 1690, NYCD, v. 3, 730.
37 Allyn to Leisler, Hartford, May 25, 1690, DHNY, v. 2, 252–253; Leder, *Livingston*, 66–72; Ritchie, *Duke's*, 223.
38 Leisler to Treat, New York, May 29, 30 and June 20, 30, 1690; Albany Council, July 31, 1690; Leisler's Commission appointing Winthrop commander, DHNY,

v. 2, 254–256, 258–259, 265, 270, 281–282; Hall, Leder, and Kammen, *Glorious*, 101; Trelease, *Indian*, 302–303.

39 Ritchie, *Duke's*, 222; Reich, *Leisler's*, 96.

40 Leisler to Shrewsbury, New York, June 23, 1690, NYCD, v. 3, 731–733; Leisler to Treat and Western Governments, New York, April 19 and May 13, 1690, DHNY, v. 2, 235, 242; Trelease, *Indian*, 115–118; Richter, *Ordeal*, 164, 166.

41 Leisler to Shrewsbury, New York, June 23, 1690, NYCD, v. 3, 731–733; Leisler to Treat and Western Governments, New York, April 19, May 13, 29, 1690, DHNY, v. 2, 235, 242, 255; Parmenter, *Edge*, 212–213; Richter, *Ordeal*, 166, 172.

Chapter 5: Roundups, Gauntlets, and Rioting in the Streets

1 Leisler and Council, New York, Jan. 3, 7, 17, 1689; Leisler to Melyn and Leisler Order, New York, Jan. 24 and Feb. 15, 1690; Leisler letters to Maryland, New York, March 4, 1690, DHNY, v. 2, 55, 59, 60, 62, 71, 181–184; Leisler and Council to Bishop of Salisbury, New York, Jan. 7, 1690; Modest Narrative; Van Cortlandt to Andros, NYCD, v. 3, 655–657, 682, 715–719; Ritchie, *Duke's*, 225.

2 Leisler letters to Maryland, New York, March 4, 1690, DHNY, v. 2, 181–184; Lovejoy, *Glorious*, 321; Foote, *Black*, 103.

3 Cal. Hist. MSS, Pt. II, 191–195; Leisler letters and Leisler and Council, DHNY, v. 2, 55, 60, 62, 71, 181–84; Modest Narrative; Blagge's Memorial, NYCD, v. 3, 654–684, 739; Lovejoy, *Glorious*, 321.

4 Leisler to Albany Agents, Fort William, May 19, 1690, DHNY, v. 2, 247; Schuyler, *Colonial*, v. 1, 169.

5 Leisler to Albany Agents, Fort William, May 19, 1690, DHNY, v. 2, 247.

6 Stahlhut, *Creating*, 54–55; Schuyler, *Colonial*, v. 1, 169; Trelease, *Indian*, 209–210; Richter, *Ordeal*, 137–138, 164–165, 177.

7 Leisler Order, New York, May 15, 1690, DHNY, v. 2, 243; Van Cortlandt to Andros, New York, May 19, 1690, NYCD, v. 3, 717; Stokes, *Iconography*, v. 4, 360; Matson, *Merchants*, 81; Lovejoy, *Glorious*, 317–319; Ritchie, *Duke's*, 236–237.

8 Ibid.

9 Address of New York Merchants, NYCD, v. 3, 748–749; Murrin, *English*, 78; Ritchie, *Duke's*, 225–227.

10 Milborne to Leisler, Albany, May 27, 1690, DHNY, v. 2, 256–257; Instructions of Governor to D'Aux; Message of Ourehouare, NYCD, v. 3, 733–736; Parmenter, *Edge*, 212; Colden, *History*, 116.

11 Albany Council, March 17–28, 1690, DHNY, v. 1, 191–202; Richter, *Ordeal*, 171–172, *Cultural*, 57–58; Greene, *History*, v. 1, 401.

12 Richter, *Ordeal*, 171.

13 Richter, *Cultural*, 57–58, *Ordeal*, 171–172.

14 Milborne to Leisler, Albany, May 27, 1690, DHNY, v. 2, 256–257; Richter, *Trade*, 125, *Ordeal*, 171–172.

15 Milborne to Leisler, Albany, May 27, 1690, DHNY, v. 2, 256–257.

16 Parmenter, *Edge*, 212; Richter, *Trade*, 125, *Cultural*, 58.

17 Colden, *History*, 109–110; Waterman, *We Must*, 25; Richter, *Ordeal*, 172.

18 Eccles, *Frontenac*, 230; Richter, *Ordeal*, 172; Pell, *Schuyler, Peter*.

19 Leisler to Shrewsbury, New York, June 23, 1690; Instructions of Governor to d'Aux; Message of Ourehouare, NYCD, v. 3, 731–736; Milborne to Leisler, Albany, May 27, 1690; Leisler to Coode, New York, June 27, 1690, DHNY, v. 2, 256–257, 266–269; Lahontan, *New Voyages*, v. 1, 154, 156–158; Parmenter, *Edge*,192, 211–212; Trelease, *Indian*, 303; Parkman, *Count*, 200–201; Richter, *Ordeal*, 150–151, 156–157, 172–173; Eccles, *Frontenac*, 181–183, 186–187, 207–208; Burleigh, *Ourehouare.*
20 Ibid.
21 Narrative 1689, 1690, NYCD, v. 9, 464–465, 469–470; Lahontan, *New Voyages*, v. 1, 154, 156–158; Richter, *Ordeal*, 150–151, 156–157, 172–173; Eccles, *Frontenac*, 181–183, 186–187, 207–208; Burleigh, *Ourehouare.*
22 Ibid.
23 Ibid.
24 Frontenac to Pontchartrain, Champigny to Pontchartrain, May 10, 1691, NYCD, v. 9, 495, 499; Lahontan, *New Voyages*, v. 1, 157–158; Leisler to Coode, New York, June 27, 1690, DHNY, v. 2, 267–268; Richter, *Ordeal*, 172–173.
25 Lahontan, *New Voyages*, v. 1, 157–158.
26 Richter, *War*, 533–535; Shannon, *Iroquois*, 33.
27 Leisler to Coode, New York, June 27, 1690, DHNY, v. 2, 267–268; Frontenac to Pontchartrain, Champigny to Pontchartrain, May 10, 1691, NYCD, v. 9, 495, 499; Lahontan, *New Voyages*, v. 1, 157–158; Parmenter, *Edge*, 212; Trelease, *Indian*, 303; Parkman, *Count*, 200–201; Richter, *Ordeal*, 172–173, *War*, 533–535; Eccles, *Frontenac*, 230; Shannon, *Iroquois*, 33.
28 Ibid.
29 Ibid.
30 Blackhawk, *Rediscovery*, 94; Staffa, *Schenectady*, 73; Richter, *War*, 530-532.
31 Blackhawk, *Rediscovery*, 94.
32 Lahontan, *New Voyages*, v. 1, 157–158; Leisler to Coode, New York, June 27, 1690, DHNY, v. 2, 267–268; Frontenac to Pontchartrain, Champigny to Pontchartrain, May 10, 1691, NYCD, v. 9, 495, 499; Parmenter, *Edge*, 212; Shannon, *Iroquois*, 33; Parkman, *Count*, 200–201; Richter, *Ordeal*, 172–173, *War*, 533–535.
33 Richter, *War*, 534.
34 Shannon, *Iroquois*, 33-34; Richter, *War*, 533–535, *Trade*, 68–96; Blackhawk, *Rediscovery*, 92–95.
35 Leisler to Coode, New York, June 27, 1690, DHNY, v. 2, 267–268.
36 Anonymous (likely John Tuder), Account, June 5–8, 1690, in Leder, *Madmen*, 409.
37 Leisler and Council, New York, June 7, 1690; Leisler Act of Assembly for Raising Three Pence in the Pound, Jan. 25, 1690; Deposition of Robert Sinclair, Feb. 23, 1691, DHNY, v. 2, 262–263, 320, 402–404; Anonymous (likely John Tuder), Account, June 5–8, 1690, in Leder, *Madmen*, 409–410.
38 Anonymous (likely John Tuder), Account, June 5–8, 1690, in Leder, *Madmen*, 409–414; Leisler and Council to Bishop of Salisbury, New York, Jan. 7, 1690; Modest Narrative; Riot Depositions, NYCD, v. 3, 654–657, 665–684; Leisler to Treat, New York, Aug. 28, 1689, DHNY, v. 2, 25–27; Ritchie, *Duke's*, 225–227; Foote, *Black*, 102–104; Schuyler, *Colonial*, v. 2, 164–166; Lovejoy, *Glorious*, 320–321; Archdeacon, *New York*, 117.

39 The following recreation of the New York City Riot of June 6, 1690, is based upon the following first-hand accounts: Anonymous (likely John Tuder), Account, June 5–8, 1690, in Leder, *Madmen*, 409–414; Riot Depositions, NYCD, v. 3, 740–746; Leisler and Council, New York, June 7, 1690, DHNY, v. 2, 262–263. Also see Leder commentary in *Madmen*, 405–408, 414–415, and 409–414 (Footnotes).
40 Ibid.
41 Ibid.
42 Ibid.
43 Ibid.
44 Ibid.
45 Ibid.
46 Ibid.
47 Anonymous (likely John Tuder), Account, June 5–8, 1690, in Leder, *Madmen*, 412–413.
48 Blagge's Memorial, NYCD, v. 3, 739; Answer to Blagge's Memorial, DHNY, v. 2, 390; Leder, *Madmen*, 405–415; Lovejoy, *Glorious*, 321–322.
49 Leder, *Madmen*, 405–415; Anonymous (likely John Tuder), Account, June 5–8, 1690, in Ibid, 409–414; Riot Depositions, NYCD, v. 3, 740–746; Leisler and Council, New York, June 7, 1690, DHNY, v. 2, 262–263.
50 Modest Narrative; Eyck Deposition; Address of New York Merchants, NYCD, v. 3, 673, 744–745, 749; Leder, *Madmen*, 405–415.
51 Anonymous (likely John Tuder), Account, June 5–8, 1690, in Leder, *Madmen*, 414; Letter from gentleman, DHNY, v. 2, 431; Balmer, *Traitors*, 350–351; Ritchie, *Duke's*, 225.
52 Anonymous (likely John Tuder), Account, June 5–8, 1690, in Leder, *Madmen*, 413; Riot Depositions, NYCD, v. 3, 740–746; Leisler and Council, New York, June 7, 1690, DHNY, v. 2, 262–264.
53 Selyns, Varick, and Dellius to the Classis, Oct. 12, 1692; Varick to the Classis, April 9, 1693, Defense of Dellius against Bellomont charges, Oct. 31, 1699, ERNY, v. 2, 1041–1045, 1048–1053, and 1394–1397; Ritchie, *Duke's*, 225–226; Goodfriend, *Who*, 25.
54 Selyns, Varick, and Dellius to Classis, Oct. 12, 1692, ERNY, v. 2, 1041–1045; Ritchie, *Duke's*, 225–226.
55 Varick to Classis, April 9, 1693, ERNY, v. 2, 1048–1049.
56 Memorial of late occurrences; Letter from gentleman, DHNY, v. 2, 56–60, 430–432; Leder, *Madmen*, 414–415; Ritchie, *Duke's*, 225–227.
57 Newton to Nicholson, Boston, May 26, 1690, NYCD, v. 3, 721.

Chapter 6: The Invasion of New France

1 Holland Society, Records, 51; Sivertsen, *Turtles*, 25–26, 207; Hinderaker, *Hendricks*, 40–41.
2 Ibid.
3 Ibid.
4 Ibid.

5 Winthrop, *Journal*; Reasons that hindered army from going to Canada, Aug. 21, 1690; Winthrop to Governor and Council of Massachusetts, Hartford, Sept. 23, 1690; Winthrop to Governor and General Assembly of Connecticut, New London, Oct. 6, 1690, *The Winthrop Papers*, MHS *Collections* [1882], 5th series, v. 8, 309, 312–324, NYCD, v. 4, 193–196; Leisler to Shrewsbury, New York, June 23, 1690, NYCD, v. 3, 731–733; Leisler to Treat and Western Governments, New York, April 19, May 13, and May 29, 1690; Bradstreet to Leisler, Boston, May 30, 1690, DHNY, v. 2, 235, 242, 255, 259–260.

6 Ibid.

7 Allyn to Leisler, Hartford, Aug. 23, 1690; John Schuyler journal, DHNY, v. 2, 284–286; Winthrop, *Journal*; Reasons that hindered army from going to Canada, Aug. 21, 1690; Winthrop to Governor and Council of Massachusetts, Hartford, Sept. 23, 1690; Winthrop to Governor and General Assembly of Connecticut, New London, Oct. 6, 1690, *The Winthrop Papers*, MHS *Collections* [1882], 5th Series, v. 8, 312–324; Parmenter, *Edge*, 213; Trelease, *Indian*, 304; Laramie, *King*, 153–155.

8 Frontenac to Minister, Nov. 12, 1690, NYCD, v. 9, 460–461; Winthrop, *Journal*; Reasons that hindered army from going to Canada, Aug. 21, 1690; Winthrop to Governor and Council of Massachusetts, Hartford, Sept. 23, 1690; Winthrop to Governor and General Assembly of Connecticut, New London, Oct. 6, 1690, *The Winthrop Papers*, MHS *Collections* [1882], 5th Series, v. 8, 312–324; Laramie, *King*, 153–155; Parmenter, *Edge*, 213.

9 Winthrop, *Journal*, *The Winthrop Papers*, MHS *Collections* [1882], 5th Series, v. 8, 312–318, NYCD, v. 4, 193–196; Schuyler, *Colonial*, v. 2, 224; Parmenter, *Edge*, 213.

10 Proposals made by Convention, Albany, Nov. 5, 1689, DHNY, v. 2, 109–112; Schuyler, *Colonial*, v. 2, 223–224; Pell, *Schuyler, Johannes*.

11 Schuyler, *Colonial*, v. 2, 224.

12 John Schuyler journal, DHNY, v. 2, 285–286; Parmenter, *Edge*, 213.

13 John Schuyler journal, DHNY, v. 2, 285–288; Schuyler, *Colonial*, v. 2, 223–241; Pell, *Schuyler, Johannes*; Parmenter, *Edge*, 213; Laramie, *King*, 155.

14 John Schuyler journal, DHNY, v. 2, 286; Pell, *Schuyler, Johannes*; Parmenter, *Edge*, 213.

15 Schuyler, *Colonial*, v. 2, 224; John Schuyler journal, DHNY, v. 2, 286.

16 Marsh, *Birchbark*; Lienhard, *Indian*; John Schuyler journal, DHNY, v. 2, 285–287.

17 John Schuyler journal, DHNY, v. 2, 286–287; Schuyler, *Colonial*, v. 2, 224–225.

18 John Schuyler journal, DHNY, v. 2, 287; Schuyler, *Colonial*, v. 2, 225; Parmenter, *Edge*, 213–214.

19 John Schuyler journal, DHNY, v. 2, 287.

20 John Schuyler journal, DHNY, v. 2, 287; Parmenter, *Edge*, 213–214; Eccles, *Frontenac*, 232–233.

21 Narrative 1689, 1690, NYCD, v. 9, 478–479; Eccles, *Frontenac*, 232–233; Le Sueur, *Frontenac*, 260–261; Parmenter, *Edge*, 213–214.

22 John Schuyler journal, DHNY, v. 2, 287; Narrative 1689, 1690, NYCD, v. 9, 479–480; Eccles, *Frontenac*, 233; Pell, *Schuyler, Johannes*; Laramie, *King*, 155–156.

23 Eccles, *Frontenac*, 18–30, *Buade*; Parkman, *Count*, 5–13; Le Sueur, *Frontenac*, 61–64. For the most detailed scholarly works on Count Frontenac, the reader is

referred to Parkman, *Count Frontenac and New France under Louis XIV*, and Eccles, *Frontenac: The Courtier Governor.*

24 John Schuyler journal, DHNY, v. 2, 287.

25 Ibid; Narrative 1689, 1690, NYCD, v. 9, 481; Schuyler, *Colonial*, v. 2, 225; Laramie, *King*, 169.

26 John Schuyler journal, DHNY, v. 2, 287; Narrative 1689, 1690, NYCD, v. 9, 481; Eccles, *Frontenac*, 233; Parkman, *Count*, 257–258; Schuyler, *Colonial*, v. 2, 225.

27 Ibid.

28 Ibid.

29 Winthrop, *Journal*, NYCD, v. 4, 196; John Schuyler journal, DHNY, v. 2, 287; Narrative 1689, 1690, NYCD, v. 9, 481; Parmenter, *Edge*, 214.

30 Narrative 1689, 1690, NYCD, v. 9, 481; John Schuyler journal, DHNY, v. 2, 287; Pell, *Schuyler, Johannes*; Eccles, *Frontenac*, 233; Parkman, *Count*, 258; Schuyler, *Colonial*, v. 2, 225.

31 John Schuyler journal, DHNY, v. 2, 287.

32 Schuyler, *Colonial*, v. 2, 225; John Schuyler journal, DHNY, v. 2, 287; Parkman, *Count*, 258.

33 John Schuyler journal, DHNY, v. 2, 287.

34 John Schuyler journal, DHNY, v. 2, 287–288; Schuyler, *Colonial*, v. 2, 225; Eccles, *Frontenac*, 233.

35 Pell, *Schuyler, Johannes*.

36 Parkman, *Count*, 258.

37 Eccles, *Frontenac*, 233–234; Hutchinson, *History*, v. I, 354.

38 Depositions of Swyndale and another; Abstract from Lloyd, Boston, Jan. 8, 1691; Extract from Paris *Gazette* of Feb. 5, 1691; Phips's Account, April 21, 1691, CSPC, v. 13, nos. 1,245, 1,282, 1,299, and 1,417; Narrative 1689, 1690, NYCD, v. 9, 485; Walley, Walley's journal, in Hutchinson, *History*, v. I, 471.

39 Parkman, *Phips's*, 719–732, and *Frontenac*, 263; Hutchinson, *History*, v. I, 355.

40 Baker and Reid, *New*, 15–26; Mather, *Pietas*, 4–7; Sewall, *Diary*, v. 1, 203–204 (Footnote 2); Barnes, *Rise*, 273–274.

41 Mather, *Pietas*, 6, 14–15; Baker and Reid, *New*, 51–69; Hanna, *Pirate Nests*, 183; Sewall, *Diary*, v. 1, 203–204 (Footnote 2).

42 Mather, *Pietas*, 14–15; Sewall, *Diary*, v. 1, 193, 219, 321; Barnes, *Rise*, 285.

43 Leisler and Council to Shrewsbury, Oct. 20, 1690, NYCD, v. 3, 752; Baker and Reid, *New*, 86–95; Barnes, *Rise*, 290; Hanna, *Pirate Nests*, 184.

44 Bradstreet to Leisler, Boston, May 30, 1690, DHNY, v. 2, 260.

45 Abstract from Lloyd, Boston, Jan. 8, 1691; Phips's Account, April 21, 1691, CSPC, v. 13, nos. 1,282 and 1,417; Eccles, *Frontenac*, 235; Parkman, *Count*, 265.

46 Narrative 1689, 1690, NYCD, v. 9, 485–486; Abstract from Lloyd, Boston, Jan. 8, 1691, CSPC, v. 13, no. 1,282; Mather, *Pietas*, 36; Baker and Reid, *New*, 97–98; Parkman, *Count*, 265–266.

47 Narrative 1689, 1690, NYCD, v. 9, 486.

48 Abstract from Myles, Dec. 12, 1690; Abstract from Lloyd, Boston, Jan. 8, 1691; Extracts from Boston, Feb. 1691; Savage to brother, Boston, Feb. 2, 1691, CSPC, v. 13, nos. 1,239, 1,282, 1,313, and 1,314; Parkman, *Phips's*, 719–732.

49 Savage, *An Account*, 3–11; Preface; Abstract from Myles, Dec. 12, 1690; Abstract from Lloyd, Boston, Jan. 8, 1691; Extracts from Boston, Feb. 2, 1691; Savage to brother, Boston, Feb. 2, 1691; Phips's Account, April 21, 1691, CSPC, v. 13, xiii and nos. 1,239, 1,282, 1,313, 1,314, and 1,417; Parkman, *Phips's*, 719–732; Narrative 1689, 1690, NYCD, v. 9, 455–458, 487–490; Walley, Walley's journal, in Hutchinson, *History*, v. I, 471–477; Baker and Reid, *New*, 98–102; Eccles, *Frontenac*, 236–240; Parkman, *Count*, 268–283; Peckham, *Colonial*, 36–38.
50 Ibid.
51 Ibid.
52 Ibid.
53 Savage, *An Account*, 5; Narrative 1689, 1690; Champigny to Minister, May 10, 1691, NYCD, v. 9, 489–490, 497; Abstract from Lloyd, Boston, Jan. 8, 1691; CSPC, v. 13, nos. 1,282; Walley, Walley's journal, in Hutchinson, *History*, v. I, 477.
54 Preface; Phips's Account, April 21, 1691, CSPC, v. 13, xiii and no. 1,417.
55 Phips Attack on Quebec, NYCD, v. 9, 455–458; Eccles, *Frontenac*, 240–241.
56 Savage, *An Account*, 5.
57 Eccles, *Frontenac*, 240; Narrative 1689, 1690; Champigny to Minister, May 10, 1691, NYCD, v. 9, 487–490, 498.
58 Abstract from Myles, Dec. 12, 1690; Abstract from Lloyd, Boston, Jan. 8, 1691; Extracts from Boston, Feb. 2, 169, CSPC, v. 13, nos. 1,239, 1,282, and 1,313; Mather, *Pietas*, 43.
59 Preface; Depositions of Swyndale and another; Abstract from Lloyd, Boston, Jan. 8, 1691; Extract from Paris *Gazette* of Feb. 5, 1691; Extracts from Boston, Feb. 1691, CSPC, v. 13, xiii and nos. 1,245, 1,282, 1,299, and 1,313.
60 Mather, *Pietas*, 43–44; Abstract from Lloyd, Boston, Jan. 8, 1691; Address of diverse inhabitants, CSPC, v. 13, nos. 1,282 and 1,393; Barth, *Currency*, 254–255.
61 Hanna, *Pirate Nests*, 184; Barth, *Currency*, 255.
62 Lovejoy, *Glorious*, 319, 323–324; Barth, *Currency*, 254; Ritchie, *Duke's*, 224; Leder, *Livingston*, 73.

Chapter 7: The Blasphemous Privateer

1 Sloughter to Nottingham, March 27, 1691, and Sloughter to Committee, May 7, 1691, NYCD, v. 3, 756–757, 766–768; Memorial to Sidney, Oct. 16, 1691, Rotterdam, CSPC, v. 13, no. 1,842; McCormick, *Governor*, 238–252; Ritchie, *Duke's*, 229–230; Mason, *Aspects*, 177; Lovejoy, *Glorious*, 336–337.
2 Ibid.
3 Lovejoy, *Glorious*, 337.
4 Sloughter to Nottingham, March 27, 1691, and Sloughter to Committee, May 7, 1691; Commander and Council to Blathwayt, New York, Aug. 6, 1691; Memorial Leisler's Adherents; Petition Leisler to King, NYCD, v. 3, 756–757, 766–768, 794–796, 809–811, 825–826; Lovejoy, *Glorious*, 337–340; Ritchie, *Duke's*, 229–230.
5 Commander and Council to Blathwayt, New York, Aug. 6, 1691; Memorial Leisler's Adherents, Petition Leisler to King, NYCD, v. 3, 794–796, 809–811, 825–826; Ritchie, *Duke's*, 229–230.

6 Codrington to BOT, Antigua, March 1, 1690, CSPC, v. 13, no. 789; Kidd's Protest, April 11, 1700, Report on the Manuscripts of his Grace the Duke of Portland (hereafter Portland Manuscripts), v. 8, 78.

7 Dr. David Boyles, personal communication, June 2020–Sept. 2024; *Boyles Family Tree*, Ancestry.com.

8 Captain Kidd's Protest, April 11, 1700, Portland Manuscripts, v. 8, 78; New York Title and Guarantee Co., *Sea Rover*, 1–5; Geanacopoulos, *Pirate's Wife*, 43; Hinrichs, *Fateful*, 17–18; Winston, *No Man*, 114.

9 Except where noted, the listed currencies of the Early Modern Era are given in English pounds sterling with equivalent values in 2026 US dollars in parenthesis, based upon the calendar year 1690 to maintain consistency, using University of Wyoming Professor Emeritus Dr. Eric Nye's automated *Pounds Sterling to Dollars: Historical Conversion of Currency*. For the wages of mariners of the age, see Examination of John Dann, Aug. 3, 1696; Robert Snead to Sir John Houblon, Sept. 20, 1698, CSPC, v. 15, nos. 517iv and 1,331; Bellomont to BOT, New York, Sept. 21, 1698, NYCD, v. 4, 381; Hanna, *Pirate Nests*, 193–194.

10 New York Title and Guarantee Co., *Sea Rover*, 1–5; Geanacopoulos, *Pirate's Wife*, 43; Winston, *No Man*, 114.

11 Ritchie, *Kidd*, 29; Zacks, *Pirate*, 59–64; Hinrichs, *Fateful*, 18–19.

12 Marquis, *Captain Kidd*, 76; Head, Conclusion, in Head, *Golden Age*, 242; Hanna, *Well-Behaved*, 137.

13 Head, Conclusion, in Head, *Golden Age*, 241–243; Lincoln, *British*, 4; Geanacopoulos, *Pirate Next Door*, 67.

14 Stokes, *Iconography*, v. 4, 363; Ammunition and Guns delivered to Captain Kidd, Cal. Hist. MSS, Pt. II, 202; Leder, *Captain*, 48–53.

15 Leder, *Livingston*, 75–76; Ritchie, *Duke's*, 221–231; Reich, *Leisler's*, 108–116.

16 Sloughter to Nottingham, March 27, 1691, and Sloughter to Committee, May 7, 1691, NYCD, v. 3, 756–757, 766–768; Memorial to Sidney, Oct. 16, 1691, Rotterdam, CSPC, v. 13, no. 1,842; McCormick, *Governor*, 238–252; Mason, *Aspects*, 177; Geanacopoulos, *Pirate's Wife*, 67.

17 Testimony of Culliford, HCA 1/16, pt. 1, fol. 5, PRO; Depositions of Burgess, HCA 1/98, pt. 1, fol. 42–50, PRO; Testimony of Browne, June 17, 1702, HCA 1/16, pt. 1, fol. 1, PRO; Geanacopoulos, *Pirate Next*, 93–100, and *Eighteenth*, 44–52; Burgess, *Pirates'*, 220–221; Kammen, *Colonial*, 121–127; Voorhees, *Zeale*, 471–472; Stanwood, *Catholics*, 229–230.

18 Newton to Nicholson, April 8, 1691, in Leder, *Captain*, 51–52; Sloughter to King, May 7, 1691, New York, CSPC, v. 13, no. 1,463; Brooke to Southwell, April 6, 1691; Answer to Blagge Memorial, April 27, 1691, NYCD, v. 3, 757–759, 765–766; Affidavit of Van Rensselaer, March 7, 1691, NYHS *Collections* [1868], v. I, 328–331; Stokes, *Iconography*, v. 4, 362–363, 367; Zacks, *Pirate*, 80; Archdeacon, *New York*, 119–120.

19 Newton to Nicholson, April 8, 1691, in Leder, *Captain*, 50–51; Reich, *Leisler*'s, 112–113; Ritchie, *Kidd*, 34–35.

20 Ammunition and Guns delivered to Captain Kidd, Cal. Hist. MSS, Pt. II, 202; Stokes, *Iconography*, v. 4, 363.

21 Newton to Nicholson, April 8, 1691, in Leder, *Captain*, 52; Brooke to Southwell, April 6, 1691, and Sloughter to Nottingham, May 6, 1691, NYCD, v. 3, 757–759, 759–762; Draft letter Sloughter to Blathwayt, May 1691, DHNY, v. 2, 381–382; Stokes, *Iconography*, v. 4, 362–363, 367; Zacks, *Pirate*, 81.
22 Ibid.
23 Ibid.
24 Ibid.
25 Ibid.
26 Newton to Nicholson, April 8, 1691, in Leder, *Captain*, 51–52; Brooke to Southwell, April 6, 1691, and Sloughter to Nottingham, May 6, 1691, NYCD, v. 3, 757–759, 759–762; Draft letter Sloughter to Blathwayt, May 1691, DHNY, v. 2, 381–382; Stokes, *Iconography*, v. 4, 363.
27 Leisler Declaration against Ingoldsby and Council, March 16, 1691, DHNY, v. 2, 343.
28 Newton to Nicholson, April 8, 1691, in Leder, *Captain*, 52; Sloughter to Committee, May 7, 1691, NYCD, v. 3, 767; Draft letter Sloughter to Blathwayt, May 1691, DHNY, v. 2, 381–382; McCormick, *Governor*, 251–252.
29 Sloughter to Nottingham, May 6, 1691, NYCD, v. 3, 759–761; Merwick, *Being*, 392; Leonard, *History*, 112–113; Reich, *Leisler's*, 114.
30 Leisler to Sloughter, March 20, 1690–91, DHNY, v. 2, 343; Zacks, *Pirate*, 81.
31 Brooke to Southwell, April 6, 1691, and Sloughter to Nottingham, May 6, 1691, NYCD, v. 3, 757–759, 759–762.
32 Van Rensselaer, *History*, 475.
33 Stokes, *Iconography*, v. 4, 363; Leonard, *History*, 113; Merwick, *Being*, 393–394; Sloughter to Nottingham, March 27, 1691, NYCD, v. 3, 756.
34 For the comprehensive Leisler 1691 treason trial documents, see Leder, *Records*, 431–457. See also Leisler Documents, NYHS *Collections*, v. 1, 311–314; Stokes, *Iconography*, v. 4, 361–370; Historical Society, *Jacob*. For a pro-Leisler viewpoint of the proceedings and a detailed examination of Leisler's Rebellion from the aggrieved Dutch perspective, see Van Rensselaer, *History*, 368–568; Reich, *Leisler's*, 35; Leder, *Records*, 431–457; Historical Society, *Jacob*; Stokes, *Iconography*, v. 4, 361–370.
35 Leder, *Records*, 431–457; Stokes, *Iconography*, v. 4, 364–365; Law Library, *Jacob Leisler Trial.*
36 Historical Society, *Jacob*; Law Library, *Jacob Leisler Trial.*
37 Leder, *Records*, 431–457; Stokes, *Iconography*, v. 4, 364–365; Hall, Leder, and Kammen, *Glorious*, 116.
38 *Rolls*, in Leder, *Records*, 454; Hall, Leder, and Kammen, *Glorious*, 118.

Chapter 8: The Dance of Death

1 Intended Sloughter letter to Blathwayt, Aug. 6, 1691, NYCD, v. 3, 789; Burrows and Wallace, *Gotham*, 102; Van Rensselaer, *History*, 554; Zacks, *Pirate*, 86–87; Voorhees, *Zeale*, 447.
2 Ibid.
3 Dutch Church to Classis of Amsterdam, Oct. 21, 1698, NYHS *Collections* [1868], v. I, 408; Van Rensselaer, *History*, 554; Reich, *Leisler's*, 122.

4 Stokes, *Iconography*, v. 4, 367–369; DHNY, v. 1, 689; Zacks, *Pirate*, 86; Burrows and Wallace, *Gotham*, 94.
5 Intended Sloughter letter to Blathwayt, Aug. 6, 1691, NYCD, v. 3, 789; Van Rensselaer, *History*, 553.
6 Sloughter to Codrington, May 1691, DHNY, v. 2, 380–381; Leonard, *History*, 113.
7 Bayard to Nicholson, May 6, 1691, in Hall, Leder, and Kammen, *Glorious*, 119.
8 Dutch Church to Classis of Amsterdam, Oct. 21, 1698; Gouverneur Affidavit, May 15, 1699, NYHS *Collections* [1868], v. I, 407, 413–415; Merwick, *Being*, 393; Smith and Kammen, *History*, 76; Van Rensselaer, *History*, 559; Stokes, *Iconography*, v. 4, 364.
9 N. N. to Friend in Amsterdam, Aug. 6, 1691, Myers Collection, 26, New York Public Library, in Voorhees, *Zeale*, 447; Burrows and Wallace, *Gotham*, 102; Foote, *Black*, 104.
10 Van Rensselaer, *History*, 554; Reich, *Leisler's*, 122.
11 Dying Speeches of Leisler & Milborne, May 16, 1691, DHNY, v. 2, 376–380.
12 Ibid.
13 Ibid; Leder, *Livingston*, 76; Leonard, *History*, 143; Leder and Carosso, *Robert Livingston*, 18–19, 43–45.
14 Dying Speeches of Leisler & Milborne, May 16, 1691, DHNY, v. 2, 380.
15 Kierner, *Traders*, 30; Zacks, *Pirate*, 87.
16 Dying speeches of Leisler & Milborne, May 16, 1691, DHNY, v. 2, 379–380.
17 Draft of a letter from Sloughter to Blathwayt, Aug. 6, 1691, DHNY, v. 2, 382; Voorhees, *Zeale*, 447; Balmer, *Traitors*, 362; Zacks, *Pirate*, 87; Burrows and Wallace, *Gotham*, 102. Leonard, *History*, 143–144; Archdeacon, *New York*, 120–122.
18 Ibid.
19 Ibid.
20 Ibid.
21 Reich, *Leisler's*, 122–125; Balmer, *Traitors*, 362; Burrows and Wallace, *Gotham*, 102.
22 Foote, *Black*, 104; Van Rensselaer, *History*, 555.
23 Gouverneur Affidavit, May 15, 1699, NYHS *Collections* [1868], v. I, 414; Stokes, *Iconography*, v. 4, 364.

Chapter 9: Peace Offerings and War Drums

1 Frontenac to Minister, Nov. 12, 1690; Narrative 1689, 1690, NYCD, v. 9, 460–461, 490, 514; Parmenter, *Edge*, 214–215.
2 Narrative 1689, 1690; Frontenac to Minister, Nov. 12, 1690, NYCD, v. 9, 460–461, 514; Parmenter, *Edge*, 214–215.
3 Green, *New*, 106–107.
4 Trelease, *Indian*, 297–305; Green, *New*, 106–107; Parmenter, *Edge*, 206, 215.
5 Narrative 1689, 1690, NYCD, v. 9, 481; Green, *New*, 120; Parmenter, *Edge*, 214–215.
6 Phips Attack on Quebec; Narrative 1689, 1690, NYCD, v. 9, 455–458, 487–490; Parmenter, *Edge*, 214–215; Eccles, *Frontenac*, 235, 241.
7 Peckham, *Colonial*, 39; Trelease, *Indian*, 304–305; Parmenter, *Edge*, 215.

8 Bruyas to Frontenac, April 5, 1691, JR, v. 64, 57–64; Proposals of Mohawks to Sloughter and answer, June 4, 1691; Livingston to Sloughter, Albany, June 22, 1691, NYCD, v. 3, 777, 781; Champigny to Minister, May 10, 1691, NYCD, v. 9, 499; Parmenter, *Edge*, 215–216; Green, *New*, 120.
9 Ibid.
10 Bruyas to Frontenac, April 5, 1691, JR, v. 64, 59–61.
11 Ibid.
12 Green, *New*, 123.
13 Parmenter, *Edge*, 215–216; Green, *New*, 121–123.
14 Champigny to Minister, May 10, 1691, NYCD, v. 9, 499; Bruyas to Frontenac, April 5, 1691, JR, v. 64, 59–62; Parmenter, *Edge*, 215; Green, *New*, 121–127.
15 Champigny to Minister, May 10, 1691, NYCD, v. 9, 499; Parmenter, *Edge*, 215–216; Richter, *Ordeal*, 173.
16 Ibid.
17 Champigny to Minister, May 10, 1691, NYCD, v. 9, 499.
18 Sloughter's Address, June 1 and 4, 1691; Intended Sloughter letter to Blathwayt, Aug. 6, 1691, NYCD, v. 3, 773–774, 781, 790; Parmenter, *Edge*, 217; Richter, *Ordeal*, 173, *Trade*, 125; Peckham, *Colonial*, 39; Trelease, *Indian*, 305.
19 Ibid.
20 Sloughter's address and responses, June 1–5, 1691, NYCD, v. 3, 773–780; Council Minutes, Albany, May 27–June 5, 1691, NYCCM, 65; Cal. Hist. MSS, Pt. II, 206, 210; Parmenter, *Edge*, 217.
21 Proposals of Mohawks to Sloughter and answer, June 4, 1691, NYCD, v. 3, 777–778; Bruyas to Frontenac, April 5, 1691, JR, v. 64, 57–64; Reynolds, *Lawrence*; Parmenter, *Edge*, 217; Gray, *Narratives*, 141.
22 Propositions of Mohawk Sachems to Sloughter, June 4, 1691, NYCD, v. 3, 777.
23 Sloughter's address, June 1, 1691, NYCD, v. 3, 773–774.
24 Sloughter's answer, June 4, 1691, NYCD, v. 3, 778.
25 Sloughter's address, June 1, 1691; Intended Sloughter letter to Blathwayt, Aug. 6, 1691, NYCD, v. 3, 774, 790; Schuyler, *Colonial*, v. 1, 383.
26 Ohede speech, June 4, 1691, NYCD, v. 9, 780; Colden, *History*, 120.
27 Sloughter's address and responses, June 1–5, 1691, NYCD, v. 3, 773–780.
28 Proposals made by Five Nations, June 5, 1691, NYCD, v. 3, 780.
29 Answer of Five Nations to Sloughter's address, June 2, 1691; Proposals of Mohawks to Sloughter, June 4, 1691, NYCD, v. 3, 774–779; Parkman, *Count*, 289; Colden, *History*, 120.
30 Livingston to Sloughter, Albany, June 22, 1691, NYCD, v. 3, 781; Schuyler, *Colonial*, v. 1, 383; Parmenter, *Edge*, 217; Richter, *Ordeal*, 166.
31 Sloughter and Five Nations addresses and responses, NYCD, v. 3, 771–780; Parmenter, *Edge*, 217; Hart, *For*, 50; Richter, *Trade*, 125.
32 Answer of Five Nations to Sloughter's address, June 2, 1691, NYCD, v. 9, 777.
33 List of Officers in New York and their Salaries, April 20, 1693, NYCD, v. 4, 26; Council Minutes, Oct. 11, 1692, NYCCM, 77; Answer of Five Nations to Sloughter's address, June 2, 1691, NYCD, v. 9, 777; Hart, *For*, 52, 55; Hagedorn, *Brokers*, 381–382; Sivertsen, *Turtles*, 9–36; Staffa, *Schenectady*, 27, 75.

34 Ibid.
35 Propositions of Mohawks to Sloughter, May 26, 1691, NYCD, v. 3, 771–772.
36 Ibid.
37 Hart, *For*, 55–56.
38 Sloughter's Reply to Proposals of Five Nations, June 5, 1691; Livingston to Sloughter, Albany, June 22, 1691, NYCD, v. 3, 780, 781; Schuyler, *Colonial*, v. 1, 403; Sivertsen, *Turtles*, 31; Holland Society, Records, 53.
39 Holland Society, Records, 53; Sivertsen, *Turtles*, 25–26, 31, 208; Reynolds, *Lawrence*; Schuyler, *Colonial*, v. 1, 403.
40 Schuyler's journal, NYCD, v. 3, 802, 805.
41 Livingston to Sloughter, Albany, July 2, 1691; Schuyler's journal, NYCD, v. 3, 783, 805; Schuyler, *Colonial*, v. 1, 383–384; Richter, *Ordeal*, 166–167, *Trade*, 126; Parmenter, *Edge*, 218.
42 Schuyler's journal, NYCD, v. 3, 801, 802, 804; Nelson Memorial about Northern Colonies in America, Sept. 24, 1696, NYCD, v. 4, 209; Narrative 1689, 1690, NYCD, v. 9, 520, 525; Parmenter, *After*, 48, *Edge*, 218.
43 Ibid.
44 Lozier, *In Each*, 187.
45 Narrative 1689, 1690, NYCD, v. 9, 521; Schuyler's journal, NYCD, v. 3, 801; Schuyler, *Colonial*, v. 1, 384.
46 Schuyler's journal, NYCD, v. 3, 801.
47 Schuyler's journal, NYCD, v. 3, 801; Narrative 1689, 1690, NYCD, v. 9, 521; Parmenter, *Edge*, 218; Schuyler, *Colonial*, v. 1, 384.
48 Ibid.
49 Narrative 1689, 1690, NYCD, v. 9, 520–521; Schuyler's journal, NYCD, v. 3, 804; Pell, *Schuyler, Peter*; Parkman, *Count*, 290; Eccles, *Frontenac*, 248; Le Sueur, *Frontenac*, 311–312.
50 Schuyler's journal, NYCD, v. 3, 803; Schuyler, *Colonial*, v. 1, 385; Pell, *Schuyler, Peter*; Laramie, *King*, 169.

Chapter 10: The Battles of La Prairie

1 Schuyler's journal, NYCD, v. 3, 803; Schuyler, *Colonial*, v. 1, 385.
2 Narrative 1689, 1690, NYCD, v. 9, 521; Parkman, *Count*, 290; Eccles, *Frontenac*, 248; Laramie, *King*, 169–170; Le Sueur, *Frontenac*, 312.
3 Ibid.
4 Schuyler's journal, NYCD, v. 3, 803; Laramie, *King*, 169–170.
5 Parkman, *Count*, 290.
6 Narrative 1689, 1690, NYCD, v. 9, 521.
7 Schuyler's journal, NYCD, v. 3, 803.
8 Schuyler's journal, NYCD, v. 3, 803–804; Narrative 1689, 1690, NYCD, v. 9, 521; Pell, *Schuyler, Peter*; Parkman, *Count*, 290; Eccles, *Frontenac*, 248; Le Sueur, *Frontenac*, 312; Peckham, *Colonial*, 40.
9 Schuyler's journal, NYCD, v. 3, 803–804; Narrative 1689, 1690, NYCD, v. 9, 521–522; Parmenter, *Edge*, 218; Parkman, *Count*, 290–291; Eccles, *Frontenac*, 248, *Clément*; Pell, *Schuyler, Peter*; Le Sueur, *Frontenac*, 312–313; Peckham, *Colonial*,

40; Colden, *History*, 123; Laramie, *King*, 169–171; Schuyler, *Colonial*, v. 1, 385–386.

10 Ibid.

11 Ibid.

12 Schuyler's journal, NYCD, v. 3, 804.

13 Parkman, *Count*, 291.

14 Schuyler's journal, NYCD, v. 3, 803–804; Narrative 1689, 1690, NYCD, v. 9, 521–522; Eccles, *Frontenac*, 248, *Clément*.

15 Ibid.

16 Ibid.

17 Narrative 1689, 1690, NYCD, v. 9, 521; Gélinas, *Role*, 21–22.

18 Narrative 1689, 1690, NYCD, v. 9, 521; Parkman, *Count*, 291–292; Eccles, *Frontenac*, 248, *Clément*; Le Sueur, *Frontenac*, 313.

19 Schuyler's journal, NYCD, v. 3, 804; Narrative 1689, 1690, NYCD, v. 9, 522; Laramie, *King*, 171.

20 Narrative 1689, 1690, NYCD, v. 9, 517, 521, 523; Burleigh, *Ourehouare*; Le Sueur, *Frontenac*, 315; Parmenter, *Edge*, 218.

21 Schuyler's journal, NYCD, v. 3, 804; Narrative 1689, 1690, NYCD, v. 9, 522; Eccles, *Frontenac*, 248, *Clément*; Parkman, *Count*, 291–292.

22 Ibid.

23 Schuyler's journal, NYCD, v. 3, 804.

24 Narrative 1689, 1690, NYCD, v. 9, 521; Schuyler's journal, NYCD, v. 3, 804; Gélinas, *Role*, 21–22; Schuyler, *Colonial*, v. 1, 386–387; Colden, *History*, 123; Peckham, *Colonial*, 40; Parkman, *Count*, 291–292; Eccles, *Frontenac*, 248, *Clément*; Pell, *Schuyler, Peter*; Le Sueur, *Frontenac*, 313–314; Laramie, *King*, 171–172.

25 Ibid.

26 Ibid.

27 Parmenter, *Edge*, 218.

28 Schuyler's journal, NYCD, v. 3, 804.

29 Parkman, *Count*, 292.

30 Narrative 1689, 1690, NYCD, v. 9, 522.

31 Schuyler's journal, NYCD, v. 3, 804; Narrative 1689, 1690, NYCD, v. 9, 521; Eccles, *Frontenac*, 248–249, *Clément*; Pell, *Schuyler, Peter*; Le Sueur, *Frontenac*, 313–314; Gélinas, *Role*, 21–22; Laramie, *King*, 171–173; Parkman, *Count*, 292–293; Peckham, *Colonial*, 40; Schuyler, *Colonial*, v. 1, 386–387.

32 Ibid.

33 Narrative 1689, 1690, NYCD, v. 9, 520.

34 Narrative 1689, 1690, NYCD, v. 9, 520; Schuyler's journal, NYCD, v. 3, 803–804.

35 Parkman, *Count*, 292–293; Richter, *Ordeal*, 37–38, *War*, 536–537.

36 Richter, *War*, 536–537.

37 Colden, *History*, 123.

38 Narrative 1689, 1690, NYCD, v. 9, 523.

39 Schuyler's journal, NYCD, v. 3, 804.

40 Schuyler's journal, NYCD, v. 3, 804; Parkman, *Count*, 293; Peckham, *Colonial*, 40; Schuyler, *Colonial*, v. 1, 387; Le Sueur, *Frontenac*, 314.

41 Narrative 1689, 1690, NYCD, v. 9, 522–523.
42 Schuyler's journal, NYCD, v. 3, 800–805; Schuyler, *Colonial*, v. 1, 384–388.
43 Parkman, *Count*, 293.
44 Schuyler's journal, NYCD, v. 3, 805; Schuyler, *Colonial*, v. 1, 387–388; Eccles, *Frontenac*, 249, *Clément*; Pell, *Schuyler, Peter*; Richter, *Ordeal*, 167; Colden, *History*, 123; Laramie, *King*, 172–174.
45 Peckham, *Colonial*, 40–41.
46 Schuyler's journal, NYCD, v. 3, 804–805.
47 Council Minutes, Aug. 24 and 27, 1691, NYCCM, 67–68.
48 Report of Ingoldsby and Council to BOT, July 29, 1691, NYCD, v. 3, 791; Stokes, *Iconography*, v. 4, 369–370; Van Rensselaer, *History*, 563.
49 Stokes, *Iconography*, v. 4, 369–370; Report of Ingoldsby and Council to BOT, July 29, 1691, NYCD, v. 3, 791; Leder, *Livingston*, 80.
50 Schuyler's journal, NYCD, v. 3, 801, 802, 805; Parmenter, *After*, 47–48.
51 Narrative 1689, 1690, NYCD, v. 9, 523; Schuyler's journal, NYCD, v. 3, 804–805; Parmenter, *Edge*, 218–219.
52 Sloughter's Address, June 1 and 4, 1691; Intended Sloughter letter to Blathwayt, Aug. 6, 1691; Propositions of Senecas and Mohawks and answer, Sept. 4, 1691, NYCD, v. 3, 773–774, 781, 790, 805–809; Parmenter, *Edge*, 219; Trelease, *Indian*, 306.
53 Measures for better defense of Canada, NYCD, v. 9, 510–512; Richter, *Ordeal*, 173; Parmenter, *Edge*, 219; Trelease, *Indian*, 306–307.
54 Measures for better defense of Canada, NYCD, v. 9, 510–512; Parmenter, *Edge*, 219.
55 Report on Affairs of Canada, NYCD, v. 9, 527–530; Schuyler, *Colonial*, v. 1, 389; Peckham, *Colonial*, 41.
56 Eccles, *Frontenac*, 250.
57 Report on Affairs of Canada; Memoir Christian Iroquois in Canada, Nov. 1, 1692, NYCD, v. 9, 527–530, 540; Schuyler, *Colonial*, v. 1, 389; Eccles, *Frontenac*, 249–250.
58 Schuyler, *Colonial*, v. 1, 389; Richter, *Trade*, 126–127.
59 Richter, *Trade*, 126.

Chapter 11: Borderland Killing Fields

1 Officers to Commander-in-Chief, Albany, Dec. 30, 1691, NYCD, v. 3, 814–816; Narrative Military Operations 1691, 1692, NYCD, v. 9, 534; Lozier, *In Each*, 195; Sivertsen, *Turtles*, 31–32; Parmenter, *Edge*, 221; Laramie, *King*, 178; Richter, *Ordeal*, 173; Green, *New*,137.
2 Ibid.
3 Sivertsen, *Turtles*, 31.
4 Officers to Commander-in-Chief, Albany, Dec. 30, 1691, NYCD, v. 3, 814–816; Lozier, *In Each*, 195; Green, *New*,137; Richter, *Ordeal*, 173; Laramie, *King*, 178; Sivertsen, *Turtles*, 31–32.
5 Richter, *War*, 547, *Ordeal*, 173; Parmenter, *Edge*, 221.
6 Parmenter, *Edge*, 221.
7 Parmenter, *Edge*, 221; Green, *New*, 104–139; Richter, *War*, 547.
8 Officers to Commander-in-Chief, Albany, Dec. 30, 1691, NYCD, v. 3, 816.
9 Ibid, 814–816.

10 Ibid, 816.
11 Ibid, 815.
12 Schaick and Wessels to Speaker of Assembly, NYCD, v. 3, 817–818; Brandão and Starna, *Treaties*, 214–215; Trelease, *Indian*, 307; Staffa, *Schenectady*, 76.
13 Propositions of Senecas and Mohawks and answer, Sept. 4, 1691, NYCD, v. 3, 805–809.
14 Propositions of Senecas and Mohawks and answer, Sept. 4, 1691, NYCD, v. 3, 805–809; Richter, *Trade*, 124–129, *Ordeal*, 173, 178; Parmenter, *Edge*, 219; Brandão and Starna, *Treaties*, 214–216; Trelease, *Indian*, 306–307.
15 Albany to Commander-in-Chief, New York, June 30, 1692, CSPC, v. 13, no. 2,256.
16 Reynolds, *Albany*, 110; Schuyler, *Colonial*, v. 1, 302.
17 Valentine, *Manual*, 634; Kammen, *Colonial*, 28–30; Earle, *Colonial*, 70; Van Rensselaer, *History*, 67; Archdeacon, *New York*, 46, 78–96; Foote, *Black*, 79–83; Geanacopoulos, *Pirate's Wife*, 35, 43.
18 Geanacopoulos, *Pirate Next*, 76; Zacks, *Pirate*, 82; Marquis, *Captain Kidd*, 86–87; Bradley, *Before*, 180.
19 Goodfriend, *Who*, 27, 33–36, *Before*, 40–48, 60–64; Archdeacon, *New York*, 32–96; Bonomi, *Factious*, 24–26; Matson, *Merchants*, 49–56.
20 Ibid.
21 Bullivant and Andrews, *Glance*, 61–63; Burrows and Wallace, *Gotham*, 21, 35–37, 63–64, 91–98; Earle, *Colonial*, 70–71; Merwick, *Being*, 404; Zimmerman, *Women*, 26–29.
22 Albany to Commander-in-Chief, New York, June 30, 1692, CSPC, v. 13, no. 2,256; Schuyler, *Colonial*, v. 1, 392.
23 Officers to Commander-in-Chief, Albany, Dec. 30, 1691; Propositions of Commander-in-Chief to Five Nations and responses, June 6, 1692, NYCD, v. 3, 815–816, 840–844.
24 Parmenter, *Edge*, 222.
25 Albany to Commander-in-Chief, New York, June 30, 1692, CSPC, v. 13, no. 2,256; Schuyler, *Colonial*, v. 1, 392.
26 Albany to Commander-in-Chief, New York, June 30, 1692, CSPC, v. 13, no. 2,256.
27 Ibid; Schuyler, *Colonial*, v. 1, 392.
28 Schuyler, *Colonial*, v. 1, 392.
29 Albany to Commander-in-Chief, New York, June 30, 1692, CSPC, v. 13, no. 2,256.
30 Ibid.
31 Ibid; Stahlhut, *Creating*, 19.
32 Ibid.
33 Schuyler, *Colonial*, v. 1, 392.

Chapter 12: The Reckoning

1 Parmenter, *Edge*, 223; Schuyler, *Colonial*, v. 1, 392.
2 Schuyler Propositions to Five Nations, Schenectady, Aug. 12, 1692, in Leder, *Livingston Indian*, 162–168; Schuyler, *Colonial*, v. 1, 392.
3 Reynolds, *Albany*, 110; Sivertsen, *Turtles*, 7; Staffa, *Schenectady*, 19, 26-27; Hagedorn, *Friend*, 241.
4 Staffa, *Schenectady*, 324.

5 Albany Council, March 29, 1690, DHNY, v. 2, 199–202.
6 Burke, *Leisler's*, 408, 415; Sivertsen, *Turtles*, 3; Staffa, *Schenectady*, 59-61, 75.
7 Midtrøød, *Flemish*, 88–100; Staffa, *Schenectady*, 69-61, 75; Burke, *Leisler's*, 408, 415; Sivertsen, *Turtles*, 3.
8 Ohede answer for Five Nations, June 6, 1692, NYCD, v. 3, 844; Hagedorn, *Friend*, 23, 73–76; Midtrøød, *Flemish*, 94–96; Richter, *Cultural*, 52–53.
9 Ohede answer for Five Nations, June 6, 1692, NYCD, v. 3, 844.
10 Schuyler propositions to Five Nations, Aug. 12, 1692, in Leder, *Livingston Indian*, 162–164; Parmenter, *Edge*, 216–218, 222.
11 Schuyler propositions to Five Nations, Aug. 12, 1692, in Leder, *Livingston Indian*, 162–163.
12 Ibid.; Green, *New*, 104–147.
13 Schuyler propositions to Five Nations, Aug. 12, 1692, in Leder, *Livingston Indian*, 162–164; Parmenter, *Edge*, 222–223; Green, *New*, 104–147.
14 Measures for better defense of Canada, NYCD, v. 9, 510–512; Parmenter, *Edge*, 219–220; Green, *New*, 104–155.
15 Schuyler propositions to Five Nations, Aug. 12, 1692, in Leder, *Livingston Indian*, 163.
16 Ibid, 164.
17 Ibid.
18 Ibid.
19 Answer of Five Nations to Schuyler, Aug. 14, 1692, in Leder, *Livingston Indian*, 164–165; Sivertsen, *Turtles*, 20–21; Silverman, *Thundersticks*, 23.
20 Answer of Five Nations to Schuyler, Aug. 14, 1692, in Leder, *Livingston Indian*, 164–165.
21 Ibid.
22 Schuyler's reply to Five Nations, Aug. 14, 1692, in Leder, *Livingston Indian*, 165–166.
23 Answer of Five Nations and Adogaounwa to Schuyler, Aug. 14, 1692, in Leder, *Livingston Indian*, 164–166.
24 Schuyler to Ingoldsby, Aug. 17, 1692, in Leder, *Livingston Indian*, 166–168; Parmenter, *Edge*, 223.
25 Schuyler to Ingoldsby, Aug. 17, 1692, in Leder, *Livingston Indian*, 167.
26 Ibid.
27 Narrative 1692, 1693, NYCD, v. 9, 555–556.
28 Ibid, 556; Parmenter, *Edge*, 223–224; Green, *New*, 137; Sivertsen, *Turtles*, 31.
29 Narrative 1692, 1693, NYCD, v. 9, 555–557; Green, *New*, 137–138; Parmenter, *Edge*, 223–224.
30 Narrative 1692, 1693, NYCD, v. 9, 556.
31 Ibid; Green, *New*, 138; Parmenter, *Edge*, 223–224.
32 Parmenter, *Edge*, 224.
33 Narrative 1692, 1693, NYCD, v. 9, 556.
34 Narrative 1692, 1693, NYCD, v. 9, 556–557; Eccles, *Frontenac*, 251; Green, *New*, 138–139; Parmenter, *Edge*, 223–224.
35 Narrative 1692, 1693, NYCD, v. 9, 556.
36 Narrative 1692, 1693, NYCD, v. 9, 556–557; Parmenter, *Edge*, 224; Green, *New*, 138–139.

37 Narrative 1692, 1693, NYCD, v. 9, 556–557; Eccles, *Frontenac*, 251.
38 Parmenter, *Edge*, 224.
39 Narrative 1692, 1693, NYCD, v. 9, 556.
40 Shannon, *Iroquois*, 30–36, 46–47; Parmenter, *After*, 39; Richter, *Trade*, 70–88, *War*, 528–559; Blackhawk, *Rediscovery*, 94.
41 Shannon, *Iroquois*, 32–38; Richter, *War*, 544, 548–549; Parmenter, *After*, 39–76.
42 Laramie, *King*, 188; Green, *New*, 138–140.
43 Fletcher to Blathwayt, New York, May 30, 1696, NYCD, v. 4, 158.
44 Eccles, *Frontenac*, 251.
45 Narrative 1692, 1693, NYCD, v. 9, 565; Eccles, *Frontenac*, 251–252; Parmenter, *Edge*, 216.
46 Narrative 1692, 1693, NYCD, v. 9, 556–557; Parmenter, *Edge*, 223–224.
47 Memoir Christian Iroquois in Canada, Nov. 1, 1692, NYCD, v. 9, 539.
48 Ibid, 540.
49 Narrative 1692, 1693, NYCD, v. 9, 550.
50 Parmenter, *Edge*, 223–224; Green, *New*, 138–141.
51 Narrative 1692, 1693, NYCD, v. 9, 557.
52 Ibid.

Chapter 13: Benjamin Fletcher

1 Fletcher to Blathwayt, New York, Sept. 10, 1692, NYCD, v. 3, 846, and CSPC, v. 13, no. 2,459.
2 Ranlet, *Safe*, 41; Boatfield, *Fletcher*, 315–316.
3 Commission of Fletcher, NYCD, v. 3, 827–833; Ritchie, *Kidd*, 47–48; Hanham, *Blathwayt*; Boatfield, *Fletcher*, 315–316.
4 Davis, *Administration*, 213–215; Kammen, *Colonial*, 138.
5 Commission of Fletcher, March 18, 1692, NYCD, v. 3, 830–831.
6 Fletcher to Blathwayt, New York, Sept. 10, 1692, CSPC, v. 13, no. 2,460.
7 House of Representatives to Fletcher, New York, Sept. 6, 1692, CSPC, v. 13, no. 2,443.
8 Leamon, *Governor*, 527.
9 Council Minutes, Sept. 1, 1692–Feb. 26, 1693, July 20, 1693, June 11, 1696, NYCCM, 75–8, 86, 115; Council Minutes, Sept. 1, 1692–March 20, 1693, JLCNY, 19–34; Stokes, *Iconography*, v. 4, 376–377; Leder, *Livingston*, 85; Kammen, *Colonial*, 138.
10 Instructions to Fletcher, March 1692, NYCD, v. 3, 818; Burgess, *Pirates'*, 89.
11 Fletcher to Nottingham and Blathwayt, New York, Sept. 10, 1692, NYCD, v. 3, 847, 848.
12 Fletcher to Blathwayt, New York, Sept. 10, 1692, NYCD, v. 3, 848; Archdeacon, *New York*, 125; Ranlet, *Safe*, 43.
13 Archdeacon, *New York*, 124–125.
14 Fletcher to Blathwayt, New York, Sept. 10, 1692, NYCD, v. 3, 848; Hall, Leder, and Kammen, *Glorious*, 115–116; Ritchie, *Duke's*, 237–239; Smith and Kammen, *History*, 123–124.
15 Rights and Privileges of New Yorkers, May 13, 1691, in Hall, Leder, and Kammen, *Glorious*, 121–123; Hall, Leder, and Kammen, *Glorious*, 115–116; Burgess, *Politics*, 36–38.

16 Mason, *Aspects*, 178.
17 Foote, *Black*, 105–106; Stanwood, *Empire*, 189; Archdeacon, *New York*, 123; Ritchie, *Duke's*, 237–239.
18 Miller, *Description*, 51.
19 Fletcher to Nottingham and Blathwayt, New York, Sept. 10, 1692, NYCD, v. 3, 847, 848; Howe, *Bayard*, 61–64; Ritchie, *Duke's*, 238–239; Burrows and Wallace, *Gotham*, 101–105. 14; Archdeacon, *New York*, 124–125; Ranlet, *Safe*, 43.
20 Ibid.
21 Kammen, *Colonial*, 128, 142.
22 Fletcher to Blathwayt, New York, Sept. 10, 1692, NYCD, v. 3, 848.
23 Council Minutes, Sept. 10, 1692, CSPC, v. 13, no. 2,444.
24 Council Minutes, Sept. 9–10, 1692, NYCCM, 76; Fletcher to Blathwayt, New York, Sept. 10, 1692, NYCD, v. 3, 848.
25 Bradley, *Before*, 180, 188–189.
26 Marquis, *Captain Kidd*, 78; Burgess, *Pirates'*, 193; Bialuschewski, *Pirates*, 54; Taylor, *American Colonies*, 258; Geanacopoulos, *Eighteenth*, 24–25.
27 Bradley, *Before*, 187–190; Woodard, *American*, 62–63.
28 Bradley, *Before*, 187–190.
29 Ibid, 189.
30 Ibid, 189–190.
31 Ibid, 190–191.
32 Bradley, *Before*, 189–191; Schuyler, *Colonial*, v. 1, 496.
33 Reynolds, *Albany*, 110; Schuyler, *Colonial*, v. 1, 394–395; Greene, *History*, v. 1, 408.
34 Schuyler, *Colonial*, v. 1, 394–395; Greene, *History*, v. 1, 408.
35 Council Minutes, Oct. 11, 1692, NYCCM, 77; List of Officers in New York and their Salaries, April 20, 1693, NYCD, v. 4, 26; Hart, *For*, 52, 55; Hagedorn, *Brokers*, 381–382; Chet, *Colonists'*, 39.
36 Waterman, *We Must*, 26.
37 Schuyler, *Colonial*, v. 1, 394.
38 Answer of Five Nations to Sloughter's address, June 2, 1691, NYCD, v. 9, 777; List of officers in New York and their salaries, April 20, 1693, NYCD, v. 4, 26; Council Minutes, Oct. 11, 1692, NYCCM, 77; Hart, *For*, 52, 55; Hagedorn, *Brokers*, 381–382; Sivertsen, *Turtles*, 9–36.
39 James and Jameson, *Journal*, 211.
40 Ibid, 204.
41 Hart, *For*, 54.
42 Ibid.
43 Richter, *Trade*, 118; Hart, *For*, 54; Hagedorn, *Brokers*, 381–382.
44 James and Jameson, *Journal*, 205.
45 Hinderaker, *Hendricks*, 50.
46 Queen to Phips, Oct. 11, 1692; Draft of Fletcher's commission as governor of Pennsylvania, Oct. 21, 1692, NYCD, v. 3, 855–860; Stokes, *Iconography*, v. 4, 377–378; Peckham, *Colonial*, 45; Trelease, *Indian*, 308.
47 Commission of Fletcher, March 18, 1692; Queen to Phips, Oct. 11, 1692; Draft of Fletcher's Commission as Governor of Pennsylvania, Oct. 21, 1692, NYCD, v. 3, 827–833, 855–860.

48 Fletcher to Blathwayt, New York, Sept. 10, 1692, CSPC, v. 13, no. 2,459; Commission of Fletcher, March 18, 1692, NYCD, v. 3, 827–833; Ranlet, *Safe*, 41; Leamon, *Governor*, 538.
49 Brooke to Fletcher, Boston, Aug. 2, 1693, NYCD, v. 4, 58.
50 Leamon, *Governor*, 528.
51 Gouverneur to parents, Boston, Oct. 12, 1692; Fletcher to Phips, New York, Jan. 7, 1693; Phips to Fletcher, Boston, Jan. 27, 1693, NYCD, v. 4, 3, 4, 6; CSPC, v. 13, no. 2,548.
52 Brodbent to Nicholson, New York, June 21, 1692, CSPC, v. 13, no. 2,283; Norton, *Devil's*, 315–317; Wood, *Invented*, 322.
53 Haefeli, *Dutch*, 278, 303, 306, 307; Ranlet, *Safe*, 38–43.
54 Cary's account of wife's examination, in Boyer and Nissenbaum, *Salem*, v. 1, 210.
55 Baker and Reid, *New*, 152–156; Ranlet, *Safe*, 41–43; Peckham, *Colonial*, 45.
56 Leamon, *Governor*, 527–531; Davis, *Administration*, 216–222.

Chapter 14: The 1693 Frontenac Expedition

1 Champigny, Narrative Military Operations 1692, 1693, Quebec, Aug. 17, 1693; Narrative 1692, 1693, NYCD, v. 9, 550, 557; Schuyler's report to Fletcher, March 8, 1693, NYCD, v. 4, 16, 17; Richter, *Ordeal*, 173–174; Eccles, *Frontenac*, 252; Blain, *Ailleboust.*
2 Champigny, Narrative Military Operations 1692, 1693, Quebec, Aug. 17, 1693, NYCD, v. 9, 550.
3 Ibid, 551; Lozier, *In Each*, 198.
4 Parmenter, *After*, 48.
5 Parmenter, *Edge*, 224.
6 Narrative 1692, 1693, NYCD, v. 9, 557; Eccles, *Frontenac*, 250–251; Richter, *Ordeal*, 173.
7 Narrative 1692, 1693, NYCD, v. 9, 557; Parmenter, *Edge*, 224.
8 Parkman, *Count*, 310; Parmenter, *Edge*, 224; Eccles, *Frontenac*, 252.
9 Champigny, Narrative Military Operations 1692, 1693, Quebec, Aug. 17, 1693; Narrative 1692, 1693, NYCD, v. 9, 550, 558.
10 Ingoldsby to Fletcher, Albany, Feb. 11, 1693; Schuyler's report to Fletcher, March 8, 1693, NYCD, v. 4, 6, 16; Champigny, Narrative Military Operations 1692, 1693, Quebec, Aug. 17, 1693; Narrative 1692, 1693, NYCD, v. 9, 551, 559; Parmenter, *Edge*, 225.
11 Champigny, Narrative Military Operations 1692, 1693, Quebec, Aug. 17, 1693; Narrative 1692, 1693, NYCD, v. 9, 550, 558; Trelease, *Indian*, 311; Parmenter, *Edge*, 224–225; Green, *New*, 141; Parkman, *Count*, 310–311; Eccles, *Frontenac*, 252.
12 Narrative 1692, 1693, NYCD, v. 9, 558.
13 NYCD, v. 9, 550, 558.
14 Parmenter, *Edge*, 224–225; Green, *New*, 141–142; Le Sueur, *Frontenac*, 321–322.
15 Schuyler's Report to Fletcher, March 8, 1693, NYCD, v. 4, 16; Champigny, Narrative Military Operations 1692, 1693, Quebec, Aug. 17, 1693; Narrative 1692, 1693, NYCD, v. 9, 550–551, 558; Parmenter, *Edge*, 224–225.
16 Narrative 1692, 1693, NYCD, v. 9, 558.
17 Champigny, Narrative Military Operations 1692, 1693, Quebec, Aug. 17, 1693; Narrative 1692, 1693, NYCD, v. 9, 550–551, 558–559; Eccles, *Frontenac*, 252; Richter, *Ordeal*, 174; Parmenter, *After*, 48–49; Green, *New*, 142; Sylvester, *History*, 37.

18 Champigny, Narrative Military Operations 1692, 1693, Quebec, Aug. 17, 1693; Narrative 1692, 1693, NYCD, v. 9, 550–551, 558–559; Eccles, *Frontenac*, 252; Parmenter, *After*, 48–49; Green, *New*, 142.
19 Ingoldsby to Fletcher, Albany, Feb. 11, 1693; Schuyler's report to Fletcher, March 8, 1693, NYCD, v. 4, 6–7, 16; Schuyler, *Colonial*, v. 1, 395–396.
20 Schuyler's report to Fletcher, March 8, 1693, NYCD, v. 4, 17, and CSPC, v. 14, no. 179v; Champigny, Narrative Military Operations 1692, 1693, Quebec, Aug. 17, 1693; 1692, 1693, NYCD, v. 9, 551–552, 558–560; Trelease, *Indian*, 311; Schuyler, *Colonial*, v. 1, 398–401; Eccles, *Frontenac*, 252–253; Richter, *Trade*, 126, *War*, 549; Parmenter, *Edge*, 225; Snow, Gehring, and Starna, *In Mohawk*, 225–230.
21 Ibid.
22 Ibid.
23 Schuyler's report to Fletcher, March 8, 1693, NYCD, v. 4, 17–18.
24 Ibid; Champigny, Narrative Military Operations 1692, 1693, Quebec, Aug. 17, 1693, NYCD, v. 9, 551.
25 Champigny, Narrative Military Operations 1692, 1693, Quebec, Aug. 17, 1693; Narrative 1692, 1693, NYCD, v. 9, 551, 560.
26 Parkman, *Count*, 312–313.
27 Schuyler's report to Fletcher, March 8, 1693, NYCD, v. 4, 18; Champigny, Narrative Military Operations 1692, 1693, Quebec, Aug. 17, 1693, NYCD, v. 9, 551.
28 Schuyler's report to Fletcher, March 8, 1693, NYCD, v. 4, 18.
29 Parmenter, *Edge*, 225.
30 Narrative 1692, 1693, NYCD, v. 9, 560; Parmenter, *Edge*, 225.
31 Schuyler's report to Fletcher, March 8, 1693, NYCD, v. 4, 18.
32 Narrative 1692, 1693, NYCD, v. 9, 560.
33 Schuyler's report to Fletcher, March 8, 1693, NYCD, v. 4, 18–19; Eccles, *Frontenac*, 253; Snow, Gehring, and Starna, *In Mohawk*, 229.
34 Schuyler's report to Fletcher, March 8, 1693, NYCD, v. 4, 18–19, and CSPC, v. 14, no. 179v; Snow, Gehring, and Starna, *In Mohawk*, 228–229.
35 Champigny, Narrative Military Operations 1692, 1693, Quebec, Aug. 17, 1693; Narrative 1692, 1693, NYCD, v. 9, 552, 558–560.
36 Schuyler's report to Fletcher, March 8, 1693, NYCD, v. 4, 18.
37 Ibid; Schuyler, *Colonial*, v. 1, 401; Trelease, *Indian*, 311; Snow, Gehring, and Starna, *In Mohawk*, 229; Eccles, *Frontenac*, 253.
38 Ibid.
39 Narrative 1692, 1693, NYCD, v. 9, 560; Parkman, *Count*, 314; Eccles, *Frontenac*, 253.
40 Schuyler's report to Fletcher, March 8, 1693, NYCD, v. 4, 18–19.
41 Colden, *History*, 142; Richter, *Ordeal*, 36; Schuyler, *Colonial*, v. 1, 402–403; Parkman, *Count*, 313.
42 Narrative 1692, 1693, NYCD, v. 9, 560; Eccles, *Frontenac*, 253; Parkman, *Count*, 314.
43 Narrative 1692, 1693, NYCD, v. 9, 560; Le Sueur, *Frontenac*, 322.
44 Eccles, *Frontenac*, 253–254.
45 Champigny, Narrative Military Operations 1692, 1693, Quebec, Aug. 17, 1693; Narrative 1692, 1693, NYCD, v. 9, 552, 560; Eccles, *Frontenac*, 254; Le Sueur, *Frontenac*, 322–323.

46 Champigny, Narrative Military Operations 1692, 1693, Quebec, Aug. 17, 1693; Narrative 1692, 1693, NYCD, v. 9, 552, 561; Eccles, *Frontenac*, 254; Parmenter, *Edge*, 226.
47 Eccles, *Frontenac*, 254.
48 Narrative 1692, 1693, NYCD, v. 9, 561; Parmenter, *Edge*, 225–226.
49 Parmenter, *Edge*, 225–226.
50 Van Cortlandt and Bayard 1693 journal, 9; Schuyler, *Colonial*, v. 1, 402; Parkman, *Count*, 315; Eccles, *Frontenac*, 254; Parmenter, *Edge*, 226.
51 Schuyler, *Colonial*, v. 1, 402.
52 Parkman, *Count*, 315; Eccles, *Frontenac*, 254; Parmenter, *Edge*, 226.
53 Journal of Fletcher's expedition, New York, March 7, 1693, NYCD, v. 4, 14–15; Council Minutes, Feb. 13, 1693, NYCCM, 81; Trelease, *Indian*, 312; Davis, *Administration*, 220; Snow, Gehring, and Starna, *In Mohawk*, 221–224.
54 Ibid.
55 Schuyler, *Colonial*, v. 1, 403.
56 Address of mayor of Albany to Fletcher and Five Nations answer, Albany, Feb. 24 and 25, 1693, NYCD, v. 4, 20, 22; Snow, Gehring, and Starna, *In Mohawk*, 221–225; Davis, *Administration*, 220; Trelease, *Indian*, 312; Parmenter, *Edge*, 226.
57 Five Nations answer, Albany, Feb. 25, 1693, NYCD, v. 4, 22; Richter, *War*, 549, *Ordeal*, 174; Hart, *For*, 22–23; Davis, *Administration*, 220.
58 Fletcher's speech to Sachems, Albany, Feb. 25, 1693, NYCD, v. 4, 20–22; Hagedorn, *Brokers*, 401; Hart, *For*, 23.
59 Fletcher's Speech to Sachems and Five Nations answer, Albany, Feb. 25, 1693, NYCD, v. 4, 20–24; Richter, *War*, 549; Davis, *Administration*, 220–221; Hart, *For*, 23; Eccles, *Frontenac*, 255.
60 Five Nations answer, Albany, Feb. 25, 1693, NYCD, v. 4, 23.
61 Fletcher's speech to Sachems and Five Nations answer, Albany, Feb. 25, 1693, NYCD, v. 4, 20–24; Trelease, *Indian*, 312–313; Hart, *For*, 23.
62 Schuyler's report to Fletcher, March 8, 1693, NYCD, v. 4, 19; Richter, *Trade*, 126–127; Parmenter, *Edge*, 226; Trelease, *Indian*, 313.
63 Richter, *Ordeal*, 177.
64 Fletcher speech to Five Nations, Albany, July 3, 1693, NYCD, v. 4, 40–42; Parmenter, *Edge*, 227; Schuyler, *Colonial*, v. 1, 406–407; Hagedorn, *Brokers*, 401.
65 Sivertsen, *Turtles*, 18, 36; Parmenter, *Edge*, 227.
66 Fletcher Speech to Five Nations, Albany, July 3, 1693, NYCD, v. 4, 40–42.
67 Richter, *Ordeal*, 177.
68 Fletcher and Five Nations, Albany, July 4, 1693, NYCD, v. 4, 43–44; Richter, *Ordeal*, 178–179; Trelease, *Indian*, 314.
69 Trelease, *Indian*, 314; Richter, *War*, 550, *Ordeal*, 179.
70 Richter, *Ordeal*, 180, *War*, 550; Parmenter, *Edge*, 226.
71 Parmenter, *Edge*, 226.

Chapter 15: Imperial Warfare, Iroquois Peace

1 New York Council Minutes, Dec. 11, 1693, CSPC, v. 14, no. 733; Report from Oneida by Mohawk Joseph, Dec. 2, 1693; Schuyler to Fletcher, Dec. 4, 1693; Message of Onondagas to governor, Onondaga, Nov. 22, 1693; Dellius to Fletcher,

Albany, Jan. 12, 1694; Fletcher to BOT, Jan. 22, 1694; Schuyler journal, NYCD, v. 4, 74–79, 81–83; Trelease, *Indian*, 314–315; Parmenter, *Edge*, 226–234; Richter, *Ordeal*, 175–181; Schuyler, *Colonial*, v. 1, 415.

2 Ibid.

3 Trelease, *Indian*, 315.

4 Richter, *Trade*, 125–127; Trelease, *Indian*, 315.

5 New York Council Minutes, Sept. 4 and 25, Oct. 6, Nov. 27, Dec. 11, 1693, CSPC, v. 14, nos. 538, 582, 606, 698, 733; Trelease, *Indian*, 315; Schuyler, *Colonial*, v. 1, 404–415.

6 Trelease, *Indian*, 315.

7 Schuyler to Fletcher, Albany, May 14,1696, NYCD, v. 4, 151–152.

8 Greene, *Old*, 7–291; Greene, *History*, v. 1, 4; Schuyler journal, NYCD, v. 4, 81, CSPC, v. 14, no. 991v.

9 Schuyler journal, NYCD, v. 4, 81–82, CSPC, v. 14, no. 991v.

10 Schuyler journal, NYCD, v. 4, 81–82, CSPC, v. 14, no. 991v; Shannon, *Iroquois*, 38–62; Parmenter, *Edge*, 181–266; Schuyler, *Colonial*, v. 1, 415–417.

11 Report from Oneida by Mohawk Joseph, Dec. 2, 1693; Schuyler to Fletcher, Dec. 4, 1693; Message of Onondagas to governor, Onondaga, November 22, 1693; Dellius to Fletcher, Albany, Jan. 12, 1694; Fletcher to BOT, Jan. 22, 1694; Schuyler journal, NYCD, v. 4, 74–79, 82; Schuyler, *Colonial*, v. 1, 415.

12 Narrative 1692, 1693, NYCD, v. 9, 566.

13 Schuyler journal, NYCD, v. 4, 82.

14 Schuyler journal, NYCD, v. 4, 82, CSPC, v. 14, no. 991v; Schuyler, *Colonial*, v. 1, 414–415.

15 John Pynchon Deposition, Springfield, Mass., June 2, 1693, in Leder, *Livingston Indian*, 170; Council Minutes, July 14, 1693, NYCCM, 86; Fletcher to Five Nations, July 3, 1693, NYCD, v. 4, 41; Parmenter, *Edge*, 228 (Footnote 127), 360; Richter, *Ordeal*, 177.

16 Hagedorn, *Brokers*, 383; Parmenter, *Edge*, 228.

17 Parmenter, *Edge*, 228 (Footnote 127), 360; Richter, *Ordeal*, 177; Hagedorn, *Brokers*, 383.

18 Schuyler journal, NYCD, v. 4, 82, CSPC, v. 14, no. 991v; Schuyler, *Colonial*, v. 1, 415.

19 Ibid.

20 Earle, *Colonial*, 122, 131, 143, 160–161.

21 Schuyler journal, NYCD, v. 4, 82–83, CSPC, v. 14, no. 991v.

22 Ingoldsby to Fletcher, Albany, Jan. 12 and 15, 1694, Schuyler journal, NYCD, v. 4, 80–83, CSPC, v. 14, no. 991v, vi; Schuyler, *Colonial*, v. 1, 415.

23 Propositions of Five Nations; Schuyler's answer to the Five Nations; Five Nations reply to Schuyler's answer; Schuyler's answer to the Five Nations' reply; Speaker of Five Nations to Schuyler; Three Belts of Wampum, Albany, Feb. 2–9, 1694, NYCD, v. 4, 85–92, CSPC, v. 14, no. 991viii.

24 Account of meeting of Schuyler and Five Nations, CSPC, v. 14, no. 991viii; Richter, *Ordeal*, 180; Shannon, *Iroquois*, 52.

25 Colden, *History*, 150.

26 Propositions of Five Nations, Albany, Feb. 2, 1694, NYCD, v. 4, 85–88, CSPC, v. 14, no. 991viii; Schuyler, *Colonial*, v. 1, 415–416.

27 Propositions of Five Nations, Albany, Feb. 2, 1694, NYCD, v. 4, 88.
28 Schuyler's answer to Five Nations, Albany, Feb. 3, 1694, NYCD, v. 4, 88–89.
29 Ibid.
30 Schuyler's answer to Five Nations; Five Nations' reply to Schuyler's answer; Schuyler's answer to the Five Nations' reply; Speaker of Five Nations to Schuyler; Three Belts of Wampum, Albany, Feb. 2–9, 1694, NYCD, v. 4, 88–92, CSPC, v. 14, no. 991viii.
31 Schuyler to Fletcher; Livingston to Fletcher; Ingoldsby to Fletcher, Albany, Feb. 14, 1694, CSPC, v. 14, no. 991xi, xii, xiii; Parmenter, *Edge*, 234; Richter, *Ordeal*, 180–181; Schuyler, *Colonial*, v. 1, 415–416.
32 Narrative 1694, NYCD, v. 9, 577–585; Parkman, *Count*, 398–399; Parmenter, *Edge*, 234; Schuyler, *Colonial*, v. 1, 419–420.
33 Richter, *Ordeal*, 180–181.
34 Narrative 1694, NYCD, v. 9, 577–585.
35 Narrative 1694, NYCD, v. 9, 577–585; Colden, *History*, 161–171; Shannon, *Iroquois*, 51–52; Parmenter, *Edge*, 235–236; Richter, *Ordeal*, 181–182; Parkman, *Count*, 398–399.
36 Narrative 1694, NYCD, v. 9, 581.
37 Narrative 1694, NYCD, v. 9, 577–585; Parmenter, *Edge*, 235–236; Schuyler, *Colonial*, v. 1, 418–420; Trelease, *Indian*, 316–317.
38 Message from governor of Canada to Five Nations and answer, Onondaga, Jan. 31–Feb. 4, 1695; NYCD, v. 4, 120–122; Narrative 1695, 1696, NYCD, v. 9, 640–649; Richter, *Ordeal*, 183–185; Eccles, *Frontenac*, 259–264; Parkman, *Count*, 406–407.
39 Trelease, *Indian*, 314–320.

Chapter 16: Wiping Away the Tears

1 Fletcher to BOT, Aug. 22, 1696, NYCD, v. 4, 173-174; Expedition to Albany, Aug. 1696, DHNY, v. 1, 340; Narrative 1695, 1696, NYCD, v. 9, 649–655; Stokes, *Iconography*, v. 4, 396–397; NYCCM, 117; Parmenter, *After*, 49, *Edge*, 246; Blackhawk, *Rediscovery*, 78.
2 Council Minutes, New York, July 9 and 31, 1696, DHNY, v. 1, 323–325; Trelease, *Indian*, 320; Kammen, *Colonial*, 138; Davis, *Administration*, 214–224.
3 Stokes, *Iconography*, v. 4, 379, 382, 383, 397; Goodfriend, *Who*, 29.
4 Stokes, *Iconography*, v. 4, 397.
5 Council Minutes, Aug. 2, 1696, NYCCM, 117.
6 Ibid; Stokes, *Iconography*, v. 4, 397.
7 Council Minutes, June 10, 1696, NYM, v. 1, 405–406; Stokes, *Iconography*, v. 4, 395; Zacks, *Pirate*, 13.
8 *Minutes of Supreme Court of Judicature*, April 4, 1693 to April 1, 1701, NYHS *Collections* (1912), v. 45, 55, 56, 62, 63, 65, 68, 73; Brooke to [Blathwayt] and accompanying letters, New York, November 24, 1694, CSPC, v. 14, nos. 1,546 and 1,546i–iv, and CO 5/1038, fols. 421–422, PRO; Hamlin and Baker, *Supreme Court*, NYHS *Collections* [1945–47], v. I, 150, 163–164; Leder, *Livingston*, 90, 93–95.
9 Commissioners of Records, Index of Conveyances Recorded in Office of Register of City and County of New York: Grantees, v. "L," 219; Graham to Blathwayt, New York, May 29, 1695, Blathwayt MSS, v. 10, HL; Marquis, *Captain Kidd*, 60–62, 82; Leder, *Livingston*, 93; Geanacopoulos, *Pirate's Wife*, 53.

10 Agreement between Bellomont, Livingston, and Kidd; Kidd and Livingston Performance Bonds, NYCD, v. 4, 762–764; Commission from Admiralty (Commission of Reprisals upon the French); Commission for Cruising against Pirates, *State Trials*, v. 14, 169–173; Commons *Journals*, v. 13, 12; Anonymous, Full Account, 5; Marquis, *Captain Kidd*, 77–78, 117.

11 Marquis, *Captain Kidd*, 95; Wilson, *Piracy*, 29; Lincoln, *British*, 121.

12 Kidd's Protest, April 11, 1700, Portland manuscripts, v. 8, 79; *State Trials*, v. 14, 208–209.

13 Baer, *Pirates*, 120.

14 Council Minutes, Aug. 4, 1696, NYCCM, 117; Brooke and Nicoll to BOT, Whitehall, Aug. 26, 1696, NYCD, v. 4, 181–182; Stokes, *Iconography*, v. 4, 395, 397.

15 Fletcher to BOT, Aug. 22, 1696; Expedition to Albany, Aug. 1696, DHNY, v. 1, 339–340; NYCD, v. 4, 174.

16 Fletcher to BOT, Aug. 22, 1696; Expedition to Albany, Aug. 1696, DHNY, v. 1, 339–340; Schuyler, *Colonial*, v. 1, 452; Colden, *History*, 180–182.

17 Richter, *Ordeal*, 186.

18 Meeting of Sachems of Five Nations, Albany, Oct. 1, 1696, DHNY, v. 1, 349; Richter, *Ordeal*, 186.

19 Commission and Instructions of Board of Commissioners of Indian Affairs, Aug. 10, 1696, NYCD, v. 4, 177–178; Trelease, *Indian*, 320; Schuyler, *Colonial*, v. 1, 452.

20 Narrative 1695, 1696, NYCD, v. 9, 653–656; Schuyler, *Colonial*, v. 1, 449.

21 Fletcher to BOT, Aug. 22, 1696, NYCD, v. 4, 173–174, 180–181; Narrative 1695, 1696, NYCD, v. 9, 652–656; Green, *New*, 153; Parmenter, *Edge*, 246–247; Blackhawk, *Rediscovery*, 102.

22 Ibid.

23 Narrative 1695, 1696, NYCD, v. 9, 654; Colden, *History*, 182; Eccles, *Frontenac*, 266; Le Sueur, *Frontenac*, 351–352.

24 Narrative 1695, 1696, NYCD, v. 9, 657.

25 Fletcher to BOT, Aug. 22, 1696, NYCD, v. 4, 174; DHNY, v. 1, 339, 340, 345, 355; Council Minutes, Aug. 18, 1696, NYCCM, 117; Stokes, *Iconography*, v. 4, 397; Parmenter, *Edge*, 247, *After*, 49–50; Trelease, *Indian*, 320.

26 Commission and Instructions of Board of Commissioners of Indian Affairs, Aug. 10, 1696, NYCD, v. 4, 177–178, and DHNY, v. 1, 343–345; Stokes, *Iconography*, v. 4, 396–397; Trelease, *Indian*, 309; Schuyler, *Colonial*, v. 1, 452–453; Richter, *Trade*, 127.

27 Report on Livingston's Commission, New York, Sept. 15, 1696, NYCD, v. 4, 203–204.

28 Ibid.; Leder and Carosso, *Robert Livingston*, 18–45; Kierner, *Traders*, 33–36, 46–47; Trelease, *Indian*, 209–210, 309–310.

29 Trelease, *Indian*, 211.

30 Fletcher to Brooke and Nicoll, Albany, Dec. 20, 1696, NYCD, v. 4, 251.

31 Brooke and Nicoll to BOT, Whitehall, Aug. 26, 1696; Peter Delanoy to [BOT], New York, June 13, 1695, NYCD, v. 4, 181–182, 221–224; CSPC, v. 14, no. 1,892; Berlin and Harris, *Slavery*, 63; Davis, *Administration*, 245–247; Leamon, *Governor*, 536–537.

32 NYCD, v. 4, 157–172.

33 Goodfriend, *Before*, 55.
34 NYCD, v. 4, 157–172; Ritchie, *Kidd*, 63.
35 Petition of widow of Leisler; Petition to King to Reverse Attainders; Proceedings of Privy Council on Petition of Leisler and Gouverneur, Feb. 28, 1694; Petition of Leisler and Governeur to House of Lords, NYHS *Collections* [1868], v. I, 335–340; Statement of Leisler and Gouverneur, Sept. 25, 1696, CSPC, v. 15, nos. 262 and 263.
36 Reversing Leisler's attainder, April 22 and 30, 1695, Commons *Journals*, v. 11, 312, 328, 329; Order of King, Referring the Petition of Leisler and Governeur, Whitehall, Feb. 28, 1695, CSPC, v. 14, no. 1,689; Leamon, *Governor*, 531–532.
37 Runcie, *Problem*, 194.
38 Shrewsbury to BOT, March 16, 1697, NYCD, v. 4, 261; Ritchie, *Kidd*, 50.
39 Shrewsbury to Blathwayt, Whitehall, July 13, 1697, *Report on the Manuscripts of the Duke of Buccleuch and Queensberry*, v. II, pt. 2, 492; Leamon, *Governor*, 538.
40 Fletcher's answer to charges, New York, Aug. 22, 1696; Bellomont to BOT, New York, May 8, 1698, and May 18, 1698, addenda; Report of BOT on New York, October 19, 1698, NYCD, v. 4, 179, 302–310, 385–389; Leamon, *Governor*, 536–538; Ritchie, *Kidd*, 50.
41 Fletcher to Blathwayt, New York, Sept. 18, 1696, NYCD, v. 4, 204.
42 Fletcher to Blathwayt, New York, Sept. 18, 1696; Journal of the Fletcher Expedition; Meeting of Sachems of Five Nations and responses, Albany, Sept. 29, Oct. 1–3, 1696, DHNY, v. 1, 347–355; NYCD, v. 4, 234–241; Trelease, *Indian*, 321; Parmenter, *Edge*, 247; Schuyler, *Colonial*, v. 1, 454.
43 Ibid.
44 Meeting of Sachems of Five Nations, Albany, Oct. 1, 1696, DHNY, v. 1, 350.
45 Meeting of Sachems of Five Nations and responses, Albany, Oct. 1–3, 1696, DHNY, v. 1, 349–355; NYCD, v. 4, 235–241; Fletcher to Shrewsbury and to BOT, Nov. 9, 1696; BOT to Fletcher, Whitehall, Feb. 1, 1697, NYCD, v. 4, 232–235, 256; Trelease, *Indian*, 321; Schuyler, *Colonial*, v. 1, 454.
46 Ibid.
47 Hart, *For*, 23–24; Richter, *Ordeal*, 188; Green, *New*, 145–155; Parmenter, *After*, 49–50.
48 Colden, *History*, 109–110; Waterman, *We Must*, 25; Richter, *Ordeal*, 172.
49 Hagedorn, *Friend*, 83.
50 Trelease, *Indian*, 310; Richter, *Trade*, 127; Hinderaker, *Hendricks*, 43, 44, 49.
51 Hart, *For*, 29–30.
52 Hinderaker, *Hendricks*, 44.
53 Hart, *For*, 30.
54 Richter, *Trade*, 127–128, *Ordeal*, 186–187.
55 Jennings, *Ambiguous*, 205; Hinderaker, *Hendricks*, 47.
56 Hart, *For*, 28.
57 Fletcher to Shrewsbury, BOT, and Blathwayt, Nov. 9, 1696; Meeting of Sachems of Five Nations and responses, Albany, Oct. 1–3, 1696, NYCD, v. 4, 232–241, 243; Hinderaker, *Hendricks*, 40, 41, 47; Richter, *Ordeal*, 180, *Trade*, 127–128; Brandão and Starna, *Treaties*, 209–217; Green, *New*, 145–155; Hart, *For*, 23–25.
58 Ibid.
59 Hart, *For*, 25.

60 Fletcher to Shrewsbury, BOT, and Blathwayt, Nov. 9, 1696; Fletcher to Brooke and Nicoll, Albany, Dec. 20, 1696, NYCD, v. 4, 232–235, 243, 246–247; NYCCM, 119; Buffinton, *Policy*, 348; Trelease, *Indian*, 322; Schuyler, *Colonial*, v. 1, 455; Hart, *For*, 23.
61 Fletcher to BOT, [Late September 1696], NYCD, v. 4, 275.
62 Fletcher to Brooke and Nicoll, Albany, Dec. 20, 1696, NYCD, v. 4, 247; Schuyler, *Colonial*, v. 1, 455–456.
63 Conference between Fletcher and River Indians, Dec. 20, 1696, NYCD, v. 4, 248; Davis, *Administration*, 223; Trelease, *Indian*, 322.
64 Trelease, *Indian*, 322.
65 Fletcher to Shrewsbury, BOT, and Blathwayt, Nov. 9, 1696; Fletcher to Brooke and Nicoll, Albany, Dec. 20, 1696, NYCD, v. 4, 232–235, 243, 246–247; Richter, *Trade*, 127–128; Trelease, *Indian*, 322; Staffa, *Schenectady*, 76.
66 Buffinton, *Policy*, 348–349; Richter, *Trade*, 128.
67 Schuyler, *Colonial*, v. 1, 456; Davis, *Administration*, 224–225.
68 Fletcher to BOT, [Late Sept. 1696], NYCD, v. 5, 275; Trelease, *Indian*, 322; Davis, *Administration*, 224–225.
69 Richter, *Ordeal*, 189; Buffinton, *Policy*, 348–350; Davis, *Administration*, 225; Schuyler, *Colonial*, v. 1, 456; Shannon, *Iroquois*, 54–55; Parmenter, *Edge*, 248.

Chapter 17: The Treaty of Ryswick

1 Stokes, *Iconography*, v. 4, 405; Fletcher's neglect to write governor of Canada about peace, NYCD, v. 4, 338; Laramie, *King*, 279–280.
2 Clark, *Character*, 168–182; Peckham, *Colonial*, 52–55; Trelease, *Indian*, 323; Laramie, *King*, 283–288.
3 Richter, *Ordeal*, 187, 191, 193; Trelease, *Indian*, 323; Crouse, *French*, 145; Peckham, *Colonial*, 54–55.
4 Parkman, *Count*, 452; Brandão and Starna, *Treaties*, 214–217; Richter, *Cultural*, 61–63, *Ordeal*, 187–193; Parmenter, *Edge*, 253; Laramie, *King*, 283–285; Trelease, *Indian*, 323; Lozier, *In Each*, 208–209.
5 Ibid.
6 Ibid.
7 Trelease, *Indian*, 323.
8 Shannon, *Iroquois*, 54.
9 Richter, *Cultural*, 61–63; Brandão and Starna, *Treaties*, 214–217.
10 Richter, *Cultural*, 61.
11 Lozier, *In Each*, 208–209; Brandão and Starna, *Treaties*, 214–217; Richter, *Cultural*, 61–63.
12 Richter, *Ordeal*, 188.
13 Peckham, *Colonial*, 53.
14 Number of inhabitants in Albany 1689, NYCD, v. 4, 420; Richter, *Ordeal*, 188; Peckham, *Colonial*, 53; Trelease, *Indian*, 323.
15 Trelease, *Indian*, 323; Peckham, *Colonial*, 53; Snyderman, *Behind*, 41.
16 Richter, *Ordeal*, 188.
17 Trelease, *Indian*, 323; Parmenter, *Edge*, 250–251.
18 Trelease, *Indian*, 323–324.

19 Christians departed from Albany since beginning of War, NYCD, v. 4, 421; Depositions of Swyndale and another; Abstract from Lloyd, Boston, Jan. 8, 1691; Extract from Paris *Gazette* of Feb. 5, 1691; Extracts from Boston, Feb. 1691, CSPC, v. 13, nos. 1,245, 1,282, 1,299, and 1,313; Peckham, *Colonial*, 53; Report on Affairs of Canada; Memoir Christian Iroquois in Canada, Nov. 1, 1692, NYCD, v. 9, 528, 540; Eccles, *Frontenac*, 250, 268; Trelease, *Indian*, 323–324.
20 Christians departed from Albany since beginning of war, NYCD, v. 4, 421; Peckham, *Colonial*, 53; Trelease, *Indian*, 323.
21 Leder, *Livingston*, 134–135, 137; Peckham, *Colonial*, 54.
22 Fletcher's neglect to write governor of Canada about peace, NYCD, v. 4, 338; Narrative 1697, 1698, NYCD, v. 9, 680; Eccles, *Frontenac*, 268–269; Parmenter, *Edge*, 250.
23 Stokes, *Iconography*, v. 4, 401, 406. Lord Bellomont's official governor's commission, signed at Westminster, went into effect on April 2, 1698, the day of his arrival in New York when Governor Benjamin Fletcher's commission became "void."
24 Stokes, *Iconography*, v. 4, 406; Sewall, *Diary*, v. 1, 4, 476; De Peyster, *Bellomont*, 31; Ritchie, *Kidd*, 169; Burgess, *Pirates'*, 189–190.
25 Commission for cruising against pirates, *State Trials*, v. 14, 169–173.
26 Bellomont to Lords of Treasury, Boston, Sept. 8, 1699, CSPC, v. 17, no. 769xiv; Rowlands, *Coote*; Handley, *Coote*; Finnegan, *Pirates*, 134–136; De Peyster, *Life*, 5–6; Stackpole, *History*, 200; Ritchie, *Kidd*, 47.
27 De Peyster, *Life*, 5; Hinrichs, *Fateful*, 28; Geanacopoulos, *Pirate's Wife*, 73.
28 Journal of BOT, Shrewsbury announcing appointment of Bellomont as governor of Massachusetts, June 14, 1695; Bellomont's Draft Commission for Governorship of Massachusetts, Whitehall, June 27, 1695, CSPC, v. 14, nos. 1,893 and 1,917; Rainbolt, *Creation*, 103–106; Handley, *Coote*; Finnegan, *Pirates*, 138–139.
29 NYM, Dec. 28, 1697, v. 2, 25; De Peyster, *Life*, 31.
30 Bellomont to BOT, Jan. 8, 1697; Bellomont to BOT, New York, May 8 and 18, 1698; NYCD, v. 4, 296, 302–306; Runcie, *Problem*, 194; Rainbolt, *Creation*, 117.
31 Burgess, *Pirates'*, 193; Marquis, *Captain Kidd*, 78.
32 Matson, *Merchants*, 50; Kammen, *Colonial*, 151–152; Burgess, *Pirates'*, 193–194.
33 Bellomont to BOT, New York, May 8 and 18, 1698, and June 22, 1698, NYCD, v. 4, 306–310, 320–326; Burgess, *Pirates'*, 189–190.
34 Burgess, *Pirates'*, 193–194.
35 Lincoln, *State*, 75; Burgess, *Pirates'*, 189–190.
36 Bellomont, *Proclamation of His Excellency Richard Earl of Bellomont, New York, April 2, 1698*, and in Rainbolt, *Creation*, 119.
37 Bellomont to BOT, Oct. 17, 1700, NYCD, v. 4, 720; Bellomont to BOT, Boston, Sept. 7, 1699, cited in Palfrey, *History*, v. 4, 171; Zacks, *Pirate*, 107, 254, 318; De Peyster, *Life*, 32.
38 New York, *Proclamation of His Excellency Richard Earl of Bellomont, New York, April 2, 1698*, and in Rainbolt, *Creation*, 119.
39 Vernon, instructions and additional instructions to Bellomont, Whitehall, Aug. 31 and Sept. 9, 1697; Bellomont to BOT, New York, May 8 and 18, 1698; NYCD, v. 4, 284–292, 302–306; Burgess, *Pirates'*, 189–190.

40 Council Minutes, New York, May 8, 1698, CSPC, v. 16, no. 433; Bellomont to BOT, New York, May 8, 1698, NYCD, v. 4, 303; Burgess, *Pirates'*, 189–190; Nanfan, Portland manuscripts, v. 8, 337.
41 Schuyler, *Colonial*, v. 1, 461.
42 Address to Fletcher from inhabitants of New York, May 18, 1698, CSPC, v. 16, no. 472v, and CO, 5/1040, fol. 162, PRO; Bellomont to BOT, New York, May 18, 1698, NYCD, v. 4, 310; Burgess, *Pirates'*, 192; Runcie, *Problem*, 194.
43 Bellomont to Frontenac; Bellomont to Callière; Bellomont's instructions to Schuyler and Dellius, New York, April 22, 1698, NYCD, v. 4, 338–341, NYCD, v. 9, 690; Schuyler, *Colonial*, v. 1, 463.
44 Schuyler and Dellius report, New York, July 2, 1698, NYCD, v. 4, 347–351; Winthrop, *Journal*, NYCD, v. 4, 194; Laramie, *King*, 153, 154; Schuyler, *Colonial*, v. 1, 463.
45 Schuyler and Dellius report, New York, July 2, 1698, NYCD, v. 4, 347.
46 Lozier, *In Each*, 278.
47 Schuyler and Dellius report, New York, July 2, 1698, NYCD, v. 4, 347, 351; Richter, *Cultural*, 63; Parmenter, *Edge*, 251–252.
48 Schuyler and Dellius report, New York, July 2, 1698, NYCD, v. 4, 347; Schuyler, *Colonial*, v. 1, 463; Lozier, *In Each*, 279–280.
49 Schuyler and Dellius report, New York, July 2, 1698, NYCD, v. 4, 347.
50 Ibid; Laramie, *King*, 153; Schuyler and Dellius report, New York, July 2, 1698, NYCD, v. 4, 348.
51 Bellomont to Callière, New York, April 22, 1698; Callière to Bellomont, Montreal, June 17, 1698; Schuyler and Dellius report, New York, July 2, 1698, NYCD, v. 4, 339–340, 344–345, 348; Trelease, *Indian*, 334–335; Parmenter, *Edge*, 251–252; Schuyler, *Colonial*, v. 1, 463; Parkman, *Count*, 422.
52 Schuyler and Dellius report, New York, July 2, 1698, NYCD, v. 4, 348.
53 Ibid.
54 Schuyler and Dellius report, New York, July 2, 1698, NYCD, v. 4, 348; Trelease, *Indian*, 334–335; Parmenter, *Edge*, 251.
55 Schuyler and Dellius report, New York, July 2, 1698, NYCD, v. 4, 348.
56 Narrative 1697, 1698, NYCD, v. 9, 682; Callière to Bellomont, Montreal, June 17, 1698; Schuyler and Dellius report, New York, July 2, 1698, NYCD, v. 4, 344–345, 348; Trelease, *Indian*, 334–335; Laramie, *King*, 281; Eccles, *Frontenac*, 268–269; Schuyler, *Colonial*, v. 1, 463–464; Parkman, *Count*, 422–424.
57 Bellomont to Frontenac, New York, April 22, 1698, NYCD, v. 4, 338–339, NYCD, v. 9, 690.
58 Narrative 1697, 1698, NYCD, v. 9, 682; Schuyler and Dellius report, New York, July 2, 1698, NYCD, v. 4, 348–349; Schuyler, *Colonial*, v. 1, 463–464.
59 Narrative 1697, 1698, NYCD, v. 9, 682; Schuyler and Dellius report, New York, July 2, 1698, NYCD, v. 4, 348–351; Schuyler, *Colonial*, v. 1, 464–465; Parkman, *Count*, 422–424; Trelease, *Indian*, 335; Eccles, *Frontenac*, 268–269; Laramie, *King*, 281–282.
60 Ibid.
61 Schuyler and Dellius report, New York, July 2, 1698, NYCD, v. 4, 349–350.
62 Ibid.
63 Ibid, 350; Trelease, *Indian*, 335.

64 Schuyler and Dellius report, New York, July 2, 1698, NYCD, v. 4, 350.
65 Narrative 1697, 1698, NYCD, v. 9, 682; Schuyler and Dellius report, New York, July 2, 1698, NYCD, v. 4, 348–351; Schuyler, *Colonial*, v. 1, 464; Eccles, *Frontenac*, 268–269.
66 Schuyler and Dellius report, New York, July 2, 1698, NYCD, v. 4, 351; Narrative 1697, 1698, NYCD, v. 9, 682; Parmenter, *Edge*, 251–252.
67 Lozier, *In Each*, 278; Richter, *Cultural*, 63, *Trade*, 128.
68 Schuyler and Dellius report, New York, July 2, 1698, NYCD, v. 4, 351.

Chapter 18: The Wrath of Lord Bellomont

1 Instructions to Bellomont, Whitehall, Aug. 31, 1697, NYCD, v. 4, 284–292; Leder, *Livingston*, 136; Runcie, *Problem*, 194–195; Burgess, *Pirates'*, 192.
2 Address to Fletcher from inhabitants of New York, May 18, 1698, CSPC, v. 16, no. 472v, and CO, 5/1040, fol. 162, PRO; Bellomont to BOT, New York, May 18, June 22, 1698, NYCD, v. 4, 320–326, 384.
3 Stokes, *Iconography*, v. 4, 408.
4 Complaints against Fletcher, Nov. 28, 1698, NYCD, v. 4, 433–434; Rainbolt, *Great*, 337–338; Zimmerman, *Women*, 174.
5 Bellomont to BOT, New York, June 22, 1698; Report of BOT on affairs of New York, Whitehall, Oct. 19, 1698; NYCD, v. 4, 323–324, 389, 396.
6 Bellomont to Popple, New York, June 27, 1698, NYCD, v. 4, 327; Stokes, *Iconography*, v. 4, 405.
7 Hanna, *Pirate Nests*, 286–291.
8 Bellomont to BOT, New York, May 15, 1699, and Oct. 17, 1700, NYCD, v. 4, 520, 720; Goodfriend, *Who*, 27–35, *Before*, 81–110; Kammen, *Colonial*, 128–151; Burrows and Wallace, *Gotham*, 107–112.
9 Rainbolt, *Great*, 333–348; Bonomi, *Factious*, 77–78.
10 Bellomont to BOT, Oct. 21, 1698, and May 15, 1699; NYCD, v. 4, 400–401, 523; Stokes, *Iconography*, v. 4, 405; Ritchie, *Kidd*, 171; Reich, *Leisler's*, 149.
11 Burrows and Wallace, *Gotham*, 112; Zacks, *Pirate*, 229.
12 Accusations against Bellomont, March 11, 1700; Petition of merchants of New York, March 1700; NYCD, v. 4, 534, 620–624; Runcie, *Problem*, 194–196; Leamon, *Governor*, 539.
13 *Propositions Made by the Five Nations of Indians*, July 20, 1698, published by William Bradford (hereafter Five Nations propositions), 1–22; Bellomont to BOT, Sept. 14, 1698, NYCD, v. 4, 362–363, CSPC, v. 16, nos. 822, 822i; Trelease, *Indian*, 336; Richter, *Ordeal*, 191–192; Parmenter, *Edge*, 253.
14 Five Nations propositions, 4–5; Bellomont to BOT, Sept. 14, 1698, NYCD, v. 4, 362–363, CSPC, v. 16, nos. 822, 822i; Richter, *Ordeal*, 191; Parmenter, *Edge*, 253.
15 Trelease, *Indian*, 336.
16 Five Nations propositions, 4.
17 Five Nations propositions, 4–12; Parmenter, *Edge*, 253; Schuyler, *Colonial*, v. 1, 467.
18 Five Nations propositions, 6–7; Trelease, *Indian*, 336; Richter, *Ordeal*, 191–192.
19 Five Nations propositions, 7.
20 Five Nations propositions, 1–22; Trelease, *Indian*, 336–337; Richter, *Ordeal*, 192.
21 Bellomont to BOT, Sept. 14, 1698, NYCD, v. 4, 362–363, CSPC, v. 16, no. 822.
22 Five Nations propositions, 1–22; Stokes, *Iconography*, v. 4, 410.

23 Fletcher to BOT, [Late Sept. 1696], NYCD, v. 5, 275; Richter, *Ordeal*, 191–192; Schuyler, *Colonial*, v. 1, 466.
24 Bellomont to BOT, Sept. 14, 1698, NYCD, v. 4, 362.
25 Richter, *Ordeal*, 192.
26 Depositions of Hendrick and Joseph, May 31, 1698, CSPC, v. 16, no. 822ii; Fraudulent purchase, May 31, 1698; BOT on affairs of New York, Oct. 19, 1698; Bellomont to BOT, Oct. 21, 1698, NYCD, v. 4, 345–347, 391–395, 398; Defense of Dellius, Oct. 31, 1699, ERNY, v. 2, 1401–1408; Leder, *Livingston*, 127; Hinderaker, *Hendricks*, 51; Parmenter, *Edge*, 252; Richter, *Ordeal*, 192.
27 Fraudulent purchase, May 31, 1698; Memorial of Bleeker and Schermerhorn, Sept. 6, 1698; Bellomont to BOT, Sept. 14 and 16, 1698, NYCD, v. 4, 330, 346, 362–367; Depositions of Hendrick and Joseph, May 31, 1698, CSPC, v. 16, no. 822ii; Parmenter, *Edge*, 252; Hinderaker, *Hendricks*, 51.
28 Five Nations propositions, 1–22; Bellomont to BOT, Sept. 14 and 16, 1698; BOT on affairs of New York, Oct. 19, 1698, NYCD, v. 4, 362–367, 393.
29 Minutes Bellomont and Mohawks, Albany, July 25, 1698, CSPC, v. 16, no. 822ii; Bellomont to BOT, Sept. 14, 1698, NYCD, v. 4, 362–365; Hinderaker, *Hendricks*, 50–55; Richter, *Trade*, 128–129, *Ordeal*, 192; Parmenter, *Edge*, 252.
30 Hinderaker, *Hendricks*, 56.
31 Defense of Dellius, Oct. 31, 1699, ERNY, v. 2, 1401–1408; Hinderaker, *Hendricks*, 55–56; Trelease, *Indian*, 338–340.
32 Trelease, *Indian*, 338; Hinderaker, *Hendricks*, 51, 55; Richter, *Trade*, 128–129.
33 Bellomont to Somers, Boston, March 7, 1700, Portland manuscripts, v. 8, 73.
34 Leder, *Livingston*, 134.
35 Defense of Dellius, Oct. 31, 1699, ERNY, v. 2, 1401–1408; Richter, *Trade*, 128–129, *Ordeal*, 192; Trelease, *Indian*, 338–339; Hinderaker, *Hendricks*, 55–58.
36 Trelease, *Indian*, 339.
37 Romer to Bellomont, Albany, June 13, 1698, NYCD, v. 4, 329.
38 Minutes Bellomont and Mohawks, Albany, July 25, 1698, CSPC, v. 16, no. 822ii.
39 Bellomont to BOT, Sept. 14, 1698, NYCD, v. 4, 364.
40 Romer to Bellomont, Albany, June 13, 1698; fraudulent purchase, May 31, 1698; NYCD, v. 4, 329, 346; Richter, *Trade*, 129, *Ordeal*, 193; Trelease, *Indian*, 212; Hinderaker, *Hendricks*, 56–57.
41 Richter, *Trade*, 129; *Ordeal*, 193; Hart, *For*, 58.

Chapter 19: The End of an Era

1 Commissioners of Indian Affairs, Albany, Dec. 16, 1698, propositions by Sachems of Onondaga and Oneida, NYCD, v. 4, 491–494; Richter, *Cultural*, 64–65, *Ordeal*, 189, 192–195; Trelease, *Indian*, 340–342; Brandão and Starna, *Treaties*, 215–217; Green, *New*, 161–167; Hinderaker, *Hendricks*, 64–65.
2 Ibid.
3 Richter, *Ordeal*, 193.
4 Parmenter, *Edge*, 253–256; Eccles, *Frontenac*, 328; Richter, *War*, 550, *Ordeal*, 193–194.
5 Encroachments of English on New France, NYCD, v. 9, 703; Richter, *War*, 550–551, *Ordeal*, 193–194, *Trade*, 129–130; Eccles, *Frontenac*, 328–330; Trelease, *Indian*, 240–342.

6 Commissioners of Indian Affairs, Albany, Dec. 16, 1698, NYCD, v. 4, 491; Colden, *History*, 190.
7 Richter, *Ordeal*, 195–196; Eccles, *Frontenac*, 325–329; Parmenter, *Edge*, 255.
8 Encroachments of English on New France, NYCD, v. 9, 703.
9 Ibid; Parmenter, *Edge*, 255.
10 Bellomont to BOT, Boston, May 29 and 31, 1699, ERNY, v. 2, 1313–1315; Bellomont to BOT, New York, Oct. 24, 1698; Romer Report, Aug. 6, 1698; Bellomont to BOT, April 13, 1699, NYCD, v. 4, 409–410, 440–441, 487–488; Trelease, *Indian*, 340; Parmenter, *Edge*, 256; Richter, *Ordeal*, 194–195; Eccles, *Frontenac*, 329.
11 Parmenter, *Edge*, 256.
12 Richter, *Ordeal*, 194–195.
13 Bellomont to BOT, Boston, Feb. 28, 1700 and April 20, 1700, NYCD, v. 4, 607–612, 637–638; Bellomont to Commissioners for Indian Affairs; Bellomont's instructions to Schuyler, Livingston, and Hansen, Boston, March 21, 1700, CSPC, v. 18, no. 345xi, xii; Schuyler, *Colonial*, v. 1, 484.
14 Negotiation of Commissioners, NYCD, v. 4, 654–661; Livingston to Bellomont, Albany, April 8, 1700, CSPC, v. 18, no. 345xiv; Onondaga distance from Albany, Leder, *Livingston Indian*, 175.
15 Schuyler, Livingston, and Hansen to Bellomont, Albany, May 3, 1700, NYCD, v. 4, 653.
16 Trelease, *Indian*, 209–210; Leder, *Livingston*, 90, 94, 130.
17 Trelease, *Indian*, 209–210.
18 Livingston to Bellomont, Albany, April 8, 1700, CSPC, v. 18, no. 345xiv; Onondaga distance from Albany, Leder, *Livingston Indian*, 175.
19 Sivertsen, *Turtles*, 36.
20 Onondaga distance from Albany, Leder, *Livingston Indian*, 175.
21 Livingston's report of journey to Onondaga, Albany, May 3, 1700, NYCD, v. 4, 650–651; Onondaga distance from Albany, Leder, *Livingston Indian*, 175; National Park Service, *Timeline*.
22 Negotiation of commissioners, NYCD, v. 4, 654–661.
23 Ibid, 656; Onondaga distance from Albany, Leder, *Livingston Indian*, 175.
24 Negotiation of commissioners, NYCD, v. 4, 654–657; Leder, *Livingston*, 151–152.
25 Negotiation of commissioners, NYCD, v. 4, 656.
26 Ibid, 654–657.
27 Parmenter, *Edge*, 260.
28 Negotiation of commissioners, NYCD, v. 4, 657–659; Richter, *Cultural*, 64–65, *Ordeal*, 201.
29 Ibid.
30 Negotiation of commissioners; Propositions of Five Nations to commissioners of Indian Affairs, NYCD, v. 4, 658–661, 694; Richter, *Ordeal*, 201.
31 Negotiation of commissioners, NYCD, v. 4, 658–661; Trelease, *Indian*, 345; Richter, *Ordeal*, 201.
32 Negotiation of commissioners, NYCD, v. 4, 661.
33 Richter, *Ordeal*, 201.
34 Livingston's report; Schuyler, Livingston, and Hansen to Bellomont, Albany, May 3 and 11, 1700; Negotiation of commissioners, NYCD, v. 4, 648–661; Richter, *Ordeal*, 200–201; Schuyler, *Colonial*, v. 1, 484.

35 Negotiation of commissioners, NYCD, v. 4, 661; Richter, *Ordeal*, 200–201.
36 Livingston's report; Schuyler, Livingston, and Hansen to Bellomont, Albany, May 3 and 11, 1700; Negotiation of Commissioners, NYCD, v. 4, 648–661; Onondaga Distance from Albany, Leder, *Livingston Indian*, 175; Trelease, *Indian*, 345–346; Schuyler, *Colonial*, v. 1, 484–485; Parmenter, *Edge*, 258–259.
37 Ibid.
38 Leder, *Livingston*, 151–152.
39 Livingston's report, NYCD, v. 4, 650.
40 Bellomont to Lords of Trade, New York, July 26, 1700, NYCD, v. 4, 689.
41 Ibid; Richter, *Ordeal*, 200–201; Parmenter, *Edge*, 260.
42 Death of Bellomont, New York, March 5 and 6, 1701, Cal. Hist. MSS, Part II, 280; Bayard to Meadows, March 8, 1701; Council of New York to BOT, March 10, 1701, NYCD, v. 4, 848, 850–851; Stokes, *Iconography*, v. 4, 428; De Peyster, *Life*, 57.
43 Council of Nevis to Blathwayt and Nevis to Vernon, Nevis, May 18, 1699, CSPC, v. 13, no. 136, and v. 17, no. 404; Instructions of Vernon, Whitehall, Nov. 23, 1698; Kidd narrative, July 7, 1699; Blathwayt, Piracies in East Indies, Commons *Journals*, v. 13, 16, 32, 35, 36; Kidd protest, Portland manuscripts, v. 9, 405.
44 Emott testimony Massachusetts Council, June 19, 1699, CO 5/787, fols. 214–215, PRO; Memorial of Campbell, June 19, 1699; Bellomont to Kidd, June 19, 1699; Kidd to Bellomont, June 24, 1699; Examination of Barlycorne, Parrot, and Wood, July 8, 10, and 21, 1699; Bellomont to BOT, July 8 and 26, 1699; Narrative of Gardiner, Boston, July 1699; Blathwayt, Piracies in East Indies, Commons *Journals*, v. 13, 18, 19, 21–23, 25, 27, 29, 30–31, 35; BOT to Lords Justices, Sept. 12, 1699, NYCD, v. 4, 583–584.
45 Lorrain, *Ordinary*; *Post Boy*, May 24, 1701, 1; *Flying Post* or *Post Master*, May 24, 1701, 1; Ritchie, *Kidd*, 227; Zacks, *Pirate*, 392.
46 ADM 2/1048, fol. 29; 1/3666, fols. 210–211; HCA 1/29, fols. 288–289, PRO; Ritchie, *Kidd*, 228; Lincoln, *British*, 37–38; Konstam, *Sacrifice*; Zacks, *Pirate*, 392–393.
47 Bellomont to Vernon, July 29, 1700; Bellomont to BOT, Oct. 17, 1700; Bellomont to Vernon, Oct. 18, 1700; Bellomont to BOT, Nov. 28, 1701; BOT to Bellomont, April 29, 1701; NYCD, v. 4, 697–698, 712–726, 759–761, 781–797, 852–857; Burgess, *Pirates'*, 238.
48 Bellomont to BOT, Oct. 17, 1700; Bellomont to Vernon, Dec. 6, 1700; Bellomont to BOT, Jan. 2, 1701; BOT to Bellomont, Feb. 11, 1701; NYCD, v. 4, 712–726, 815–818, 820–827, 840–845; Burgess, *Pirates'*, 238.
49 Bayard to Meadows, March 8, 1701, NYCD, v. 4, 848; Council to Beeckman, Polhemus, and Laurence, New York, March 17, 1701, Cal. Hist. MSS, Part II, 281; Stokes, *Iconography*, v. 4, 428–429; De Peyster, *Life*, 57.
50 Finnegan, *Pirates*, 156–157; Rainbolt, *Great*, 340–351.
51 Burgess, *Pirates'*, 238; Bishop of London to BOT, Nov. 1, 1700; Bayard to Meadows, March 8, 1701, NYCD, v. 4, 774, 848; Finnegan, *Pirates*, 156–157; Rainbolt, *Great*, 348–351.
52 Council Minutes, March 5, Aug. 30, Nov. 10, and Dec. 24, 1701; Jan. 29, April 13, and Sept. 12, 1702, NYCCM, 153, 158, 161, 163, 165, 173; Cal. Hist. MSS, Part II, 292, 296, 309; Livingston to BOT, New York, May 13, 1701; BOT to Cornbury, Whitehall, Feb. 22, 1703; BOT to Cornbury, Whitehall, April 7, 1703; Thrale and

Mercer on Lady Bellomont's accounts, April 19, 1703; Cornbury to BOT, New York, Oct. 7, 1703, NYCD, v. 4, 876, 1029–1030, 1038, 1039–1040, 1072–1073.

53 Cornbury to BOT, New York, Dec. 1702, NYCD, v. 4, 1003; Zacks, *Pirate*, 403.

54 NYCD, v. 4, 851; Zacks, *Pirate*, 403; Finnegan, *Pirates*, 134–135.

55 Nanfan conference with Indians, Albany, July 10–21, 1701, NYCD, v. 4, 896–908; Peace between French and Indians, NYCD, v. 9, 722–725; Jennings, *History*, 165–166; Brandão and Starna, *Treaties*, 209–244; Blackhawk, *Rediscovery*, 103–104; Richter, *Ordeal*, 210–211, *Trade*, 129–132; Parmenter, *Edge*, 266–273; Hinderaker, *Hendricks*, 68–69; Trelease, *Indian*, 361–363; Eccles, *Frontenac*, 331–333; Shannon, *Iroquois*, 55; Buffinton, *Policy*, 350.

56 Peace between French and Indians, NYCD, v. 9, 722–725; Shannon, *Iroquois*, 59–60; Richter, *Ordeal*, 210–211, *Trade*, 129–132; Hinderaker, *Hendricks*, 68–69; Trelease, *Indian*, 361–363; Blackhawk, *Rediscovery*, 103–104.

57 Nanfan conference with Indians, Albany, July 10–21, 1701, NYCD, v. 4, 896–908; Jennings, *History*, 165; Brandão and Starna, *Treaties*, 223–229; Hinderaker, *Hendricks*, 69.

58 Reynolds, *Albany*, 110.

59 Sivertsen, *Turtles*, 7; Hagedorn, *Friend*, 241.

60 Nanfan conference with Indians, Albany, July 10–21, 1701, NYCD, v. 4, 896–908; Parmenter, *Edge*, 268; Hinderaker, *Hendricks*, 69.

61 Nanfan conference with Indians, Albany, July 10–21, 1701, NYCD, v. 4, 896–908; Richter, *Ordeal*, 211, *Trade*, 130; Hinderaker, *Hendricks*, 69–70; Brandão and Starna, *Treaties*, 223–229; Shannon, *Iroquois*, 61.

62 Five Nations reply to Nanfan, July 19, 1701, NYCD, v. 4, 905.

63 Deed from Five Nations to King, July 19, 1701, NYCD, v. 4, 908–911; Richter, *Ordeal*, 212; Brandão and Starna, *Treaties*, 225; Parmenter, *Edge*, 268–269; Trelease, *Indian*, 362; Shannon, *Iroquois*, 61–62.

64 Deed from Five Nations to King, July 19, 1701, NYCD, v. 4, 908–911; Richter, *Ordeal*, 212; Parmenter, *Edge*, 268–269; Trelease, *Indian*, 362; Shannon, *Iroquois*, 61–62; Hinderaker, *Hendricks*, 70.

65 Five Nations reply to Nanfan, July 19, 1701, NYCD, v. 4, 905; Brandão and Starna, *Treaties*, 228; Parmenter, *Edge*, 268; Shannon, *Iroquois*, 62.

66 Richter, *Cultural*, 59, *Trade*, 129, *Ordeal*, 177.

67 Schuyler, *Colonial*, v. 2, 90; Bradley, *Before*, 188–190; Richter, *Ordeal*, 177.

68 Richter, *Cultural*, 65, *Trade*, 130–131; Jennings, *Ambiguous*, 213.

69 Shannon, *Iroquois*, 62; Jennings, *Ambiguous*, 210–213; Parmenter, *Edge*, 268–269; Hinderaker, *Hendricks*, 70–71; Brandão and Starna, *Treaties*, 209–244; Trelease, *Indian*, 362–363.

70 Hagedorn, *Friend*, 55–90; Hinderaker, *Hendricks*, 70–71; Richter, *Cultural*, 59–67, *Ordeal*, 177, *Trade*, 118–132.

71 Richter, *Trade*, 131–132, *Cultural*, 66–67; Shannon, *Iroquois*, 62.

72 Parmenter, *Edge*, 270–273; Trelease, *Indian*, 363; Shannon, *Iroquois*, 62–63; Jennings, *Ambiguous*, 213.

Afterword

1 Hinderaker, *Hendricks*, 83; Schuyler, *Colonial*, v. 1, 302–304, 323–324.

2 Albany Council, July 14–19 and Aug. 12, 1709, Leder, *Livingston Indian*, 206–214; Examination of Indians, June 22, 1709; Cockerill to Popple, July 5, 1709; Hunter to BOT, Nov. 30, 1709, NYCD, v. 5, 80, 81, 85–87, 113; Dudley and others to Sutherland, Boston, Oct. 24, 1709, CSPC, v. 25, no. 794; McCully, *Catastrophe*, 441–456; Richter, *Ordeal*, 226; Peckham, *Colonial*, 68–70; Hinderaker, *Hendricks*, 82–83; Muller, *Palace*, 32.

3 Congress of colonial governors; address of governors to Queen, Oct. 14, 1709, CSPC, v. 25, nos. 794i, 794ii; McCully, *Catastrophe*, 448–456; Leder, *Livingston*, 206–207; Richter, *Ordeal*, 227.

4 Albany Council, July 2–3, 1710, in Leder, *Livingston Indian*, 215–216; Sivertsen, *Turtles*, 59–68; Muller, *Palace*, 32–35; Hawkins, *Across*, 39–46; Hinderaker, *Hendricks*, 83–84; Schuyler, *Colonial*, v. 2, 224; John Schuyler journal, DHNY, v. 2, 286.

5 Hinderaker, *Hendricks*, 84–96; Sivertsen, *Turtles*, 66–69; Hawkins, *Across*, 52–54, 65–66; Richter, *Ordeal*, 227; Schuyler, *Colonial*, v. 2, 33–36, 224.

6 Staggs, *Calvinists*, 215–216; Blackhawk, *Rediscovery*, 78; Hawkins, *Across*, 52–64; Muller, *Palace*, 27–31, 34–43; Hinderaker, *Hendricks*, 88–91; Sivertsen, *Turtles*, 66–68.

7 Schuyler, *Colonial*, v. 2, 37.

8 Jennings, *Ambiguous*, 260–262; Schuyler, *Colonial*, v. 2, 33–36; Richter, *Ordeal*, 227–228; Lavin, *Dutch*, 119; Peckham, *Colonial*, 71–73; Muller, *Palace*, 44.

9 Schuyler, *Colonial*, v. 2, 90; Trelease, *Indian*, 336.

10 Schuyler, *Colonial*, v. 2, 90–92.

11 Richter, *Cultural*, 59, *Trade*, 129, *Ordeal*, 177.

12 Hart, *For*, 24.

13 Grant, *Memoirs*, 75.

14 Hendrick to Albany Council, June 28, 1754, DHNY, v. 2, 576.

15 Sullivan, *Papers*, v. 9, 177.

16 Richter, *Ordeal*, 177, 226.

17 Richter, *Ordeal*, 213.

18 Sivertsen, *Turtles*, 25–26, 227.

19 Grems-Doolittle, *Stockade*; Giacalone, *Looking*; Farrell, *Little*; Gleason, *Lawrence*; Gilmore, *Lawrence*.

20 Ibid.

21 Staggs, *Calvinists*, 213; Sivertsen, *Turtles*, 7–10, 50–56; Hagedorn, *Friend*, 76, 83, 90, 182; Midtrøød, *Flemish*, 94.

22 Deed to Hilletie van Olinda, Oct. 24, 1704, applications for land grants, 1642–1803, New York State Archives, Series A0272–78, v. 4, p. 27b; Midtrøød, *Flemish*, 95–96.

23 Staffa, *Schenectady*, 75.

24 Staggs, *Declarations*, 60–61; Bradley, *Before*, 188–192; Sivertsen, *Turtles*, 20, 21, 26, 42, 48, 50; Midtrøød, *Flemish*, 91, 94–96; Richter, *Cultural*, 53, 61; Staffa, *Schenectady*, 27, 75.

25 Ibid.

26 Sivertsen, *Turtles*, 6–7.

27 Bradley, *Before*, 190–191.

INDEX

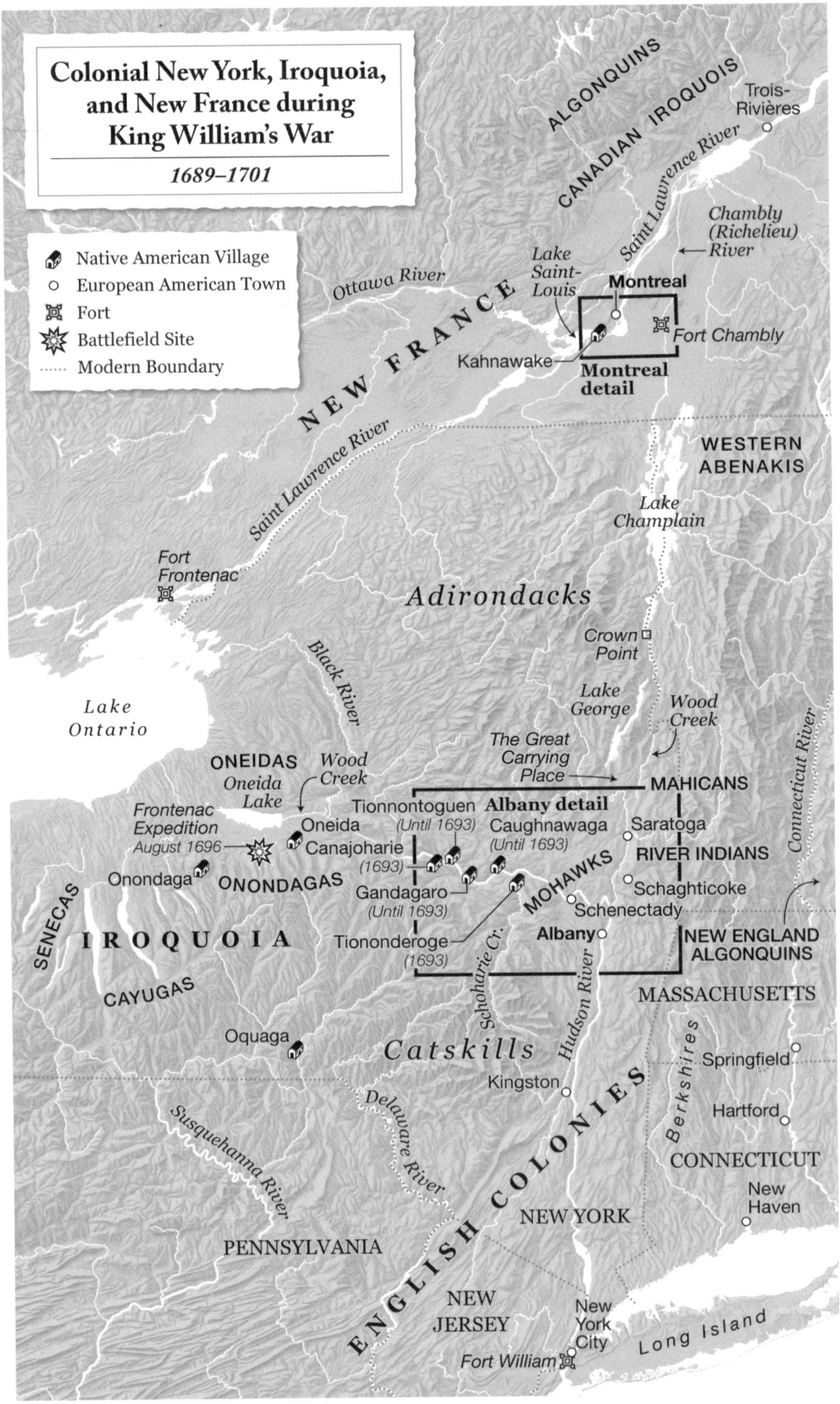

Colonial New York, Iroquoia, and New France during King William's War
1689–1701
Native American Village
European American Town
Fort
Battlefield Site
Modern Boundary
ALGONQUINS
CANADIAN IROQUOIS
Trois-Rivières
Saint Lawrence River
Chambly (Richelieu) River
Lake Saint-Louis
Montreal
Ottawa River
NEW FRANCE
Fort Chambly
Kahnawake
Montreal detail
Saint Lawrence River
WESTERN ABENAKIS
Lake Champlain
Fort Frontenac
Adirondacks
Crown Point
Black River
Lake George
Wood Creek
Lake Ontario
The Great Carrying Place
ONEIDAS
Wood Creek
Oneida Lake
MAHICANS
Frontenac Expedition
August 1696
Tionnontoguen
(Until 1693)
Albany detail
Caughnawaga
(Until 1693)
Oneida
Canajoharie
(1693)
Saratoga
RIVER INDIANS
Onondaga
ONONDAGAS
MOHAWKS
Schaghticoke
Gandagaro
(Until 1693)
Schenectady
SENECAS
IROQUOIA
Tiononderoge
(1693)
Albany
NEW ENGLAND ALGONQUINS
Connecticut River
Schoharie Cr.
Hudson River
CAYUGAS
MASSACHUSETTS
Oquaga
Catskills
Berkshires
Springfield
Kingston
Hartford
Delaware River
Susquehanna River
ENGLISH COLONIES
CONNECTICUT
New Haven
NEW YORK
PENNSYLVANIA
NEW JERSEY
New York City
Long Island
Fort William